Electronic Globalized Business and Sustainable Development Through IT Management:

Strategies and Perspectives

Patricia Ordoñez de Pablos
University of Oviedo, Spain

Miltiadis Lytras
American College of Greece, Greece

Waldemar Karwowski
University of Central Florida, USA

Rongbin W.B. Lee
The Hong Kong Polytechnic University, Hong Kong

BUSINESS SCIENCE REFERENCE

Hershey · New York

Director of Editorial Content:	Kristin Klinger
Director of Book Publications:	Julia Mosemann
Acquisitions Editor:	Lindsay Johnston
Development Editor:	Dave DeRicco
Publishing Assistant:	Jamie Snavely
Typesetter:	Casey Conapitski
Production Editor:	Jamie Snavely
Cover Design:	Lisa Tosheff

Published in the United States of America by
Business Science Reference (an imprint of IGI Global)
701 E. Chocolate Avenue
Hershey PA 17033
Tel: 717-533-8845
Fax: 717-533-8661
E-mail: cust@igi-global.com
Web site: http://www.igi-global.com/reference

Library of Congress Cataloging-in-Publication Data

Electronic globalized business and sustainable development through IT management : strategies and perspectives / Patricia Ordonez de Pablos ... [et al.], editors.
      p. cm.
 Includes bibliographical references and index. Summary: "This book provides fresh ideas on how IT and modern management can contribute to societal and economic objectives and the significant role of IT for global challenges and international collaboration"--Provided by publisher. ISBN 978-1-61520-623-0 (hbk.) -- ISBN 978-1-61520-624-7 (ebook) 1. Information technology--Management. 2. Computer-assisted instruction. 3. Knowledge management. I. Pablos, Patricia Ordonez de. HD30.2.E435 2010
 004.068--dc22

                              2009053535

British Cataloguing in Publication Data
A Cataloguing in Publication record for this book is available from the British Library.

Table of Contents

Detailed Table of Contents

Chapter 1
    Robert D. Tennyson, University of Minnesota, USA

Improving learning in a global environment is major goal for advanced technology growth. Web-based instructional systems offer learners simultaneous information regardless of their home environment. As the world cultures become more integrated, instruction designs can bridge the information gap and enhance world learning. Management strategies include a learning climate that encourages diversified workers to participate in active learning situations that reflect the global nature of their work. This chapter focuses on the role that simulations can provide in both the effectiveness and efficiency of training and education. Simulations offer the means to improve learning by enhancing initial and on-the-job learning. Simulation approaches are presented within the framework of learning sciences. These include technical simulations, business simulations, modeling, role-playing exercises, case studies, micro-worlds, and animations.

Chapter 2
    Robert D. Tennyson, University of Minnesota, USA
    Robert L. Jorczak, University of Minnesota, USA

Impressed by the motivation and effort displayed by players of complex and highly interactive electronic games, psychological researchers seek to apply gaming techniques to enhance globalization of diverse populations in problem solving and decision making. Researchers are interested in identifying characteristics of entertainment games that influence player motivation and learning. From the perspective of Interactive Cognitive Complexity theory, researchers need to examine how game variables relate to key learning components, including learner affect, cognitive strategy, and knowledge/skill acquisition. From a learning perspective, video simulation games are primarily a series of problem solving interactions set in a specific virtual context and using various learning aids that support the solving of problems to achieve the object of the game. Cognitive problem solving factors and strategies are; therefore, key independent variables for learning game studies. In creating such a framework, we propose five conceptual categories of instructionally relevant game variables: (1) virtual context, (2) problem specification, (3) interaction and control, (4) learning support, and (5) social interaction. Proposed is that electronic gaming methodology, founded in cognitive learning theory, will enhance efficient and effective development efforts to improve learning of global management strategies.

Chapter 3

Human Factors in Knowledge Management: Building Better Systems by Employing Human
Tareq Z. Ahram, University of Central Florida, USA
Waldemar Karwowski, University of Central Florida, USA
Chris Andrzejczak, University of Central Florida, USA

This chapter introduces Human Systems Integration (HSI) practices and applications, relating them to the framework of Knowledge Management (KM). In addition, the chapter presents practical tools and applications in the HSI and KM domains. Practices within the discipline of systems engineering have brought great strides to the systems development lifecycle (SDLC) process. The field of Human Factors has created a liaison method where the system is not viewed in a bubble away from the operators, maintainers, and other affected parties. Human Systems Integration (HSI) practices form a framework and suggest heuristics for integrating human elements along with more traditional physical and performance-based design requirements. Systems complexity has forced designers to consider Knowledge Management, and develop methods to systematically creating, sharing, retaining, and transferring skills, facts, limitations, capabilities, and experiences. The authors describe the importance of and benefits resulting from good HSI and KM practices.

Chapter 4

Irene Samanta, Technological Education Institute of Piraeus, Greece
P. Kyriazopoulos, Technological Education Institute of Piraeus, Greece

The research examines whether the changes that have taken place in the global business environment have modulated the way firms do business or whether it is simply transient details that have caused such excitement. Should firms be wary of any proclamations of 'new' ways of doing business? Or should they ignore changes of the business environment? Semi-structured in-depth interviews were conducted in three focus groups of managers from three major firms operating in Greece. The influence of globalization, the intense competition and new technologies in B2B e-commerce are external factors that raise problems and complexities in the future direction of Greek firms. There is also a gap caused by the lack of an innovation culture between top and lesser management. Businesses are required to modernise their practices to move from their present situation at the level of the 2nd industrial revolution of "old economy" to the 3rd industrial revolution of "new era economy". The results of this research can be used to assist companies to move to e- business taking into consideration account the external and internal factors with regard to the ways in which e-relationships can be modulated.

Chapter 5

Jon G. Hall, The Open University, UK

This invited chapter offers a new view on the wickedness of problems, and employs a new problem solving approach to show how problems tangle together to form complex problems, which shows how they might be untangled. The focus then changes from being general problems to being those of an economy. A complete taxonomy of problem overlaps is given, illustrated with examples of how economic value is or might be delivered by those involved in problem solving.

Chapter 6

Jussi Kantola, Korea Advanced Institute of Science and Technology (KAIST), Republic of Korea
Waldemar Karwowski, University of Central Florida, USA
Hannu Vanharanta, Tampere University of Technology, Finland

In this chapter, the authors address the Evolute methodology (Kantola, 2005) that attempts to enhance understanding of MOs to all stakeholders thereby making management more systematic and efficient. By clarifying the conceptual structures of MOs to all stakeholders, decisions are based on the proper and relevant concepts. This ontology-based approach aids understanding and managing the whole clearer than previous methods. Also, the change becomes transparent easy to visualize. Such transparent and visualized change enables the use of meta-knowledge to direct the mosaic towards the desired outcome.

Chapter 7

Masoud Mohammadian, University of Canberra, Australia

Development and management of IT systems are complex, demanding, and yet crucial to an organization success and its competitive position in the marketplace. Due to rapid changes in emerging technologies there is a need for constant improvement and adjustment to IT systems. There are a large number of processes involved in IT system development and monitoring. The interdependencies of these processes make it very difficult for Chief Information Officers (CIOs) to comprehend and be aware of effect of inefficiencies that may exist in development of these processes in their organization. This chapter considers the implementation of a Fuzzy Cognitive Maps (FCM) to provide facilities to capture and represent complex relationships in an IT management model and their related processes to improve the understanding of CIOs about the systems and its associated risks. By using FCMs CIOs can regularly review and improve their IT systems and provide greater improvement in development, monitoring and maintenance of IT facilities. CIOs can perform what-if analysis to better understand vulnerabilities of their designed system.

Chapter 8

Thanos Kriemadis, University of Peloponnese, Greece
Theodore Pelagidis, University of Piraeus, Greece

This chapter contributes to an understanding of the organizational culture of the industrial spin-off knowledge-based enterprises, which operate within the Science and Technology Parks in Greece. In this context, a critical number of questionnaires have been distributed to the spin-offs to examine whether firms born within the parks have developed a functional, innovative organizational culture, one that provides a solid foundation for organizational effectiveness and business excellence. The paper presents the results of a quantitative analysis of the data collected in a fieldwork study. It also includes the necessary policies for the spin-offs to overcome organizational culture problems and adopt the culture of innovation and business excellence.

The value of social computing and its application in business has not received much attention in literature. However, this chapter reveals that social computing principles may have important business value, as they can help lower transaction costs. This makes the social computing development here to stay, instead of another hype. This chapter describes social computing with nine technological and social principles, obtained by comparing both Internet and academic sources in this field. Relating them to a business model reveals that social computing provides most support in those aspects of business where connections with the environment exist; the relations with partners and customers. This chapter will explain what social computing is, and how one can use it to increase business value.

This chapter examines how incumbent firms respond to the industrial pricing dynamics with the adjustment of their own pricing strategies so as to create and sustain their market share dominance. The empirical context of this chapter is the strategic behavior of online game operators (i.e. the companies who operate online games) in the Chinese online game market – the most active market in the world with strong network effects. This chapter introduces Velu's business model theory in the market with strong networks. Further, in this research, the authors extend Velu's research by challenging some of his propositions by a careful observation of pricing dynamics in the Chinese online game industry since 2000 and how dominant and non-dominant incumbent firms adjust their pricing strategy. In the Findings Part, this chapter explains why acquisition is regarded by main dominant game operators as the most effective way to complement their pricing model revolution.

The study aims to uncover the influence of classroom technology (i.e. a variety of audio-visual and online equipment) on an individual's (i.e. student's) learning attitude. The antecedents that were considered relevant in the early post implementation phase were: (1) experience with Information and Communication Technologies (ICTs), (2) enhanced communications, (3) learner independence and (4) ease of technology use. The original concept for the research was derived from Technology Acceptance Model (TAM) which has been a source of numerous studies exploring user attitude towards technology. The outcome indicated a positive and significant relationship between learner independence and individual learner attitude; enhanced communications and individual learner attitude and ease of technology use and individual learner attitude. However the relationship between ICTs experience and individual learner attitude was non-significant. The study outcome implicated that use of classroom technology, in the introduction stage, does increase with the degree of perceived and encountered ease of use and extended capacity for self-directed learning.

Chapter 12
Seppo J. Hänninen, Helsinki University of Technology, Finland

The 'perfect technology syndrome' has a strong effect on the success of the high-technology companies. The objective of the chapter is to create a better understanding of the impact of the dominance by technological knowledge base. The study builds on knowledge base theory, which has its underpinnings in the knowledge company theory. The present study is based on interviews within 8 companies that have business operations in Finland and that have participated in the Usix technology program financed by the Finnish Funding Agency for Technology and Innovation Tekes. All the companies were small or medium sized. Because of the small size of the sample, the study is to some extent a multi-case study. The interviewees from companies were technology directors or research and development directors as well as general directors of the companies. According to the results, investing only in technological development leads less to successful commercializing process than investing also in, for example, branding and usability. This result gives support to the proposition that the technological knowledge base is not only needed for the successful innovation commercializing process. In parallel, the results give confirmative evidence that the four knowledge bases of innovation have a positive correlation with successful innovations. There were two additional interesting results as regards to the objective of creating a better understanding of the impact of knowledge bases in the innovation commercializing process. Networking with key stakeholders and aligning vertically. These results may be a sign that there do exist innovation commercializing process tools which can create with various stakeholders, including competitors, win-win partnerships. These tentative empirical results are in line with the essential nature of absorptive capacity of a company.

Chapter 13
Vladimir Stantchev, Berlin Institute of Technology, Germany
Martin Goernitz, Krallmann AG, Germany

The Information Technology Infrastructure Library's (ITIL) is widely used as a model for IT service processes mainly due to its general nature. A drawback of this generality is that it greatly hinders the conversion of best practices into specific implemental processes. To assess such processes for their completeness and to find and overcome possible weak-spots in the design, this work proposes an in-depth comparison with available best practice frameworks that relate to and extend the ITIL, such as the Microsoft Operations framework (MOF). The comparison and evaluation method is presented and verified exemplarily with an actual pilot-phase process implementation.

Chapter 14

The authors of the chapter exploring E-Marketing practices by Egyptian small business enterprises as a tool for globalisation. An organized systematic examination of the published work related to E-Marketing practices by small business enterprises is discussed and illustrated. Moreover, the chapter demonstrates that although many Egyptian small business enterprises seems to conduct E-Marketing activities, only very small number of these enterprises conduct an effective and efficient E-Marketing activities for expanding globally. The chapter illustrates an exploratory research to explore the current aspects related to E-Marketing adoption and implementation by Egyptian small business enterprises as a tool for globalisation. The main aim of conducting such exploratory study is to achieve a deep and reflective understanding of E-Marketing practices by Egyptian small business enterprises as a tool for globalisation.

Chapter 15

The chapter employs a hypercube innovation model to analyze the differences in technology and learning models in conventional (face-to-face) classroom learning and E-learning environments. The results of the analyses indicate that the innovation from traditional classroom learning to E-learning is radical for both the learner and instructor, leading to drastic changes in the technology and learning model. For education institutions, the technology is a fundamental change, while the learning model is reinforced. From the dynamic capability perspectives, a set of core capabilities needed for successfully exploiting E-learning is identified. These results provide insight for learners, instructors, and education institutions for enhancing their understanding of E-learning innovation and provide guidelines to help E-learning stakeholders adapt from conventional classrooms to E-learning environments.

Chapter 16

The chapter discusses instructional design strategies to improve student learning satisfaction. Conformation factor analysis was performed to test the reliability and validity of the measurement model. The partial least squares method was used to evaluate the causal model. The results indicated that the learning climate, perceived value and perceived ease of use significantly affected learning satisfaction. Computer self-efficacy had a strong impact on perceived behavioral control; computer self-efficacy, perceived behavioral control and social interaction had significant effects on perceived ease of use. System functionality, content feature and social interaction significantly affected perceived value. Social interaction had a significant effect on learning climate. This chapter provides initial insights into those factors that are likely significant antecedents for planning and implementing a blended e-learning system to enhance student learning satisfaction.

Preface

In a world where traditional business practices are reconsidered, economic activity is performed in a global context, new areas of economic development are recognized as the key enablers of wealth and income production, and the quest for collaboration and exploitation of synergies is recognized as an Information Technologies Primer, this book brings together academics, researchers, entrepreneurs, policy makers and government officers aiming to contribute to the debate on Sustainable Development and Strategic Management through Information Technology.

This book is timely responding to the high demand of our society to adopt Emerging Technologies in all the aspects of Business and Economic activity towards innovative solutions to research problems and high performance systems. The key characteristic of the book is that brings together the experts of the IT industry, IT practitioners and researchers in High Tech Research centres and Academia promoting a sound contribution to the IT literacy as demanded by real users.

The book has a clear editing strategy:

- To be the reference edition for all those interested on the strategic role of IT and Management towards sustainable development [with main emphasis to be paid on practical aspects].
- To be the reference edition for all those (policy makers, government officers, academics and practitioners) interested in understanding Business and Globalization.
- To become a reference edition for people thirsty for globalised electronic business, sustained development and Information Systems.

The proposed book with the presented strategy will:

- Provides fresh ideas on how IT and Modern Management can contribute to societal and economic objectives.
- Shows the significant role of IT for Global Challenges and International Collaboration.
- Exploits synergies between disciplines and cultures.
- Influence the way theory meets practice and creates business opportunity and wealth.
- Illustrates how IT can support humanistic visions, etc.

The audience for this book is:

- Politicians
- Academics
- Policy Makers
- Government officers
- Students
- Corporate heads of firms
- Senior general managers
- Managing directors
- Board directors
- Academics and researchers in the field both in universities and business schools
- Information technology directors and managers
- Quality managers and directors
- Human resource directors
- Libraries and information centers serving the needs of the above

Patricia Ordoñez de Pablos
Miltiadis Lytras
Waldemar Karwowski
Rongbin W. B. Lee

Editors

Chapter 1
Simulation Technologies in Global Learning

Robert D. Tennyson
University of Minnesota, USA

ABSTRACT

Improving learning in a global environment is major goal for advanced technology growth. Web-based instructional systems offer learners simultaneous information regardless of their home environment. As the world cultures become more integrated, instruction designs can bridge the information gap and enhance world learning. Management strategies include a learning climate that encourages diversified workers to participate in active learning situations that reflect the global nature of their work. This chapter focuses on the role that simulations can provide in both the effectiveness and efficiency of training and education. Simulations offer the means to improve learning by enhancing initial and on-the-job learning. Simulation approaches are presented within the framework of learning sciences. These include technical simulations, business simulations, modeling, role-playing exercises, case studies, micro-worlds, and animations.

INTRODUCTION

Simulations have been an area of interest and development since the early days of computer-based instruction and learning (1960s). Biological, physical, economic and social phenomena have been depicted within *simulation models* that are executable on a computer. Such phenomena can be derived from a real, a theoretical or a ficti-tious context. Regardless of context, a more or less sophisticated interaction component enables learners to access the model, to change parameters, to modify routines, or even to modify the structure; and, to receive feedback on the status of the model reflecting the various types of interventions (Lierman, 1993; O'Neil & Perez, 2008). The interaction between the learner and the model occurs in a sequence over time. From interactions over time, the learner acquires knowledge, skills,

DOI: 10.4018/978-1-61520-623-0.ch001

and/or strategies about the content depicted and its dynamics (Breuer, Molkenthin, Tennyson, 2006)

From those early simulations, there has been a continuous stream of developments enhancing and creating new design approaches (de Jong 1991; Edwards, 1995; Kass, Burke, & Fitzgerald, 1996; van der Boom, Paas, van Morriënboer, & van Gog, 2004). Outcomes of these efforts over the past decades are readily seen in the application of simulations in technical skills education and training. For example, railroad engineers are trained to run today's high-speed trains via simulators. Mechanics are certified for the utilization of CNC (Computer Numerically Controlled)-technologies based on exercises with simulators. Business executives improve their decision making in complex, dynamic markets based on business market simulators. Students acquire knowledge and skills in subject matter domains based on (simulated) micro-worlds. There is application variance in respect to levels of fidelity between simulations. The successful integration of analogue media into the digital format is an example of contemporary differences. The level of fidelity presented within simulations has been extended to the full multi-media repertoire.

In addition, improved learning based on simulations is shown by the growing use of simulations as research and development tools (Mayer, 2006). An example from research is given in the studies on complex problem solving abilities performed in educational psychology (Tennyson & Breuer, 2002). Experimental subjects are requested to cope with complex, dynamic environments represented by means of micro-worlds. The research end is not findings in instructional design but the study of human problem solving abilities. This includes the study of learning activities within problem solving activities, but not primary from an educational perspective.

Given the above background and the growing technological milieu, there is no surprise about the extension of simulation-based instructional approaches into web-based formats. The formats allow the dissemination of simulations throughout the Internet to users at any workstation within the web environment. The lower level application formats provide for downloading of simulation programs. This makes use of the Internet as a distribution platform. More enhanced approaches target the interactive use of a simulation via the Internet. The technical solution has been achieved since the development of the World Wide Web in the early 1990s.

Learning Theory Foundations

At its core, the interactive solution comprises three basic elements: A simulation model is run as a resident on a central server. A data exchange process is established via the Internet or an intranet providing the necessary interaction between the user and the model. The network-connection makes use of a standard browser providing a Graphical User Interface (GUI). The GUI represents the status of the model and the variables on which the participant can make her or his decisions. The three elements, a model on a server, a network-connection, and a GUI within a browser, establish the necessary technical basis for using simulations at any workstation on the web or on any notebook in a wireless LAN. The realization of such a set-up is not a trivial task but from the authors' perspective it does not provide an educational asset in itself. The technical platform is a necessary prerequisite; any educational approach is dependant from its functionality. Meaningful instructional and learning activities however need more than a technical platform. They require a foundation in learning-instructional theory (Tennyson, 2002). Web-based simulations need design approaches making use of both simulation tools and learning foundations to achieve significant objectives of learning. This orientation defines the perspective of this presentation.

The proposed approach looks first at the framework of objectives for using simulations in educational environments. It addresses basic types of simulations in accordance with such objectives. It reflects on the approach to use simulations as a tool for problem-based learning activities. It refers to the notion of adaptivity for customized interaction processes. Such interaction may be established by using real-time, intelligent 4th generation instructional design evaluation (Tennyson & Foshay, 1998). This demand feeds back into requirements for the architecture of web-based simulations. A basic assumption of our thesis is that the web-based approach to simulations can bring a major technical advantage. The use of a central server can make available processing speed and processing capacity with almost no limits for web-based simulations.

The background of my thesis is derived from three disciplines. First there is a root in educational psychology. Second, there is a link to educational technology. And, third, there is a tie to vocational education and training (VET). The latter may result in specific arguments and examples that differ from general education. I trust that the reader has a chance for drawing generalizations and for transfer into other educational domains.

Objectives for Instructional-Learning Processes Based on Web-Simulations

The spectrum of potential learning activities is extensive. Among these activities there are the acquisition and recall of knowledge, the automation of motor as well as of cognitive skills, the construction of problem solving strategies, the elaboration of methods for learning or meta-cognition, the development of transfer strategies, the shaping of attitudes, the enhancement of motivation and interest, the creation of mental models, and the modification of behavior. From an instructional design perspective (Koedinger & Corbett, 2006), this variety of learning activities should be analyzed to identify distinct classes of outcomes and then define specific instructional

methods and strategies that will effectively result in the desired outcome of learning.

My perspective on the use of web-based simulations is that in general they do not focus on narrow, specific results of learning. They rather open up a spectrum of potential objectives, which can be targets of learning. The set-up of web-based simulation approaches needs a major investment in educational design and development as well as in information technology. The latter will provide its best return when instructional approaches are open and when they allow options for the set-up of learning environments. The options can stress different objectives. An example may be given by the time a simulation becomes used in a learning activity. That is, a web-based simulation can be offered at the beginning of a learning activity as a source of motivation for follow-up study efforts on the subject matter. Within that approach a web-based simulation may also function as an *advance organizer* for follow-up learning.

A web-based simulation may be used for studying the model that it is based on. This way a core objective can be the development of an appropriate mental model, which allows perceiving the variables involved, their interrelations, and the corresponding dynamics. The mental model may become the basis for decision-making processes within the simulated as well as in the real, depicted environment.

A simulation may also be used at the end of a learning activity for assessing the level of performance achieved by a student. This can be done, for example, by exposing participants to a scenario at a specific level of difficulty. The three approaches (advance organizer, mental model, and assessment) may make use of the same simulation environment. The decision for using a specific approach is up to the *user* given that the simulation environment allows such an open approach.

The use of web-based simulation-environments can target different objectives. Without the attempt at being a comprehensive list, such objectives may include:

- Acquisition of structural knowledge,
- Development of domain-specific problem-solving competencies,
- Elaboration of holistic views toward complex phenomena (systems thinking),
- Fostering of subject-matter interest and/or meta-cognitive competencies (self-regulation, self-monitoring),
- Support for the ability of role-taking, and
- Build-up of the ability for coping with dynamics.

The acquisition of structural knowledge points to the need of making knowledge and skills applicable in a flexible way. Concepts, which become merely memorized, can hardly be used in the process of explaining a certain situation. Likewise, skills, which become acquired as a mechanical, not situated procedure, can hardly be used for performing within a specific context (Renkl, Gruber, Mandl, & Hinkhofer, 1994). Such components of knowledge have to be linked within semantic networks. They have to be contextualized. In addition to the conceptual and the procedural facets of knowledge, learning needs the contextual or conditional component (Tennyson, in press). Knowledge becomes applicable in a flexible mode, when it becomes used in varying situations. When students can apply concepts and procedures within different situations and can elaborate on the usefulness and appropriateness of such experiences, they can construct a flexible, structured knowledge base. One efficient way of providing respective contexts can be through the use simulations in learning environments.

The ability to perform in specific (work-place) situations is certainly but not only rooted in the availability of elements of knowledge. It also needs approaches of how to tackle tasks and how to proceed through a sequence of steps. An early model illustrating this problem-solving concept is the TOTE unit defined by Miller, Galanter, and Pripram (1960). Based on a sequence of status explorations (tests) and operations a person per-

forms in a larger task, the overall task becomes decomposed into sub-tasks. A specific sub-task is executed (operated on) until it has been accomplished (test and exit). This includes the knowledge of when to test what against which standards. The result is to start working on the next sub-task. Such sequences of performance can become automated. The result is the built-up of schemata in the sense of Piaget, which can be used adaptively to varying situations. The development of schemata needs to be repeated in experiences within varying contexts. Simulations are one approach to provide the necessary repetition in the required variations. When schemata become applied to newly encountered needs they provide a basis for domain-specific problem-solving activities.

Human problem-solving activities have a tendency for failure (Doerner, 1996). Among the reasons for potential failure are the tendencies for sequential, causal inferences as well as the neglecting of side effects and undesired long-term effects within decision-making for complex, dynamic environments. Approaches for counteracting this tendency are given within *system dynamics* (Forrester, 1968) and within *system thinking* (Senge, 1990). Both highlight the specifics of complex, dynamic environments, which incorporate, among others, delays over time, non-linear interrelations between variables and feedback processes within systems and thus are likely to confront problem-solvers with counter-intuitive system behavior. System thinking highlights the notion of systemic, not just systematic, structures of complex processes. System dynamics adds the aspect of modeling to these structures for the purpose of simulating the corresponding dynamics. Both refer to the concept of mental models (Johnson-Laird, 1983, 1988) as basis for action within solving complex, dynamic problems. In this respect, Senge points out that, "*Mental models* are deeply ingrained assumptions, generalizations, or even pictures or images that influence how we understand the world and how we take act action (1990, p. 8)." Such mental models are highly resistant against changes. For modification, they need alternative, powerful models which may be provided by active modeling and simulation-based learning activities (Hillen, 2004).

The motivational effect of simulation-based learning activities is well recognized (Jonassen & Tennyson, 1997). This is one reason for their long-term use in education. The strength of such motivational effects becomes obvious from reports on flow-experiences within simulation-based learning processes. Motivation is considered to contribute to problem-solving activity in a significant way (O'Neil, 1999). Processes of planning and of self-monitoring can be elicited within simulation-based learning activities. They can give room for self-reflection and for external feedback on such processes. This construct of motivation is beyond conventional objectives for teaching. Nevertheless, I consider motivation to constitute one specific potential of educational simulation use.

Web-based simulations can give access to problem-solving processes from different perspectives. For a single learner this may be achieved by being assigned to different activities within a given simulation. In local networks this can be extended to assigning activities to different learners who have to compete or to collaborate in respect to the objectives of the simulation. Web-based installations can extend this option for role taking into the distance. This can be accomplished both in an asynchronous as well as in a synchronous design. Role-players can compete or collaborate in indirect or in direct electronic contact with their co-agents. In this respect technology can provide a significant contribution to this field.

Finally, a primary objective of educational simulations from its first roots shall not be omitted. That is, the exposure of learners to the dynamics of processes. Whether there is a market-process, a chemical process, a physical process or a technical process, in each case there is a development of a system over time that a learner can experience

and into which she or he can intervene by means of given variables. Such dynamics in many cases can hardly be studied in real settings, due to their restricted accessibility. This can allow for learning processes at the skill level, it can allow for problem-solving activities, it can allow for processes of self-reflection, it can represent a subject matter in a mode which attracts attention and evokes motivation and/or interest. This can result in the development of specific skills in a playful as well as in a serious approach.

WEB-BASED APPROACHES TO SIMULATION DESIGN

In the early applications, simulations were used primarily within military, political, and economic scenarios for the purpose of decision-making support. That way, risky and costly strategies could be analyzed and evaluated in respect to probable consequences. The option of testing and evaluating the probable results of decisions without being faced with the outcomes from failure made simulations an interesting tool for education and training. For instructional purposes, the significant structures of a real world environment can be depicted within a model. Learners can intervene into the model by means of decisions and can observe and evaluate the consequences of these decisions. The conclusions of each decision (or set of decisions) constitute the basis for follow-up decision-making. The model used can be defined at a qualitative as well as at a quantitative level. For example, in an economic model the effect of workers' wages are often more related to quality of the work environment (i.e., qualitative) than monetary variables (quantitative). In reference to Wilbers (2001), I will address web-based approaches of technical simulations, business simulations, modeling, role-playing exercises, case studies, micro-worlds, and animations.

Technical Simulations

Simulators represent a *technical simulation* system within a model. The learner can manipulate the variables of the model directly. For that, the model depicts the regulation and adaptation processes within the real system. That way, the learner can improve through training the handling (process control as well as maintenance) of the system. Specific procedures can be trained and automated. Errors in handling the system have no impact on the real system and thus do not cause negative consequences such as cost, damage, or loss. This allows for testing of new procedures as well as of risky or dangerous ones. CNC-simulators, which represent the functions of automated drilling, metal shaping or wood processing machines, can include the option for transferring *debugged* procedures of code to a real machine. This provides realistic feedback to the trainee. In *virtual* laboratories, the performance of the real equipment, based on the learner's commands, is represented by means of animations. This includes handling and measurement processes and can reduce the need for manipulative skills on the learner's side. Because these approaches are computer-based to begin with, this makes it possible to represent the learner/system interaction in a web-based approach, given the necessary IT-technology.

Business Simulations

Two defining features represent the *business simulations* approach. There are a model-based simulation component and a social component. The model-based defines the task environment with its basic structures. This does not include the social aspects of the situation. Learners who have to perform in respect to the given knowledge base, the defined communication, and the decision-making processes control the social variables (Capaul, 2001). The outcomes from these processes, the *decisions*, are entered into the simulation model. Decision results are calculated and represent

the *environmental* conditions for the follow-up period of social interaction. This may comprise only one or more social parties competing against each other on a virtual market in a sequence of several periods. As there are a huge variety of such simulations and games, reflecting all kinds of markets, industries, strategies, and highlighting the two sides of the approach, there is the distinction between *tactical-decision simulations* and *social process simulations* (Gredler, 1992). The first highlights the systematic approach to information retrieval and uses within decision-making. This approach is included in many business games. The category of social process simulations stresses the interaction between learners and their references to attitudes and values. Learners have to act upon a defined role within a social framework and are requested to solve a given problem by means of specific interaction processes (Haritz & Breuer, 1995). Technological support can be given to this approach by means of web-based discussion groups and by video conferencing. However, there may be restrictions to personal interaction processes especially in respect to non-verbal communication. Highflying technologies based approaches in military systems and in corporate settings, are referring to this approach in terms of an electronic *war-room*.

Modeling

The *modeling* approach refers to the active development and/or elaboration of models to represent a given system. Within this approach, the previously addressed approaches of *system thinking* and especially of *system dynamics* come into play (Sterman, 2000). Following the modeling of a system is the study of its dynamics in simulation runs. A simulation construction process includes the analysis of the system behavior, which may provide reason for redefining or enhancing the model in respect to the representation of a certain aspect. Alessi (2000) refers to these two activities by applying the labels, *building and using models*.

Both activities are considered to contribute to the development of refined mental models for acting within the respective system (Hillen, 2004). Of special relevance here is the aspect that both technical and business simulations are based in models of the underlying system. The construction of the model is a necessary prerequisite for the simulation of the system. What makes a difference, however, is the degree of transparency that is associated with the modeling approach. Most technical and business simulations are based on *black-box* models, which are defined by their programming language code. Such code in addition becomes compiled and is stored in binary format. There is no need for explanation in respect to the *readability* of it for any user. The alternative is to make use of a systems dynamics based modeling tool. This allows for the development of *glass-box* models or at least *opaque* ones, which the user may access for elaboration of her or his mental model on the simulated system (Berendes & Breuer, 1999). That way, in addition to the process of building and refining models, the system itself can be of educational relevance. Open, glass-box models can also support participants using technical and business simulations in the process of developing valid mental models for their decision-making process in running such simulations.

Role-Playing Exercises

As stated in respect to business simulations, the social aspects of decision-making processes can be considered in simulations (Haritz & Breuer 1995). For example, a learner takes over a role, which he or she is not yet familiar with, and experiences a situation from an unknown perspective. This is meant to improve the ability for empathy (Capaul, 2001). A significant aspect of role-playing exercises is the option for a repeated experience of social situations and their analysis in respect to alternative interpretation and perception. Role-playing exercises do not necessarily depend on a technical platform. The web comes

into play when there is support from discussion groups (Wilbers, 2001) or when interactions become based in video-clips offering options to the learner for tactical decisions in social processes. This for example is used for the training of sales strategies or for counseling processes (Schwarzer & Buchwald, 2001).

Case Studies

The fifth approach, *case studies,* originates from law-studies and is based in the casuistic methodology. At the Harvard Business School the approach has been adopted to business administration studies. From that basis there is transfer into additional subjects especially for fostering problem-solving abilities (Frey, 1995). Cases represent authentic, that is from specific professional demands, derived problems. Students are to solve these by defining respective measures. Here too the decision-making situation is handled in the approach of a simulation. Also, there is no direct need for technical support. There are, however, more and more approaches for support of the case study approach within the Internet by means of corresponding web pages and by video clips.

Micro-Worlds

The concept of computer-based micro-worlds has been introduced in education from at least two perspectives. One is from the context of the first *revival* of computer-based instructional and learning activities in the early 1980s based on the newly emerging microcomputer technology (Breuer, 1983). In this respect the statements on simulators and on business simulations and games given above can be applied without essential differences. The technical platform has been stand-alone microcomputers. The options for graphical representation were low level but were emerging. The major educational advantage can be considered in the better accessibility of the technology within educational settings, which could provide an interactive access to simulation-based learning activities. This has been one of the lines of developments already addressed in the introductory statements.

The second perspective is from psychological research on complex-problem solving as initiated by the workgroup of Dietrich Doerner (1996) in Germany. For a brief orientation on these works the reader can refer to O'Neil (1999) and Frensch and Funke (1995) respectively. The basic purpose of this approach concerns the performance of individuals or of small-groups of people in complex, dynamic, and at least partly transparent environments, as many all-day situations people have to act in are considered to be. This approach too was based in the emerging microcomputer technology. It has made use of simulation programs in order to represent the problem-solving space the subjects of research have been confronted with. In the beginning subjects had no direct access to the respective computer-based model, but have been monitored and advised by a mediator. This has been modified with the emerging user-friendliness of technology and with the transfer of the approach into the field of management diagnostics (Frensch & Funke, 1995) and into the field of instructional/learning activities (Breuer, 1983; Breuer, 1985; Breuer & Kummer, 1990).

Here too there is no basic difference to the characteristics given before in respect to business simulations. In fact some of the simulations used for complex problem-solving research have been grounded in scenarios from business administration.

Animations

Computer-based *animations*, from a surface glance, can look similar to the interfaces (GUIs) of computer-based simulations. Looking at animations representing chaos systems for example, gives evidence that they are also based in simulation models. Additionally, there are options to vary parameters within the simulation model,

which results in the modification of the dynamic pattern on a simulation's interface. In respect to virtual laboratories, this I have already stated that the real equipment becomes represented by means of animations. Thus, there is no clear division-line between computer-based simulations and computer-based animations. I may define a distinction in respect to the stress that is given to the purpose to the underlying model. In case that it serves as a driver for an animation, I would not consider that to be a computer-based simulation. On the other hand, in cases that the animation represents features of the problem-space a user has to cope with, I would refer to that as a simulation. This however remains a weak point and is included in this line of argument for purposes of a more comprehensive view towards the field of simulations.

The six approaches to computer-based simulations have in common the following two features: they allow the learner to explore decision-making outcomes; and, second, the problem solving space is free of risks for the learner and her or his environment. The results of errors may be experienced, but they are not associated with real costs. That way, options for action as well as hypotheses on the outcomes of measures taken can be tested, and hypothesis-based approaches for solving complex, dynamic problems can be encountered. *Errors* experienced by a learner can become a driving source for additional learning-activities (Kriz, 2001).

The distinctions given between the approaches to simulations only highlight the variability of the concept. A sharp differentiation cannot be achieved. Especially, with regard to business simulations, this becomes obvious because they include elements of role-playing and case studies (Capaul, 2001). Learners become assigned to a specific task as part of the role of a decision-maker or a problem-solver. Within a market simulation this, for example, may be the role of a marketing manager. This role of a manager has to be performed within a given scenario. Such a scenario can be considered to be the *case* of the simulation. In consequence, there has to be a close correspondence between the paper-based scenario and the model that is driving the simulation for the calculation of the future system statuses. Each new system status represents a variation of the starting scenario and gives cause for new learning activities to define new measures of action in order to modify a given less desirable system status into a more desirable one. This constitutes the dynamics of the simulation environment. The description given closely matches the concept of micro-worlds. These are learning environments, which aspects of a segment of reality are represented within a simulation model and which allow students to explore the environment including the model it is based upon (Edwards, 1995).

Due to the tradition of the case approach within the concept of simulations and games I will use this label within our follow-up thesis. I'll stress the tactical-decision-making approach, because this is in large part based on a computer-based model of the represented environment. I will focus on the functions which simulations and games should have as part of learning environments and which specifics can be enhanced by means of web-based approaches. Again, I assume that the reader can transfer to the field of technical simulations and to related approaches.

PROBLEM-ORIENTED SIMULATION ENVIRONMENTS

Approaches to instructional design differ. They have developed over time and have stressed different perceptions of the learning process. Major effects on the discussions have come from the paradigmatic orientation within learning theories. Differences are due in large part to the cognitive shift in learning theories and, following that, to the constructivist view (Reimann-Rothmeier & Mandl 1996). This is not the place to elaborate on this development. Instead I follow two orientations.

The first is to base our web-based simulations approach in an up-to-date orientation. The second is to refer to an orientation that is in accordance with the underlying assumptions, which have at least partly been addressed already in respect to learning activities, grounded in computer-based simulations.

I refer to the pragmatic approach published by the working-group around Heinz Mandl at Munich that takes up a mediating position between the constructivist and the preceding cognitive approach (Reinmann-Rothmeier & Mandl, 1999). This pragmatic approach provides room for teaching activities that support individual processes of knowledge construction.

One basic orientation for web-based simulations is that of a problem-oriented approach (Tennyson, in press). Learning activities should be based in problems, which either are authentic in themselves or which at least refer to authentic problems situations, which are of relevance for the learner, which are based in present general or individual significance, and which evoke personal involvement. This orientation is based on the assumption that such problems result in four main effects:

- Lead to an active enquiry of the issue by the learner.
- Result in self-regulated learning activities.
- Evoke situated cognitions in the respect that inferences, solutions, points of view and interpretations are related to the problem situation.
- Allow for developing solutions by means of social interaction.

Behind these expectations, there is the concept of a learner that is predominantly active out of her or his own efforts and is receptive only for interim phases. The teaching environment in reverse should be able to switch between a mostly supportive and to a limited degree active performance. This position clearly objects to teaching approaches that favor unguided discovery activities on the one hand and externally directed learning activities on the other hand to avoid over-strain which can cause a decrease in motivation and hence lower learning outcomes. Problem-oriented learning activities are centered on five instructional design principles and corresponding objectives (Table 1).

The interpretation of this orientation in respect to learning with computer-based simulations is biased in favor of the simulation approach. There are, however, some rather obvious features to relate to at first glance. Simulation environments are set up for active explorations and interventions into the simulation model. They share the notion of active learners, who regulate their processes of orientation, learning, decision-making and/or problem solving.

Simulations represent a problem-space the learner can engage in. So, by definition, this is a problem-oriented approach. The degree of *authenticity* of the problem space will vary across context; this can be considered and planned for during the development of the simulation environment. This should be done in respect to the case(s) a simulation is grounded in and in respect to the features of the model(s) that drive the simulation. Given the multi-media features of contemporary computer systems, authenticity may also be supported by the inclusion of realistic and authentic images and video clips. Taking this approach would mean that there should be no simulations that merely represent a subject matter per se without providing for the opportunity to embed it into an authentic problem. This can also be considered as another claim for open designs, which allow for multiple uses of a simulation model. Realism also can be used in designing the GUI for a simulation. Students may look at features and information in a simulation as these can be *seen* in reality. A simple example may be the presentation of a gains and loss calculation on the financial status of a company. For that information, there is a professional format in business administration. Thinking for example of trainees in business administration to be a target group for a simulation, the information can be presented in the professional format. This is not only an issue of authenticity but can be considered also from the perspective of the ecological validity of the simulation system.

Multiple contexts can be offered by a variation of cases (scenarios) which simulations can be embedded. There is also the chance to have students actively relate from a simulation to their real (vocational or business) environment in respect to the structures and processes simulated.

Multiple perspectives are for the most part a defining feature of simulations based in their dynamics. For example, over time systems achieve different statuses of variables and thus have to be interpreted differently. This holds true for a single status representation. The level of a variable can or has to be read differently from different perspectives.

There is also a *social context* approach to this principle from having students' assigned to different activities in a simulation. In a single-user approach this can be accomplished by default parameter settings to a set of variables while the

Table 1. Principles and objectives of problem-oriented learning activities

Principle of learning	Objective
Authentic problems in a situated orientation	Applicability of new knowledge
Multiple contexts	Usability of knowledge; reduced adherence of knowledge to specific situations
Multiple perspectives	Extended flexibility of knowledge
Social context	Reduced idiosyncrasies, social entrenchment and knowledge
Instructional support	Reduced risk of failure, efficiency and effectiveness

student is in charge of one specific variable. This provides a certain perspective on the system to the student, which will become different when she or he become in charge of another variable. In a multi-user approach this can be accomplished by assigning students to different activities and then having them rotate on these assignments in a sequence of simulation runs. Each change in assignments provides a different perspective toward the system and to the actions taken by the co-participants.

The fifth principle, *instructional support*, is effective within simulation environments at a basic level as they are responsive to the decision-making processes of students. An input into the system generates an output. Students can figure out whether this output is reasonable and conclude from that on the appropriateness of their perception of the system. For such support a simulation-system would need a diagnostic component, which is not yet available. On that I will elaborate in the next section, taking into account the potentials of a web-based approach.

DIAGNOSTIC WEB-BASED BUSINESS SIMULATIONS

The thesis presented thus far can be condensed into on overview toward what simulations can contribute to the problem-oriented learning and instructional approach. Table 2 represents essentials from the authors' view, but does not claim to be comprehensive. In respect to most specifics of the web-based enhancements I cannot elaborate on all these within this presentation. I propose to make cross-references within this book for that. Instead the thesis will turn to the specific issue of online diagnostic support for web-based simulations based on assumptions in respect to the computer infrastructure within educational environments. The web-based approach targets at providing computer-based simulations to a wider audience within the educational system or within training organizations. This orientation has to take into account the average infrastructure, which today is, and in the near future supposedly will be, given within such settings.

Table 2. Problem-oriented learning activities and online-simulations

Principle of learning	Simulations & Games	Web-based Enhancements
Authentic problems in a situated orientation	- Starting case(s), - Multimedia representation(s) - Glass-box (opaque) models	- Downloads for starting cases - Downloads for multimedia features - Model-based GUIs - Pop-ups - Flash animations
Multiple contexts	- Multiple scenarios - Variations of models	- Access to multiple scenarios - Access to varying models
Multiple perspectives	- Feedback on dynamics - Role-taking within different activities of a simulation	- Online feedback to dynamics - GUI-based representation of different activities - Role-taking within different activities - (Asynchronous; synchronous)
Social context	- Collaborative problem-solving	- Distributed collaboration (Asynchronous, synchronous)
Instructional support	- Interactivity (feedback on system-statuses) - Diagnostic features	- Online feedback to dynamics - Dedicated web-pages - Web-based discussion groups (asynchronous, synchronous) - Web-tutoring - Online-diagnostics

Schools, training institutes and training departments today have computer laboratories giving students and teachers access to computing resources. Such computer labs are linked to the web. Workstations are equipped with standard software products. Among these is a standard browser for navigating in the web. For installation of additional, specific software there are restrictions in respect to administrative privileges and to financial resources. Access to the Internet is via a technology, which is shared for all the workstations within a lab. This causes a bottleneck for data exchange. In addition there are firewalls and/ or software installations for security against the hazards within the Internet. That way the user side of web-based simulations is to be considered a constrained environment with little options only for the use of sophisticated technology. This side should be served in a lean approach.

On the side of the provider, however, there are options for scaling the computer recourse needs. Computing power and speed for a server center can become available today with almost no restrictions. Different to the situation for the side of the many users this is a single need only. Restrictions on the server side again are in respect to security issues. The server needs control of access and defense against pirates in the Internet at the server side too. The conclusion from the technical perspective is, that requirements for the educational settings should be limited to the standard features available and that the process of data exchange should be designed for a lean and secure approach. Options for scaling the needs are on the side of the provider for web-based simulations. I will refer to this background in respect to three aspects of the design of web-based simulations:

• Design of a glass-box access to simulations.
• Implementation of a basis for online-diagnostics for simulation runs.
• Introduction of a process-perspective to the use of simulations.

The rational of a glass-box view on the model driving a simulation has been previously presented. In short, it is a method to provide the basis for the exploration of the complexity and the structural dynamics of the model. This can support the development of a holistic, systemic view toward the simulation, help for elaborations of the knowledge base, and support processes of meta-cognitive control. I approach that objective by means of the design of the GUI for a simulation game.

The approach is grounded in the use of a system dynamics-based simulation model. Such models can be designed in a graphical format on the computer screen. A necessary requirement is the use of system-dynamics-based modeling software. The model can be developed in a graphical representation and can drive the corresponding simulation directly due to the underlying mathematical integration procedures (Berendes, 2002). I discussed this in the preceding section on web-based approaches to simulation within the paragraph on modeling. Recent research has come up with the finding that such models can be read by students and can foster the development of higher-level cognitive processes that cover a systemic view toward the simulation model (Hillen, 2004). On that basis, Molkenthin (2003) has developed a GUI-based approach for using the model within the Internet. There is a prototype-system running now at the Johannes-Gutenberg-University Mainz, which can be accessed, on request. Factually, the GUI is made up from a set of corresponding pages that become presented to the user with a standard browser after a login at the simulation server.

The basis for online-diagnostics in simulation runs is defined in the set-up of the simulation-server. Between the simulation-driver and the user there is a data bank server. All communication from the simulation model to the user and vice versa becomes channeled through the data bank. This allows for keeping track of all exploratory actions a learner takes when working with the GUI. All decisions a learner enters into the system become recorded before they are entered into the simulation model. Likewise, all information on the status of the simulation model becomes stored in the database. This covers essential information available on the use of a simulation, which can be collected within a run of the system.

The content of the data bank can be accessed in parallel to the simulation run and processed by a diagnostic routine in respect to structural information. This can refer to the patterns within the exploratory activities of a learner as basis for her or his decision-making process. An approach for the retrieval of such pattern is given within the works of Streufert and co-authors (Streufert & Satish, 1997; Breuer & Streufert 1995). The moves of the user within her or his exploratory activities can be displayed and mirrored back to the user. This provides information for fostering self-reflection on the individual decision-making processes. In addition, a set of parameters can be calculated, which represent qualities within the processes. Examples here may be given by the breadth of the information search, which is applied, by the level of initiative a user takes or by the follow-through within the individual decision-making processes. Streufert and coauthors have defined such measures. They will have to be re-validated within the given context. Such process-related information can become available in addition to the standard system-status related information, which has always been given to the user since the early days of educational simulation uses. The interrelation between the two sets of information will be a focus for our future research efforts. The approach is considered to be an implementation of fourth generation measurement as defined by Bunderson, Inouye, and Olsen (1993).

In a medium perspective, the diagnostic information may become useful for instructional support to the learner. Feedback and feed-forward on decisions could as well be accomplished as the adaptation of simulation runs to the level of abilities individual learners can perform at. This however is an issue of research and developmental activities still to come.

CONCLUSION

Web-based simulations and games have been implemented in a variety of examples. They make use of features provided by technology. The application of principles of instructional design up to now does not seem to by a key issue in the field. This may in part result from the technical problems that have to be solved in the set-up of web-based simulations. The solution of such problems is essential. Beyond that there is the need for substantial foundation of the web-based approach in teaching/learning theory. The mere use of technical options can have an exploratory meaning. This however cannot be the level of professional developmental activities, which have to be grounded in principles of instructional systems design. I have outlined such an approach. Further I have tried to elaborate on the potentials that can be derived from that in respect to the implementation of diagnostic procedures, which can provide on-line information in respect to significant objectives of learning to the user.

The learning principle underlining our thesis is that thinking strategies are acquired in reference to employment of the learner's own knowledge base and that they are not independent thinking skills (Tennyson & Breuer, 2002). Our instructional principle is that, because cognitive complexity is ability, it can be developed and improved with instructional intervention. As this presentation indicates, problem-oriented simulations focus on the improvement and development of higher-order thinking strategies (i.e., problem solving within the context of employing the knowledge base).

Following this line of argumentation, I can look at two major perspectives. The first refers to research on learning processes which make use of computer-based simulations. Diagnostic procedures can be used to collect information on such learning processes. Unlike *blind* tracing procedures from information technology, the approach defined has a direct link to information on the content within a simulation. Working with controlled groups under experimentally controlled conditions can provide new insights into learning and teaching processes. Such research can take place in the field, given the accessibility of core elements of the learning-environment via the web. This can include additional data collection in a web-based approach. Our second perspective is defined within large-scale assessment of learning outcomes. Given the use of simulations in the diagnostics of managerial competences and for the measurement of problem-solving skills this could be extended to the diagnosis of competencies in the vocational respectively business administration field.

REFERENCES

Alessi, S. (2000). Building versus using simulations. In Spector, J. M., & Andersen, T. M. (Eds.), *Integrated and holistic perspectives on learning, instruction and technology: Improving understanding in complex domains* (pp. 175–196). Dordrecht, The Netherlands: Kluwer.

Berendes, K. (2002). *Lenkungskompetenz in komplexen ökonomischen Systemen*. Wiesbaden, Germany: Gabler.

Berendes, K., & Breuer, K. (1999). Potentiale von systemdynamisch basierten Mikrowelten. In Hohmann, G. (Ed.), *Simulationstechnik* (pp. 113–116). Erlangen, Germany: SCS Publishing House.

Breuer, K. (1983). Lernen mit computersimulierten komplexen dynamischen Systemen. In Lechner, E., & Zielinski, J. (Eds.), *Wirkungssysteme und Reformansätze in der Pädagogik* (pp. 341–351). Frankfurt, Germany: Peter Lang.

Breuer, K. (1985). Computer simulations and cognitive development. In Duncan, K. A., & Harris, D. (Eds.), *The proceedings of the world-conference on computers in education 1985 WCCE/85* (pp. 239–244). Amsterdam: North Holland.

Breuer, K., & Kummer, R. (1990). Cognitive effects from process learning with computer-based simulations. *Computers in Human Behavior, 6,* 69–81. doi:10.1016/0747-5632(90)90031-B

Breuer, K., Molkenthin, R., & Tennyson, R. D. (2006). Role of simulations in Web-based learning. In O'Neil, H., & Perez, R. (Eds.), *Web-based learning* (pp. 307–326). Mahwah, NJ: Erlbaum.

Breuer, K., & Streufert, S. (1995). Strategic management simulations in the German case. In Mulder, M., Nijhoff, W. J., & Brinkerhoff, R. O. (Eds.), *Corporate training for effective performance* (pp. 195–208). Norwell, MA: Kluwer.

Bunderson, C. V., Inouye, D. K., & Olsen, J. B. (1993). The four generations of computerized educational neasurement. In Linn, R. L. (Ed.), *Educational measurement* (pp. 367–407). Phoenix, AZ: Oryx Press.

Capaul, R. (2001). Didaktische und methodische Analyse der Planspielmethode. *Erziehungswissenschaft und Beruf, 1,* 3–14.

de Jong, T. (1991). Learning and instruction with computer simulations. *Education and Computing, 6,* 217–229. doi:10.1016/0167-9287(91)80002-F

Doerner, D. (1996). *The logic of failure: Why things go wrong and what we can do to make them right* (1st ed.). New York: Metropolitan Books.

Edwards, L. D. (1995). Microworlds as representations. In DiSessa, A. A., Hoyles, C., & Noss, R. (Eds.), *Computers and exploratory learning, computer and systems sciences* (pp. 127–154). Berlin: Springer.

Forrester, J. W. (1968). *Principles of systems*. Cambridge, MA: MIT Press.

Frensch, P. A., & Funke, J. (1995). *Complex problem solving. The European perspective*. Hillsdale, NJ: Erlbaum.

Frey, K. (1995). *Die Projektmethode* (6th ed.). Weinheim, Germany: Beltz.

Gredler, M. E. (1992). *Designing and evaluating games and simulations. A process approach.* London: Kogan Page.

Haritz, J., & Breuer, K. (1995). Computersimulierte und dynamische Entscheidungssituationen als Element der multikulturellen Personalentwicklung. In Scholz, J. M. (Ed.), *Internationales change-mangement* (pp. 109–120). Stuttgart, Germany: Schäffer-Poeschel.

Hillen, S. (2004). *Systemdynamische Modellbildung und Simulation im kaufmännischen Unterricht.* Frankfurt, Germany: Peter Lang.

Johnson-Laird, P. N. (1983). *Mental models. Towards a cognitive science of language. Inferences and consciousness.* Cambridge, MA: University Press.

Johnson-Laird, P. N. (1988). *The computer and the mind. An introduction to cognitive science.* Cambridge, MA: University Press.

Jonassen, D., & Tennyson, R. D. (Eds.). (1997). *Handbook of research on educational communications and technology.* Washington, DC: Association for Educational Communications and Technology.

Kass, A., Burke, R., & Fitzgerald, W. (1996). How to support learning from interactions with simulated characters. In Gorayska, B., & Mey, J. L. (Eds.), *Cognitive technology: In search of a human interface.* Amsterdam: Elsevier. doi:10.1016/S0166-4115(96)80030-6

Koedinger, K. R., & Corbett, A. (2006). Technology bringing learning sciences to the classroom. In Sawuer, R. K. (Ed.), *The Cambridge handbook of the learning sciences* (pp. 61–77). New York: Cambridge Press.

Kriz, W. C. (2001). Die Planspielmethode als Lernumgebung. In Mandl, H., Keller, C., Reiserer, M., & Geier, B. (Eds.), *Planspiele im Internet: Konzepte und Praxisbeispiele für den Einsatz in Aus- und Weiterbildung* (pp. 41–64). Bielefeld, Germany: Bertelsmann.

Lierman, B. C. (1993). Designing laboratory and simulation instruction. In Piskurich, G. M. (Ed.), *The ASTD handbook of instructional technology* (pp. 24.1–24.12). New York: McGraw-Hill.

Mayer, R. (2006). Ten research-based priniciples of multimedia learning. In O'Neil, H., & Perez, R. (Eds.), *Web-based learning* (pp. 371–390). Mahwah, NJ: Erlbaum.

Merrill, M. D. (1997). Instructional transaction theory: An instructional design model based on knowledge objects. In R. D. Tennyson, F. Schott, N. Seel, & S. Dijkstra (Eds.), *Instructional design: International perspectives. Vol. 1: Theory and research* (pp. 381-394). Hillsdale, NJ: Erlbaum.

Miller, G. A., Galanter, E., & Pripram, K. H. (1960). *Plans and the structure of behaviour.* London: Holt, Rinehart & Winston. doi:10.1037/10039-000

Molkenthin, R. (2003). *Zur Entwicklung einer systemdynamischen Unternehmenssimulation als Komponente von e-Learning.* Unpublished master's thesis, Johannes Gutenberg-University, Mainz, Germany.

O'Neil, H. F. (1999). Perspectives on computer-based performance assessment of problem solving. *Computers in Human Behavior, 15,* 269–282.

Reimann-Rothmeier, G., & Mandl, H. (1996). Lernen auf der Basis des Konstruktivismus. Wie Lernen aktiver und anwendungsorientierter wird. *Computer und Unterricht, 23,* 41–44.

Reimann-Rothmeier, G., & Mandl, H. (1999). *Unterrichten und Lernumgebungen gestalten.* Göttingen, Germany: Hogrefe.

Renkl, A., Gruber, H., Mandl, H., & Hinkhofer, L. (1994). Hilft Wissen bei der Identifikation und Steuerung eines komplexen ökonomischen Systems? *Unterrichtswissenschaft, 22,* 195–202.

Schwarzer, C., & Buchwald, P. (2001). Beratung. In Krapp, A., & Weidenmann, B. (Eds.), *Pädagogische Psychologie* (4th ed., pp. 565–600). Weinheim, Germany: Beltz Psychologie.

Senge, P. (1990). *The fifth discipline.* New York: Doubleday.

Sterman, J. D. (2000). *Business dynamics. System thinking and modeling for a complex world.* Boston: McGraw-Hill.

Streufert, S., & Satish, U. (1997). Graphic representations of processing structure: The time-event matrix. *Journal of Applied Social Psychology, 27,* 2122–2131. doi:10.1111/j.1559-1816.1997.tb01644.x

Tennyson, R. D. (2002). Linking learning theories to instructional design. *Educational Technology, 42*(3), 51–55.

Tennyson, R. D. (2005). Learning theories and instructional design: An historical perspective of the thinking model. In J. M. Spector, C. Ohrazda, & A. Van Schaak (Eds.), Innovations in instructional technology: Essays in honor of M. David Merrill (pp. 219–235). Mahwah, NJ: Erlbaum.

Tennyson, R. D., & Breuer, K. (2002). Improving problem solving and creativity through use of complex-dynamic simulations. *Computers in Human Behavior, 18,* 650–668. doi:10.1016/S0747-5632(02)00022-5

Tennyson, R. D., & Foshay, W. R. (1998). Instructional systems development. In Dean, P. J., & Ripley, D. E. (Eds.), *Performance improvement interventions: Methods for organizational learning* (*Vol. 2*, pp. 64–106). Washington, DC: The International Society for Performance Improvement.

van der Boom, G., Paas, F., van Morriënboer, J., & van Gog, T. (2004). Reflection prompts and tutor feedback in a web-based learning environment: effects on students' self-regulated learning competence. *Computers in Human Behavior, 20,* 551–568. doi:10.1016/j.chb.2003.10.001

Wilbers, K. (2001). E-Learning didaktisch gestalten. In Hohenstein, A., & Wilbers, K. (Eds.), *Handbuch E-Learning: Expertenwissen aus Wissenschaft und Praxis.* Köln, Germany: Fachverlag Deutscher Wirtschaftsdienst.

Chapter 2
Electronic Games Improve Adult Learning in Diverse Populations

Robert D. Tennyson
University of Minnesota, USA

Robert L. Jorczak
University of Minnesota, USA

ABSTRACT

Impressed by the motivation and effort displayed by players of complex and highly interactive electronic games, psychological researchers seek to apply gaming techniques to enhance globalization of diverse populations in problem solving and decision making. Researchers are interested in identifying characteristics of entertainment games that influence player motivation and learning. From the perspective of Interactive Cognitive Complexity theory, researchers need to examine how game variables relate to key learning components, including learner affect, cognitive strategy, and knowledge/skill acquisition. From a learning perspective, video simulation games are primarily a series of problem solving interactions set in a specific virtual context and using various learning aids that support the solving of problems to achieve the object of the game. Cognitive problem solving factors and strategies are; therefore, key independent variables for learning game studies. In creating such a framework, the authors propose five conceptual categories of instructionally relevant game variables: (1) virtual context, (2) problem specification, (3) interaction and control, (4) learning support, and (5) social interaction. Proposed is that electronic gaming methodology, founded in cognitive learning theory, will enhance efficient and effective development efforts to improve learning of global management strategies.

INTRODUCTION

The popularity of video and computer-based entertainment games, the high level of player effort displayed in learning the games, and the amount of learning that occurs in mastering a game, have led learning researchers to hypothesize that the techniques of such electronic games can be used to increase motivation and learning of decision making and problem solving outcomes (Garris, Alhers, & Driskell, 2002; Gee, 2005; Habgood, Ainsworth, & Benford, 2005; Prensky, 2001). Adult educa-

DOI: 10.4018/978-1-61520-623-0.ch002

tors are also interested in learning via electronic games because of the instructional trends toward learner-centered education wherein adult learners have increased involvement in learning activities and are given more control over learning goals and resources (Breuer, Molkenthin, & Tennyson, 2006; Dembo, Junge, & Lynch, 2006).

Designers of learning activities (learning resources) hope to significantly improve adult learning by merging the content of education (or training) with the format and techniques of entertainment games, thereby designing electronic or instructional games that often are computer-based. Educational researchers are interested in identifying the characteristics of entertainment games that influence player motivation and promote learning that could be incorporated into electronic instructional games. In addition, researchers are interested in how instructional games can be used to promote *higher level* learning outcomes such as problem solving and decision making (Kafai, 2001). To help instructional designers in the task of creating electronic games that are intrinsically motivating and enable players to achieve desired learning outcomes, educational researchers want to establish how variables of game design and play affect learning.

ELECTRONIC GAME DESIGN AND USE

Electronic games are not new, but research into the effectiveness of gaming is not extensive. Some empirical evidence suggests that games can efficiently promote learning (Cordova & Lepper, 1996; Henderson, Klemes, & Eshet, 2000; Moreno & Mayer, 2005; Ricci, Salas, Cannon-Bowers, 1996), but research into electronic game characteristics has been unfocused in regard to how games can promote learning (Dempsey, Lucassen, Haynes, & Casey, 1996; Habgood, et al., 2005; Kafai, 2001; Moreno & Mayer, 2005). Much of past and current research into the effects of games

tends to look at social factors suspected of being detrimental, such as whether video games increase violent behavior of players or socially isolate them (Anderson & Bushman, 2001; Emes, 1997; Mitchel & Savill-Smith, 2004).

While the fact that entertainment games are highly motivating and are often successful at helping players achieve game mastery is clear, just what makes them so, and whether or not those factors can be applied to improve adult learning in decision making and problem solving is not clear. Educators and instructional game designers would like to see students apply a similar amount of effort to learning school subjects as they see applied to entertainment games, but they are not sure how to use game techniques to achieve high learner motivation and also achieve meaningful learning. The current situation is summarized by Garris, et al. (2002, p. 442): "Unfortunately, there is little consensus on game features that support learning, the process by which games engage learners, or the types of learning outcomes that can be achieved through game play." Educators and instructional game designers need the input and direction of information provided by empirical studies to make good choices about applying the lessons of video games to learning activities. To design studies that answer key questions about learning via game play, researchers need to focus on characteristics of games that are suspected of playing a role in motivation and learning. The identification of such characteristics is not easy because games are complex and include many variables.

Conceptual Framework in Designing Electronic Games

A conceptual framework that identifies key variables of games that affect learning outcomes and relates those variables to learning theory can help focus design on factors that lead to the effective use of electronic games for adult learners in diverse global populations. The value of such a conceptual framework is how well it suggests design strategies and raises questions of interest to designers A framework can best suggest direction to designers if it identifies potential independent variables for design of instructional games, and places such variables in a theoretical context understood by learning theorists and researchers. A useful conceptual framework identifies, categorizes, and links game variables likely to affect learning to a learning model specified by a learning theory.

An example of a current learning theory is the Interactive Cognitive Complexity (ICC) Learning Model (Tennyson & Breuer, 1997). ICC is integrative information processing learning theory that views learning as the result of complex and non-sequential interactions of internal and external variables on the cognitive systems of a learner. According to the ICC model, the components of the cognitive system include learner affect, cognitive strategy, and a knowledge base, in addition to executive control and internal processing components. Each component of the ICC model has specific sub components (see Figure 1).

The *knowledge base* of the ICC model is the repository for all previously acquired information including declarative, procedural and contextual knowledge. Declarative knowledge includes concepts, rules, and principles, i.e., "knowing that…" Procedural knowledge is "knowing how" to use declarative knowledge to accomplish tasks and solve problems. Contextual knowledge is "knowing why, when, and where" of using declarative and procedural knowledge. Contextual knowledge is knowledge most used in association with cognitive strategies. Tennyson and Breuer (1997) see the structure of the knowledge base as complex networks of concepts and propositions (domains) that are organized into meaningful associations (schemata). For organizations with global aspects, a common knowledge base and cognitive strategies for employees is essential for success. Given the complexity of global industry and commerce, effective and efficient education and training employing instructional games and simulations is possible.

Cognitive strategies are processes that learners apply in elaborating and altering their knowledge

Figure 1. Interactive cognitive complexity (ICC) learning model

base and include differentiation, integration, and construction. The cognitive strategies of the ICC model are similar to a model of "multimedia learning" used by Monreno and Mayer (2005) in which the learner interacts meaningfully with materials that promote the cognitive processes of selecting relevant information, organizing information into coherent representations, and integrating the representations with existing knowledge. In the ICC model, cognitive strategies are used, in association with a learner's affect and executive control, to create and elaborate information in the knowledge base

In addition to declarative, procedural, and strategic cognitive outcomes, Garris et al. (2002), for example, include "skill based" (i.e., motor skills) and affective outcomes as potential learning outcomes. The ICC model finds the separation of affect and cognitive domains "somewhat arbitrary" and includes affect as directly influencing traditional cognitive processes (Tennyson & Breuer, 1997). The *affect component* of the ICC model includes motivation in addition to other constructs such as cultural diversity, attitudes, emotions, self-efficacy, and values. An instructional game may have the explicit goal of establishing or changing the affect of the learner (e.g., learner attitudes about the game subject) or the game may influence a player's affect in a way that indirectly affects learning in the cognitive domain. Global management strategies are in large part the affect and require interaction with knowledge and cognitive strategies domains.

The *executive control component* (ECC) actively (volitionally) and automatically regulates other components of the ICC model. Primary functions of the ECC include perception, attention, and resource allocation. Information from internal or external sources (the latter from sensory receptors) is assessed for potential value by the ECC which then directs attention and internal resources accordingly. Resource allocation functions include encoding into the knowledge base, storage processes that increase the strength of existing internal information, retrieval processes

that obtain knowledge (intentionally and automatically) from the knowledge base, and maintenance processes that keep information active within the ECC (Tennyson & Breuer, 1997).

All components of the ICC interact with each other and with sensory information from an external source, such as an instructional game, to elaborate the individual's knowledge base. The process is iterative as information enters the cognitive system from the senses continually, affecting the system components in combination with internally stored information (from the knowledge base) and various internal state variables (of, for example, the affective or executive control systems). New states and knowledge result from the operation of cognitive strategies on new and stored information. The cognitive system continually cycles through the process of updating internal states and information based on external and internal information. This chapter proposes a framework for designing the effects of instructional games on learning by suggesting how categories of game variables may affect the cognitive system of the learner as modeled in the ICC theory.

A key point in creating a useful framework based on game variables that affect learning is the distinction between the variables in the cognitive system of the learner and the variables in the game. The framework we present here focuses primarily on game variables that may affect the cognitive systems of the individual. Individual differences are found within the cognitive system, such as different information in the knowledge base (prior knowledge), different self-esteem, etc. The overall operations of the system, and the nature of the system components, however, are assumed to be the same for everyone. The states of individual variables of the cognitive system vary significantly among individuals and the state of those variables can and do affect motivation and learning—these are the "internal variables" of the ICC model. Thus, the state of internal variables primarily determines individual differences in this model.

Motivation and Learning

Malone and Lepper (Lepper & Malone, 1987; Malone, 1981; Malone & Lepper, 1987) proposed taxonomy of intrinsic motivation based in part on studies of characteristics of instructional computer games. Malone and Lepper (1987) propose that intrinsic motivation consist of individual motivations and interpersonal motivations (motivations that depend on other people). Within individual motivations, the researchers list challenge, curiosity, control, and fantasy as the major categories of intrinsic motivations. A useful framework for studying instructional games would link game characteristics (variables) to such motivations, which are established by interactions of various cognitive components in the ICC model.

Researchers studying games as potential learning tools tend to look at a how games motivate players because they assume that increased motivation will positively affect learning. Lepper and Malone (1987) note that motivation can affect learning by merely affecting time-on-task (i.e., more motivated learners will spend more time on the learning task). They suggest, however, that differences in motivated learning not related to the amount of time the learner spends on the task has greater theoretical significance. Lepper and Malone review various theories of how increased motivation can improve learning (e.g., increased arousal, attention, depth-of-processing, etc.) but the theorists note that "virtually nothing is known about this very fundamental question (Lepper & Malone, p.260)." The researchers suggest that the study of instructional games offers a practical avenue in which to study the connection of motivation to learning. Within a global environment, motivation is directly linked to cultural diversity. Therefore, in addition to the conventional variables associated with motivation, game design should reflect motivation differences among workers of diverse cultures.

INITIAL CONCEPTS AND DEFINITIONS OF ELECTRONIC GAMES

To begin the task of identifying gaming variables related to cognitive systems of the ICC model and therefore tie such variables to learning, some basic concepts must be defined. Unfortunately, many of the concepts associated with games and game-like learning activities do not have precise or even generally-accepted definitions. The concept of a *game* itself is not well-specified and there are several competing definitions in the literature of instructional games (Dempsey et al., 1996; Garris et al., 2002; Mitchel & Savill-Smith, 2004). Games are often associated with play, which can be defined as pleasing activity disassociated from direct consequences in the real management world (Fabricatore, 2004).

There also is no generally accepted taxonomy of *game types*. Mitchel and Savill-Smith (2004) review some ways games are categorized. Some games have characteristics similar to simulations. Both games and simulations have a set of rules governing interaction between the simulation (and game) and the user. Garris et al. (2002) distinguish games from simulations in stating that simulations represent real-world systems and games do not. Probably a more specific distinction is that games often have artificial consequences (such as amassing points) that are not realistic if used in simulations attempting to mimic real systems. Also, simulations are sometimes used to test hypotheses while games usually have distinct goals. We find the distinctions between simulation-like games and simulations of little value in determining how to use games to promote learning and prefer to view games and simulations as falling somewhere on a continuum of contextual realism.

What is of more value for instructional game analysis is examining what simulations and entertainment games have in common. Both involve a presentation to a user of a virtual context determined by the state (specific values) of a set of variables. The values of some or all of the state variables are presented to the simulation user (output) so that the user gets a sense of the current condition of the system being simulated. For example, a simulation might represent the state of a nuclear power reactor by presenting, on a computer display, representations of instruments and indicators found in an actual reactor control room (which indicate the state of reactor variables). Simulation users observe the output and determine an action (input) that changes the state of the simulation toward a desired state determined by the simulation user (or to tests hypotheses). Users observe the effects of their actions and input additional changes. (In the above example, the user might adjust reactor control rods to maintain a safe temperature within the reactor.) This process of observing the effect of actions and taking new action is iterative and defines the interaction cycle of a simulation. In short, users of a simulation game repeatedly observes the state of various simulation variables and responds interactively in determining changes and move the state of the game closer to achievement of the gaming goal (a targeted end state). This basic looping process establishes the essential interactive nature of simulations including simulation type games. In playing a simulation game, a player gathers information regarding the virtual world (the context) of the game, analyzes it, makes decisions, and acts to change the status of the gaming world and thus initiating a new interactive cycle (Breuer, Molkenthin, & Tennyson, 2006).

The interaction cycle of a simulation complements the internal cycle of the cognitive system specified by the ICC model (i.e., iterative update of stored information based on input and the state of internal variables). The output of the simulation is the input of the cognitive system and the output of the cognitive system (behavior) provides input to the simulation. The state of the simulation is altered toward a desired goal, and the internal state of the user (e.g., learning) is altered by interacting with the simulation. This compatibility is not surprising as simulations are meant to mimic real environments that the human cognitive system has evolved to deal with. The intrinsic attraction of simulation type games may, in part, be due to the fact that the human cognitive systems is most engaged when dealing with complex processes that mimic real world situations.

In *role playing games* (RPGs), a type of simulation game, players assume specific roles associated with game characters (avatars) that have various characteristics in terms of appearance, abilities, and affect. The roles available to and preferred by players in RPGs are of interest to entertainment game designers (Edwards, 2004) and may also be significant variables affecting motivation in instructional games that include roles (Habgood et al., 2005).

Educational or *instructional games* have specific learning outcomes as primary goals. For example, Garris et al (2002) propose a model of an instructional game that includes learning outcomes as goals and the interactive cycle described above, but also includes specification of a game context that includes both game characteristics and instructional content. This model raises an immediate issue. How distinct are instructional content and game characteristics in instructional games? In some simple instructional games, instructional content is not related to game characteristics. For example, an instructional game may drill a student on math problems set in a fantasy context with no connection between the math operations and the fantasy context. Such instructional games may not be as effective as games that have a virtual context related to the learning outcomes or that incorporate instructional objectives in game choices and interactions. Fabricatore (2000, p.14) states, "… the most common picture in the edutainment market is that there is the game and the cognitive task, and usually there is no cohesion between the two, meaning that the cognitive task has little or no contextual relevance in terms of game-play."

With effective entertainment games, "entertainment content" is found within the game characteristics, suggesting that instructional games in which game characteristics, including context and interactions, are closely tied to instructional content (i.e., content that supports achievement of targeted learning outcomes) may be more instructionally effective. The degree to which instructional content is contained within game characteristics is not easy to quantify but may be a key variable of games relative to game learning effectiveness because this linking of learning goal to context and interaction makes game play meaningful to the player. The importance of connecting game characteristics to learning objectives is supported by ICC theory in that the various components of the cognitive system interact and work with each other. Such integration of function suggests that input that is related in terms of context, action, and cognition will be more easily processed.

The types of learning outcomes that can effectively be targeted by instructional games is an open question. Orbach (1977) posits that simulation type games are more effective in addressing application of knowledge and attitudinal change than knowledge acquisition. The ICC model suggests that all learning outcomes necessarily involve learner cognitive strategies, affect, and existing knowledge. Altering a learner's affect can be a specific goal of an instructional game, but more often a game would use affect to more effectively add to the learner's knowledge base (e.g., motivated learners learn better). Improvements in learners' cognitive strategies can also be directly addressed as a learning outcome, but again, requiring that a learners exercise their cognitive strategies is often done to promote better and deeper learning of declarative, procedural, and contextual knowledge. The ICC model, and many instructional game enthusiasts, does not view games as being limited in addressing any types of learning outcomes.

Simulation games are complex and provide a rich environment that can best mimic real, authentic learning environments which most engage the cognitive systems of students. ICC theory supports the view that simulation games offer the highest potential as instructional games. Such games also provide the most comprehensive and flexible means to study instructional game characteristics.

ENTERTAINMENT GAMES AND LEARNING

Entertainment games that are simulations have characteristics that are intrinsically motivating to many players, resulting in high player effort in acquiring game skills and knowledge about the game. What variables of game design affect motivation? Simulation games used for entertainment seem to be motivating because they let humans do in a virtual world what they are designed to do in the real world: interact with rich environment to achieve a goal. This characterization of simulation games suggests that "rich environment" and "interaction" are concepts that need further examination. A rich environment can be achieved without interaction as when readers become cognitively and emotionally immersed in an imaginative and detailed story (which can be delivered by various media such as text, video, etc.). Activity and interaction without a rich immersive environment can also be achieved as when students *drill and practice* activities out of a meaningful context. A rich environment and interaction can be motivating independently, but the combination of the two may be much more motivating than merely the sum of their independent motivation.

Another characteristic of instructional interest is the way some entertainment games enable players to improve their performance and move towards goal achievement in small steps starting from low competence and knowledge. Instructional strategies also seek to gradually move novices to mastery. How do entertainment games achieve this gradual progression toward mastery? The structure of the progression of game play from easy tasks to harder task is certainly one factor, but games also include components specifically designed to aid and teach players (i.e., learning support components). This design strategy is interestingly based in behavioral psychology. That is, moving small, incremental steps followed by positive reinforcement. Success of simple tasks is followed by increasingly complex steps. The ICC theory is in part uniquely associated with behavioral components.

Rich virtual environments (complex and elaborated contexts), high interactivity within that environment, and a carefully constructed progression of challenges in obtaining a goal are the focus of interest in producing a framework of salient instructional game characteristics that affect motivation and learning. Questions about the motivational and instructional characteristics of games can best be answered by game research that uses a conceptual framework that links game variables to cognitive components of learners and categories game variables based on the characteristics of entertainment games mentioned above. In creating such a framework, we propose five conceptual categories of instructionally relevant game variables: (1) *virtual context*, (2) *problem specification*, (3) *interaction and control*, (4) *learning support*, and (5) *social interaction*.

Virtual Context

Most entertainment games are played in highly-contextualized virtual environments comprising the basic story and virtual setting of the game. While the virtual contexts of entertainment games are not always realistic, in the sense of simulating real world as opposed to imaginary situations, game contexts are internally consistent and logically elaborated to make the contexts seem authentic, even for imaginary settings. Game players use and acquire skills that seem very authentic because representations and events of the game; and the skills, tasks, and consequences required to achieve the game goals, are consistent with the context of the game (i.e., game play is

meaningful). Such consistency makes game play seem authentic and authentic tasks are thought to positively affect learning (Jonassen et al., 1999; Ormrod, 2004). Learning theorists recognize the importance of context in learning, a recognition associated with theoretical perspectives of situated learning and supported by the ICC model in that learners respond to authentic tasks by using learner-specific information in the knowledge base and engaging cognitive, affective, and volitional sub processes.

Context Type. The specification of a real world (e.g., WWII combat) or imaginary (e.g., interstellar combat) context is an aspect of game design that can affect player interest in the game. Educational games are successful in motivating players by offering virtual contexts that are intrinsically motivating to the target audience (Kirriemuir, 2003). The Becta (2001, p.7) study of computer games in education makes an explicit connection between context and learner interest: "The over-riding appeal of the games in lessons was the way in which learning opportunities and skills were presented in the context of a situation attractive to young people."

So what contexts are attractive to students? This is an area of potential investigation by researchers. It is likely that some contexts are inherently interesting to most students in a specific age group but the appeal of a context may be related to learner-specific preferences and needs. Gender differences have also been found regarding game context (e.g., Malone & Lepper, 1987). The ICC model suggests that aspects of learner affect (e.g., motivation) are influenced by how game content matches the state of the learner's cognitive system, for example, information already present in a learner's knowledge base. Learner-specific variables, such as existing declarative knowledge, may influence a learner's interest in contexts of specific types. For example, a learner may respond positively to a game situated in ancient Rome if that learner is somewhat knowledgeable about ancient Roman history. Differences in affective variables such as self-efficacy, self-image, etc. also influence the appeal of game contexts according to the ICC model.

Intrinsic and Extrinsic Fantasy. Game context has previously been investigated in terms of intrinsic and extrinsic fantasy. Malone (1981a) studied the connection between game fantasy (similar to game context, but constructed in the mind of the player) and motivation, based on whether the fantasy suggested by the game is intrinsic (connected to instructional goals of the game). Malone and Lepper (1987) studied student use of simple computer games in which the fantasy component was altered or eliminated and found that presence of fantasy affects motivation. Habgood et al. (2005) suggest that game fantasy is important in initially engaging a player's interest, but that other game characteristics, such as game operations and interactions, are more important for continuing motivation during game play. The relative importance of game context on motivation and learning in comparison to other game factors is still an open question.

Point of View. Players interact with entertainment simulation games from various *points of view*. In *first person* games the player literally sees through the eyes of the character in the virtual game context. In other points of view of entertainment games, the player controls a character they can see from various perspectives in the virtual space of the game (e.g., from behind the game character). The influence of point of view on learner motivation and learning is another potential area of investigation by instructional game researchers. In addition to physical points of view, role-playing games have functional and attitudinal perspectives that are assumed by players. In assuming attitudes different from the players' own attitudes, new perspectives open to the player, enabling learning that might be otherwise difficult or impossible (Gee, 2005).

Media Fidelity and Mood. The use of multiple media modalities (e.g., audio and video) seems to increase both interest and attention of game players. Another variable is the *fidelity* of a medium used to establish a virtual context. Entertainment games impress players with a visual representation of the virtual context that is detailed and realistic. Entertainment games use increasingly realistic graphics and animations to add to the realism and interest of the virtual context. The degree to which game media is real and complex (context fidelity) depends on the subjective perception of the player, but quantitative parameters such as maximum resolution of graphics and frame rates of animations are assumed by game designers to be related to visual fidelity.

Qualitative factors such as the artistic style of graphics, the graphic design of scenes, and genre of music, may contribute to increased affective qualities that players associate with the game. These qualitative characteristics, can, for example, establish a mood that promotes the targeted emotions of the game (e.g., creepy) which likely heightens player involvement.

Dynamic Media. Entertainment games use multiple media to great effect but emphasize visual stimuli, often by presenting a graphically realistic and highly dynamic three-dimensional virtual environment. Thus, the entertainment gaming medium is very different than the static and often text-based media used in many cooperate training and educational activities.

Habgood et al. (2005) suggest that research on how to represent information for learning identifies two key ways that representations can support learning: (1) by using representations that make key domain features explicit and (2) by using dynamic and interactive features. Game contexts which include representations that are related to the targeted learning domain are particularly those that serve to clarify or provide metaphors, may be beneficial to learning. Animated graphics increase player motivation and are preferred by game players (Rieber, 1991). Highly dynamic 3D visual stimuli may be inherently more interesting to students because they increase the realism of the virtual reality of the game and make games more experiential. Increased *use of multiple dynamic media* is a potential variable for examination by researchers studying the effect instructional games on learner affect and cognition. For example, Malone and Lepper (1997) found that students preferred games with audio effects. Increasing media type and dynamism also engage more cognitive systems and resources (e.g., sensory inputs) which may influence amount and depth of learning. An important feature of the ICC model is the concept that the cognitive system is highly receptive to all sensory inputs. It seems that a rich external environment is beneficial to gaining learner attention in the executive control function.

The type of context or story of a game, the point of view of the player, the fidelity of its presentation, and the dynamism of its media are all potential variables of context that can contribute to motivation and are therefore targets of investigation by researchers in relation learning. How context variables affect the cognitive system components (i.e., the affective, cognitive strategy, knowledge base, and volitional functions the ICC model) are key questions of the design of instructional games.

Problem Specification

Popular entertainment games do not depend only on interesting contexts for their appeal; games pose challenging problems for players to solve via their virtual actions. Many entertainment games are essentially a series of problem solving challenges in which problems are solved with knowledge and skills acquired by playing the game and manipulating the virtual environment. A problem, in this context, is loosely defined and ranges from virtual physical actions and motor skills (e.g., avoiding being killed by a game agent) to complex puzzles requiring a series of actions or responses by the player.

Learning theorists view problem solving as relatively high-level learning that has the potential to engage learners in the construction of solutions using their cognitive strategies and knowledge base (Tennyson & Breuer, 1997). Problem-based learning activities let learners direct and control actions in dealing with a presented problem in a specific context. The characteristics of real-world problem solving activities are the same factors observed in the virtual contexts and interactions of entertainment games. Problem solving may be inherently motivating to learners because it provides an environment in which learners can apply some or all of their cognitive strategies in achieving meaningful goals. In attempting to solve problems, a learner often must choose from their current knowledge, integrate new knowledge acquired about the problem, and construct a solution. Potentially, problem solving can employ all cognitive strategies noted in ICC theory.

From a learning theory perspective, the components of problems are known to include givens, goals, and operations (Ormrod, 2004). These components are also primary concerns of entertainment game designers in specifying game problems. *Givens* include the context of the game in addition to the many virtual objects and situations of the game. Game *goals* are often the solutions to problems presented by the game or achievement of a targeted end state. In many simulation-type entertainment games, problems are presented at various levels from the overall problem (the solution of which is the major goal of the game) to solutions of smaller-scale problems that prevent the player from proceeding toward the overall goal (and be forced to repeat the subordinate problem). Game *operations* include all the actions that a player can take, the objects or abilities players can acquire, and the results of actions taken. Game operations, therefore, include *rules* governing game interactions including what options are available for solving problems (i.e., the potential solutions to a problem and the consequences of correct or incorrect solutions).

All three components of problem specification (givens, goals, and operations) offer variables for study based on traditional research questions related to problem solving. For example, Malone and Lepper (1997) found that computer-games with goals had the highest correlation with student game preference compared to other game characteristics. Malone and Lepper (1997) also distinguish fixed goals from emergent goals that are found in open-ended games in which players define their own goals. Game with emergent goals (e.g., The Sims) better fit into a constructivist learner-centered instructional approach. (Goal selection or creation by learners is discussed further in regard to learner control in the section on learner control.)

Gee (2005) speculates that the motivation of a game is related to the ability of the game to provide pleasantly frustrating challenges (i.e., doable tasks with gradually increasing difficulty). Related to this variable is Fabricatore's (2004) contention that videogames necessarily include some type of opposition the player must struggle against in attaining game goals. He finds that "most of the products that crowd the educational games market cannot be defined as videogames at all since they lack the element of struggle, which deeply compromises the challenge that the player faces during the game-playing (Fabricatore, 2004, p.13)." The assertion is that instructional game designers are reluctant to hinder learning tasks with active game opposition and therefore design games that are less challenging and fun. Lepper and Malone (1997) include challenge as one category of intrinsic motivation in instructional games. They see challenge as the presentation of performance goals whose attainment is uncertain but likely to contribute to enhanced self-esteem of the players. They further suggest that uncertainty in goal achievement is based on difficulty levels and the inclusion of a random element. These variables of challenge are used extensively in entertainment games and their affect upon learning games is a potentially key area of study.

Problem *organization* or *structure* is another variable of potential study. Gee (2005) recommends that learners should not be "set adrift" to solve complex problems, but rather presented with problems they are currently equipped to solve (with

the domain knowledge in their knowledge base). Malone and Lepper (1997) note the importance of an optimal level of problem challenge in motivating game players and suggest the level at which a player succeeds 50 percent of the time (the highest level of uncertainty) is the most motivating. Successful games are adept at presenting a sequence increasingly challenging problems that are within the ability of the progressing player to solve. By this means, players are challenged to gradually move toward competence.

Other variables associated with problem solving include: the complexity of required problem-solving algorithms or heuristics, well-defined versus ill-defined problems, type of problem solving strategies (e.g., trial and error) required to solve game problems, and the type cognitive resources involved problem solving (Ormrod, 2004). For example, a study could attempt to correlate motivation with the types of problems presented by an instructional game, such as those with solutions requiring motor skills, mental puzzles, or those requiring a specific sequence of actions. Games requiring a specific type of problem solving strategy probably are best for teaching that type of problem solving, but other learning outcomes, such as acquisition of declarative domain knowledge, many be linked with the type of problem solving strategy required in a game.

Malone and Lepper (1997. p. 234) hypothesize that instructional environments that pose high-level goals (such as problem solving) can use "natural cognitive motivation to optimize existing mental procedures" to achieve high motivation (and, therefore, improved learning). They posit that adults naturally choose goals and challenge levels based on probability and perceived value of success and to maximize information about themselves. Thus, properly designed instructional games with goals appealing to the target learners and properly organized problems of carefully sequenced increases in challenge, will likely be motivating and prove efficient at helping players learn.

We propose also that the human cognitive system includes curiosity (similar to challenge but not involving self-esteem). One type of curiosity, sensory curiosity is attraction to unexpected sensory stimuli and the other, cognitive curiosity, attempts to achieve completeness, consistency, and parsimony in cognitive structures (such as the ICC knowledge base). Designers of games must consider the potential of game problems to stir the curiosity of the targeted audience of learners.

Adult learner affect, measured by reports of satisfaction, frustration, and perceived arousal and enjoyment, can be measured in regard to challenge, opposition, goal orientation, and difficulty levels of game problems. These variables are related to differences in affect and can be presumed to affect learning by the ICC model. Also, the retention and comprehension of declarative, procedural, and contextual information may differ with variations of instructional game problem specification.

Learner Control

Learner control is another category of variables that may affect players' motivation, cognition, and learning when using instructional games. Learner control variables include interactivity (e.g., choice of action) and personalization (e.g., choice of representation) and can extend to the selection or specification of game goals.

Entertainment game environments are highly interactive. Interaction involves the transfer of information between the game and the cognitive system of the player. Players observe the virtual environment and input information or manipulate that environment to solve problems or meet challenges. Players receive consistent, realistic feedback for their actions. Designers of computer-delivered instruction have long believed that high levels of interaction in computer-assisted learning correlate with more and better learning (e.g., Northup, 2002). Some theorists believe that learning requires (or is equated with) activity itself (e.g., Jonassen, 2002). So, it is reasonable to expect that a highly interactive environment of simulation type instructional games can have positive effects on learning. High levels of interaction involve players in the game (e.g., demand high levels of resource allocation, such as attention) and gives players a sense of empowerment and control because the players' actions are seen to affect the game (solve problems and resolve situations), which, for example, can affect the learner's self-efficacy and self-esteem, factors known to affect learning (Bandura, 1993).

Learner control in simulation games often manifests as the ability of players to choose or control virtual activity (i.e., operations). In entertainment games, players are given much discretion in choosing virtual tools (e.g., weapons), initiating actions of a player avatar (e.g., jumping, climbing, picking up objects), selecting directions in which to move and explore, and other volitional actions. Game designers specify problems and potential solutions, but players determine how problems are solved. High interactivity combined with many choices results in players feeling empowered. Players control their own fate, and this empowerment seems related to the general appeal of entertaining simulation games.

In their taxonomy of intrinsic motivation in instructional games, Malone and Lepper (1987) state that the amount of control a learner has depends on (a) the range of outcomes possible in an environment and, (b) the extent to which a outcome is contingent on responses available to the learner. Control can be viewed as interaction in which reaction of the simulation (feedback) is contingent on learner actions (input). Malone and Lepper (1997) point out that range of choice (e.g., number of choices) and power of choice (the strength or extent of a choice) are two parameters of choice and therefore are potential variables of instructional games that may affect learning.

When playing complex simulation games, adult players must use their cognitive processes, such as the differentiation and integration strategies of the ICC model, to deal with game-presented problems. These cognitive processes are used in reorganizing, elaborating, or constructing declarative, procedural, and contextual knowledge acquired from the game. In their experiment involving a multimedia instructional game, Moreno and Mayer (2005) speculated that problem-solving interactions involve the cognitive processes of organizing and integrating. The study found evidence that a simple interaction (choosing via a multiple choice question) promotes cognitive activity to a deeper level than simply being told a correct answer.

Control extends beyond a player's ability to choose actions and direction within the game. *Personalization* involves the players choosing non-operational attributes, such as the appearance of their avatar or a name used in the game. *Customization* involves the player's ability to change aspects of game contexts or operations (rules). The ability to choose how a game looks or operates can give players a strong perception of control which may relate to player motivation. Some research indicates that increased personalization and customization results in better learning (e.g., Cordova & Lepper, 1996, Malone & Lepper, 1987).

Higher levels of learner control could include having the adult players set their own game goals. Constructivist learning theorists posit that learners learn more deeply when they can choose their own learning goals and learning activities (Jonassen, Howland, Moore, & Marra, 1999). Gee (2005) calls this setting of goals and rules by game players "co-design". Kafai (2001) identifies "games-to-learn" as games that are created or designed by students (as opposed to "games-that-teach" designed with fixed goals by others). She sees game creation as more compatible with constructivist perspectives in letting students choose game goals and construct a means to address those goals via play. Letting the adult learner choose learning goals and activities enables that student to elaborate from his or her existing knowledge base or construct new knowledge by employing

the integration and construction cognitive strategies specified by the ICC model. This approach would offer learners in international organizations with diversity in the practice of their cultural differences. That way, management strategies would reflect the uniqueness of each culture and indicate that no one strategy is correct for all cultures. That is, it can be shown that the path to success is multivariate.

Interactivity and learner control are game variables that do not lend themselves to easy quantification. But such variables play an important part in how instructional games can affect learner cognitive strategies and affect. Researchers need to examine how variations in perceived player control in instructional games influences the affective component (e.g., challenge and frustration) of the player's cognitive systems, and also influence the use of cognitive strategies (e.g., the types of interaction that better support integration and construction). Exposing students to variations of games similar in all respects except variables of interactivity and learner control is one way that instructional games can prove to be a valuable tool for learning research with adults of different cultures.

Learner Support

Ideally, entertainment games support the learning of game rules and functions implicitly by having players explore game context via the game's problem-solving interactions. The interactions are designed to teach the game simply by playing it. As the games tasks and challenges are carefully designed to reveal how to play the game. Entertainment games employ implicit learning by a gradual and sequenced increase in problem difficulty by breaking down complex tasks in to smaller component task and presenting those tasks in a logical sequence much as is recommended by systematic design of instructional material. Ideally, an instructional game would also impart its instructional content to learners through the problem-solving interactions of game play.

Rarely, however, is a game so well crafted that satisfactory learning occurs only by playing the game. Many entertainment games, therefore, explicitly support learning with various techniques and components including the presentation of tutorial and reference textual and graphic information. Explicit learning support of computer-based games is accomplished in ways traditionally used in supporting software applications including user manuals, "on demand" information (e.g., online help) and "just-in-time" information that is presented as needed. Information presented just in time is usually context sensitive (relevant only to the player's current situation), players are presented (or given access to) information when it is required within the sequence of game play. Requested information is often more comprehensive and players choose relevant information. Game players need not read a reference manual an attempt to store all relevant information about rules, game context, operations, and game scenarios if information is available in context and/ or on demand. In using context-sensitive learning support, entertainment games avoid problems of cognitive overload in learning the rules of complex game and present information in a context which makes it meaningful. "Human beings are quite poor at using verbal information (i.e. words) when given lots of it out of context and before they can see how it applies in actual situations. They use verbal information best when it is given 'just in time' (when they can put it to use) and 'on demand' (when they feel they need it) (Gee, 2005, p. 7)." Because context-sensitive information is more meaningful it is, presumably, easier to accommodate in the learner's knowledge base.

The presentation of learning support information related to solving virtual problems is a source of important variables of instructional games. The use of on-demand or context-specific learning support by instructional games may be more effective than traditional instructional or training presentations such as lectures and tutorials and suggests several variables for investigation of instructional games. For example, Moreno and Mayer (2005) found that "guidance," in the form of explanatory feedback, improved learning transfer. Leutner (1993) found that, under specific conditions, system-initiated adaptive (context sensitive) and on-demand non-adaptive learning support can improve learning of domain knowledge.

In their study of the reactions of adults to 40 instructional games, Dempsey et al., (1996) found that players would at first try a trial-and-error strategy and then look for instructions or "hint screens" within the game. The researchers recommended that games clearly state goals and objectives to engage players and examples of how to play.

The use of simulation games for learning can be criticized as lacking in teaching function and teaching presence. This concern may reflect a feeling that students cannot learn domain-specific declarative knowledge from games that do not include traditional didactic instructional strategies. Explicit learning support components can provide information in a format more like traditional direct instruction. The need or value of such explicit learning components in a well-designed instructional game is, of course, an open research question.

Other ways entertainment games explicitly support the learning of game functions and rules is with game scenarios (sub contexts) that are specifically designed for learning game basics or practicing game skills. Gee (2005) labels these functions "fish tanks" (simplified game scenarios) and "sandboxes" (safer game scenarios). These practice scenarios help players learn game operations and by practicing the game with less complex problems and interactions. Such practice seems most useful for learning motor skills, but the usefulness of such practice scenarios for learning targeted management strategy domain knowledge maybe value in a multi-cultural organization.

Feedback, in its basic form, is the change in state of a system that can be observed by the person interacting with a simulation. Simulation game designers choose what information is displayed to players. The type and amount of information displayed affects the player understands of how the simulation is responding to input. Feedback information that better enables a user to understand the operation or state of the simulation is said to make the simulation more "transparent" (Leutner, 1993). How to increase transparency of instructional simulation games and the effect of doing so on learning is a clear area of potential investigation by instructional game researchers. Leutner (1993) investigated the effect of explicit learning support on learning simulation transparency.

Within instructional activities, feedback has an additional definition. Feedback is information (usually text) that performs a specific pedagogical role, usually providing information about the "correctness" of a learner's response (e.g., answer to a question). Feedback has many variables, it can be as simple as a single word (e.g., correct/incorrect), a statement the expected response; or it can be more complex in explaining why and response is correct or not. This type of feedback is a form of just-in-time context-sensitive explicit learning support as it is presented in association with learners' interactions and contains information specific to the particular input of the learner.

In their study of types of learner support in an instructional game, Moreno and Mayer (2005) examined the differential effect of simple feedback (telling the learner if their answer was correct or not) and more complex feedback that provided guidance to the correct answer. Guidance feedback included a discussion of why the player's response was incorrect based on a set of principles that are the main instructional content of the game. The guidance was delivered by a computer-based "agent" who assumed the role of an instructor. This study is a good example of an experiment that addressed specific variables of gaming related to explicit learner support

(feedback and guidance) in regard to specific model-based cognitive processes. It is worth noting that the effects of the use of agents on learner affect and performance in instructional games is another area of potential study.

Some theorists speculate that explicit teaching processes make games more instructionally effective, but more studies examining specifically what instructional support is effective and what cognitive processes are affected are needed, especially in light of concerns about too much didactic content reducing the appeal and instructional effectiveness of games.

Social Characteristics

Many learning theorists stress the value of social interaction in learning (e.g., Jonassen et al., 1999). The social characteristics of entertainment games vary greatly. Games can be used to promote social skills as the targeted outcome of the game or take support collaboration that targets specific content domain outcomes.

Various types of multi-user entertainment games can be found on the Internet (e.g., MUDs, MOOs, and MMORPGs). Socialization occurs within popular games by the interaction among game players in clubs, Internet sites, etc., forming an affinity group for specific games (Gee, 2003). Multi-user entertainment games can be played with or against other players. Game play is often competitive, but it can also be cooperative, both goal formats increase player social interaction. Instructional games have the same social variables and can be used to support cooperative and collaborative learning. "Learning is a social activity, and computers can support the social construction of knowledge, with computer games providing environments which can demand collaboration of the people using them (Becta 2001, p.9)."

Game players understand that social interaction with other players will help support the learning of complex game rules. Discussion of game play within a community of players is a means of scaffolding game learning (i.e., it is a form of learning support). Game playing communities are examples of distributed knowledge and, as such, communities promote social interaction as players improve their game knowledge by interacting with others in the community. Learning to socially interact with others is a major side benefit of games. Gaining status within a group via game knowledge and skill is an additional motivation for playing games and may boost self-efficacy and self-esteem.

Gee (2003) makes a strong case that what people think and learn is determined by their interactions with other people who are members of their social group. This assertion implies that researchers may need to consider how student membership in various social and cultural groups affects motivation and learning when using games. Adult students are in some obvious social groups (Gee calls them "affinity groups") such as being employees in a specific job situation but in different locations. Students, however, are also members of various other social groups (e.g., those who play sports) and can form social groups in regard to games.

Malone and Lepper (1987) include interpersonal motivations in their taxonomy of intrinsic motivation in games. Interpersonal motivations (those depending on other people) include cooperation and competition. The strength of these motivations may be very dependent on individual differences or related to personal traits such as gender. As with game context, problems, and interactions; interpersonal game functions may or may not be directly tied to learning outcomes. Cooperation or competition may be an important targeted learning outcome, may be essential to the targeted learning outcome, or may be unrelated to the learning outcome. Malone and Lepper (1987) also identify recognition (e.g., by peers) as an important social motivator.

CONCLUSION

Ron Edwards, an influential entertainment game designer, has formulated the GNS theory which posits that game players fall into three categories: gamists, narrativists, and simulationists, who have quite distinct goals in playing a game. Gamists seek competition and challenge; narrativists seek story and characters; and, simulationists like exploration and experience (Edwards, 2004). Edwards finds that games cannot be designed to meet the expectations of all three types of players. Edwards' player types can be viewed as having a primary motivation tied to major categories in the framework we propose: gamists are primarily motivated by aspect of game goals (problems), narrativists by game context and, simulationists by game interactions and representations. If true, these game player categories suggest a player-specific trait related to player motivation that also may have significance for the instructional games. Specific game goals will align with the motivations of only a subset of the target audience of the instructional game and may be less effective for those learners with a different goal orientation.

Dempsey, et al. (1996) recognize that educational researchers will be increasingly asked how to incorporate games in to learning environments and that they may be "perplexed" about how to answer the question through research studies. Some theorists and researchers also posit that the variables of the game-player interaction are so numerous, and so hard to measure and control, that a systematic study of gaming variables may not be productive or even possible (Dempsey et al., 1996; Quinn, 1997). We believe, like Gee (2005, p. 1) that "Good game designers are practical theoreticians of learning…" While good game design is currently an art more that a science, game designers intuitively attend to gaming variables that influence player affect and learning for specific audiences. Variables of interest to entertainment game designer can serve to indicate potential instructional game variables for systematic study.

A more systematic study of electronic games can result from a conceptual framework that suggests categories of instructional game variables that are related to learning as suggested by a modern cognitive learning theory such as Interactive Cognitive Complexity theory. We suggest that it is useful to view instructional gaming variables from the perspectives of virtual context, problem specification, learner control, learner support, and social characteristics. More and more focused studies are required to guide instructional designers in creating electronic games that work within the international work force. Clear rationales for the design of electronic games and evidence that they are effective learning resources will further the use of games in traditional learning environments.

REFERENCES

Anderson, C. A., & Bushman, B. J. (2001). Effects of violent video games on aggressive behaviour, aggressive cognition, aggressive affect, physiological arousal, and prosocial behaviour: A metaanalysis of the scientific literature. *Psychological Science, 12,* 353–359. doi:10.1111/1467-9280.00366

Bandura, A. (1993). Perceived self-efficacy in cognitive development and functioning. *Educational Psychologist, 28,* 117–148. doi:10.1207/s15326985ep2802_3

Becta, D. A. (2001). Computer games in education. *Project Report.* Retrieved July 20, 2005, from http://www.becta.org.uk/page_documents/research/cge/report.pdf

Breuer, K., Molkenthin, R., & Tennyson, R. D. (2006). Role of simulation in Web-based learning. In O'Neil, H. F., & Perez, R. S. (Eds.), *Web-based learning: Theory, research, and practice* (pp. 307–326). Mahwah, NJ: Erlbaum.

Cordova, D. I., & Lepper, M. R. (1996). Intrinsic motivation and the process of learning: Beneficial effects of contextualization, personalization, and choice. *Journal of Educational Psychology, 88,* 715–730. doi:10.1037/0022-0663.88.4.715

Dembo, M. H., Junge, L. G., & Lynch, R. (2006). Becoming a self-regulated learner: Implications for Web-based education. In O'Neil, H. F., & Perez, R. S. (Eds.), *Web-based learning: Theory, research, and practice* (pp. 185–202). Mahwah, NJ: Erlbaum.

Dempsey, D. V., Lucassen, B. A., Haynes, L. L., & Casey, C. S. (1996). *Instructional applications of computer games.* Paper presented at the 1996 annual meeting of the American Educational Research Association, New York.

Edwards, R. (2004). *System does matter.* Retrieved July 28, 2005, from http://www.indie-rpgs.com/_articles/system_does_matter.html

Emes, C. E. (1997). Is Mr. PacMan eating our children? A review of the effect of video games on children. *Canadian Journal of Psychiatry, 42,* 409–414.

Fabricatore, C. (2000). *Learning and videogames: An unexploited synergy.* Retrieved June 20, 2005, from www.learndev.org/dl/Fabricatore-AECT2000.pdf

Garris, R., Ahlers, R., & Driskell, J. E. (2002). Games, motivation, and learning: A research and practice model. *Simulation & Gaming, 33,* 441–467. doi:10.1177/1046878102238607

Gee, J. P. (2003). *What video games have to teach us about learning and literacy.* New York: Macmillan.

Gee, J. P. (2005). Learning by design: Good video games as learning machines. *E-learning, 2*(1), 5–14. doi:10.2304/elea.2005.2.1.5

Habgood, M. P. J., Ainsworth, S. E., & Benford, S. (2005). Endogenous fantasy and learning in digital games. *Simulation & Gaming, 36*, 483–498. doi:10.1177/1046878105282276

Jonassen, D. H. (2002). Learning as activity. *Educational Technology, 42*(2), 45–48.

Jonassen, D. H., Howland, J., Moore, J., & Marra, R. (1999). *Learning to solve problems with technology–A constructivist perspective.* Columbus, OH: Merrill Prentice Hall.

Kafai, Y. B. (2001). *The educational potential of electronic games: From games-to-teach to games-to-learn.* Retrieved May 16, 2006, from http://www.culturalpolicy.uchicago.edu/conf2001/papers/kafai.html

Kirriemuir, J. (2003). *The relevance of video games and gaming consoles to the higher and further education learning experiences.* Techwatch Report: TSW 02-01. Retrieved June 30, 2005, from http://www.jisc.ac.uk/uploaded_documents/tsw_02-01.rtf

Lepper, M. R., & Malone, T. W. (1987). Intrinsic motivation and instructional effectiveness in computer-based education. In Snow, R. E., & Farr, M. J. (Eds.), *Aptitude, learning and instruction: III. Conative and affective process analyses* (pp. 255–286). Hillsdale, NJ: Erlbaum.

Malone, T., & Lepper, M. R. (1987). Making learning fun: A taxonomy of intrinsic motivation for learning. In Snow, R. E., & Farr, M. J. (Eds.), *Aptitude, learning and instruction: III. Conative and affective process analyses* (pp. 223–253). Hillsdale, NJ: Erlbaum.

Malone, T. W. (1981). Toward a theory of intrinsically motivating instruction. *Cognitive Science, 5*, 333–369. doi:10.1207/s15516709cog0504_2

Mitchel, A., & Savill-Smith, C. (2004). *The use of computer and video games for learning: A review of the literature.* Retrieved June 30, 2005, from http://www.lsda.org.uk/files/PDF/1529.pdf

Moreno, R., & Mayer, R. E. (2005). Role of guidance, reflection, and interactivity in an agent-based multimedia game. *Journal of Educational Psychology, 97*, 117–128. doi:10.1037/0022-0663.97.1.117

Northup, P. (2002). A framework for designing interactivity into web-based instruction. *Educational Technology, 41*(2), 31–41.

Orbach, E. (1977). Some theoretical considerations in the evaluation of instructional simulation games. *Simulation & Games, 8*(3). doi:10.1177/003755007783003

Ormrod, J. E. (2004). *Human learning* (4th ed.). Upper Saddle River, NJ: Merrill Prentice Hall.

Prensky, M. (2001). *Digital game based learning.* New York: McGraw-Hill.

Quinn, C. N. (1997). Engaging learning. *Instructional technology forum.* Retrieved July 30, 2005, from http://it.coe.uga.edu/itforum/paper18/paper18.html

Ricci, K., Salas, E., & Cannon-Bowers, J. A. (1996). Do computer-based games facilitate knowledge acquisition and retention? *Military Psychology, 8*, 295–307. doi:10.1207/s15327876mp0804_3

Rieber, L. P. (1991). Animation, incidental learning, and continuing motivation. *Journal of Educational Psychology, 83*, 318–328. doi:10.1037/0022-0663.83.3.318

Tennyson, R. D., & Breuer, K. (1997). *Psychological foundations for instructional design theory.* In R. D. Tennyson, F. Schott, N. Seel & S. Dijkstra (Eds.), *Instructional design: International Perspective, Volume 1: Theory, research, and models* (pp. 113-133). Mahwah, NJ: Erlbaum.

Chapter 3
Human Factors in Knowledge Management:
Building Better Systems by Employing Human Systems Integration Methods

Tareq Z. Ahram
University of Central Florida, USA

Waldemar Karwowski
University of Central Florida, USA

Chris Andrzejczak
University of Central Florida, USA

ABSTRACT

This chapter presents an overview of key Human Systems Integration (HSI), Human Factors (HF), and Knowledge Management (KM) methods that support building user-centered systems. The chapter stresses that KM can benefit the systems design process by reducing rework and duplication of effort. In addition, tools aiding KM implementation within the HSI and Human Factors (HF) domains are discussed. HSI practices created and employed within the discipline of Systems Engineering (SE) have brought positive changes to the systems development lifecycle (SDLC) process, affording increasingly complex and smarter systems to be built. These increases in systems complexity have created a need for systems designers and program managers to apply KM principles to systematically create, share, retain, and transfer workforce skills, facts, processes, capabilities, and experiences in a systematic fashion. The authors describe the importance and benefits of integrating HSI and KM practices to build better and smarter systems.

DOI: 10.4018/978-1-61520-623-0.ch003

INTRODUCTION

Knowledge Management

Knowledge Management (KM) is a multidisciplinary practice spanning fields such as information systems and business administration. It has many applications in industry. Knowledge Management focuses on identifying, employing, storing, and distributing available resources on a project to generate expertise, insight, and information during the development of a product, service, or model. The process of KM incorporates elements of knowledge acquisition, its creation, and its transition into the information stores of society (Phoha, 2001). Studies indicate that the effects of a changing, diverse, and mobile workforce result in companies having an increasingly difficult time retaining knowledgeable employees (Ryan, 2000). The integration of Human Factors in Knowledge Management entails capturing and retrieving information relevant to human capabilities and limitations to build new knowledge or extend current knowledge. This process is inextricably bound and inseparable from human cognition, introducing all sorts of bias. It is a classic problem of psychology, where the cognitive agent must study its own workings, complete with biases, limitations, and perceptual qualities.

Therefore, the management of knowledge occurs within a biased behavioral, cultural, and personal context. This context may vary greatly between individuals. Past research in KM has revealed the importance of considering human cognitive and physical factors when designing knowledge management systems. Human factors practitioners study and apply knowledge relative to human physical, cognitive, and sensory capabilities and limitations to design better products, processes and interfaces (Karwowski, 2006a). KM is especially important in situations where tacit (as opposed to implicit) knowledge exists. Tacit knowledge is not consciously known or recallable by a subject performing a task (he or she "just

knows how to do it"), while implicit knowledge is knowledge which is easily transferred by the subject to others, and thus, can be easily documented (Alavi & Leidner, 2001). The advantages of adopting KM practices include:

- Rapid formation of subjective, objective, and empirical knowledge
- Knowledge integration
- Accessibility and conductivity to collaborative problem solving

Human Systems Integration (HSI) is pertinent to systems engineering, specifically, the human component of every system. HSI aims to prevent system designs that do not adequately consider human capabilities and limitations. Thus, HSI is the choice interdisciplinary process for integrating human capabilities and limitations within and across all system elements, i.e. an essential enabler to systems engineering practice. The goal of HSI is to optimize total system performance while accommodating both select and general characteristics of the end user population that will operate, maintain, and support the system in an effort to minimize overall system lifecycle costs and enhance human-system compatibility (Folds et al., 2008). Throughout system design, development, fielding, sustainment, and retirement processes, HSI experts work to ensure the consideration and accommodation of human capabilities and limitations. Within systems engineering, the human is recognized as an integral element of each system through the HSI component, which ensures that human factors have a prominent place throughout the total system lifecycle. Good design practices include the human element within requirements, reliability, and maintainability processes.

The attention to HSI in system development programs have resulted in hundreds of human-centered design improvements and enhanced human-system compatibility. Efforts were concentrated on maximizing total system performance through improvements in workload management, safety, maintenance, and reliability. These efforts resulted in billions of dollars saved and the prevention of hundreds of possible system related safety issues (Booher and Minninger, 2003).

Karwowski (2000) stated that system-human compatibility should be considered at all levels, including physical, perceptual, cognitive, emotional, social, organizational, and environmental considerations. This requires quantification of the inputs and outputs that characterize a set of system-human interactions. Karwowski (2000) stated "*at the present time, no universal matrix for measurement of such compatibility exists*". A new science deemed 'Symvatology' has been introduced based on investigations of human-system compatibility. Symvatology was proposed to help to advance the progress of the ergonomics discipline by providing a methodology for system design for compatibility.

The Human Factors Engineering (HFE) field of study is concerned with studying human capabilities and limitations to improve work performance, safety, and efficiency (Dempsey et al., 2006) (Karwowski, 2006). The array of work human factors and ergonomics professionals perform has been discussed in detail by Karwowski (2005; 2006) and Salvendy (2006). The primary focus for HFE is to consider human capabilities and limitations within system design to achieve optimal levels of total system performance across factors such as operation, maintenance, repair, and disposal. Comprehensive task analysis are utilized by HFE to help define system functions and, in turn, allocate those functions to meet system requirements.

Benefits of Knowledge Management to Organizational Workforce and Global Economy

The rapid changes inherent in globalization, increasing pressures in terms of reduced resources, increased complexity in the design process, and influx of regulations have all forced organizations to adapt their operations. The most critical

resources are no longer material in nature, but exist within the human mind. Ideas such as human capital, workforce retention, and workforce development now are prevalent in industry. The formation of the Knowledge Management field seems to mirror the ergonomic movement during the Second World War. Human labor was no longer seen as expendable, and so practices and regulations were put into effect to first protect workers from acute and cumulative stress injuries and to maximize their efficiency. Human physical limits were measured and understood, and work processes were tailored around these limitations and capabilities. As with the human cultural development, once the physical needs of people are attended to, the cognitive needs soon are placated.

KM can be considered analogous to this process. The knowledge, skills, experience, and capabilities of the workforce must now be employed with the greatest efficiency while understanding and accounting for limitations on the social and cognitive levels. There are fewer and fewer opportunities to be a "jack of all trades," and it is impossible to be an expert on everything, even within a given industry. Information sharing and transfer are more important than ever. Duplication of effort across organizations and recreating previous discoveries and solutions waste organizational time and resources. KM provides the tools and processes to prevent such inefficiencies.

The global economy has increased pressures to outsource and distribute a workforce in the interest of recruiting the best talent at the best price. This action forces organizations to develop a plan for transferring knowledge to these outlying branches (Baum and Greve, 2001). Knowledge is a resource, and the best use of this resource leads to increased competitive advantage for an organization (Argote and Ingram, 2000). A good example of using distributed teams for competitive advantage is that of global software engineering. Thanks to time zone differences, a 24-hour development process is attainable. However, this process must be managed effectively and work handed off appropriately to reduce possible overhead that would erode the seemingly non-stop workday benefit (Gorton and Motwani, 1996). A good analogy is a relay race; the individual runners must time their handoffs with minimal losses in time, thus maximizing their intense energy outputs. Just as in a relay race, however, proper "handoffs" of work outputs are critical.

Today's economic pressures force many smaller organizations to merge. Many of these mergers fail for cultural reasons, both on a corporate and national level. When two culturally dissimilar corporations merge, performance generally decreases as individuals within the merged new entity tend to overestimate the performance level of the new organization based in its new size and capability. They blame the lack of actual performance on the members of the other organization rather than the actual cause created by the conflicting culture and overhead costs introduced (Weber and Camerer, 2003).

KM attempts to understand and overcome social issues as well. Individual expertise levels affect knowledge sharing within heterogeneous groups. For example, Thomas-Hunt et al. (2003) found that expertise as well as social isolation level affects an individual's tendency to share their own knowledge as well as acknowledge the contributions of others. Individual expectations, as well as notions of social connectedness affect perceptions and ultimately actions in group activities. Good practices encourage sharing by all members, not just the well-connected and positively perceived experts.

Knowledge Management Best Practices

KM best practices seek to understand, employ, and overcome our inherent social tendencies and streamline the group process. In times of tough global economies and scarce resources, managing the most important resource, the knowledge or human capital resource, becomes critical. Knowledge

work processes are structured around four main categories, capturing knowledge, transferring knowledge, knowledge creation, and knowledge integration (see Figure 1). Knowledge integration can be thought of as the end product of the process. Integration requires inputs from the other three activities with the results of the integration process driving the remaining three. In the first stage of most projects, the focus is capturing knowledge from all resources. Over time, focus starts to shift to transferring knowledge to more stable processes and activities after which fruitful knowledge creation and implementation occurs. In this model, knowledge integration happens at any stage to foster value creation and positive impacts on systems design and usage.

Experts in the HSI domain contribute to KM by ensuring that human capabilities and limitations are identified and considered early in system design phase. It has become clear from real world application that treating the system as separate from the users results in poor performance and potential failure in the operational setting of the system. Continued growth in technology alone while neglecting user population characteristics and needs has not delivered desired results. Systems engineers and other disciplines are beginning to understand the role humans play in technology systems. The core challenge is to balance successful hardware and software solutions with human capabilities and needs. To this end, the human element must be considered as a part of the system, and included within the entirety of the design process.

To define the requirements of humans as a fundamental system component, it is essential to understand the inherent capacity of end user populations and their typical operational environment (Booher, 2003). A description of a population's capacity incorporates more than the basic anthropometrics or the cognitive capability of the average member of the user population (Chapanis, 1996). For example, the U.S. Air Force HSI program has been designed to support mission

*Figure 1. Human factors knowledge work process-
es (Extended model based on original framework
by Back, 2005)*

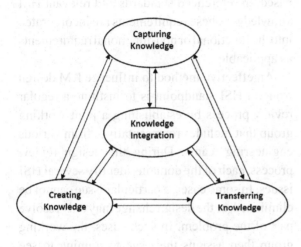

*Figure 1. Human factors knowledge work process-
es (Extended model based on original framework
by Back, 2005)*

critical operations by incorporating systems that optimize human performance at every level. Two studies conducted by the U.S. Air Force Science Advisory Board (AF SAB, 2005) indicated that the increased need on human operators negatively affected the accuracy of decisions, decreased occupational safety and increased the total lifecycle cost of the system. This is generally caused by increased volume and complexity of information, limited amounts of decision time, varying job demands and decreased manpower constraints (i.e. fewer operators allowed). Recommended actions included the importance of strengthening HSI methods during the systems engineering processes. Paul Kaminski, a United States Air Force subject matter expert, stressed the need for systems engineering and incorporating HSI knowledge management methods in the following statement:

"The central problem is a breakdown in the most basic element of any big military project: accurately assessing at the outset whether the technological goals are attainable and affordable, then managing the engineering to ensure that hardware and software are properly designed, tested and integrated. The technical term for the discipline is

systems engineering. Without it, projects can turn into chaotic, costly failures." (Taubman, 2008)

Failure to incorporate HSI methodology within systems engineering processes may result in failure to meet desired system objectives, poor design, unnecessary burdens on the workers, and in some cases negative environmental impacts that could affect public health and safety. The owner of the system may incur unnecessarily high costs in connection with total ownership. The long-term success of the system and customer satisfaction rely heavily upon demonstrated effectiveness of the total system inclusive of its operators, maintainers, supported customers, sustainers, and the support network. In all systems, failure to address long-term lifecycle issues can result in lost customer confidence, decreased market share, product liability, and a decrease in repeat business. The aforementioned methodologies include the familiar, carefully structured approach to meeting functional and non-functional requirements. The systems engineering team relies on a multidisciplinary approach to assist in analyzing customer requirements.

The study of human factors in KM is concerned with capturing, organizing, and retrieving information in order to build knowledge. The field is further focused on fostering human factors in organizational learning, organizational memory, workplace design, and expertise management. Human factors methods and practices have become more commonplace especially within the past three decades. Current research in KM is limited in areas that focus on human cognitive, social, and behavioral factors. In a recent study, Thomas et al., (2001) stated the following:

"Knowledge is bound up with human cognition, and it is created, used, and disseminated in ways that are inextricably entwined with the social milieu. Therefore, we argue that knowledge management systems must take both human and social factors into account... we describe a number of

the research findings and applied techniques that motivate our work. We believe that these pieces are vital parts of any picture of knowledge management. At the same time, we acknowledge that there are undoubtedly other missing pieces to the KM puzzle, and that many distinct, but still valid, pictures of KM are possible" (Thomas et al., 2001).

Large organizations falsely conclude that by simply making information widely available without context or organization will solve most KM problems. Knowledge storage is only as good as the ability to recall and use it. IBM has found one approach in which to correct this issue. The IBM management-training program is very scenario-based and is one of the few examples of successful interactive KM implementation. A typical training scenario asks trainees to make choices in realistic situations common to those systems designers and managers face. These scenarios are based on analysis of real cases. They assume that when the individual makes a wrong decision, it motivates the person to read and understand the rationale behind the concept of a specific design. The advantage of such simulations is that even if the individual learner is sitting alone in front of a computer console, learning is influenced by individual cognitive and social contexts. These contexts of application that provide much of the motivation, interest, and guidance on what constitutes a good system design decision. Recent work at IBM Research Labs has focused on developing a comprehensive mixture of strategies for enhancing creativity and knowledge creation (Thomas et al., 2001).

Elements of Human Systems Integration and Knowledge Management are derived from requirements for performance, efficiency, safety, environment, operation, maintenance, and training. Some of the relevant human-centered requirements can be nested deep within design requirements (e.g. mechanical and electrical requirements). During the requirements analysis phase of the project, systems engineering elicits requirements from the various engineering teams. HSI team members will have to work with systems engineers to develop additional well-defined requirements based on referenced standards and relevant HSI knowledge. These requirements are incorporated into the functional or non-functional requirements as applicable.

An effective method to influence KM design from an HSI standpoint is to institute a regular review process by establishing a joint working group that includes representatives from various engineering teams. During the design review process, each of the domains identify several HSI issues. In some cases, a particular issue cannot be eliminated, or the design change may only resolve part of the problem. In such cases, the working group then assigns the issue to training to see if it is feasible to develop a standard operating procedure (SOP) that will minimize the impact to the human and the system. This should not be construed as a license to shift the responsibility (and cost burden) from design to training. Rather, it should be regarded as a joint process or even better a last-resort that requires an authorized deviation from requirements. It is important for experts in the KM domain to build relationships with members of the integration team and continue supporting the systems engineering team in order to rejoin the project at the right time to help support the integration process.

A critical component for HSI and KM methodology should be the verification and validation process that provides a clear way to evaluate the success of the system. The HSI team should develop a test plan that can easily be incorporated into the systems engineering test plan. Performance of the human in the system must be validated as part of the overall system. Nowadays, systems engineering practitioners need a stand-alone testing method for KM to show the interaction between the user and the controls or displays as well as user performance on a specific task. The key objective is to develop a close relationship between KM and systems engineering. This methodology can address the performance of the human operator, maintainer, or both with respect to the overall system. The HSI and KM practitioners find it difficult to convince program managers of the full value of implementing KM or HSI applications (Booher and Minninger 2003). Nowadays, the requirements and technologies have changed and, as a result, systems and engineering strategies that worked with past systems may not work with present or future systems. Best practices can be applied to KM and HSI scope of activities in order to maximize the return on investment, starting with the point when key technologies are matched to a basic set of user requirements. According to Walker (2000), best practices divide the product development stage into two phases—system integration and system demonstration. Figure 2 illustrates a HSI system development phase incorporating best practices.

In order to achieve optimal system design, best practices used by commercial firms indicate that optimal results can be achieved by the concurrent completion of product/system development with low rate production. Achieving low rate production could allow the firm to verify when a product has met user requirements while under Statistical Process Control (SPC), and satisfy HSI requirements in both operational conditions and manufacturing processes. Best practices used by HSI practitioners provide early risk reductions which improve quality while reducing cost and schedule.

For example, the Comanche Rotor System Design (CRSD) program provides excellent lessons learned for industry on the benefits that can accrue when KM best practices and recommendations are adopted.

"The Boeing-Sikorsky design team had originally considered a rotor blade design that met government specifications but one for which MANPRINT and ILS contractor personnel had raised maintainability and transportability concerns. Because the team was still in competition with McDonnell Douglas, it was reluctant to expend extra design resources where they were not required by government specifications. Nevertheless, by bringing the full focus of the domains together on this issue, MANPRINT/ILS persevered, and the team decided to develop a new modular design that was easier to maintain, reduced the potential for installation error, and eliminated close-fit tolerance for transportability" (Booher and Minninger 2003).

The amount of additional effort needed in the analysis, testing, drawing change, and evaluation for the Comanche Rotor System Design was reported as approximately 395 man-hours, with the total cost below $50,000. However, when a life-cycle cost analysis was conducted, approximately $150 million was avoided due to improvements in the design. Savings would be in the area of manpower, and specifically, requirements reductions

Figure 2. Product development phases with HSI knowledge mapping to ensure mature design (Modified from original model by Walker, 2000)

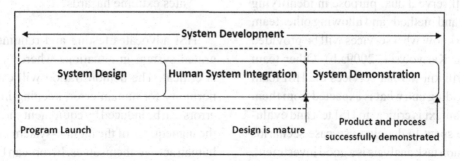

in skill and numbers, due to reduced maintenance on the rotor system and reductions in transportation requirements (Booher and Minninger, 2003). In estimating HSI and KM return on investment, program managers encounter the problem of making a decision on whether or not to pursue further HSI implementations. This involves selecting an alternative over a set of choices based on specific HSI performance measures as discussed in the next section.

HUMAN SYSTEMS INTEGRATION KNOWLEDGE MANAGEMENT COMPONENTS

Successful integration of HSI and KM into the system design process starts at the very beginning of a project with the development of a comprehensive human systems engineering strategy, employing both joint systems engineering and HSI working groups. The strategy clearly articulates project roles to ensure that all team members understand the role of each HSI team member and how each of these roles relates to the integration of the human into the overall system. The strategy will go on to define how HSI and KM as a whole will impact the systems engineering process. In order for the HSI plan to be effective it should include a detailed method along with a description of how each of the domains within HSI will interface with all the other project team elements (including project management, various engineering teams, along with systems engineering and support services, such as integrated logistics support). A HSI strategy will serve a dual purpose in identifying the process and methods and allowing other team members to know what services will be provided (Ahram and Karwowski, 2009a,b). Other team members will know what services the HSI team will be providing and what is expected from them in return. Context is critical to HSI test and evaluation. Time spent to develop use-case scenarios during mission task analysis is a good investment.

Scenarios chosen for HSI demonstration should be those that are critical for mission and maintenance success (Ahram and Karwowski, 2009).

Figure 3 shows a KM model with three main components: Human Factors, Systems and Processes, and Technology Integration (sometimes referred to as knowledge sharing technology) which includes data repositories (i.e. web based material repositories and digital libraries). KM components are connected together with a networking medium (i.e. communication systems, discussion forums, email).

In Figure 3, HSI forms the center of three KM components (Human Factors, Systems and Processes and Technology Integration); each of these components interacts with each other to promote knowledge generation. The interaction is dynamic and the structure of the interactions depends on the focus and goals of a particular task or system functionality. External factors, such as environmental factors (i.e. community of practice and best practices in industry), contribute by capturing external knowledge related to the system while the internal factors (i.e. organization internal knowledge systems) refer to extracting knowledge in order to identify what is relevant to system design and to the overall integration task. Here are some questions that HSI analysts commonly investigate:

- Which conditions are people the most fatigued?
- What are the critical decisions?
- What are their triggers?
- What combination of circumstances generates extreme hazards?

HSI advocates testing and running the integrated system in situations where performance is critical. The demonstration will evaluate opportunity for human error, keeping in mind that errors can be induced by equipment shortcomings, the inadequacy of the human-system interface, or human actions themselves. Errors can be captured during the demonstration by trained observers, system databases that record system status during executions of tasks, or usability tools that track keystrokes and eye movements or user reports. Many "human error" accidents were the result of hardware and software designs that neglected HSI. The HSI evaluation must also demonstrate the resilience of the integrated system and answer the following:

- When the equipment fails, does the system provide information enabling the operator to formulate and execute remedial actions, or does the operations concept call for evacuation and abandonment?

- Has the information support plan been modified without human systems integration review to remove data sets that would otherwise enhance the ability of the operator and maintainer to diagnose and respond to anomalies?

Moving on to knowledge management, current challenges include the failure of many KM efforts associated with huge organizational losses and high cost in some cases (Davenport et al., 1998). The reasons for current KM problems have to do with treating knowledge similar to information or referring to knowledge as an asset that could be generated at no cost (Ladd & Ward, 2002). Researchers also note that a conflict between the goals of KM, environmental and organizational culture might cause a major conflict, reducing the effectiveness of projects (Davenport et al., 1998) (Ladd & Ward, 2002). Ladd and Ward (2002) referred to this conflict in KM and organizational culture as the reason to study a possible relationship between organizational culture and knowledge transfer.

Developing KM test parameters, as shown in Table 1, can be an effective strategy for defining and executing initial KM practices at the system level. Managing these parameters during task analysis establishes traceability (Ahram et al., 2009). Parameters are evaluated against objective, physical criteria while others require evaluation in the context of use-case scenarios in order to be meaningful. Subjective evaluation is required for the more general parameters, which can be accomplished by using rating scales or by administering questionnaires developed by HSI specialists and can also be supplemented with interviews. Thus, it is clear that HSI is an important aspect of systems engineering that brings human considerations into

Figure 3. HSI knowledge management components

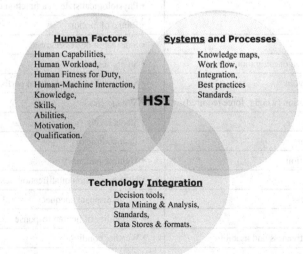

the system design process and seeks to maintain the human elements of the system.

MODEL-BASED HUMAN-SYSTEMS INTEGRATION FOR KNOWLEDGE MANAGEMENT

The model-based HSI approach for knowledge management system differentiates between human performance effectiveness criteria. These criteria determine the total system mission performance and acceptability that is directly attributable to specific actions allocated to human performance metrics (Ahram et al., 2009). These indicators measure which performance effectiveness criteria are met. The basic steps for the HSI-KM approach are summarized below:

1. **Human Systems Integration KM Process:** Apply a standardized approach that is integrated with systems processes.

2. **Top-Down Requirements Analysis:** Conduct this type of analysis at the beginning of the design process and continue the process to decide which steps to include in the optimization of workforce and system performance.

3. **Human Systems Integration Strategy:** Incorporate inputs into system processes throughout the lifecycle.

4. **Knowledge Management Integration Plan:** Prepare and update HSI plan regularly to facilitate implementing various activities.

5. **Human Systems Integration Risks:** Identify, prioritize, track, and mitigate factors that will adversely affect human performance.

6. **Knowledge Management Metrics:** Implement practical metrics in specifications and operating procedures to evaluate progress continually.

7. **System Interfaces:** Assess the relationships between the individual, the equipment, the

Table 1. Sample human systems integration KM test parameters (Source: Folds et al., 2008)

• Access to amenities	• Illumination conditions
• Acoustics	• Maintenance/installation safety
• Atmosphere (temperature, pressure, humidity, quality, etc)	• Maintenance/installation time to complete
• Auxiliary equipment and attire form, fit, function	• Motivation of performance
• Decision correctness	• Physiological state as a function of time (fatigue, stress)
• Decision, time to make	• Range of motion
• Disorientation and awareness	• Safe, rapid ingress/egress
• Effectiveness of error prevention or mitigation designs	• Safety restraints
• Effectiveness of workspace layout	• Sound, vibration effects on performance
• Equipment handling by population (weight, force required)	• Storage space
• Error rate per unit time	• Stress levels
• Error recovery rate per unit time	• Task complexity
• Fault identification and correction	• Training adequacy
• Food and water availability	• User population qualification / experience
• G-forces or zero-G effectiveness	• Waste disposal adequacy
• Hazard protections	• Variability of human response
• Human-system interface effectiveness and usability	• Weather conditions
• Information transfer	• Workload

individual, between the individual (or organization) and the organization to optimize physiological, cognitive, or socio-technical operations.

8. **Modeling:** Use simulation and modeling tools to evaluate tradeoffs.

Knowledge Management Modeling using Systems Modeling Language (SysML)

This chapter emphasizes the importance of human factors in knowledge management in an effort to build better systems through Human Systems Integration (HSI). The manner in which to apply human factors knowledge to achieve safe and efficient engineering practices is the goal of HSI. A model-based human systems integration framework based on Systems Modeling Language (SysML) will be presented in order to facilitate human factors knowledge extraction, organization, and management.

Systems Modeling Language (SysML) borrows heavily from the Unified Modeling Language (UML), and several diagram similarities between the two languages exist. The Object Management Group (OMG) (http://www.omgsysml. org/) defines systems Modeling Language (OMG SysML) as:

"a general-purpose graphical modeling language for specifying, analyzing, designing, and verifying complex systems that may include hardware, software, information, personnel, procedures, and facilities. In particular, the language provides graphical representations with a semantic foundation for modeling system requirements, behavior, structure, and parametrics that are used to integrate with other engineering analysis models. SysML represents a subset of UML 2 with extensions needed to satisfy the requirements of the UML for Systems Engineering RFP as indicated" (OMG SysML specification, 2007)

Figure 4 depicts a typical SysML diagram taxonomy with KM model considerations. The KM capabilities have been identified under both the behavior and structure diagrams. This serves as a placeholder for a human capabilities diagram and task requirements with respect to human performance diagram. Figure 5 provides a summary for the system model with HSI methods as a framework for analysis and traceability.

In Model-Based Systems Engineering (MBSE), human behavior model libraries and behavior analysis can be integrated with user-domain model libraries. Friedenthal *et al.* (2008) stated:

"Model-based systems engineering (MBSE) is the formalized application of modeling to support system requirements, design, analysis, verification, and validation activities beginning in the conceptual design phase and continuing throughout development and later life cycle phases."

The KM model shown in Figure 6 extends the three main components for Human Factors Knowledge work processes:

1) Capturing Knowledge with the following functions:
    ◦ Task Descriptions
    ◦ Task Flows
    ◦ Goal Oriented Task List
    ◦ Decision and Task priorities
    ◦ Product Points Design Scenarios
    ◦ Functional Analysis
2) Creating Knowledge and design synthesis with the following functions:
    ◦ HSI Requirements and Specification
    ◦ Rapid Prototyping
    ◦ Decision Support Tools
    ◦ Usability Testing
    ◦ HSI Improvements
3) Transferring Knowledge with the following functions:

Figure 4. Extended SysML diagram taxonomy incorporated with HSI and KM considerations (Extended model based on original framework by Friedenthal et al, 2008)

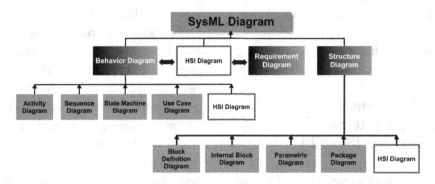

- ○ HSI modeling
- ○ Design improvements
- ○ Model testing
- ○ Model requirements
- ○ HSI software design
- ○ Evaluation
- ○ Testing and proof of concept
- ○ Updates to model

KNOWLEDGE MANAGEMENT SOFTWARE IMMPLEMENTATIONS

Human Factors in KM is challenging, especially for large organizations with complex projects involving multiple disciplines. Despite our increasing ability to communicate and share knowledge, it seems that many engineering groups do not share their findings outside of their group (Stasser

Figure 5. Extended system model incorporating HSI-KM as a framework for analysis and traceability (Extended model based on original framework by Friedenthal et al., 2008)

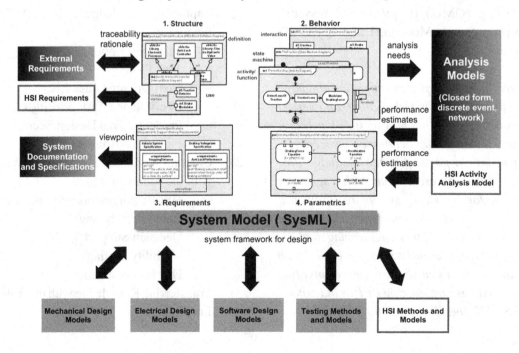

Figure 6. Human systems integration knowledge management model components

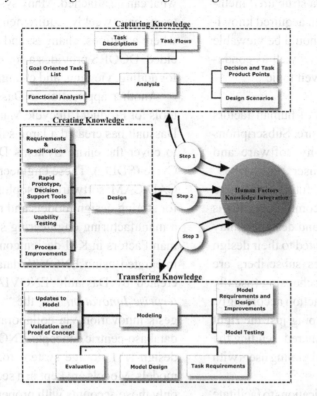

and Stewart, 1992). Certain groups or individuals acquire a skill or trade and keep it, employing it when called upon. Such groups rarely leave a legacy or ability to transfer this knowledge to their replacements, forcing the organization to re-learn and re-create that which it already knew. Obviously, this is counter-productive to the fast-paced design world.

Human Factors Engineering groups and systems engineering practitioners have realized the importance of skill acquisition problems and coined the term "Lessons Learned." This concept tracks significant findings found during the design process. These findings are categorized, and organized logically into a database. This database can take many forms, from Commercial-Off-The-Shelf (COTS) synthetic environment database solutions to highly specified custom coded internal database. Newly hired systems engineers and practitioners transferred onto the design program are encouraged to review the database,

to avoid the dreaded "duplication of effort." The market has realized the importance of KM, and thus a few software products have been created to assist organizations with this effort. Successful KM practices (and thus software based on these practices) require:

- *Ease of use* – it is unlikely that something awkward or difficult to use will be used
- *Varied format input* – aside from scribbling on notebook paper, the software should accept many document and file formats
- *Traceability* – inputs should be traced to their owner
- *Security* – all users may not require access to all elements of the knowledge database; proprietary, secret, and competitiveness concerns must be addressed
- *Routine* – inputs should be encouraged while the idea, solution, or process is still fresh in the creator's mind

- *Organization* – without a structured method of entry or search, then acquired knowledge is meaningless, it should be viewable top-down, or searchable as well as conducive to browsing on a given topic

A key feature for analysis of human factors in KM is the subscription feature. Subscriptions are implemented across many software and networking applications. A user "subscribes" to an item, and is notified of future updates to that item. Within the design community, this is critical. Individual engineers and designers may subscribe to a specific part related to their design area. When that part changes subscribers are notified via the means of their choosing (usually e-mail). They are free to take action accordingly. This facilitates design by keeping just the right amount of information being shared, sending the relevant updates without overwhelming users with unnecessary information.

Currently there are few applications to facilitate Human Factors in KM integration and requirements allocation. One of the software applications that support a full HSI and KM within a systems engineering process is IBM® Rational DOORS. DOORS stands for Dynamic Object Oriented Requirements System. DOORS facilitates requirements entry, organization into hierarchies, and display. Users make changes and link any given requirement to sub requirements and related requirements. DOORS requires individual users to have accounts. Each account can be restricted to elements of the database, and given read-only or administrative-level rights. Changes made are tracked at the user level, allowing managers to trace changes. Test plans and verification methods are also linkable. For sharing purposes, this information can be output to common office software such as Microsoft Excel. Furthermore, documents can be attached to the DOORS database, actual drawing files from CAD/CAM software, text analysis results, statistical software outputs, images, and web pages are examples of

what can be attached. Many systems engineering teams have weekly requirements review sessions where additions, changes, and test plans are decided. DOORS provides a structured framework for adding, viewing, and changing requirements.

Another application is Dassualt V5 Suite of tools for Product Lifecycle Management (PLM). Dassualt has created a large suite of tools aimed to cover the entire Systems Development Life Cycle (SDLC). These engineering tools contain CAD/CAM software, a sophisticated database for storing design models and related items, and a manufacturing engineering solution tool. Human Factors in KM design components are also integrated using ENOVIA database application created by Dassault. ENOVIA stands for *Enterprise Innovation Via*, the "via" element suggests innovation via collaboration representing database-centric concepts. ENOVIA is a complex design KM storage system for 3D CAD/CAM models. Models are kept in a secure database and only those accounts with proper permissions can access data. Along with model storage, entries within the ENOVIA database can have additional documents attached to them such as human performance analysis results, human-based requirements lists, biomechanical, structural or system design images, or other related media.

The Computer Aided Three Dimensional Interactive Application (CATIA), made by *Dassault Systems* and distributed by IBM®, is an integrated suite of Computer Aided Design (CAD), Computer Aided Engineering (CAE), and Computer Aided Manufacturing (CAM) applications for digital product definition and simulation. Figure 7 depicts a CATIA session for designing modern car seats with position prediction based on human factors engineering and ergonomics guidelines as discussed in the Handbook of Human Factors and Ergonomics Standards and Guidelines (Karwowski, 2006). Figure 7 also illustrates a CATIA session for designing modern car dashboard and console based on human factors work envelope principles. CATIA allows manufacturers to

Figure 7. CATIA session for designing modern car dashboard and seats with position prediction based on human factors engineering and ergonomics guidelines

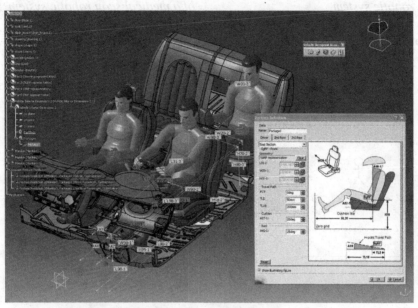

simulate all the industrial design processes, from the pre-project phase, through detailed design, analysis, simulation, assembly, and maintenance. CATIA is primarily used by the automotive and aerospace industries for automobile and aircraft design.

The above examples are tools that can help achieve these goals. Ultimately, organizations are responsible for employing a process or a set of processes for human factors knowledge creation, implementation, and utilization. With proper practices in place, duplication of effort is minimized, and the system design cycle is streamlined.

CASE STUDY: HUMAN-SYSTEMS INTEGRATION MODEL DEVELOPMENT FOR MEDICAL ROBOTS

The following case study demonstrates the advantages and costs savings resulting from implementing HSI and KM model components with SysML in the design and operation of medical robots.

Human specialists sharing the workspace with the robot led to the integration of human factors needs in robotics used in the medical field. Human components have to be integrated early in the development process. Modeling languages such as SysML provided very useful tools for modeling systems and facilitating the implementation of the HSI model. In this example, SysML was chosen as the primary language to communicate the critical need for consideration of human capabilities (Ahram et al., 2010). SysML supports the analysis of a medical robot and functional allocation, task analysis, and leveraging human error in systems engineering. SysML diagrams not only detail all interactions between actors and the system, but also between actors themselves.

An actor is defined as an outside user or related set of users who interact with the system. It is also possible for an actor to be a human user or an external system. This type of modeling facilitates the handling of interactions for safety and regulatory studies. In the example, there is a robotic system with two components, a robotic system controller and the robot scanner or probe.

Figure 8. Example of class diagram for the HSI and KM model implementation in the design of a medical scan robotic system

Class Diagram

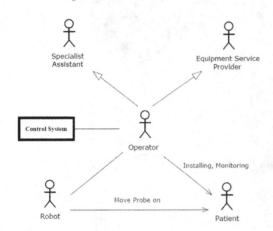

Figure 9. Example of use case diagram for the HSI and KM model implementation in the design of a medical scan robotic system

Use Case Diagram

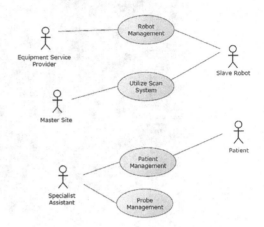

The robotic system controller interacts and takes actions from the actor specialist who is responsible for the examination. This process is detailed in Figure 8 and 9.

A significant barrier in current robotic medical applications is that many formal languages and analysis techniques are unfamiliar, difficult to understand, or delve deeply into requirements analysis. Systems engineering processes combined with HSI practices aims to include human factors considerations in systems design. This supports the position that medical robots developers must also integrate and contain the requirements of medical specialist throughout the system's definition. The use-case patient management diagram shown in Figure 9 provides scenarios of communication between the patient and the medical expert that are essential to a successful scan examination. This led to a design solution to include a two-way video-audio real time communication system. The Equipment service provider is the person (actor) in charge of the robot management and involved in the task achievement.

Human factors in safety aspects and HSI requirements are a major concern during safety analysis of medical robotic systems. In this case study, SysML was used in order to guarantee consistency of information between engineers, doctors, human factors specialists, and other professionals throughout the development process with a particular emphasis on the requirements analysis, validation and verification. Throughout the human factors analysis major advantages can be identified such as integrating safety concerns during system design, using supporting models to identify and analyzing human errors.

CONCLUSION

Knowledge Management (KM) and Human Systems Integration (HSI) are quickly becoming a critical element of the systems engineering process. This chapter has presented an overview of a growing body of knowledge, as well as advances in human factors and new technologies that developed to capture critical aspects of KM. The development of a KM framework for Human Systems Integration with Systems Modeling Language (SysML) will enable teams to collaborate better by providing a common language and process to distribute KM models and share information. By employing KM practices, systems engineers will be able to recognize the human as an integral element of every system in a more systematic, organized fashion that organizes, retains, and sustains knowledge elements for future use.

REFERENCES

Ahram, T. Z., & Karwowski, W. (2009a). Measuring Human Systems Integration Return on Investment. In *The International Council on Systems Engineering – INCOSE Spring 09 Conference: Virginia Modeling, Analysis and Simulation Center* (*VMASC*), Suffolk, VA, USA.

Ahram, T. Z., & Karwowski, W. (2009b). Human Systems Integration Return on Investment. Presentaton to the U.S. Department of Defense Human Systems Integration and Human Factors Engineering Technical Advisory Group meeting 61 HFE/HSI (DoD TAG). Seattle, Washington (May 11-14, 2009). Retrieved from http://www.hfetag.com/meetings/docs/program_meet_61.pdf

Ahram, T. Z., Karwowski, W., Amaba, B., & Andrzejczak, C. (2010). User-centered Smarter Robotic Medical Systems. In Halimahtun, K., Hedge, A., & Ahram, T. (Eds.), *Advances in Ergonomics & Usability Evaluation*. NJ: Taylor & Francis.

Ahram, T. Z., Karwowski, W., Amaba, B., & Obeid, P. (2009). Human Systems Integration: Development Based on SysML and the Rational Systems Platform. In *Proceedings of the 2009 Industrial Engineering Research Conference*, Miami, FL. USA.

Alavi, M., & Leidner, D. E. (2001). Review: Knowledge Management and Knowledge Management Systems: Conceptual Foundations and Research Issues. *Management Information Systems Quarterly*, *25*(1), 107–136. doi:10.2307/3250961

Argote, L., & Ingram, P. (2000). Knowledge transfer in organizations: A basis for competitive advantage in firms. *Organizational Behavior and Human Decision Processes*, *82*, 150–169. doi:10.1006/obhd.2000.2893

Back, A., Krogh, G., Seufert, A., & Ellen, E. (2005). *Putting Knowledge Networks Into Action: Methodology, Development, Maintenance*. Berlin: Springer-Verlag. doi:10.1007/b138845

Baum, J. A. C., & Greve, H. R. (Eds.). (2001). *Multiunit Organizations and Multiunit Strategy: Advances in Strategic Management*. Oxford, UK: Elsevier.

Booher, H. (Ed.). (2003). *Handbook of human systems integration*. Hoboken, NJ: Wiley. doi:10.1002/0471721174

Booher, H. R., & Minninger, J. (2003). Human systems integration in army systems acquisition. In Booher, H. (Ed.), *Handbook of human systems integration* (pp. 663–698). Hoboken, NJ: Wiley. doi:10.1002/0471721174

Burns, J., & Gordon, J. (2005). *Human Systems Integration*. Sonalysts, Inc. Presentation to Orlando INCOSE 09 June 2005.

Chapanis, A. (1996). *Human factors in systems engineering*. Hoboken, NJ: Wiley.

Davenport, T. H., DeLong, D. W., & Beers, M. C. (1998). Successful knowledge management projects. *Sloan Management Review*, *39*(2), 43–57.

Dempsey, P. G., Wogalter, M. S., & Hancock, P. A. (2006). Defining Ergonomics/Human Factors. In Karwowski, W. (Ed.), *The international Encyclopedia of Ergonomics and Human Factors* (2nd ed.). Boca Raton, FL: CRC Press.

Folds, D., Gardner, D., & Deal, S. (2008). Building Up to the Human Systems Integration Demonstration. *INCOSE INSIGHT, 11*(2).

Friedenthal, S., Moore, A., & Steiner, R. (2008). *A Practical Guide to SysML: The Systems Modeling Language*. San Francisco: Morgan Kaufmann, Elsevier Science.

Gorton, I., & Motwani, S. (1996). Issues in co-operative software engineering using globally distributed teams. *Information and Software Technology, 38*, 647–655. doi:10.1016/0950-5849(96)01099-3

Handley, H. A., & Smillie, R. J. (2008, May). Architecture framework human view: The NATO approach. *Systems Engineering, 11*(2), 156–164. Retrieved from http://dx.doi.org/10.1002/sys.v11:2. doi:10.1002/sys.20093

Hardman, N., Colombi, J., Jacques, D., & Hill, R. (2008). What Systems Engineers Need to Know About Human – Computer Interaction. *INCOSE INSIGHT, 11*(2).

Karwowski, W. (2000). Symvatology: The science of an artifact-human compatibility. *Theoretical Issues in Ergonomics Science, 1*, 76–91. doi:10.1080/146392200308480

Karwowski, W. (2005). Ergonomics and human factors: the paradigms for science, engineering, design, technology and management of human-compatibility systems. *Ergonomics, 48*, 436–463. doi:10.1080/00140130400029167

Karwowski, W. (Ed.). (2006). *International Encyclopedia of Ergonomics and Human Factors* (2nd ed.). Boca Raton, FL: CRC Press. doi:10.1201/9780849375477

Karwowski, W. (Ed.). (2006). *Handbook of Human Factors and Ergonomics Standards and Guidelines*. New York: Lawrence Erlbaum Publishers.

Karwowski, W. (2006). The Discipline of Ergonomics and Human Factors. In Salvendy, G. (Ed.), *Handbook of Human Factors & Ergonomics* (3rd ed., pp. 1–25). New York: John Wiley. doi:10.1002/0470048204.ch1

Karwowski, W. (2006a). The discipline of ergonomics and human factors. In Salvendy, G. (Ed.), *Handbook of Human Factors and Ergonomics* (3rd ed., pp. 3–31). Hoboken, NJ: John Wiley & Sons. doi:10.1002/0470048204.ch1

Ladd, A., & Ward, M. A. (2002). An Investigation Of Environmental Factors Influencing Knowledge Transfer, Air Force Institute of Technology (AFIT)/ENV. *Journal of Knowledge Management Practice*. Retrieved from http://www.tlainc.com/articl38.htm

OMG SysML specification. (2007). Retrieved from http://www.omgsysml.org/

Phoha, V. V. (2001). *An Interactive Dynamic Model for Integrating Knowledge Management Methods and Knowledge Sharing Technology in a Traditional Classroom*. Presented at SIGCSE.

Potomac Institute Study. (2008). *New Concepts in Human Systems Integration*.

Ryan, M. (2000, September 5). *Retention and Recruiting Update*. Air Force Commanders' Notice to Airmen 00-4.

Salvendy, G. (Ed.). (2006). *Handbook of Human Factors and Ergonomics* (3rd ed.). Hoboken, NJ: John Wiley & Sons. doi:10.1002/0470048204

Sherehiy, B., & Karwowski, W. (2006). Knowledge Management for Occupational Safety, Health and Ergonomics. *Human Factors and Ergonomics in Manufacturing, 16*(3), 309–320. doi:10.1002/hfm.20054

Stasser, G., & Stewart, D. D. (1992). Discovery of hidden profiles by decision- making groups: Solving a problem versus making a judgment. *Journal of Personality and Social Psychology, 63*, 426–434. doi:10.1037/0022-3514.63.3.426

Taubman, P. (2008). Top Engineers Shun Military, Concerns Grow. *The New York Times*. Retrieved from http://www.nytimes.com/2008/06/25/us/25engineer.html

Thomas, J. C., Kellogg, W. A., & Erickson, T. (2001). The knowledge management puzzle: Human and social factors in knowledge management. IBM Systems Journal, Knowledge Management, 40*(4)*.

Thomas-Hunt, M. C., Odgen, T. Y., & Neale, M. A. (2003). Who's Really Sharing? Effects of Social and Expert Status on Knowledge Exchange within Groups. *Management Science*, *49*(4), 464–477. doi:10.1287/mnsc.49.4.464.14425

Weber, R. A., & Camerer, C. F. (2003). Cultural Conflict and Merger Failure: An Experimental Approach. *Management Science*, *49*(4), 400–415. doi:10.1287/mnsc.49.4.400.14430

Chapter 4
Can Global Environment Influence B2B Relationships?

Irene Samanta
Technological Education Institute of Piraeus, Greece

P. Kyriazopoulos
Technological Education Institute of Piraeus, Greece

ABSTRACT

The research examines whether the changes that have taken place in the global business environment have modulated the way firms do business or whether it is simply transient details that have caused such excitement. Should firms be wary of any proclamations of 'new' ways of doing business? Or should they ignore changes of the business environment? Semi-structured in-depth interviews were conducted in three focus groups of managers from three major firms operating in Greece. The influence of globalization, the intense competition and new technologies in B2B e-commerce are external factors that raise problems and complexities in the future direction of Greek firms. There is also a gap caused by the lack of an innovation culture between top and lesser management. Businesses are required to modernise their practices to move from their present situation at the level of the 2nd industrial revolution of "old economy" to the 3rd industrial revolution of "new era economy". The results of this research can be used to assist companies to move to e- business taking into consideration account the external and internal factors with regard to the ways in which e-relationships can be modulated.

INTRODUCTION

According to Philip et al. (1999) the business environment for most organizations is rarely a stable state. There is no certainty that the future will follow the pattern of the recent past. For B2B companies operating in a low-tech, low-scale envi-

ronment, adaptation to change may be quite easy, but for a large organization which has to invest heavily for the future, the risks can be enormous.

The Internet is more than just another sales channel or marketing medium, it is also an entirely new business model. In order for B2B firms to be successful it is therefore essential for them appreciate the sea-change the Internet is bringing about in marketing strategy. It soon becomes apparent

DOI: 10.4018/978-1-61520-623-0.ch004

that B2B e-commerce itself represents an entirely new game-plan for the e-marketer to consider.

The structure and politics of an organization affect the manner in which it responds to environmental change. The internal culture of an organization, as Jones (1996) states, can greatly affect the way it responds to organizational change. Organizational culture can be shared in a number of ways, including the way the work is organized and experienced; how authority is exercised and delegated; how people are rewarded, organized and controlled; and the roles and expectations of staff and managers. Employees are the biggest cause of delay in responding to change, it therefore becomes apparent that having the right staff in the right place at the right time is more likely to enable to firm to share in the threats and opportunities which environmental change presents through the Internet. Consequently every organization can be considered to comprise an internal marketplace where employees engage in exchanges between each other making it possible for the organization to respond to environmental change in a rapid and coordinated manner.

Business-to-Business firms have received widespread attention by adopting an Internet marketing strategy, as it consists of one of the key drivers to face the changes of the business environment and in building and sustaining an organization's competitive advantage. Technology provides obvious benefits for organizations, such as the ability to carry out transactions around the clock, and also increase confidence of business partners due to their online transaction ability, and enhance relationships (Ratnasingam & Pavlou, 2003). It can also have a detrimental effect if the appropriate strategy is not applied. B2B Internet usage is growing in popularity for many reasons, ranging from cost savings to gaining benefits in the value within a supply chain. This allows businesses to extend their relationships with customers, suppliers, retailers, brokers, co-producers, employees and shareholders, and achieve a more personalized relationship with them. The develop-

ment of such personalized relationships is a key goal of marketing, because they tend to be more sustainable (Kalacota & Robinson 1999).

Recently the European Information Technology Observatory (EITO) it has been estimated that the value of B2B e-commerce activities for the year 2007 will reach approximately $6.4 trillion US dollars, indicating that a third of all B2B purchases will have been carried out online and B2B markets are expected to dominate the world of online trading. As a result, (EITO) estimated that transactions would reach $3.4 trillion US dollars by the end of 2007. There is a growing trend for some companies to refuse to transact with companies that do not use web facilities in their operations, which shows the importance of using Internet facilities in Business-to-Business relationships (Furnell & Karwenti, 1999).

According to Bondra and Davis (1996) there are five marketing strategies that can lead to a sustainable competitive advantage in relation to e-commerce:

- Actively collaborating with supply chain partners
- Extending the company's reach up and down the supply chain
- Changing the supply chain flow path
- Growing revenue
- Transforming capabilities into new business.

Most of these elements involve benefits filtering to the supply chain and are therefore relevant when assessing B2B relationships.

The way in which a business adapts to the changes of the business environment and addresses each of these marketing strategies has an impact on its B2B relationships and it is therefore important that this is sufficiently assessed by the organization. These various changes have fundamentally reshaped marketing strategies due to globalization via the Internet. The present research tries to verify whether the structure of the business environment has changed because of the new economy. This study also analyses how external and internal factors evolve in Greek markets and especially in the areas of B2B relationships.

THREATS AND OPPORTUNITIES OF GLOBALIZATION

According to Whipple (2000) globalization can be considered as a process of transformations in the organization of transactions and social relations around the globe, bringing interregional flows, activity networks, interactive environment and power. The following types of change describe it adequately: it extends the economic, political and also the social activities across regions, nations or even continents; it supports the substantial connection among different nations and the growing magnitude of flows of trade, culture, investment, movement of population; it quickens the transactions and the processes between nations, since the new technology of communication and transportation makes any transmission of information, goods or people easier and faster every day; it creates an environment where every incident (no matter how significant it may be) may affect other communities elsewhere. The consequences of a local event can be spread to the whole globe, making it clear that the frontiers of every country cannot seclude it from this system of globalization (Parkhe, 1992). According to Kotler (2003) global business firm operates in more than one country and ensures advantages of research and development, production, distribution, marketing and finances in respect to its expenses and status that the purely domestic competitors do not have. Globalization has affected firms around the world, which have managed impressive reductions in the barriers of trade and have established important agreements to promote the trade of products, services and investment globally. Therefore, a major characteristic of globalization is that it forms an international

industrial and financial business structure (Lado et al., 1998; Pearse, 1997; Lei, 1991).

A very interesting statement issued by UNCTAD (2003) shows the effects of globalization on small and medium-sized firms. In this study it is estimated that a great number of firms are in jeopardy and will face difficulties of orientation. It is mentioned that in 2005 about 40% of the firms will not survive in their present form without making significant changes in their operation costs, in the quality of their products and their management practices. Only one-third of the business firms are capable of becoming competitive internationally and of making proper use of the increasing globalization phenomenon.

Global competition has reached a point where the competition policies in most advanced countries and regions assume an international and cooperative character. The harmonization came about precisely because national competition policy was unable to keep up with globalization. The competitive environment that globalization has created complicates the survival and the self-adjustment of medium-sized companies (Vissi, 1997).

MOVING FROM "OLD TO NEW WORLD OF BUSINESS"

E-business has been in the forefront of change during the past decades, bringing new products, transforming the way of life and changing the rules of the marketplace.

The trends shaping e-business will have a significant impact on the way technology is used to conduct business in the future, and the nature of business itself. There are essentially two arguments. The first holds that although e-business will have a significant impact on organizations and the conduct of business in the future, the fundamental imperatives and underlying business principles will remain the same. Shapiro and Varian (1999), attest to the durability of economic principles, despite the fact that some of these principles are relatively new. The second is the counterclaim that the old imperatives of business will become obsolete, creating a fundamental paradigm shift in the nature and operation of organizations in the future, and a fundamentally new business environment. The latter is the more realistic in light of the current trends that are shaping and altering the conduct of e-business. In this light, organizations must constantly monitor, respond and adapt to the environment to ensure that they are not left behind in the face of intense competition. Market and technical expertise are intertwined and will be equally important in those organizations that achieve success. The new business paradigm emerging in the domain of e-business has resulted in the significant restructuring of organizations (Blumenthal & Haspeslagh, 1994). This raises complex economic, strategic, legal, and social and conflict management issues, as well as major changes in both organizational and technological practices. The new business paradigm emerging is one that requires a rethinking and redesign of core business processes and new organizational forms. The new business models emerging are relationship-focused and, hence, involve a more collaborative process that focuses on customer needs and wants and the building of business relationships. The move to relationship-focused business models therefore involves a return to basics. This includes identifying the significance of existing business relationships and real customer service, so advantages can be enhanced through collaboration. Generally, companies are now centring on procedural effectiveness and the need to utilize resources in deploying and raising business relationships. The implication is that there are many key areas that organizations will have to manage in the future (Burn & Robins, 2003).

Malhotra (2001) suggests there are three phases of technology that enable change from 'old' to 'new' world of business:

- **Automation:** for increased operational efficiency
- **Rationalisation of procedures:** streamlining of procedures and elimination of bottlenecks
- **Re-engineering:** thorough redevelopment of procedures and work flows with the use of technology.

Knowledge management is the closest approach that can facilitate all the procedures of an organization. Using the knowledge along with the technology and the potentiality of the employees, an organization can come to much better outcomes. A firm in order to overcome the barriers and enhance e-business implications is required to manage the changes. These changes in patterns have a consequence on the following:

Role of Senior Management

The character of management will be changed from 'command and control' to 'sense and respond', emphasizing the building commitment to the organizational vision while also the organization, treated as a 'human community', could vary substantially according to the information produced from technological systems. This demands additional skills of managers to anticipate the consequences of the introduction of such technology. The three trends – globalization, time compression and technology integration – require managers to adopt a global perspective, enhance organizational speed of response, and work with other organizations to adapt to technological changes as well as to fully exploit the potential of new technology. Nevertheless, it is crucial that managers are fully cognisant with the management of technology, particularly in such a changing environment.

Job Content and Tasks

The development of e-business requires changes in work processes and automated routine tasks. This will allow to organizations to reduce staff levels and re-engineer job descriptions and the business structure. Through the maintenance of e-business employees learn new work processes and skills to fulfil their expanded roles. It is the responsibility of the human resource departments to acknowledge the impact of technology and e-business on employee satisfaction, morale, status, productivity and training.

Use of Technology

Current information systems tend to be inflexible, especially where there are static assumptions supporting transaction processing; there will be an inclination towards communication building and people networks as well as the on-the-job learning.

Organizational Knowledge Processes

In the past it was assumed that problems were a given and that a solution was based on understanding of the business environment; the shift will be towards a characterization of the given difficulty from the current knowledge of each time, while any divergence of meanings will converge around the organizational mission.

Organizational Design

There will be a shift from where 'best practices' are institutionalized with a high level of structure and control to a relative lack of structure, external control, plenty of freedom and only some determinate information; assumptions will be constantly under review with a continuous pursuit of 'better practices'. This will result in the world of 'e-everything'. Organizations will constantly question and adapt operating assumptions and logic. There will be less focus on predefined rules

and more on adapting to changes in the rules, and the game itself. It would be true to say that yesterday's best practices become today's core rigidities. Therefore, organizations should have the skill to produce and afterwards adopt easily new knowledge. This will be achieved in part with ongoing renewal of existing archived knowledge.

Role Ambiguity

Technology has changed the role and tasks employees perform in organizations, creating new positions while making others redundant. Individuals may experience role confusion, with organisational departments unsure who will be responsible for the implementation, use and maintenance of e-business Zinkhan, (2002).

Breakdown of Relationships

Also e-business influence the way organizations, customers and employees communicate. Before the creation of e-business, sales staff built a relationship with customers in an effort to produce a sale. These relationships were built with the salesperson taking responsibility for servicing the customer's business requirements.

Process Technology

Process technology pertains to the techniques of producing and marketing goods and services. It also includes work methods, equipment, distribution and logistics, process technology changes that are much less visible in the marketplace. Such changes are much more difficult to detect either by a firm's customers or by its competitors. Changes in process technology may bring about changes in the organization, including its human resource practices, logistics and marketing functions.

The development of technology and e-business in organizations requires a change in management thinking and practice. It means a change in job content and task, role ambiguity, changes in technology and communication requirements, changes in management and supervision style, availability of information and breakdown of relationships.

MANAGEMENT E-BUSINESS

With such a chaotic and unpredictable business environment, there are many implications for the management of change that distinguish it from other stable and predictable situations. The technological environment is dynamic and needs to be tracked on an ongoing basis. From an open-systems perspective, management of organizations, including technology, should be predicated on the environment facing organizations. The domino effect on the strategies for change is particularly evident with such change (Bensaou & Earl, 1998). Tracking technological changes whether it is in the external or internal environment, requires managers to penetrate the organizations and networks that conduct and facilitate technology development. There are significant implications for this change management strategy. Successful management of technology requires that the problem solving within the organization should take into account both technical and market considerations. Also, learning through environmental intelligence, innovation and imitation are central to effective problem solving. Therefore, change interventions which consider globalization, time compression and technology integration as vital are positioned to heighten the need for faster and more effective problem solving. Managing technology in a changing environment is not a daunting experience – it is a fact of life. For change agents, the development of problem solutions can be accomplished either within the organization in collaboration with others, or simply by adopting innovations from outside. But the method of organizational development should be a deliberate and informed managerial choice.

In order to change management, one should bear in mind the factors of failure or success, the application of the knowledge of the executive staff and also the methodologies needed for those applications. The strategies thus have to be developed for all the stages before, during and after that implementation. The company can make some procedures easier at the corporate level (Karuppuarachchi et al., 2002) by creating a project organization plan, supporting the team work by establishing teams that work over the company's needs, building an information system or even providing employees with adequate training for the project. In facilitating the successful implementation of e-business into an organization, leaders must develop effective methods for managing employee resistance. Individuals resist change for three predominant reasons; a lack of information, a lack of understanding, or mistrust of the changes occurring. Resistance can be demonstrated by stop-work action, protests, lockouts, go-slows, high turnover rates, absenteeism and theft. The development of technology and e-business in an organization can cause resistance if leaders do not address employee concerns. Employees resist change because they feel inadequately consulted, their job may be threatened, their job description and task may change or simply they fear the unknown. Organization leaders must implement training programmes and communication, which will allow employees to be kept well informed and address their concerns (Coltman et al., 2001).

BUSSINSS-TO-BUSINESS IN E-BUSINESS NETWORK

As have we considered the factors that relate to the e-business implementation as key components to successful marketing implementation in order to meet the needs of the present research, the importance of Business-to-Business relationships are researched in a e-marketing context. In this point,

B2B firms are defined as markets where a firm sells goods and services to another business firm for internal use, or for resale to other customers (Wright, 2004). According to Wilkinson and Young (2002), there are five groups of factors that need consideration in relation to business networks. These characteristics refer to the relationships and interactions in which a firm is involved, the characteristics of the firm's relationship partners, the characteristics of connected relations and their interactions, the characteristics of a firm's network positions and the characteristics of the network as a whole (Wright, 2004). These factors influence the potential success and longevity of a relationship. In general, B2B relationships tend to be relatively long term and stable. Overall, it is the interaction of the stakeholders that influences exchanges in such relationships.

Ultimately, the understanding of the changes from the business environment is becoming imperative, and has been defined as the subjective probability by which an organization believes that the underlying technology infrastructure and control mechanisms are capable of facilitating inter-organizational transactions (Wright, 2004). Therefore, according to Bennet (1997), the development of e-marketing strategies in B2B transactions has affected relationships quite drastically, allowing more competition and more control over processes and employees. According to Earle and Keen (2000), the value trust networks (VNTs) will develop into collaborative networks in which related companies will be motivated to work together based upon the mutual creation of value. Consequently, the rapid alterations of the business environment mainly influence B2B relationships and this qualitative research is an attempt to identify the firms' intentions to deal with these changes. Based on strategic issues focused on marketing, proportionately to the positive or negative response of B2B firms, we can then identify how firms move from the traditional to the new era in order to develop successful relationships.

THE GREEK BUSINESS ENVIRONMENT

In this contemporary business environment, therefore, the question is whether Greece is ready to seize the opportunities and reinforce its competitiveness and productivity. Greece is still far from the northern countries that monopolize the research and technology industry, spending large sums of money in this area. More specifically, according to recent Eurostat data, Greece has the lowest access to the new economy and the information society of all the countries in the European Union, given that it has the lowest expenditure on research and technology.

Furthermore, the lack of specialized executives in positions concerning new technologies and electronic business constitutes a very important issue for all countries and especially for countries with a high development rate, such as Greece. Last but not least, incorporating new technologies in the activities of the Greek companies is viewed, at least at present, as unsatisfactory. According to the annual Report of Competitiveness from the International Institute for Management Development (IMD), the application of electronic commerce is not adequately developed in creating business opportunities (Greece is rated 44th out of 49 countries). The incorporation of new technologies in informatics is not part of companies' demands (Greece is rated 41st out of 49 countries). The lack of cooperation in technologies between companies is also noted (Greece is rated 39th out of 49) (McDonald, 2005).

To settle these problems, more extended cooperation between the state and the business world is required. The Greek companies must keep up with the new business requirements in what concerns new technologies, towards reinforcing their technological infrastructure and offering wider training of their executives. In order to meet the expectations and changes of the business environment, contemporary companies have to react positively to competition by accepting and undertaking the risks of entrepreneurship, which means continuously undertaking new initiatives and adopting innovations, organizing access in business or departmental networks and adjusting production to the international models, by putting into action the techniques of benchmarking. Also, by changing their structure, the companies will succeed in becoming cross-national while also addressing the continuous improvement of the cost by taking measures for increasing productivity and full visibility of the supply chain while orientating on the world market. When the companies focus on the above efforts, they should take into account the constant widening of the knowledge of their personnel and investing in it, by understanding that knowledge constitutes today the strongest advantage for competitiveness, in order to move to broad applications of informatics and new technologies.

On the other hand, the state has to reinforce constantly the companies' efforts in establishing adequate corporate and extra-corporate infrastructures, in order to accomplish the much desired progress and international awards. Actions and measures that will have to do with the reassessment of the framework that today still creates boundaries (deregulation of the markets, cutback of the civil services, motivation for mergers, creation of venture capital etc.) are required, with the development of the capital markets for making the financing of these adjustments easier. The improvement of the information networks for on-time information concerning the international changes and the importance of adjustments as well as radical restructures in education and training, stressing new systems of informatics and the positive connection of education and production, are also two additional actions that are required.

As a conclusion, the new economy seems to be changing the world dramatically. It creates new possibilities for development in countries such as Greece. It creates a global economy obliging everyone to be properly prepared to confront the pressures of international competition. The

responsibilities of both the state and the business world are immense and any delays will have a negative effect on both industry and government. In this significant part of the 'brave new world', businesses in Greece are asked to answer the call for further development and modernization of their practices. From this standpoint, a qualitative research was been conducted to provide a better understanding of the issues at stake.

RESEARCH METHODOLOGY

In the present research the qualitative method was used through focus groups to create a base for a deeper and more complete understanding of the studied phenomenon.

A case-study methodology was considered to be the most appropriate because of the qualitative nature of the data collected. Relationships are complex and dynamic by nature and their study necessitates in-depth knowledge of the organisational context. Yin (1994) defines a case study as an empirical enquiry that investigates a contemporary phenomenon within its real-life context, especially when the boundaries between phenomenon and context are not clearly evident.

To achieve that goal it was important to have the largest possible variation among the samples. It was also crucial to use respondents who were expected to have a profound knowledge of the studied phenomenon. A group of managers from three firms operating in Greece where selected. Therefore, the sample used consists of representatives from three firms: The first was from firm Alpha, a leading multi-national firm producing a wide range of consumer goods which was chosen as one of the target companies for this purpose. Their biggest sellers and customers are equally big corporations from a multitude of industries. Firms Beta is a multi-national company in the consumer goods arena. The third firm Gamma is a leading Greek domestic firm into producing a wide range of consumer goods, whose biggest sellers and customers are equally big corporations from a multitude of industries.

The steps in conducting every focus group was first the preparation for each group, second the selection of a focus group facility, third the recruitment of participants and finally the creation of a discussion guide. In total three focus groups were carried out over a six-month period. The interviews that were conducted were semi-structured, and encompassed a discussion of buyer-seller relationship dimensions. The participants were staff from high and middle management. The selection was based on their position and duties within the organisations. The participants had responsibilities for external relations with regard to purchasing and supply and their position varied along the hierarchical structure. These provided multiple sources of evidence bearing in mind that the complex interactions that take place between organisations cover a wide range of functions and activities in the firm. The researcher was aided by an interview framework. This warranted internal validity (Yin, 1994) and ensured the comparability of data collected. In order to ensure internal validity (Yin, 1994) and avoid subjective and personal held views by the interviewees, the researcher ensured that the documented perceptions were supported with evidence. Reliability was enhanced through the taping of discussions. This ensured the traceability of data (McCutcheon & Meredith, 1993). These were later transcribed, documented and coded.

The questions were direct and to the point. The response from one person stimulated other responses. The time allowed was one hour for each focus group. The goal was to learn and understand what executives have to say and to allow questions formulated in the focus groups to be accurately recorded to use in interviews where appropriate. The emphasis also was upon encouraging the executives to talk in detail. The survey took place in the area of Attica where four firms are established. The research took place in September 2005 and February 2006.

The questionnaire was developed for the accomplishment of the research objectives, taking into account external factors of the economic environment of Greece. Participants are asked to respond on questions included issues that influence their main relationships with their partners and to reflect on the interactions they have with them. More analytically, the questions are relative to the internal environment of firm as well as to external raised to managers that would allow them to express their views are summarized in the following:

- Does the globalization influence firms' strategy and culture?
- Which variables affecting the organizational structure that the B2B firm could adjust or change to suit its changing environment (innovation diffusion)?
- Which changes in the business environment that create threats and opportunities are usually beyond the control of management?
- Can the existing planned of the organization hold relationships of seller–buyer together?
- Do the managers recognize the potential benefits of e-commerce applications?
- What organizational change factors are necessary for successfully deploying B2B relationships? Has the firm a strategic vision for utilizing Internet technologies?

Firms' Profiles

The three firms studied in this research are briefly introduced. A concise description of their background is presented due to limitations of space. For reasons of confidentiality, the identity of case-organisations is expressed anonymously.

Alpha is a leading multi-national firm producing a wide range of chemical consumer goods and has a history that goes back fifty years. In the Greek subsidiary it has around three hundred employees and trades well-known brands. Clients can choose from a large array of categories of products. The firm is very effective in its delivery and always manages to keep delivery dates as promised to its clients. Alpha is organised along a rigid hierarchical structure. The firm purchases materials and products used in the production process on a Just in Time (JiT) basis exclusively from local suppliers. Every purchase is registered through a purchase order with the supplier who then delivers as per specific instructions.

Beta is a leading Greek domestic firm into producing a wide range of agriculture consumer goods, whose biggest sellers and customers are equally big corporations from a multitude of industries employing around two hundred employees. The majority of their staff is technical and well educated personnel. Beta produces its own quality brand and has a strong R&D department. It has been established for sixty years. Beta's purchases from the local suppliers consist mainly of laboratory equipment, consumables, spare parts and packaging material. It also buys technical expertise in the form of maintenance and calibration for all its equipment. Beta is "ready to build a supplier/customer relation" because time is an important factor especially when technical expertise is required.

Gamma is a fully owned subsidiary of a multinational organisation involved in the consumer chemical goods. Gamma has been established for twenty-five years and employs around three hundred highly skilled employees. The firm main purchases from Greek suppliers consist of packaging material, machine tools and printed-matter. They consider it easier to make these purchases from local firms both from an operational point of view (JIT) and because they can solve occurring problems faster and with less hassle because suppliers can visit in a relatively short time. They believe that their key suppliers are their partners in their continual effort to deliver quality products to their clients world-wide. They work 'hand in-hand" with their suppliers and expect them to be

involved in the R&D of their product and in the reengineering of their processes

DATA ANALYSIS

Guided by the literature, analysis yielded some main themes as identified in this research is reproduced below. At first we examined the factors from the business environment that have been recognized by B2B firms as crucial in order to develop 'new' ways of doing business and adopt an e-marketing strategy. It was discovered that a very significant motive of those questioned is globalization and the free market economy, as the global economy requires an understanding of the foreign marketing environment. With the international delivery availability, it is important for the firms to design a logistical system that allows them to deliver their products/services across nations efficiently.

Firm Beta represents a very significant motive of the B2B collaboration for successful relationships. Marketing manager says: *"The enlargement of business relations in the new economy will reinforce the development of interactive e-relationships involving real customer relationships, as it contributes to forming the exchange of the required information among B2B firms."* Customer acceptance is another significant motive relevant to external-related factors and including all the special efforts to motivate their partners to make the move to an online environment. The use of new technologies appears to be of crucially important, while globalization and the reduction of natural distances because of the e-commerce is the second reason. Also the competition is of extremely importance.

Summarizing the aspects of three focus groups relevant to the motives that lead the industries to their activation to the digital environment the findings add up some statements which are generated from:

- The pressure in order to lessen the working costs,
- The pressure from collaborators, who have proceeded in electronic operational solutions,
- The pressure from competitive threats, as they are formed at the digital environment,
- The pressure for the exact monitoring and satisfaction of the request,
- The pressure for the reinforcement of the relationships with the customers, and
- The pressure for better financial circles between offer and demand.

Apart from the several external factors that may urge a business firm to adopt a B2B e-marketing strategy, there are, as well, the most crucial internal motives that seemed to play a great role. According to firm Beta the most important were contribution to the process cost, along with the impact on the speed of activities and business internal co-ordination that such a strategy might have. Rather crucial, seemed to be the contribution to Customer Relationships Management and the contribution to the development of competitive advantage and added-value.

Obvious benefits from firm Alpha delivered by new economy principles is cost savings as well as benefits in the value chain. E-commerce provides the ability to carry out transactions around the clock, in addition to increasing confidence of business partners due to their online transaction ability. Firms' expectations with regard to the benefits which are achievable by using e-marketing applications appear to be high. The organizations surveyed agreed that e-business will provide opportunities to reduce the cost base. The respondents believe that e-business will enable the enlargement of business relations and the clientele.

The adaptation of an e-marketing strategy contributes to the regulation of the prices. It also contributes to a better control of the supply chain and influences the speed of the processes in the internal environment of the organization and increase the growth rate between the departments. It helps to organize the production and to collaborate successfully with supply, marketing and sales department.

The respondents consider that e-marketing doesn't contribute absolutely to relationship management and their retention. There is not plenary of trust among B2B firms. They are cautious to the dispersion of the information which is more personal than professional. The implementation of an e-marketing strategy offers time reduction and saving money but it can't be achieved to the short run. There is an ambiguity that the use of technology through e-marketing is not able to acquire buyers but they consider that it can more operate to acquire customers of raw materials. However e-marketing assist the products to be upgraded because it contributes to be discovered any weaknesses. Consequently, the major advantage is the cost reduction, the supply management, time reduction of the distribution of goods. In addition they consider the personalization and customization that firm implements to respond to their customers' needs doesn't succeed through e-marketing as most of customers have a lot of features. The organization is responded to the customer needs as the most of the partners in Greece operate in a traditional way keeping their own structure.

Based on strategic issues with a focus on marketing, proportionately to the positive or negative response of B2B firms, we can then identify how firms move from the traditional to the new era in order to develop successful relationships.

The participants agree that an adequate information technology infrastructure is considered a vital factor in successful B2B e-marketing implementation; hence the availability of equipment for access and services is required. Therefore the implementation of e-marketing practices creates a shared vision for an operational website. The results of the research show that firm Beta uses Intranet technologies and ERP system.

Firm's Alpha department of information technology is in a reformation stage and regarding to the use of Electronic Data Interchange (EDI) is an embryonic stage. Firm Gamma had defined the launch of EDI system but the parent company decided to establish EDI system, finance and organize by own.

Currently firm Gamma establish "VELUM" system through Internet which is fund by the subsidiary in Greece. The main characteristic of the system is that communicate with agents in a national level who are responsible for firm's customers. This system operating cost is low while it gives an add value to the organization reducing the cost.

Two years ago the new manager in firm Alpha introduced a new vision to the organization in order to be e-business oriented. As the decision of the high management was to progress the necessary procedures to change from the "old" to the "new" world of business they faced the resistance from the low management. This situation created a gap between high and low management and as a result several employees to transfer from the marketing department while other employees abandoned their jobs because they couldn't adapt to the new regulations.

High management of the firm Beta future plans, which it is a domestic one, is to adopt an e-marketing strategy because it has the experience from the firm's participation in an e-marketplace. The benefits for the firm were the company promotion, information on partner activities, and exchange of standardized information such as: orders, price lists, and bills of sales, research for possible suppliers or buyers and participation in online auctioning.

In order to deal with these changes in the operational environment that has affected B2B relationships, companies have to take into account the employees' resistance to e-business changes. Actually, the participants in the study in totally agree that the most difficult task they face is of encouraging an innovative culture of sharing

and networking to the employees, while at the same time maintaining a high level of individual expertise and excellence.

They accord that have to lead and encourage the employees to the development of an innovation culture in the firm's internal processes motivating them. Organizations that participated in this research stated that a lot of modifications have to take place and they have to change their structure in order to adopt and implement e-business standards. Therefore investments in IT infrastructure are required in order to facilitate networking.

Concertedly, they emphasize that the transition of the firm to e-business change the way that B2B relationships occurred. The participants classified some important criteria to accomplish effective e-relationships between B2B firms and their partners: The distribution and communication of relevant private and secure information. The need to re-align their marketing strategy with new perspectives to increase the 'lifetime value' of relationships.

DISCUSSION

Globalization creates vast new opportunities for firms. National boundaries have become meaningless in the business world due to globalization, and the managerial process in global companies has changed to reap the rewards of this new climate. Firms in the industrial sector taking advantage of the new environment pursue the increasingly universal objective of wealth generation through globalization.

Companies who want to use the Internet to do business internationally have to revise their operations, strategies, and business models in order to exploit the opportunities offered by the Internet to their full potential.

Since companies have identified the external factors that force them to be global, then it is necessary to be considered the factors that relate to the internal environment include technological infrastructure, internal/innovation culture, and the importance of training programmes. It means how Marketing activities through the internet can should be coordinated by the general strategic perspective of the industry to the successful implementation and strengthening to the new era.

The completion of those activities with the marketing activities which take place in traditional markets is the best way in order to encompass the efficient exploitation of the chances, which are given in the electronic environment. According to Porter (2001), the weakness of reconciliation of the electronic with the natural activities to the strategic frame of operational development comprises one of the main reasons of failure of the electronic markets. Moreover, many industries have not succeeded in understanding the strategic environment of the internet and have tried to operate their electronic expressions with mechanisms of natural market, a fact that led quickly to operational failures.

The organization must understand and conform to the new values, management processes and communication styles and strategies applied aim to associate innovation with business targets, and the application of the innovation values into the firm's internal environment. The fieldwork sought to define the firm's innovative core and create frameworks to integrate innovation throughout the range of enterprise leaders and teams in order to sustain the level of innovation by generating and implementing ideas, strategies and plans that cultivate a thinking organization.

CONCLUSION

The findings introduce the concepts of globalization, the Internet and the technological changes that have impacted the business environment, forcing B2B firms to develop an e-commerce strategy. This research has gone some way in the exploration of how B2B e-commerce can fundamentally change the inter-organizational processes

at the buyer–seller interface. More specifically, it emphasizes the importance of developing a Business-to-Business e-marketing strategy. It has been shown that electronic B2B marketing can provide support for e-relationships. At one end of the continuum, electronic marketing can create joint, inter-organizational processes, while at the other end creating increased efficiency and reduced transaction costs with partners. The development of close business partnerships to optimize inter-organizational processes remains one of the most difficult aspects as well as problems are met related to business culture. The need for the firms to answer the following questions prior to any attempt for operational activation at the internet is of a crucial important:

- What does the industry try to succeed out of its activation at the electronic markets?
- Which is the focal point of the electronic activation?
- Which are the necessary additional substructures for its presence in the internet?
- How is the electronic expression completed by the actual operational activities?
- What kind of marketing outline is it needed for the reassurance that the realization of the marketing programme won't be affected by the unstable electronic environment?

REFERENCES

Barbian, J. (2000). IT in 2000 and beyond. *Computer User, 19*(1).

Bensaou, M., & Earl, M. (1998). The right mindset for managing information technology. *Harvard Business Review, 76*(5).

Blumenthal, B., & Haspeslagh, P. (1994). *Toward a definition of corporate transformation.* Sloan Management Review.

Burn, J., Marshall, P., & Barnett, M. (2002). *E-business Strategies for Virtual Organisations*. Oxford: Butterworth-Heinemann.

Burn, J., & Robins, G. (2003). Moving towards e-government: a case study of organizational change processes. *Logistics Information Management, 16*(1), 25–35. doi:10.1108/09576050310453714

Burnes, B. (2000). *Managing Change: A Strategic Approach to Organizational Dynamics*. London: Pearson Education.

Cao, L. (2002). Corporate and product identity in the post national economy: rethinking US trade laws. *California Law Review, 90*(2), 401–484. doi:10.2307/3481283

Coltman, T., Devinney, T., Latukefu, A., & Midgley, D. (2001). E-business: revolution, evolution or hype? *California Management Review, 44*(61).

Day, G., & Schoemaker, P. (2000). Avoiding the pitfalls of emerging technologies. *California Management Review, 42*(52).

European Commission. (2000). *SMEs Access to the Digital Economy*. Brussels: Directorate C of DG Information Society.

Evans, P., & Warster, T. S. (1999). *Blown to Bits: How the New Economic of Information Transforms Strategy*. Boston, MA: Harvard Business School Press.

Jones, R. (1996). Digital equipment corporation: creating new business. In *The Internet Strategy Handbook, Lessons from the New Frontier of Business*. Boston, MA: Harvard Business School Press.

Kalakota, R., & Robinson, M. (1999). *E-business, Roadmap for Success*. Reading, MA: Addison-Wesley.

Kanter, R., Stein, B., & Jick, T. (1992). *The Challenge of Organizational Change: How Companies Experience It and Leaders Guide It*. New York: Maxwell Macmillan Int.

Kotter, J. (1996). *Leading Change*. Boston, MA: Harvard Business School Press.

Kuruppuarachchi, P., Mandal, P., & Smith, R. (2002). IT project implementation strategies for effective changes: a critical review. *Logistics Information Management, 15*(2), 126–137. doi:10.1108/09576050210414006

Lado, A. A., Boyd, N. G., & Hanlon, S. C. (1997). Competition, cooperation, and the search for economic rents: a syncretic model. *Academy of Management Review, 22*(1), 110–141. doi:10.2307/259226

Lawrence, E., Corbitt, B., Fisher, J., Lawrence, J., & Tidwell, A. (2000). *Internet Commerce: Digital Models for Business* (2nd ed.). Milton, Australia: John Wiley & Sons, Inc.

Lei, D. (1991). Global strategic alliances: payoffs and pitfalls. *Organizational Dynamics, 19*, 44–62. doi:10.1016/0090-2616(91)90093-O

Lei, D., & Slocum, J. W. Sr. (1992). Global strategy, competence-building and strategic alliances. *California Management Review, 35*, 81–97.

Malhotra, Y. (Ed.). (2001). *Knowledge Management and Business Model Innovation*. Hershey, PA: Idea Group.

May, P. (2000). *The Business of E-commerce: From Corporate Strategy to Technology*. New York: Cambridge University Press.

McCutcheon, D. M., & Meredith, J. R. (1993). Conducting case study research in operations Management. *Journal of Operations Management, 11*, 239–256. doi:10.1016/0272-6963(93)90002-7

Narayanan, V. (2001). *Managing Technology and Innovation for Competitive Advantage*. Upper Saddle River, NJ: Prentice Hall.

Naude, P., & Holland, C. (1996). *Business-to-business relationships, Relationship Marketing, Theory and Practice*. London: Paul Chapman Publishing.

Parkhe, A. (1991). Interfirm diversity, organizational learning, and longevity in global strategic alliances. *Journal of International Business Studies*, *22*, 579–601. doi:10.1057/palgrave.jibs.8490315

Parkhe, A. (1993). '*Strategic alliances structuring: a game theoretic and transaction cost examination of interfirm cooperation*'. *Academy of Management Journal*, *38*, 794–829. doi:10.2307/256759

Pearce, R. J. (1997). 'Toward understanding joint venture performance and survival: a bargaining and influence approach to transaction cost theory'. *Academy of Management Review*, *22*(1), 203–225. doi:10.2307/259229

Pearlson, K. (2001). *Managing and Using Information Systems: A Strategic Approach*. New York: John Wiley & Sons.

Porter, M. (1986). *Competition in Global Industries*. Cambridge, MA: Harvard Business School.

Shapiro, C., & Varian, H. (1999). *Information Rules: A Strategic Guide to the Network Economy*. Boston, MA: Harvard Business School Press.

Turban, E., King, D., Warkentin, M., & Chung, H. (2002). *E-commerce: A Managerial Perspective*. Upper Saddle River, NJ: Prentice Hall.

Turban, E., Lee, J., King, D., & Chung, H. (2000). *Electronic Commerce: A Managerial Perspective* (International Ed.). Upper Saddle River, NJ: Prentice-Hall International.

Turban, E., McLean, E., & Wetherbe, J. (2000). *Information Technology for Management: Making Connection for Strategic Advantage* (2nd ed.). New York: John Wiley & Sons Inc.

Waddell, D., Cummings, T., & Worley, C. (2000). *Organisation Development and Change*. Melbourne: Nelson Thomson Learning.

Whipple, J. M., & Frankel, R. (2000). Strategic alliance success factors. *Journal of Supply Chain Management*, 21-26.

Wilkinson, I., & Young, L. (2002). On cooperating: Firms, relations and networks. *Journal of Business Research*.

Wright, R. (2004). *Business to Business Marketing, A step by step guide*. Harlow, UK: Prentice Hall.

Yin, R. K. (1994). *Case Study Research - Design and Methods*. Thousand Oaks, CA: Sage Publications.

Zinkhan, M. G. (2002). Promoting services via the internet: new opportunities and challenges. *Journal of Services Marketing*, *16*(5), 412–423. doi:10.1108/08876040210436885

ADDITIONAL READING

Ahanotu, N. D. (1998). Empowerment and production workers: a knowledge-based perspective. *Empowerment in Organizations*, *6*(7), 177–18. doi:10.1108/14634449810242611

Cabrera, A., & Cabrera, E. F. (2002). Knowledge-sharing dilemmas. *Organization Studies*, *23*(5), 687–710. doi:10.1177/0170840602235001

Carneiro, A. (2000). How does knowledge management influence innovation and competitiveness? *Journal of Knowledge Management*, *4*, 87–98. doi:10.1108/13673270010372242

Choo, C. (1998). *The Knowing Organization: How Organizations Use Information to Create Meaning, Create Knowledge, and Make Decisions*. Oxford, UK: Oxford University Press.

Davenport, T. H., De Long, D. W., & Beers, M. C. (1998). Successful knowledge management projects. *Sloan Management Review*, *39*(2), 43–57.

Davenport, T. H., & Prusak, L. (1998). *Working Knowledge: How Organizations Manage What They Know Best*. Cambridge, MA: Harvard Business School Press.

Davenport, T. H., & Prusak, L. (2000). *Working knowledge: how organizations manage what they know*. Cambridge, MA: Harvard Business School Press, Boston.

Galbraith, J. R., & Lawler, E. E. (1993). *Organizing for the Future*. San Francisco, CA: Jossey-Bass Publishers.

Hansen, M. T. (1999). The Search- Transfer Problem: The Role of Weak Ties in Sharing Knowledge Across Organization Subunits. *Administrative Science Quarterly*, *44*(1), 82–111. doi:10.2307/2667032

Hansen, M. T. (2002). Knowledge networks: Explaining effective knowledge sharing in multiunit companies. *Organization Science*, *13*(3), 232–248. doi:10.1287/orsc.13.3.232.2771

Ingram, H. (1997). Performance management: processes, quality and team working. *International Journal of Contemporary Hospitality Management*, *9*(7), 295–303. doi:10.1108/09596119710190895

Johnson, G., & Scholes, K. (1997). *An Integrated Approach*. Boston: Houghton Mifflin Company.

Kim, D., Cameron, S., & Quinn, R. E. (1998). *Diagnosing and Changing Organizational Culture: Based on the Competing Values Framework*. Reading, MA: Addison-Wesley.

Kyriazopoulos, P. (2000). *The Modern firm in the starting of the 21st century*. Athens: Synchrony Ekdotiki.

Nonaka, I. (1994). The dynamic theory of organizational knowledge creation. *Organization Science*, *5*(1), 14–37. doi:10.1287/orsc.5.1.14

Nonaka, I., & Takeuchi, H. (1995). *The Knowledge Creating Company: How Japanese Companies Create the Dynamics of Innovation*. New York: Oxford University Press.

Orlikowski, W. J. (2002). Knowing in practice: enacting a collective capability in distributed organizing. *Organization Science*, *13*(3), 249–273. doi:10.1287/orsc.13.3.249.2776

Szeto, E. (2000). Innovation capacity: working towards a mechanism for improving innovation within an inter-organizational network. *The TQM Magazine*, *12*(2), 149–158. doi:10.1108/09544780010318415

Thomond, P., & Lettice, F. (2002). Disruptive Innovation Explored. In *9ᵗʰ IPSE International Conference on Concurrent Engineering: Research and Applications* (CE2002).

Tidd, J., Bessant, J., & Pavitt, K. (2001). *Managing Innovation*. Integrating Technological, Market and Organizational Change.

Chapter 5
The Global Knot:
How Problems Tangle in the World's Economy

Jon G. Hall
The Open University, UK

ABSTRACT

This invited chapter offers a new view on the tangling of problems, and suggests a new problem solving approach to how they might be untangled, based on a complete taxonomy of their interelatedness, illustrated with examples of how economic value is or might be delivered by those involved in problem solving.

"Oh, what a tangled web we weave..."

Sir Walter Scott

INTRODUCTION

The digital economy has opened new doors for business through its fusion of digital and material business worlds. It has opened cracks, too, not filled by traditional product and service offerings, that offer a business home for a myriad of new entrepreneurs eager to hop the tiny hurdles to marketplace entry. For the foreseeable future, all will be innovation resulting in huge engineering challenges for those involved in business: the con-

tinued delivery of transparently adequate products and services to this new tangled marketplace is an incredible challenge. Business problem solving in this new landscape depends critically on understanding the linkages between the players, their contexts and their needs.

Previously, problems like these have been called 'Wicked', and everyone knows that 'Wicked problems have no solutions.' In my opinion, that's a defeatist attitude unworthy of business and academia, we must simply find new models from which analysis, prediction and synthesis of fit-for-purpose business solutions can be forged. This essay explores how recent research, by the author and his colleague Lucia Rapanotti at The Open University, can be extended to give problem solving techniques that deal with this 'wicked' tangle of business problems.

DOI: 10.4018/978-1-61520-623-0.ch005

Copyright © 2011, IGI Global. Copying or distributing in print or electronic forms without written permission of IGI Global is prohibited.

Tangling might seem to suggest that problems are extended objects, like pieces of string, capable of wrapping themselves around themselves and each other, tending to clump together in knots. It may also be suggestive that they're difficult to follow through the tangle: focussing your gaze on only one part of the tangle and trying to follow how it weaves in and out, how it relates to the other problems, is difficult if not impossible.

THE BUTTERFLY'S TANGLE

The large blue butterfly (*Maculinea arion*) is an extraordinarily beautiful creature that lives most of its pre-butterfly life underground with a (very) distant relative, the red ant (*Myrmica sabuleti*).

Simply put—and to cut a long story short—the large blue became extinct in 1979 in various parts of the UK. Professor Jeremy Thomas didn't like the cut-short-story: it's a complex web he discovered. The butterfly, as a caterpillar, is parasitic on its red ant relative, spending quality time within their nest duping them into treating it like royalty. The butterfly cannot live without the ant.

Now, like many natives of the UK, the red ant likes the sun, but—sadly—doesn't get enough of it. As it burrows underground—under grass—it grows cooler as the grass grows its shade, as might happen, for instance, when rabbits (*Oryctolagus cuniculus*) are not grazing it. Without rabbits the ants die off. And why didn't the rabbits graze? Well, the poor things were stung in the 1970s by myxomatosis.

The butterfly needed the ant and the ant needed the sun and they got it as the rabbit grazed. No rabbits, no shade; no shade, no sun; no sun, no ants; no ants, no large blue butterfly. It's a simple chain when you've heard the story, but until Professor Thomas came along no-one understood just why the big blue butterfly was fluttering into obscurity.

It's a salutary tale: the problems of the butterfly–how to live–and the ant–needing the sun–and the rabbit–in a world with myxomatosis–tangle together. But, fixing the focus on the butterfly's problem, or the ant's or the rabbit's alone gets you nowhere. It's only understanding the tangle that solves the problem: Professor Thomas has seen that the reintroduction of the large blue is succeeding.

TANGLED PROBLEMS EXIST IN THE BUSINESS WORLD TOO

Meet Kate and Daniel—fun-loving small entrepreneurs—working full-time in organisations facing the credit crunch. They have lowered their expectations of job security. They pay their bills and taxes. They face an unsatisfactory educational and health system and choose independent schools and private healthcare for their children. They worry about green-house gases as much as anyone and want to do their bit. Their life is already a tangle of problems. But, in the spirit of innovation that characterises the best entrepreneurs, K&D make a molehill out of their mountain and begin an online energy-saving light-bulb web-store. Of course, K&D's step on-line doesn't solve their problems. Indeed for a short time it makes things much more complex: now their friends become potential customers, now they have to rely on their bank manager for advice and funds, now they have creditors and suppliers – some in the UK, some in Asia—legal and business advisors, an accountant, each of which has their own problems to solve.

K&D's problems are of a different nature to those of the butterflies/ants/rabbits. But they're still all-a-tangle: their business environment is tangled with their business is tangled with their family life is tangled with their social life is part of their business environment (see Figure 1).

To get a handle on the complexity of a tangle, we will first look at individual problems, beginning with an engineering model of a problem, adapted for the business.

Figure 1. A sketch of Kate and Daniel's tangled problems

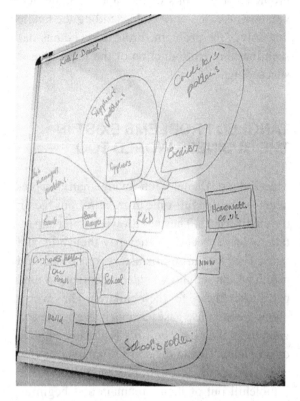

THE PROBLEM OF ENGINEERING

GFC Rogers, in his book *The Nature of Engineering*, provides a practice-based definition of engineering; he says:

'engineering refers to the practice of organising the design and construction of any artifice which transforms the physical world around us to meet some recognised need' (emphasis added)

According to Rogers, then, engineering is all about identifying the real-world environment that will be transformed, recognising a need and designing and constructing something—the artifice—that will meet it.

Current research at the Open University takes Rogers' definition, and makes that triple of Environment (the blue ENV in Figure 2), Need (the red NEED in Figure 2) and Solution (the green SOLN in Figure 2) the basis of problem solving; the breakthrough was to see that triple as an *engineering design problem* and to think of ways in which it could be solved as such. In Figure 2, there's an iconic representation of an engineering design problem that will allow us to see how they interrelate, at least for this essay.

Let's look again at K&D in the light of this research. They have their recognised need—personal financial security—and a complex real-world environment—including all the players mentioned above—and they are building their solution—their on-line light-bulb business to meet that need. They have a business problem and have developed—are developing—their solution.

As business problem solvers, K&D's designed their e-business to work within their business landscape, populated by bank managers, friends, suppliers, customers, ISPs, accountant, legal team, and family, to satisfy their need for a sustainable living wage. K&D share their business environment with others, and indeed, their e-business venture contributes to the solutions of many other's business problems: their suppliers build their business on the many businesses that use their products; their accountant and legal advisers sell their wares and services to K&D too; K&D's family get a living wage; the shops and businesses in their home town benefit from K&D's success by serving them better; even the

Figure 2. Environment, Need and Solution: The three elements of Rogers' engineering and the basis of engineering design research into problem solving at the Open University

taxman gets a bigger slice of a bigger pie. And, just as K&D solve their problems with a business, K&D's customers solve their problems—being greener—with K&D's products.

K&D's economic footprint has grown; and like the laces in K&D's sneakers, problems overlap and tie together in simple ways to tangle. In fact, here are the six basic overlaps between the three elements of two problems:

Environment/Environment Overlap: The Credit Crunch Problem

It is a fantastically fortunate business that doesn't have the current credit crunch[1] as a dominating factor in their business environment; any two businesses' fortunes will vary or co-vary as their environment experiences its ups and downs. There is no causal linkage in that variance, however, as long as they are otherwise insulated from each other in their business relationships. It's a benign relationship one to the other.

Environment/Solution Overlap: The Fashion Industry's Problem

It all started in 1858 when another Englishman, Charles Frederick Worth, opened his high fashion shop in Paris. Today, the importance of the professional designer in a changing fashion world has increased to the point when almost all clothes in almost any high street shop, from bijoux boutique to colossal chain, is inspired by their work.

But the 'fashion problem,' that of coming up with tomorrow's fashion in today's world, keeps reinventing itself. The fashion dynamic is cyclic, recurring, revisited. As Paul Smith's catwalk shows determine the new fashion, it quickly becomes the new norm in the environment of the new. The new fashion while tangled with the old and conceived in it defines the new solution—the fashion solution simultaneously solves and sustains the fashion problem.

Of course, it isn't always a single problem that tangles with itself: extended loops in which one solution enters the environment of another which is then newly solved, only to disturb another are common. Indeed, it is essentially the loops between problems that sustain creativity, business and value creation. And this makes environment/solution overlaps some of the most interesting problem tangles to look at.

Need/Environment and Need/Solution Overlap: The French President's Problems

'What should we do with the Louvre?' was the problem given to Emile Biasini, the head of the Grand Louvre project, by the President of the French Republic in the early 1980s. And when the French President wants you to solve their problem, you should probably listen! Biasini listened, attentively I guess, to the President, and tried to understand his need—in that sense, the President's need was part of Biasini's environment. In understanding and recording the need, Biasini produced the solution to his own problem, which he could then task the world-renowned architect I.M. Pei. The result, of course, was Pei's pyramid:

"The center (sic) of gravity of the museum had to be in the Cour Napoleon, that's where the public

Figure 3. Environment/environment

Figure 4. Environment/solution overlap

Figure 5. Need/environment overlap

had to come. But what do you do when you arrive? Do you enter into an underground space, a kind of subway concourse? No. You need to be welcomed by some kind of great space. So you've got to have something of our period. That space must have volume, it must have light and it must have a surface identification. You have to be able to look at it and say, Ah, this is the entrance."

Lecocq (1989)

Solution/Solution Overlap: The Software Developer's Problem

A very large collection of problems overlap on the solution, because they form the producer/consumer class of business relationships. Examples include the developer who produces software for another business: the software developer's problem of producing a sustainable business, is (one might assume) solved by the software that solves their customer's problem. Of course, the relationship isn't always sweet, and a poor 'solution' might not really solve either problem, and perhaps even both: software that crashes and burns constantly solves neither customer's nor developer's problem–although it seems that some organisations can continue to get away with it!

Need/Need Overlap: The Competitor/ Collaborators' Problem

Finally, and indicative of needing to find a closer business relationship, two problems that have overlapping needs (but not environments) suggest looking together for solutions. On the other hand, if environments are overlapping too—for instance, located within the same marketplace—that's a potentially competitive relationship, although collaboration—on standards, self-regulation, *etc.*—can still, sometimes, pay dividends.

THE SUBTLETY OF TIMINGS

Problems do not need to have a designed solution, of course: the rabbit/ant/butterfly relationship is a nature-solved problem which does without. In business, however, the moves are too quick for a purely evolutionary approach to problem solving. Business problems have to have more-or-less designed solutions, whether a new package or service, a new market for an old product, a changed maintenance regime, re-branding, a new business model, *etc*. Before a designed solution can exist, however, a real-world context and identified need must be recognised even if no detail of them is

Figure 6. Need/solution overlap

known: 'I have a dream' is a powerful statement of real-world—not dream-world—intent.

The knowledge of the need for a solution necessarily precedes the solution, but it may not precede it by very long. Although defining new problems, the digital economy provides solutions in record time: with Service-Oriented Architectures (SOAs), for instance, business problem solvers can respond ever more quickly and cost-effectively to their environment. iTunes University delivers knowledge without pesky semesters. All the web is geared for speed. Although no fit-for-purpose solution is cheap, the search for an engineered solution—let's call it siftware engineering, if you'll forgive the pun—makes rapid solution possible.

Business problem solving in this new landscape depends critically on understanding the linkages between the players, their contexts and their needs.

PROBLEMS OF THE GLOBAL ECONOMY

There aren't too many ways in which two problems can overlap: using our research into problem solving we've been able to find them all. Just as pick-up sticks[2] would be a very boring game with just two sticks, the real fun comes when there are hundred, thousands, millions of problems tangled together. Just like there are in the global economy.

Although on-line economies are beginning to appear, the real-world global economy is as big as it gets. Even so, it is driven by the simple interactions between problems that we have seen in this paper. Its highs, its lows, it twists and turns are all products of the solving of problems.

You can read more about the research described here at http://problemoriented.wikispaces.com

Figure 7. Solution/solution overlap

Figure 8. Need/need overlap

REFERENCE

Lecocq, C. (1989). *The New Louvre*. Connaissance des Arts.

ENDNOTES

[1] October 2008 to the time of writing, September 2009.

[2] An exciting traditional game for two or more players: see http://en.wikipedia.org/wiki/Pick-up_sticks

Chapter 6
Managing Managerial Mosaic:
The Evolute Methodology

Jussi Kantola
Korea Advanced Institute of Science and Technology (KAIST), Republic of Korea

Waldemar Karwowski
University of Central Florida, USA

Hannu Vanharanta
Tampere University of Technology, Finland

ABSTRACT

In this chapter, the authors address a new management methodology that attempts to enhance understanding of organizational resources to all stakeholders thereby making management more systematic and efficient. By clarifying the conceptual structures of organizational resources to all stakeholders, decisions are based on the proper and relevant concepts. This new ontology-based management approach aids understanding and managing the whole in more human-centred way than previous methods. Also, the change becomes transparent and easy to visualize. Such transparent and visualized change enables the use of meta-knowledge to direct the management mosaic towards the desired outcome.

INTRODUCTION

Managerial work serves to lead and coordinate knowledge, people, materials, and technological and financial resources required by an organization to achieve its goals (c.f. Hess and Siciliano, 1996). In this article, these organizational resources are referred as Management Objects (MOs). MOs are vague entities that individuals perceive differently from their own viewpoints. Each individual has a unique life experience and therefore has a unique base to understand the meaning of MOs.

The meaning of objects is biased by the mind's personal, varied, and unique knowledge structures. The present work situation coupled with personal circumstances has an effect on how one perceives and understands a MO. People can also envisage the future of MOs – including themselves.

Conceptual structures of MOs are not typically available to people who are working with the MOs. Therefore, it seems that people have to work with a very incomplete picture of the world around them (c.f. Ford et al., 1998). This is a big problem, since the literature supports the fact that many managerial solutions often fail due to an

DOI: 10.4018/978-1-61520-623-0.ch006

incomplete perception of the situation requiring a solution (c.f. Jackson, 2004).

Measurement aids good decision-making. This is true for tangible assets, but in the case of abstract MOs, it is impossible to measure them directly or quantitatively. The quantitative information regarding MOs would not even deliver a holistic picture required for justifiable decisions. The concepts of MOs are not numerical but rather are abstract by nature. MO concepts are interrelated in many ways. Instead of trying to measure MOs numerically we can ask people who have knowledge of MOs to evaluate them using natural language. To achieve this, a holistic conceptual structure of MOs is needed. Zadeh claims that human ability to make precise and meaningful statements about a system's behaviour decreases as the complexity of a system increases (Zadeh, 1973). Taking into account a systems perspective, MOs are systems with interrelated parts.

The wide range of MOs forms a very difficult field for the management. An illustrative metaphor for this problem is a Mosaic. The mosaic is fragmented at the detail level, making it difficult to see the whole. Different pieces are inter-related and together they form the whole picture when viewed holistically. If a detailed, in-depth view is taken, the meaning of the whole is not apparent. An even greater difficulty arises if we assume a dynamic mosaic making it that more difficult to know to which direction the mosaic is moving and how its parts should be developed in order to achieve its goals. Today, it is common that business is made far from management. Business is moving abroad, becoming global, and therefore disconnected somewhat from management hubs. This means additional strain on management activities as there are separations in geography and time. Global business means the involvement of several cultures as well. Cultural differences cause MOs to be understood very differently. Clearly, new methods are needed; as a collective involvement of stakeholders is necessary to actuate the business and change. What is needed to view mosaic at the

correct level of abstraction, seeing its meaning without focusing on individual details?

Linguistic (language-based) methods are becoming helpful in understanding the whole. Language-based methods can be made as on-line software applications. The goal is to make the management easier and more accurate, while allowing informed and justifiable decisions to be made. Managing the mosaic is becoming a new way to succeed in business.

In this article, we present the Evolute methodology (Kantola, 2005) that attempts to enhance understanding of MOs to all stakeholders thereby making management more systematic and efficient. By clarifying the conceptual structures of MOs to all stakeholders, decisions are based on the proper and relevant concepts. This ontology-based approach aids understanding and managing the whole clearer than previous methods. Also, the change becomes transparent easy to visualize. Such transparent and visualized change enables the use of meta-knowledge to direct the mosaic towards the desired outcome.

Employing this method, workers can operate (manage, work, learn, co-operate, etc.) with a more complete picture of their situation than the managerial methods employed currently. The proposed method can be used for management, development, and co-operational activities as well as for teaching and training purposes. The Evolute methodology is already being successfully used in several countries in academic and business organizations. The following chapters describe the theory and practise of the Evolute methodology.

THEORETICAL FRAMEWORK OF THE EVOLUTE METHODOLOGY

Ontologies

Ontology is defined as the specification of the conceptualisation of a domain (Gruber, 1993). Conceptualisation is an idea regarding an element of the world that a person or persons can have (Gomez-Perez, 2004). Ontology defines the common words and concepts (meanings) that describe and represent an area of knowledge (Obrst, 2003). Ontologies thus represent a method of formally expressing a shared understanding of information (Parry, 2004). The main parts of ontologies are classes (concepts), relations (associations between the concepts in the domain), and instances (elements or individuals in ontology) (Gomez-Perez, 2004).

Using ontologies results in several benefits, such as interoperability, browsing and searching, and reuse and structuring of knowledge (Menzies, 1999). Ontologies also enable computational processing of information. Ontologies are becoming increasingly important in fields such as knowledge management, information integration, co-operative information systems, information retrieval, and e-commerce (Baader et al., 2004). Ontologies serve needs such as storage, exchange of data corresponding to ontology, ontology-based reasoning or ontology-based navigation (Crubezy and Musen, 2004; Oberle et al., 2004).

Ontologies provide an approach to specify and manage concepts of MOs in a holistic way. Without utilizing ontologies it is difficult for a manager to perceive, manage and develop MOs in the right way. Without the use of ontologies, management cannot follow the classification and structure of MOs. Ontologies promise a shared and common understanding of a domain that can be communicated between people and application systems (Davies et al., 2003). In addition, ontologies enable computer processing to retrieve and use information. The two above mentioned aspects, combined with opportunities provided by contemporary Internet programming technology makes constructing MOs as ontologies a very attractive approach to position and manage current and future organizational resources. The discerning of meaning from the mosaic would be impossible without utilizing ontologies.

Helpful Metaphors in Ontology Interpretation

The following three metaphors aid in understanding how and why individuals perceive MOs ontologies uniquely. These metaphors are useful in designing applications where ontologies are utilized in working, managing, learning and teaching contexts. In the context of managing the mosaic, these metaphors lead us to the conclusion that the mosaic is collectively formed in the minds of stakeholders. The whole exists collectively in the minds of people!

A Holistic Concept of the Man Metaphor

The Holistic Concept of Man (HCM) is a human metaphor. The basic dimensions of the metaphor consist of a body, mind, and a situation (Rauhala 1986; 1995). A human being is an organism that employs thinking processes utilized in particular and individually formed situations (Maslin, 2001). The human being constitutes three modes of existence simultaneously based on the above basic dimensions of the HCM, inseparable from each other. HCM depicts the holistic nature of the human being. These modes of existence of the human being are called (1) corporeality, or existence as an organism with organic processes (the body) (2) consciousness, or existence as a psychic-mental phenomenon, as perceiving and experiencing (the mind), (3) situationality, or existence in relation to reality (the situation), Figure 1. The first mode of existence, corporeality, describes the basic physical processes of existence and implements the physical activities of the human being. The human brain and sense organs (internal and external) are required when observing objects and concepts in a specific situation, these create meanings for the observer (Vanharanta et al., 1997) Consciousness processes afford the human being experiences, perceptions and understanding of phenomena encountered through activities such as pattern recognition and the formation of meaning. Stimuli

Figure 1. The three modes of existence in the HCM metaphor

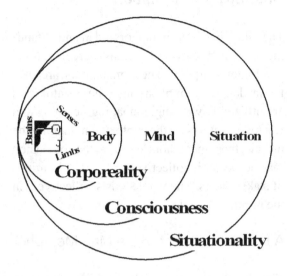

from the environment provide consciousness with possibly meaningful content, the human being understands this content, i.e. perceives the corresponding construct(s) or object(s) or concept(s) to be "something." Understanding results in the formation of a relationship, meaning or meanings.

Situationality is the third dimension of human existence. Situationality emphasizes that a human being exists not only "as such," in a vacuum or isolation, but rather in relation and interrelation to reality containing a multitude of aspects. The world, our reality, is all that exists concretely or ideally, i.e. the world with which people in general can relate to. Situation (or the situation of life) is that part of the world with which a particular human being forms relationships and interrelationships (Maslin, 2001). Situationality is always unique to each individual. Individuals understand the same object(s) in their situation differently.

The Theater Metaphor

The HCM metaphor, or the idea of the human being in a specific situation as a totality, is not sufficient alone. The metaphor lacks the new,

current research findings on the unconscious part of the human brain. Baars (1997) has combined psychology with brain science and the old conception of the human mind to create a metaphor based on the workspace of the mind. The totality can be explained through the theatre metaphor, where the self is an agent and behaves as if on a theatre stage. Close to the stage is the unconscious part of the brain (the audience), divided into four main areas: the motivational system, automatic systems, the interpreting system, and the memory system. The spotlight controller, context, and theatre director are also present.

The Circles of Mind Metaphor

A combination of the HCM and the theatre metaphor of Baars (1997) led to a new and very practical metaphor. This was named the *Circles of Mind* metaphor (Vanharanta, 2003). The Circles of Mind metaphor was also designed as a physical entity so the metaphor could be used for design purposes. This has led to the idea of a brain-based system, which contains the physical body following Cartesian mind-body relationships, i.e. as a thinking thing and an extended thing (Maslin, 2001). One version of the Circles of Mind metaphor is presented in Figure 2.

The metaphor contains various elements: Res cogitans / A Thinking Thing (mind) is evident here, yielding four main parts for the architecture of new computer applications. Res extensa / An Extended Thing (body) represents the other dimension of man, which physically uses the computer keyboard and gives the power of functionality to the computer applications to be used on the stage. This article posits that different management objects (MOs) are sent to the conscious experience on the stage. Next, the agent perceives and understands them from different angles and views. This action results in a holistic view of the current and future stage. Adding personal, individual, views and perceptions develops the collective understanding of management objects. A high level view of the management mosaic emerges.

Creative Tension and Proactive Vision

The Human Resource Management (HRM) department in every organization strives to apply efficient tools in order to develop and manage the competencies of its workforce in a rapidly changing business environment fraught with intense competition. The fundamental challenge for managers in contemporary enterprises is to meet both the individual and organizational objectives and requirements. The integration of individuals and organizational goals is very important, but also difficult to achieve. How can any executive, manager or supervisor be aware of employee personal goals and wishes? To answer this question, it is important to develop an awareness of the present situation. The realistic assessment of a current reality is a starting point for any future visioning activity. Senge (1994) named this future visioning "creative tension." It is the force behind the concept of personal mastery, which includes continuous learning by generating and sustaining of a perception of life. The creative tension is a dynamic interaction between the envisioning of the future and the idea of current reality. It is close to the concept of psychological energy that moves a person toward the reality of his/her vision. The collective creative tension of individuals, in turn, has the power to move organizations from one (business) position to another. In the context of work roles, the first requirement for the human resource development is to identify and visualize the creative tension of individual employees. This knowledge can be used to integrate the needs and goals for individuals and organizations. In addition to developing their human capital, enterprises aim to develop their business processes as well. The bottom-up analysis of objects (business processes) being developed is crucial to the successful integration of the goals of individuals and organizations. When an object is evaluated and developed using the Evolute methodology, something similar to the energy of creative tension is perceived. This energy, or the will to develop an object, can be called the proactive vision (Paajanen et al. 2004). Creative tension and proactive vision is a crucially important element to be included in the management of the mosaic!

Figure 2.

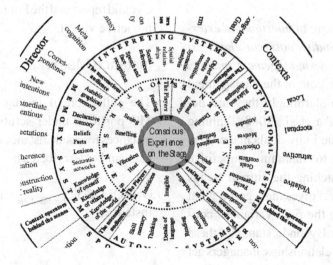

81

EVOLUTE METHODOLOGY

Instances in the Management Mosaic

Within an organization people perceive MOs – internal and external. People have personal needs and needs regarding MOs, which are based on their individual perceptions. Therefore, perception plays a very important role in an organization's management, since people think and act based upon their perception. People also envision the future of MOs – including their part. This is a very important element to consider, since this tension between current reality and envisaged future indicates the direction for peoples' thoughts and actions regarding MOs in the future. For individuals, this tension is described creative tension by Senge (1994) and for external MOs this energy can be called the proactive vision (Paajanen et al. 2004).

According to ontological engineering principles MOs can be modelled as ontologies. In this context we call such ontologies as MOOs (Management Object Ontologies) (Kantola, 2005). A MOO can be internal, describing certain aspects of an individual. In this case human perception is introspective, which refers to one's own subjectivity (Churchland, 2002). A MOO can also describe an external object (MO) perceptible to many. The perception of external ontology is called extrospection.

Capturing the meaning of internal and external objects (MOOs) to individuals (stakeholders) is the cornerstone of the management mosaic. Individuals are often left out of the management picture, or even more alarmingly they are being ignored (c.f. Nonaka et al., 2008). Valuing the contributions unique individuals make in an organization allows it to maintain competitive business activities. Catching the current trends from the bottom-up level gives managers a great opportunity to manage the right variables, concepts, and constructs. By understanding these relationships and inter-relationships, managers get

meta-understanding utilizing meta-knowledge, i.e. novel and meaningful insights regarding management of the organization.

An individual's perception of a MOO, both present and future is defined as an instance. Instances capture tacit knowledge and relate it to an ontology making it more meaningful for others to understand.

In our approach, each concept in a MOO is described with few indicative statements (Figure 3). These statements indicate what level the concept is adopted in an organization practise. A person performing the self-evaluation does not know which concept(s) the statement is indicating. The indicative statements are related to individuals' every-day work. The goal is to find statements that indicate the concepts from different "angles". Each statement is evaluated at its current level and at a targeted future level. According to Senge (1994), the accurate and sincere self-assessment of one's current reality and future goals is the cornerstone of personal mastery and the manifestation of a person's creative tension (Senge, 1994).

The following two print screens in Figure 4 depict samples of an instance as a result of an ontological evaluation pertaining to a single situation. The first ontology is project managers' competences (Cycloid), and the second sample is the knowledge creation ontology (Folium), (Figure 4). Creative tension is apparent in the Cycloid report and the Folium report demonstrates proactive vision.

Instance Matrix

The collection of instances reflects a specific MO portfolio under scrutiny. The collection of instances forms an instance matrix (Kantola, 2005) that can be described as:

ONTOLOGY $_{\text{Identifiers 1 - m}}$ (Individuals 1-n, Instance)

Figure 3. A print screen from the Evolute ontology evaluation window. The specific statement is an indicator for a specific class (concept) in the knowledge creation ontology – Folium (Paajanen, 2006).

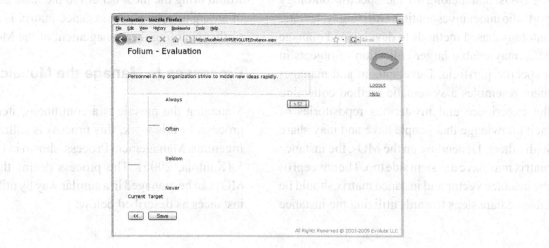

For example, personnel in an organization participate in the following MOO self-evaluations within a given time-window (c.f. Kantola et al, 2009a):

- Cardioid ontology (physical competencies) (Kantola et al., 2005)
- Cycloid ontology (project managers' competences) (Liikamaa, 2006)
- Serpentine ontology (safety culture) (Halima, 2007)
- Folium and Talbot ontologies (knowledge creation and learning environment) (Paajanen, 2006)
- Tractrix ontology (R&D project portfolio) (Naukkarinen, 2004)

$(O_{Cardioid}$ (1-50, 1),

$O_{Cycloid}$ (1-50, 1),

$O_{Serpentine}$ (1-50, 1),

O_{Foilum} (1-50, 1),

O_{Talbot} (1-50, 1),

$O_{Tractrix}$ (1-50, 1)}

The instance matrix, as a function of time, tells the story of MO development in the organization. In other words, it is the story of an organization's assets over time. It also enables the validation of targeted management cycles. The instance matrix, as a function of time, can be described as:

$ONTOLOGY_{Identifiers\ 1-m}$ (Individuals 1-n, Instances 1-k)

Using the same example as above, every six months over a three year time period, all personnel in an organization periodically participate in the self-evaluation:

$(O_{Cardioid}$ (1-50, 1-7),

$O_{Cycloid}$ (1-50, 1-7),

$O_{Serpentine}$ (1-50, 1-7),

O_{Foilum} (1-50, 1-7),

O_{Talbot} (1-50, 1-7),

$O_{Tractrix}$ (1-50, 1-7)}

The intent of the instance matrix is to match the MOs that belong to the specific ontology portfolio under investigation. Utilizing systematic ontology-based methods to develop and manage MOs may enable larger collection of objects in a specific portfolio. Development and management resembles a systematic method collecting the experience and mysterious repositories of tacit knowledge that people have and may share with others. Depending on the MOs, the instance matrix may have a system side too. The concept of the instance vector and instance matrix should be intermediate steps towards utilizing the instance

matrix over time, which is a continuous process and would bring the most benefit to the management of an organization. The instance matrix is a tool further enabling the management of the Mosaic.

Processes to Manage the Mosaic

Managing the mosaic is a continuous, iterative process. In this work, this process is called The Ingenious Management Process, shown in Figure 5 (Kantola, 2005). The process deems that all MOs can be managed in a similar way by utilizing instances as described below:

Figure 4. Two samples of visualized instances

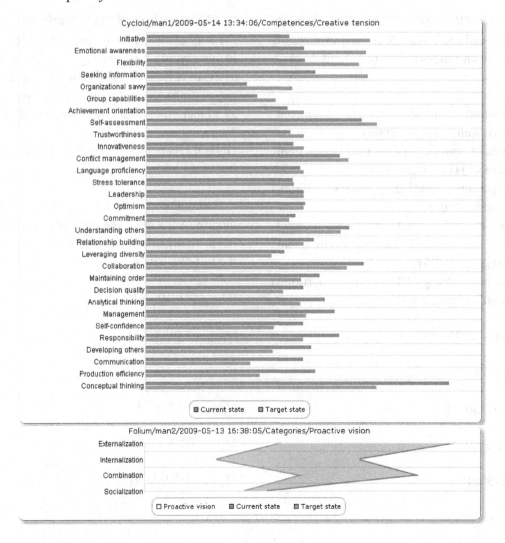

1. Collecting instances within a set time window.
2. Validating (in workshops) the perceived impact of previous development plans (if existing) and fitting them together.
   a. Unique instances
   b. Focus areas coming from the strategy of an organization and local conditions
   c. Explicit knowledge about MOs, such as important competencies in a specific work role
3. Making targeted development plans for the MOs
4. Taking action according to the plans
5. Returning to Step 1 after each development cycle (6/12 months)

These steps are generic and independent from the content of MOOs. A MOO with only a couple of sub-classes and a MOO with tens of sub-classes are handled in the same way. MOOs may have more or less hierarchy, but instances are collected in a similar fashion regardless of amount of content, allowing the visualization of the perception of MOOs. If MOOs have specified system boundary management can also apply meta-knowledge coming from the system boundary of MOs. Every cycle can be seen as different, yet all cycles can, in principle, be handled in a uniform way.

THE EVOLUTE TECHNOLOGY

Evolute technology enables the application of Evolute methodology in organizations. The technology is an on-line soft-computing platform that supports MOO development and use according to Evolute methodology (Kantola, 2005). The Evolute technology enables:

- MOO research and development in academic and business organizations
- Practical MOO application projects in academic and business organizations

The Evolute technology utilizes fuzzy logic (Zadeh, 1965) to capture abstract instances by stakeholders. The use of fuzzy sets allows for using linguistic meanings directly without conversion to numerical scale. Fuzzy logic facilitates the reasoning of the indicators to visualized outputs, Figure 4. The outputs can also be examined and studied further in numerical formats and in Self-Organized Maps (Kohonen, 2001).

EVOLUTE RESEARCH AND APPLICATION STATUS

Currently there are 19 universities and colleges (Evolute Research Centres - ERCs) in eight dif-

Figure 5. The ingenious management process (Kantola, 2005)

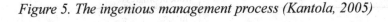

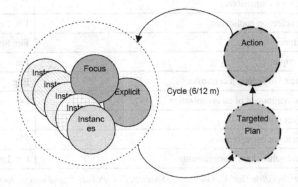

ferent countries applying Evolute methodology in MOO research. These ERCs also form number of networks that participate in international research regarding MOO. The ERCs work together with local organizations (funding bodies, authorities, etc.) and companies. Currently there are more that 25 MOOs each of which contains at minimum MS theses level of literature and empirical research. Some MOOs have been studied to PhD thesis level, and few of them will be on the PhD thesis level by the end of 2010. There are nine language versions depending on the MOO. The number of instances approaches 10,000 in 2009. The following table summarizes the current state of Evolute applications: name, content and current language versions, Table 1.

Table 1. Summary of the evolute research and application status

Name	Content	Language versions
Astroid	Competencies of sales personnel	Fin, Eng, Swe
Bicorn	Safety culture	Fin, Eng, Pol
Cardioid	Physical competencies	Fin, Eng, Swe, Spa, Cat
Cardioid kids	Kids' physical activity and competences	Fin, Eng
Cissoid	Maintenance and sales person combined	Fin, Eng, Swe, Kor
Cochleoid	Competencies of buyers	Fin
Conchoid	Competencies of maintenance personnel	Fin, Rus
No name 1	Innovative human	Work in progress
Cycloid	Competencies of project managers	Fin, Eng, Swe, Spa, Cat, Pol, Kor, Fre
Deltoid	Competencies of plant operators	Fin, Eng, Swe, Spa, Cat, Pol, Kor, Rus
Epitrochoid	Competencies of human resource managers	Fin
Folium	Knowledge creation of an organization	Fin, Eng, Swe, Spa, Cat, Pol, Kor
Helicoid	Competencies of executives	Fin, Eng, Swe
Kappa	Sales culture	Eng
Languoid	Language learning competence	Eng
Lissajous	Project business culture	Eng
Nephroid	Competencies of human work professionals	Fin, Eng, Swe, Spa, Cat, Pol
No name 2	Innovative culture	Work in progress
Rhodonea	Mega-projects	Fin, Eng
Rose	Affection, love dimensions	Eng
Sinusoid	Work role selection application	Fin, Eng
Serpentine	Safety culture	Fin, Spa, Pol
Spiric	Growth company	Fin
Strophoid	Competencies of financial controller	Eng
Talbot	Learning environment of an organization	Fin, Eng, Swe, Spa, Cat, Pol, Kor
Tractrix	R&D project portfolio	Eng
Tricuspoid	Competencies of entrepreneurs	Fin
Trifolium	Supply- and value chain management	Fin, Eng, Swe

Fin=Finnish, Eng=English, Swe=Swedish, Cat=Catalan, Spa=Spanish, Pol=Polish, Rus=Russian, Kor=Korean, Fre=French

DISCUSSION

Managing the mosaic as described in this article requires new approaches, new methodologies, and new applied techniques and tools. Most importantly, significant basic research is needed in order to develop both scientifically and empirically valid Management Object Ontologies. By making the objects more meaningful to people, work and studies become more meaningful as well. MOOs make all stakeholders (who are "operating" the objects) aware of the relevant concepts regarding their work. On the other words, we can raise the general awareness level of the right concepts of objects required at work, during studies, cooperative efforts, etc.

We have been developing the Evolute methodology, Evolute technology and MOOs for several years in many countries and we have understood the significance of MOOs. By using our approach we have been able to scientifically validate and verify the research results. There is a large international network involved in research aiding understanding of the significance and application of this approach in the management field. Many theses and articles have been written, and experts in different fields have been involved in research and practical projects. The number of people involved (the number of instances) approaches 10,000 in 2009. The developed MOOs and the practical projects in which they have been used demonstrate evidence for the importance of this new approach. We can see that ontologies live and change as they reflect the international world we work in. MOOs also develop and change over time, keeping pace. We suggest Evolute applications for scientific research for those research bodies that are interested in using the Evolute methodology and tools.

Linguistic (language-based) methodologies and tools are beginning to support existing quantitative methodologies and tools in the field of management. The use of numerical and language-based "soft" methodologies, methods, and tools together yields more reliable results than numerical approaches alone. Using both approaches is novel in the management field.

The Evolute approach can offer predictive measures and concepts allowing the capture of people's abilities benefitting the organization in an effort to reach its goals.

REFERENCES

Baader, F., Horrocks, I., & Sattler, U. (2004). Description Logics. In Staab, S., & Studer, R. (Eds.), *Handbook on Ontologies* (pp. 3–28). Berlin: Springer-Verlag.

Baars, B. J. (1997). *In the Theatre of Consciousness*. Oxford, UK: Oxford University Press. doi:10.1093/acprof:oso/9780195102659.001.1

Churchland, P. S. (2002). *Brain-Wise - Studies in Neurophilosophy*. Cambridge, MA: The MIT Press.

Crubezy, M., & Musen, M. A. (2004). Ontologies in Support of Problem Solving. In Staab, S., & Studer, R. (Eds.), *Handbook on Ontologies* (pp. 322–341). Berlin: Springer-Verlag.

Davies, J., Fensel, D., & Van Harmelen, F. (2003). *Towards the Semantic Web - Ontology Based Knowledge Management. Davies, J., Fensel, D., Van Harmelen, F.* John Wiley & Sons, Ltd.

Ford, D., Gadde, L.-E., Håkansson, H., Lundgren, A., Snehota, I., Turnbull, P., & Wilson, D. (1998). *Managing Business relationships*. Chichester, UK: John Wiley & Sons, Ltd.

Gomez-Perez, A. (2004). Ontology Evaluation. In Staab, S., & Studer, R. (Eds.), *Handbook on Ontologies* (pp. 251–273). Berlin: Springer-Verlag.

Gruber, T. R. (1993). A translation approach to portable ontologies. *Knowledge Acquisition*, 5(2), 199–220. doi:10.1006/knac.1993.1008

Halima, T. (2007). *Safety Culture Ontology - From Theory to Practice*. Licentiate thesis. Tampere University of Technology, Pori, Finland.

Hess, P., & Siciliano, J. (1996). *Management - Responsibility for Performance*. New York: McGraw-Hill.

Jackson, C. M. (2004). *Systems Thinking: Creative Holism for Managers*. West Sussex, UK: John Wiley & Sons Ltd.

Kantola, J. (2005). *Ingenious Management*. Doctoral thesis, Tampere University of Technology at Pori, Finland.

Kantola, J., Karwowski, W., & Vanharanta, H. (2005). Creative Tension in Occupational Work Roles: A Dualistic View of Human Competence Management Technology Based on Soft Computing. *Ergonomia: An International Journal of Ergonomics and Human Factors, 27*(4), 273–286.

Kantola, J., Karwowski, W., & Vanharanta, H. (2009a). *Evolute Internet pages – MOO Applications*. Retrieved July 10, 2009, from http://www.evolutellc.com/Applications.html

Kantola, J., Karwowski, W., & Vanharanta, H. (2009b). *Evolute Internet pages – Evolute Research Centres*. Retrieved July 10, 2009, from http://www.evolutellc.com/ERCs/ERCs.aspx

Kohonen, T. (2001). *Self-Organizing Maps*. Helsinki, Finland: Springer Verlag.

Liikamaa, K. (2006). *Tacit Knowledge and Project Managers' Competencies*. Doctoral Thesis, Tampere University of Technology at Pori, Finland.

Maslin, K. T. (2001). *An Introduction to the Philosophy of Mind*. Malden, UK: Blackwell Publishers Inc.

Menzies, T. (1999). Cost Benefits of Ontologies. *Intelligence, 10*(3), 26–32. doi:10.1145/318964.318969

Naukkarinen, O., Kantola, J., & Vanharanta, H. (2004). A New Qualitative Decision Support Tool for Evaluating and Managing R&D Investments. In *4th Annual Conference: Governance in Managerial Life, EURAM*, St. Andrews, Scotland, May 2004.

Nonaka, I., & Takeuchi, H. (1995). *The Knowledge-Creating Company: How Japanese Companies Create the Dynamics of Innovation*. New York: Oxford University Press.

Nonaka, I., Toyama, R., & Hirata, T. (2008). *Managing Flow: A Process Theory of the Knowledge-Based Firm*. New York: Palgrave Macmillan.

Oberle, D., Volz, R., Staab, S., & Motik, B. (2004). An Extensible Ontology Software Environment. In Staab, S., & Studer, R. (Eds.), *Handbook on Ontologies* (pp. 299–319). Berlin: Springer-Verlag.

Obrst, L. (2003). Ontologies for Semantically Interoperable Systems. In *Proceedings of the 12th international conference on Information and knowledge management*.

Paajanen, P. (2006). *Dynamic Ontologies of Knowledge Creation and Learning*. Licentiate Thesis. Tampere University of Technology, Pori, Finland.

Paajanen, P., Kantola, J., Karwowski, W., & Vanharanta, H. (2004). LITUUS: A system for the development of learning organizations. In H.-W. Chu, J. Aguilar & J. Ferrer (Eds.)., *ISAS CITSA 2004: 10th international conference on international systems analysis and synthesis*, July 21-25, 2004, Orlando, Florida, USA (pp. 412-416).

Parry, D. (2004). A fuzzy ontology for medical document retrieval. In *Proceedings of the second workshop on Australasian information security, Data Mining and Web Intelligence, and Software Internationalisation*, Dunedin, New Zealand, Australian Computer Society, Inc.

Rauhala, L. (1986). *Ihmiskäsitys ihmistyössä* [The Conception of Human Being in Helping People]. Helsinki, Finland: Gaudeamus.

Rauhala, L. (1995). *Tajunnan itsepuolustus* [Self-Defense of the Consciousness]. Helsinki, Finland: Yliopistopaino.

Senge, P. M. (1994). *The Fifth Discipline the Art and practice of the Learning Organization*. New York: Currency Doubleday.

Vanharanta, H. (2003). Circles of mind. Identity and diversity in organizations – building bridges in Europe. In *11th European congress on work and organizational psychology*, 14-17 May 2003, Lisboa, Portugal.

Zadeh, L. A. (1965). Fuzzy sets. *Information and Control, 8*, 338–353. doi:10.1016/S0019-9958(65)90241-X

Zadeh, L. A. (1973). Outline of a new approach to the analysis of complex systems and decision processes. *IEEE Transactions on Systems, Man, and Cybernetics, 1*(1), 28–44.

Chapter 7
Application of Fuzzy Cognitive Maps in IT Management and Risk Analysis

Masoud Mohammadian
University of Canberra, Australia

ABSTRACT

Development and management of IT systems are complex, demanding, and yet crucial to an organization success and its competitive position in the marketplace. Due to rapid changes in emerging technologies there is a need for constant improvement and adjustment to IT systems. There are a large number of processes involved in IT system development and monitoring. The interdependencies of these processes make it very difficult for Chief Information Officers (CIOs) to comprehend and be aware of effect of inefficiencies that may exist in development of these processes in their organization. This chapter considers the implementation of a Fuzzy Cognitive Maps (FCM) to provide facilities to capture and represent complex relationships in an IT management model and their related processes to improve the understanding of CIOs about the systems and its associated risks. By using FCMs CIOs can regularly review and improve their IT systems and provide greater improvement in development, monitoring and maintenance of IT facilities. CIOs can perform what-if analysis to better understand vulnerabilities of their designed system.

INTRODUCTION

IT processes are activities for development and maintenance of applications, supporting infrastructure (e.g., hardware, systems software, and networks), to managing human resources. Luftman (Luftman, 2004) described 38 IT processes that cover all aspects or IT management in an organization. These IT processes have been categorized in three main layers. These layers include strategic layer which focuses on the long-term goals and how IT can enable the achievement of these goals in an organization. The second layer is the tactical layer which works towards achieving the strategic goals and finally operational layer which covers day-to-day operation activities. Strategic level

DOI: 10.4018/978-1-61520-623-0.ch007

consist of strategic planning control that covers business analysis planning, architecture planning and IT strategic planning control. Figure 1 shows sub-processes of strategic layer. Tactical layer consists of management planning, development planning, resource planning and service planning. These four processes are divided into 15 sub processes. Figure 2 shows the sub-processes. The operational level consists of six processes project management, resource control, service control, development and maintenance, administration services and information services. The six processes are divided into 22 sub processes. Figure 3 shows the processes of operational layer. These processes include all stages of IT management from planning, organizing, and administering processes required to effectively and efficiently manage IT. Using the three layers approach it is possible to distinguish the sub processes and code-pendences between IT functions. It can be noted that the strategic layer impacts the tactical layer by changing the technologies, tools, and methodologies used in tactical processes. Consequently new technologies, tools, and methodologies impact the operational level by changing the requirements of staff, their training, and job functions [Luftman, 2004]. Successful completion of tactical processes impact operational layer. Using this three layer approach it is possible to note the codependences of these layers and the impact of one layer on other layers.

It should be noted that leading management-consulting firms such as Ernst & Young, Price

Waterhouse Coopers, et al as well as the Society of Information Management (SIM) provide different number of IT Processes. For example Ernst & Young have presented 70 IT processes, PricewaterhouseCoopers use 62 IT processes, Society of Information Management (SIM) has listed 40 IT processes and David Feeney lists nine major (core) categories of IT processes. CobiT and the IT Governance Institute display 34 IT processes. CobiT consists of six major categories and there is no distinction between strategic, tactical, or operational layer.

No matter which model is used there are a large number of sub processes that the Chief Information Office (CIO) needs to consider to be able to successfully manage the IT for an organization. In this paper Luftman (Luftman, 2004) 38 IT processes are considered for IT management and risk analysis in an organization. Other models can easily be substituted to discover risk in the IT management of such models.

In next section the three layers of Luftman (Luftman, 2004) model is further analyzed. Section 3 provide a brief overview of Fuzzy Cognitive Maps (FCMs) and section 4 provide simulation details of application of FCMs to this three layer IT management process. It provides the facilities that a CIO require to perform risk analysis and simulate what-if scenario that needs to be considered during the development, implementation and monitoring of IT manage processes using this three level model.

Figure 1. Sub-processes of strategic layer

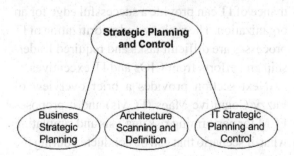

Figure 2. Sub-processes of tactical layer

Figure 3. Sub-processes of operational layer

STRATEGIC, TACTICAL AND OPERATIONAL LAYER

Strategic layer consists of processes that have long term results on an organization and therefore the benefits are attained in long term. These processes provide a competitive edge for an organization by delivering cost efficiencies and improvements to business processes.

In contrast to strategic layer the tactical layer processes are short-term and sometimes intermediate. Their impact on an organization can be observed in short term and they provide improvements to existing operations. Tactical layer processes involved majority of the IT staff and it has a largest budgets assigned to it.

Operational layer processes cover day-to-day operations and functions that are commonly the most critical to an organization. CIOs and IT executives manage and monitor IT systems and conduct IT management to improve organization's IT efficiencies and effectiveness. Some of the questions that they need to have answers on day to day bases are:

Which processes are most important? Does this reduce the importance of the remaining processes?

Who owns each of these process containers? How much resource will be applied to each process? How effective are each of these processes today?

What priority should be placed on improving each of these processes? What IT strategic processes and how they will have an impact on the pace of

technological change in an enterprise. What is the role of IT architecture in aligning the business and IT functions of an organization?

The effective IT management depends to successful application of IT processes. Some processes have more important roles and impact than other IT processes. Development of effective applications in an organization will provides competitive and strategic advantage for an organization.

IT departments and CIO need to take ownership of IT processes and develop these processes efficiently and effectively. Resource allocation for each IT process should be based on the importance and complexity of such processes. For example operational level processes provide more than 60 percent (Luftman, 2004) of IT activities in an organization. However as reported by (Luftman, 2004) less than 40 percent of the IT staff is allocated on operational activities. With careful consideration and use of new methodologies many IT processes can be improved. Improving the IT processes is costly and IT executives need to increase IT budgets while organizations are trying to reduce costs.

Finally effective management and performance of IT can provide a successful edge for an organization. The ranking and prioritization of IT processes are difficult tasks and required leadership and efforts from CIOs and IT executives.

Next section provides a brief overview of Fuzzy Cognitive Maps (FCMs) and it proposes FCM for performing risk analysis and simulating what-if scenario that can be conducted during the development of IT manage processes using this three level model.

FUZZY COGNITIVE MAPS

Fuzzy Cognitive Maps (FCM) (Kosko, 1997) are graph structures that provide a method of capturing and representing complex relationships in a system. Application of FCM has been popular in modeling problems with low or no past data set or historical information (Kosko, 1997; Kosko, 1986; Aguilar, 2005; Georgopoulous, 2002; Andreou, Mateou, & Zombanakis, 2003; Carlsson & Fuller, 1996; Tsadiras, Kouskouvelis & Margaritis, 2001). A FCM provides the facilities to capture and represent complex relationships in a system to improve the understanding of a system. A FCM uses scenario analysis by considering several alternative solutions to a given situation. Concepts sometimes called nodes or events represent the system behavior in a FCM. The concepts are connected using a directed arrow showing causal relations between concepts. The graph's edges are the casual influences between the concepts. The development of the FCM is based on the utilization of domain experts' knowledge. Expert knowledge is used to identify concepts and the degree of influence between them. A FCM can be used in conjunction Luftman model to provide CIOs with possibilities for what-if analysis to understand the vulnerability in each layers of their model and perform risk analysis and identification. Using FCM it is possible to perform what-if and scenario analysis to access the proposed model. In this paper a FCM is utilized to perform risk and scenario analysis to understanding vulnerabilities of the IT management model. Kosko enhanced cognitive maps by including fuzzy values for the relationships between concepts (Kosko, 1997; Kosko, 1986). FCM applications have been very popular in modeling for problem with low or no past data set or historical information. FCM allows capturing and representing complex rela-

tionships (Kosko, 1997; Kosko, 1986; Aguilar, 2005; Georgopoulous, 2002; Andreou, Mateou, & Zombanakis, 2003; Carlsson & Fuller, 1996; Tsadiras, Kouskouvelis, & Margaritis, 2001). A FCM describes a system as a directed graph. The concepts are connected using a directed arrow showing causal relations between concepts. The graph's edges are the casual influences between the concepts. The value of a node reflects the degree to which the concept is active in the system at a particular time.

This value is a function of the sum of all incoming edges multiplied and the value of the originating concept at the immediately preceding state. A threshold function applied to the weighted sums. Values on each edge indicate relationships between concepts. These values indicate whether one concept increases or decreases the likelihood of another concept. The edges have values in the interval range [–1, 1]. These values indicate the degree to which one concept affects another. A positive relationship between two concept 1 and concept 2 indicates an increase in the likelihood of concept 2 to occur. Negative values indicate a decrease in the likelihood of concept 2 occurring. The FCM represents the sub-processes in each layer of the IT management and monitoring model.

These relationships indicate whether one event/sub process increases or decreases the likelihood of another event/sub process (Kosko, 1997; Kosko, 1986; Aguilar, 2005; Georgopoulous, 2002; Axelrod, 1976; Carlsson & Fuller, 1996; Tsadiras, Kouskouvelis & Margaritis, 2001). The sub-processes of tactical layer as shown in Figure 2 can be converted into a FCM by considering sub-process to represent concepts of a FCM. Figure 4 shows a FCM representation of sub-processes for strategic layer, tactical layer and operational layer as a FCM with weights allocated to each edge based on opinion of experts.

CIOs and IT executives are the experts and are required to determine the weights of the different causal links and the initial activation level for each concept. In this scenario the author has carefully considered the system and provided the weights for the FCM as shown in Figure 4. The weights and the activation function value will vary for different organization based on their budget, priorities and importance of sub-processes for the given organization.

The mathematical model behind the graphical representation of the FCM consists of a $1 \times n$ state vector I. This state vector represents the values of the n concepts and $n \times n$ weight matrix W_{IJ} represents value of weights between concepts of C_i and C_j. For each concept in a FCM a value one or zero is assigned. One represents the existence of that concept at a given time and zero represent none-exist of the respective concept. A threshold function is used in FCM. The threshold function used in this paper is sigmoid function (Kosko, 1997; Andreou, Mateou, & Zombanakis, 2003; Axelrod, 1976; Carlsson & Fuller, 1996; Tsadiras, Kouskouvelis, & Margaritis, 2001).

$$C_i(t_{n+1}) = S\left[\sum_{K=1}^{N} e_{KI}(t_n)C_k(t_n)\right] \tag{1}$$

As an example the relationships in Figure 4 between C5 (Tactical Level) and C9 (Development Planning) implies, for example, that if the Development Planning increases, then Tactical Level will improve by degree of **0.2** or **20%**. A CIO can evaluate, modify the concepts and weights of an FCM based on their resources and priority of IT processes in their organization. Now FCM can be used to identify and access risks that may arise due to unavailability or shortcomings of different IT processes for a given organization. It should be emphasized the weights in FCM are calculated based on expert knowledge (CIOs, IT executives and decision makers) which shows the influences of concepts to other concepts. These weights can be changed based on CIOs and IT expert's expertise, knowledge of organization and availability of resources. The threshold function used in this paper is sigmoid function and it value is set to be 0.2.

SIMULATION

The relationships details among all concepts in Figure 4 for strategic, tactical and operational layers can be displayed using in a matrix form as follows.

$$E_{Strategic} = \begin{bmatrix} 0\ 0\ 0\ 0 \\ 0.6\ 0\ 0\ 0 \\ 0.7\ 0\ 0\ 0 \\ 0.7\ 0\ 0\ 0 \end{bmatrix} E_{Tactical} = \begin{bmatrix} 0\ 0\ 0\ 0\ 0 \\ 0.90\ 0\ 0\ 0\ 0 \\ 0.60\ 0\ 0\ 0\ 0 \\ 0.80\ 0\ 0\ 0\ 0 \\ 0.80\ 0\ 0\ 0\ 0 \end{bmatrix} E_{Operational} = \begin{bmatrix} 0\ 0\ 0\ 0\ 0\ 0\ 0 \\ 0.900000\ 0 \\ 0.800000\ 0 \\ 0.700000\ 0 \\ 0.800000\ 0 \\ 0.800000\ 0 \\ 0.800000\ 0 \end{bmatrix}$$

Figure 4. A FCM representation of sub-processes for strategic layer (a) tactical layer (b) and operational layer (c)

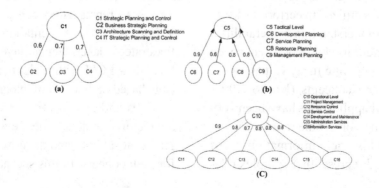

Now what-If analysis can proceed by using the above matrices. For this simulation the threshold is set to be 0.2. Consider the following scenario.

What happens if the event C9 (i.e. Management Planning) is performed successfully?

This scenario can be presented using vector I_0 representing this situation by: $I_0 = [0, 0, 0, 0, 1]$. In vector I_0 the concept C5 is represented as the fifth element in the vector and it is set to 1 and all other elements are set to be zero representing other events that has not happened. It is assumed that C5 happens and no other event has happened. Now I_0*E can provide the solution for this situation as follows: $I_1*E = [0.2, 0, 0, 0, 0] = I_1$ which conclude that if C9 happens then it will increase the possibility of success in C5 (i.e. Tactical level) to occur by 0.2 or 20%.

Are the right resources being used and are they integrated properly in tactical layer?

This scenario can be presented using vector I_0 representing this situation by: $I_0 = [0, 0, 0, 1, 0]$. In vector I_0 the concept C8 is represented as the fourth element in the vector and it is set to 1 and all other elements are set to be zero representing other events that has not happened. It is assumed that C8 happens and no other event has happened. Now I_0*E can provide the solution for this situation as follows: $I_1*E = [0.3, 0, 0, 0, 0] = I_1$ which conclude that if C8 happens then it will increase the possibility of success in C4 (i.e. Tactical level) to occur by 0.3 or 30%. Many other scenarios involving questions that can invoke several concepts at a given time can also be considered. Consider the following question:

What happens if the event C9 (i.e. Management Planning) is performed? Are the right resources being used?

This scenario can be presented using vector I_0 representing this situation by: $I_0 = [0, 0, 0, 1, 1]$. In vector I_0 the concept C8 and C9 are represented as the fourth and fifth elements in the vector and they are set to 1 and all other elements are set to be zero representing other events that has not happened. It is assumed that C8 and C9 happen and no other event has happened. Now I_0*E can provide the solution for this situation as follows: $I_1*E = [1.6, 0, 0, 0, 0] = I_1$ which conclude that if C8 and C9 happen then it will increase highly the possibility of success in C5 (i.e. Tactical level).

Other what if scenarios can easily now be performed on this FCM. Several simulations were performed using different scenarios. Table 1 displays the consequences of different scenarios based on different what if simulations.

Using scenario analysis the CIOs can identify problems before they occur. Risk assessment and risk management requires proper analysis and understanding of the threats and shortcoming in an IT system. Currently there are no facilities that can be utilized to assess the above-mentioned three layer model and to mitigate risks at this level. FCM can fill this gap in risk assessment.

Table 1. Consequences of different scenarios based different what if simulations

What if the following event occurs	Consequences
C6	$C6 \xrightarrow{20\%} C5$
C7	$C7 \xrightarrow{209\%} C5$
C8	$C4 \xrightarrow{30\%} C5$
C9	$C9 \xrightarrow{30\%} C5$
C6 & C7	$C6 \& C7 \xrightarrow{40\%} C5$
C6 & C7 & C8	$C6 \& c7 \& C8 \xrightarrow{79\%} C5$
C6 & C7 & C8 & C9	$C6\&C7\&C8\&C9 \xrightarrow{100\%} C5$

The information provided from what if scenarios can be used for risk analysis by CIOs. This approach provides a valuable tool for CIOs to evaluate risks associated with different scenarios (sub processes) in their organization. The CIOs can then confidently make decision and manipulate funding for sub processes or change tools number of staff etc to re-evaluate risks for each change. They can conduct what if analysis and make informed decisions.

It is possible using FCM to produce an exhaustive list of all possible problems in this model using scenarios to document risks in such a framework. FCM provide the risk associated with each part of the model that the CIOs like to consider. Risk analysis at different levels of IT management is useful. However the interdependencies of this three level IT management demands risk analysis based on all levels. Figure 5 shows a FCM representation of the three-level IT management combined. Now what-If analysis can proceed by using the matrix $E_{Strategic\ TacticalOperational} = E_{Strategic} + E_{Tactical} + E_{Operational}$.
What-If analysis can proceed by using the matrix $E_{Strategic\ TacticalOperational}$. to perform complicated scenarios. For this simulation the threshold is set to be 0.2.

Consider the following scenario:

What happens if the event C6 (Development Planning in tactical level is successful) and C9 (i.e. Management Planning in tactical level is performed successfully) and C11 and C15 (Project Management and administration Services are successfully performed) occur?

This scenario can be presented using vector I_0 representing this situation by:

$I_0 = [0, 0, 0, 0, 0, 1, 0, 0, 1, 0, 1, 0, 0, 0, 1, 0]$

$I_0 * E_{Strategic\ TacticalOperational} = [0, 0, 0, 0, 1.4, 0, 0, 0, 0, 1.7, 0, 0, 0, 0, 0, 0]$

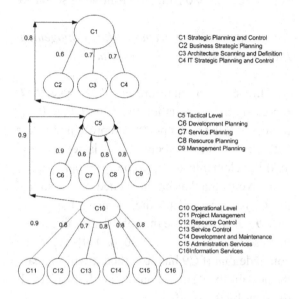

$\rightarrow I_{1} = [0, 0, 0, 0, 1, 0, 0, 0,, 0, 1, 0, 0, 0, 0, 0, 0, 0]$

$I_1 * E_{Strategic\ TacticalOperational} = [0.8, 0, 0, 0, 0.9, 0, 0, 0, 0, 0, 0, 0, 0, 0, 0, 0]$

$\rightarrow I_{2} = [1, 0, 0, 0, 0, 1, 0, 0, 0, 0, 0, 0, 0, 0, 0, 0, 0]$

which concludes that if C6, C9, C11 and C15 happens then it increases the possibility of success in C1 and C5 (i.e. Strategic level and Tactical level) to occur by 0.8 and 0.9 respectively. Many other scenarios involving questions that can invoke several concepts at different level can be considered.

Other what if scenarios can easily now be performed on this FCM. Several simulations were performed using different scenarios. Table 3 displays the consequences of different scenarios based on different what if simulations.

The information provided from what if scenarios from all three level IT management model can be used for risk analysis by CIOs. This allows to provide timely and valuable information for

Table 2. Augmented FCM matrix for the strategic, tactical and operational

	C1	C2	C3	C4	C5	C6	C7	C8	C9	C10	C11	C12	C13	C14	C15	C16
C1	0	0	0	0	0	0	0	0	0	0	0	0	0	0	0	0
C2	0.6	0	0	0	0	0	0	0	0	0	0	0	0	0	0	0
C3	0.7	0	0	0	0	0	0	0	0	0	0	0	0	0	0	0
C4	0.7	0	0	0	0	0	0	0	0	0	0	0	0	0	0	0
C5	0.8	0	0	0	0	0	0	0	0	0	0	0	0	0	0	0
C6	0	0	0	0	0.9	0	0	0	0	0	0	0	0	0	0	0
C7	0	0	0	0	0.6	0	0	0	0	0	0	0	0	0	0	0
C8	0	0	0	0	0.8	0	0	0	0	0	0	0	0	0	0	0
C9	0	0	0	0	0.8	0	0	0	0	0	0	0	0	0	0	0
C10	0	0	0	0	0.9	0	0	0	0	0	0	0	0	0	0	0
C11	0	0	0	0	0	0	0	0	0	0.9	0	0	0	0	0	0
C12	0	0	0	0	0	0	0	0	0	0.8	0	0	0	0	0	0
C13	0	0	0	0	0	0	0	0	0	0.7	0	0	0	0	0	0
C14	0	0	0	0	0	0	0	0	0	0.8	0	0	0	0	0	0
C15	0	0	0	0	0	0	0	0	0	0.8	0	0	0	0	0	0
C16	0	0	0	0	0	0	0	0	0	0.8	0	0	0	0	0	0

CIOs to evaluate risks associated with different scenarios in their organization. This approach will assist in decision making and manipulation of resources to achieve the best possible outcome for an organization.

CONCLUSION

Due to rapid changes in emerging technologies there is a need for constant improvement and adjustment of IT processes in organizations. Success of an organization is heavily dependent on the impact of IT. CIOs need to continuously monitor and analysis the performance of IT processes. They need to consider large number of activities performed by each IT processe in their organization. The interdependencies of sub processes make it very difficult for CIOs to comprehend and be fully aware of effect of inefficiencies in IT processes and skilled personnel to the whole of IT organization.

This paper considered three layers of IT management model consisting of strategic, tactical, and operational layer. With complexity of this model consisting of large number of interpedently sub processes managing and monitoring IT systems are becoming increasingly difficult and as such many IT management, developments and implementations may be flawed. IT management models do not provide any facilities to analyze and assess different risks that may exist in such models in a systematic way.

Fuzzy Cognitive Maps (FCM) is employed in this paper to provide facilities to capture and represent complex relationships in IT management models and their processes and to improve the understanding of CIOs to analyze risks. Using a FCM different scenarios are considered. The proposed FCM is used in conjunction with the proposed Luftman IT management model to provide CIOs with possibilities for what-if analysis.

By using FCMs CIOs can regularly review and improve their IT management and provide greater improvement in development, monitoring and

Table 3. Consequences of different scenarios based different what if simulations

What if the following event occurs	Consequences
C8, C7, C6	C8, C7, C6 $\xrightarrow{2.3}$ C5 $\xrightarrow{0.8}$ C1
C15, C12, C11, C3	C15, C12, C11 $\xrightarrow{2.5}$ C10 $\xrightarrow{0.9}$ C5 $\xrightarrow{0.8}$ C1 C3 $\xrightarrow{0.8}$ C1
C4, C7, C9, C10	C4 $\xrightarrow{0.7}$ C1 C7, C9, C10 $\xrightarrow{2.4}$ C5 $\xrightarrow{0.8}$ C1
C2, C8, C12, C14	C2 $\xrightarrow{0.6}$ C1 C8 $\xrightarrow{0.8}$ C5 $\xrightarrow{0.8}$ C1 C12, C14 $\xrightarrow{1.6}$ C9 $\xrightarrow{0.8}$ C5 $\xrightarrow{0.8}$ C1
C7, C8, C9, C15	C7, C8, C9 $\xrightarrow{2.2}$ C5 $\xrightarrow{0.8}$ C1 C15 $\xrightarrow{0.8}$ C10 $\xrightarrow{0.9}$ C5 $\xrightarrow{0.8}$ C1
C4, C10, C13, C15	C4 $\xrightarrow{0.7}$ C1 C10 $\xrightarrow{0.9}$ C5 $\xrightarrow{0.8}$ C1 C13, C15 $\xrightarrow{1.5}$ C10 $\xrightarrow{0.9}$ C5 $\xrightarrow{0.8}$ C1
C7, C9, C12, C13	C7, C9 $\xrightarrow{1.4}$ C5 $\xrightarrow{0.8}$ C1 C12, C13 $\xrightarrow{1.5}$ C10 $\xrightarrow{0.9}$ C5 $\xrightarrow{0.8}$ C1

maintenance of IT facilities (for example providing adequate hardware to handle existing and future applications, providing systems that are easy to learn and easy to use, providing systems that are easy to maintain and upgrade, providing adequate budgets for their IT process developments). The CIO can perform what-if analysis to find out the answer to the questions such as:

- Are the right technologies being used and are they integrated properly?
- What levels of information sharing, security, and access should be supported?
- Which applications will be developed versus which will be bought?
- Are applications, tools, and data easy to upgrade, update, and maintain?
- Who will upgrade, update, and maintain the applications, tools, and data?

- Who will assess whether the architecture will meet the firm's needs?
- Will the horizontal architecture support the horizontal processes of the firm?

REFERENCES

Aguilar, J. (2005). A Survey about Fuzzy Cognitive Maps Papers. *International Journal of Computational Cognition, 3*(2), 27–33.

Andreou, A. S., Mateou, N. H., & Zombanakis, G. A. (2003). Evolutionary Fuzzy Cognitive Maps: A Hybrid System for Crisis Management and Political Decision Making. In *Proceedings of the International Conference on Computational Intelligence for Modelling, Control and Automation*, Austria.

Axelrod, R. (1976). *Structure of Decision: The Cognitive Maps of Political Elite* (1st ed.). Princeton, NJ: Princeton University Press.

Carlsson, C., & Fuller, R. (1996), Adaptive Fuzzy Cognitive Maps for Hyperknowledge Representation in Strategic Formation Process. In *Proceedings of the International Panel Conference on Soft and Intelligent Computing*, Budapest.

Georgopoulous, V. C., & Malandrak, S. C. D. (2002). A Fuzzy Cognitive Map Approach to Differential Diagnosis of Specific Language Impairment. *Artificial Intelligence in Medicine*, 1–18.

Kosko, B. (1986). Fuzzy Cognitive Maps. *International Journal of Man-Machine Studies*, *24*, 65–75. doi:10.1016/S0020-7373(86)80040-2

Kosko, B. (1997). *Fuzzy engineering*. Upper Saddle River, NJ: Prentice Hall.

Luftman, J., Bullen, V. C., Liao, D., Nash, E., & Neumann, C. (2004). *Managing the information Technology Resources – Leadership in information age*. Upper Saddle River, NJ: Pearson Prentice Hall.

Tsadiras, A. K., Kouskouvelis, I., & Margaritis, K. G. (2001). Making Political Decision using Fuzzy Cognitive Maps: The FYROM crisis. In *Proceedings of the 8th Panhellenic Conference on Informatics*, Greece.

Chapter 8
Organizational Culture in the Greek Science and Technology Parks

Thanos Kriemadis
University of Peloponnese, Greece

Theodore Pelagidis
University of Piraeus, Greece

ABSTRACT

This chapter contributes to an understanding of the organizational culture of the industrial spin-off knowledge-based enterprises, which operate within the Science and Technology Parks in Greece. In this context, a critical number of questionnaires have been distributed to the spin-offs to examine whether firms born within the parks have developed a functional, innovative organizational culture, one that provides a solid foundation for organizational effectiveness and business excellence. The chapter presents the results of a quantitative analysis of the data collected in a fieldwork study. It also includes the necessary policies for the spin-offs to overcome organizational culture problems and adopt the culture of innovation and business excellence.

INTRODUCTION

After the Bretton Woods system collapsed in the early 70's and as, at the same time, the rigid fordist mass production-mass consumption model was reaching its limits, a new mode of business organisation began gradually to make its appearance based on flexibility in production and distribution (Piore & Sabel, 1984). The most distinctive characteristic of the so-called "flexible production" or "flexible business" systems was the encouragement, if not necessity, for close links between enterprises and research institutes and Universities. That was a critical break up with the "fordist" past where industries and Universities were quite separate fields of activities, representing organisations with quite different and separate roles within the socio-economic system. However, the new "flexible paradigm", encouraging team working and polyvalence in skills, needed highly educated workers, ready to execute diversified and high quality tasks, often changing rapidly working positions. With the appearance of the

DOI: 10.4018/978-1-61520-623-0.ch008

so-call "new economy" and the new generation of "flexible technologies", the co-operation of firms and industries with research institutes and Universities became a necessary prerequisite to adopt the culture of continuing innovation and succeed in an increasing globalized market. In the context of globalization, developing innovative products and services are critical matters. Innovation is the keyword meaning the efficiency of transferring technology from academic and research institutions into commerce and industry (British Council, 1999). Thus, the initial aim of the co-operation between scientific parks, research centres/ Universities and newly established modern firms is to commercialise the results of scientific research.

Henceforth, in the '80s and '90s, governments initiated the implementation of policies to encourage tighter links between research and production, through financing relevant infrastructure as well by promoting, through specific policies, the development of *"Science and Technology Parks"*, in an effort to have regions of high rates of productivity and growth. The development of flexible, knowledge-based companies within the parks, the so-called "spin-offs" based in a location linked to a centre of technology and innovation excellence became the primary target of national industrial and public policies, especially in the EU member-states. That is so, as *Science and Technology Parks* are said to facilitate,

- flexibility in production, new industrial activities, modernisation, and internationalisation of enterprises through technology transfer,
- accumulation of technologies and of core activities in a region,
- close links between universities and industries or small enterprises, in order for the construction of co-operation and communication networks, and last but not least,
- culture of excellence in organisation and innovation, as well as selectivity and competition.

However, *Science and Technology Parks* were originally an American phenomenon dating back to the 1960's, devised to meet the needs of entrepreneurial-minded academics. In Europe, the Science Park "movement" made its appearance first in the UK in 1971 with the formation of Parks at the Heriot-Watt University and at Cambridge University (British Council, 1999).

Research and technological poles have been also set up in Greek regions but only in the late '80s, introducing local economy into the modern international competitive environment. These infant cores of innovation have already inspired both academics and entrepreneurs to construct new models of investment planning and production. Although not yet fully developed, some of them, they have already created complex links between universities and industries, giving birth to many spin-off knowledge-based enterprises.

Firm's organisation quality and culture is one of the pillars of success in international competition. This paper focuses on examining the quality of organisational culture of the spin-off knowledge-based enterprises, within the Greek *Science and Technology Parks*, as we consider organisation culture as the cornerstone of business excellence, innovation and international competitiveness. The study also includes firms that have lately exited the parks but still have a close co-operation with them. In the following section 2 the paper focuses on the fieldwork and analyses its results. In this context, a critical number of questionnaires have been distributed to the spin-offs and the data collected was analysed quantitatively to examine whether firms born within the parks have developed a functional organizational culture, one that provides a solid foundation for organizational effectiveness and business excellence. Results are analysed in the same section. The section 3 of the paper proposes the necessary policies for the Greek Science and Technology Parks to overcome organizational culture problems and approach innovation excellence and international competitiveness.

FIELD WORK

Culture and Organization

The term culture refers to a set of beliefs, values and behaviours held by a society (Lim, 1995). Uttal (1983) defined culture as a "system of shared values (what is important) and beliefs (how things work) that interact with a company's people, organizational structures, and control systems to produce behavioural norms". Cameron and Freeman (1991) proposed the following framework of four organizational culture types: (a) Market, (b) Clan, (c) Adhocracy, and (d) Bureaucratic Hierarchy. Each culture type is characterized by a particular set of shared beliefs; style of leadership, set shared values that act as a bond for all employees within the company. The Market culture emphasizes a goal-oriented enterprise, competitive actions and achievement. The "Clan" culture is characterized by a personal place and emphasizes human resources. The "Bureaucratic Hierarchy" culture is characterized by a formalized, structured places held together by formal rules and policies emphasizing stability. Finally, the "Adhocracy" culture emphasizes a dynamic entrepreneurial place held together by a commitment to innovation and development. Most companies have elements of several types of cultures. Lund (2003) examined the impact of *organizational culture* types on job satisfaction of firms in the USA using the model of organizational cultures developed by Cameron and Freeman (1991). The author identified that job satisfaction was positively related to Clan and Adhocracy cultures and negatively related to Market and Bureaucratic Hierarchy cultures.

Hofstede (1980) stated that culture accounts for the economic performance of various countries. Schein (1990) suggested that the idea of corporate culture provides a basis for understanding the differences that may exist between successful companies operating in the same national culture. Peters and Waterman (1982) found out that suc-cessful companies possess certain cultural traits of business excellence. Ouchi (1981) reported a relationship between corporate culture and increased productivity while Deal and Kennedy (1982) argued for the importance of a "strong" culture in contributing towards successful organizational performance. Kotter and Heskett (1992) examined how changing environments affected culture and performance, and found that companies with consistently good economic performance over time tended to possess core values that emphasized the importance of an adaptive culture. They also suggested that culture might only be an intermediary of the impact of effective leadership on organizational performance. A number of studies alleged the presence of a "strong" culture as a positive influence on organizational performance (Sadri and Lees, 2001). Henceforth, after reviewing in brief the relevant literature one can easily accept that, while culture is not the only determinant of business success or failure, a positive culture can be a significant competitive advantage in the post-fordist, flexible age. So, let us now embark on the Greek Science Parks and the relevant fieldwork we worked out to examine organisation culture within them.

Research Method and Research Instrument

The Organizational Culture Assessment Questionnaire (OCAQ) was developed by Sashkin (1996) to help people identify and understand the nature of the culture in their own organization, as a first step in identifying problems and defining the sort of culture they want (and the sort of culture that will help deal with organizational problems). The data obtained by means of the OCAQ can be used to identify and find ways to deal with culture-based organizational problems.

The OCAQ is based on the work of Dr. Talcott Parsons, a sociologist at Harvard. Parsons developed a framework and theory of action in social systems. He argued that all organizations must carry out four crucial functions if they are to survive long-term. These four functions are: (a) Managing Change: Scale I of the OCAQ assesses the degree to which respondents see the organization as effective in adapting to and managing change; (b) Achieving Goals: Scale II of the OCAQ asks respondents to describe how effective the organization is in achieving goals; (c) Coordinated Teamwork: OCAQ Scale III assesses the extent to which an organization is effective in coordinating the work of individuals and groups; (d) Customer Orientation: Scale IV of the OCAQ assesses the extent to which organizational activities are directed toward identifying and meeting the needs of customers; and (e) Building a Strong Culture: Scale V of the OCAQ assesses the strength of the organization's culture, asking respondents to report on the extent to which people agree on values and examining the extent to which certain "meta values" are present such as the belief that people should support their views with facts.

Each of five OCAQ Scales has six items, with each item score ranging from 1 (low or poor) to five (high or good) and thus, the total score of the OCAQ can be as low as 30 or as high as 150. Sashkin (1996) has developed a table of norms (Table 1) showing what scores on each scale are high and what sorts of scores are low. Sashkin (1996) mentioned that the table of norms should be seen as suggestive, not as absolutely defining what is high and what is low.

Sample and Data Collection

There are four Greek Science Parks. Two of them, the Thessaloniki Technology Park (TTP)[1] and the Crete Science and Technological Park (STEP-C)[2], are considered to be relatively well-developed, while Patras[3] and Volos[4] Science Parks still have some (Volos) or most (Patras) of their infrastructure, at least partly, under construction. The data for the present study were obtained by the OCAQ mailed to a sample of 33 spin-off companies that operate within the aforementioned Science and Technological Parks. The mailing consisted of the questionnaire itself, a cover letter, and a stamped pre-addressed return envelope. As response inducement, each respondent was promised a copy of the study results on request. Of the 33 questionnaires mailed after phone contact, 33 were received, representing a 100% response rate. This high response rate was also due to the fact that companies within the Science and Technological Parks have realized the value of participating in field research conducted by the Universities and take advantage of the knowledge disseminated by them. It should be also noted that the Greek Ministry of Development contributed, at least indirectly, to the 100% response rate as it let the parks know its intention to proceed to their funding thorough the 4th framework program with a clear intention and policy goal to create the so-called "Regional Poles of Innovation", letting for the parks a core, cardinal role in this project. After the questionnaires were collected, the data

Table 1. OCAQ norms

	Managing Change	Achieving Goals	Coordinated Teamwork	Customer Orientation	Cultural Strength	Total
Very High	30	28-30	28-30	25-30	26-30	119 +
High	26-29	23-27	24-27	21-24	22-25	108-118
Average	19-25	16-22	18-23	15-20	17-21	87-107
Low	15-18	11-15	14-17	11-14	13-16	76-86
Very Low	6-14	6-10	6-13	6-10	6-12	30-75

from each were entered into the statistical testing program, the Statistical Package for the Social Sciences (SPSS-x), Version 13.

Results

Table 2 presents a summary of respondents' mean scores as well as the total score for all companies involved in this study. Regarding Managing Change, the mean score is 15.82 and is considered low compared to the corresponding mean of the table of norms. According to Sashkin (1996), this area of action concerns how well the organization is able to adapt to and deal effectively with changes in its environment. All organizations are open, to some extent, to rapid technological and social change.

The mean score for 'Achieving Goals' is 15.03 and is considered low compared to the corresponding mean of the table of norms. Sashkin (1996) stated that having a clear focus on explicit goals as been proven repeatedly to have a very strong relationship to actual success and achievement.

'Regarding Coordinated Teamwork', the mean score is 13.96, again low compared to the corresponding mean of the table of norms. Sashkin (1996) believes that long-term organizational survival depends on how well the efforts of individuals and groups within the organization are tied together, coordinated and sequenced so that people's work efforts fit together effectively.

The mean score for 'Customer Orientation' is 13.51 and is considered low compared to the corresponding mean of the table of norms. Sashkin (1996) argued that no matter how strong the culture

and no matter how well the other functions of the organization are performed, if no one wants what the organization produces, then the organization is not likely to survive and prosper.

Finally, the mean score for 'Cultural Strength' is 13.67, again low compared to the corresponding mean of the table of norms. Sashkin (1996) stated that a strong culture based on values that support the functions of managing change, organizational achievement, customer orientation, and coordinated teamwork, would provide greater stability of organizational functioning.

The total score 71.99 is very low compared to the corresponding one of the table of norms. However, Sashkin (1996) stated that the OCAQ is intended as a diagnostic aid, a first step in building better functioning organizational cultures. Through the OCAQ the company's management can probably get some feeling for what sort of numbers are "high" and what might be considered "low" from looking at Table 1. Most important is that the items that make up the scales provide concrete directions about what an organization might actually do to improve its culture.

POLICIES AND CONCLUSION

In this paper, we deal with the organizational culture of spin-off firms located in the Greek Scientific and Technology Parks. A critical number of questionnaires have been distributed to examine whether firms born within the parks have developed a functional organizational culture, one that provides a solid foundation for organizational

Table 2. Results of the study

	Managing Change	Achieving Goals	Coordinated Teamwork	Customer Orientation	Cultural Strength
N	33	33	33	33	33
MEAN	15.82	15.03	13.96	13.51	13.67
SD	2.25	2.49	3.35	2.79	3.37

Total Score: 71.99

effectiveness, innovation, competitiveness and business excellence.

All organizations have a culture based on values and beliefs usually shared by some, most or all of the organization's members (Sashkin, 1996). However, according to the results obtained through the implementation of quantitative analysis in the data collected from our fieldwork study, there seems to have been ascertained serious organisational culture weaknesses regarding "management of change" practices, goal and customer orientation, cultural strength and efficient team working. It is noted that when the culture is based on values that do not fully support the functions of managing change, goal achievement, customer orientation, and coordinated teamwork, as it is the case of the Greek spin-offs, then this culture might actually hamper organizational survival and growth. It follows that policy makers have to innovate strategic reform paths and specific appropriate policies to overcome organisational malfunctioning. Henceforth, it is of critical importance for policy makers to set general principles, guidelines as well as specific organisational reform measures and priorities to achieve efficiency and effectiveness for the Greek industrial spin-offs. For that reason, we summarize below the main policies and measures that we believe they could face spin-off's weaknesses resulted from our statistical analysis in section 2.

We summarize five methods that we believe are appropriate for the Greek spin-offs if their management intends to pursue the appropriate reforms to successfully achieve goals (Williams et al. 1993):

a. Changing 'Human Resource' management policies, management style and work environment.
b. Training employees in new skills and thus influencing their job attitudes.
c. Providing employees with training and role models appropriate to the desired culture, a culture that supports change, organizational

achievement, customer orientation, and coordinated teamwork.

d. Greater emphasis on selecting people with the desired attitudes as well as technical skills and experience. This may include the use of more sophisticated selection techniques, for example psychometric testing, assessment centres, and biodata.
e. Moving people into new jobs to break up old sub-cultures.

Accordingly, the organization should use the following strategies to meet customer needs, as Whiteley (1991) have identified:

a. Information from customers should be used in designing products/services.
b. The organization regularly asks customers to give feedback about its performance (satisfaction measures look at the extent to which customers are satisfied with the service they have received).
c. Customers' complaints are regularly analyzed in order to identify quality problems.
d. Internal procedures and systems that do not create value for the customers are eliminated.
e. Employees are encouraged to go above and beyond to serve customers well.
f. Employees who work with customers are supported with continuous training and resources that are sufficient for doing the job well.
g. Employees are empowered to use their judgement when quick action is needed to make things right for a customer.

Working as a team is a natural human behaviour that enhances cultural strength and the spirit of unity within the shop floor as well as among workers, diminishing at the same time, transaction costs. If everyone acts as part of a team, it equally acts for the good of the entire organization, minimizing, simultaneously, cases where competition inside an organisation structure that functions counterproductively. Verespej (1990) stated that the most important benefits to working in teams are:

a. Improved involvement and performance.
b. Positive morale, and
c. Sense of ownership and commitment to the product/service that teams create.

The establishment of quality circles is a good example of teamwork. Quality circles consist of small groups of employees who meet to uncover and solve work-related problems. Members get together regularly to learn interpersonal skills and statistical methods associated with problem solving and to select and solve real problems. Members meet an hour a week both during regular and outside of regular working hours. A group leader chairs meetings. The leader is a discussion moderator who facilitates the problem-solving process. Problems are not restricted to quality, but also include productivity, cost, safety, morale, environment and other topics (Crocker, Charney & Chiu, 1984).

As the results of the fieldwork have indicated, Greek spin-off industrial firms need to adopt new, innovative management approaches and systems in attempting to change and manage effectively their organizational culture. If so, we argue that they should take seriously into account the general rules, guidelines and prescriptions extracted from the relevant literature and presented above. Indeed, those specific elements of culture such as customer focus, teamwork and goal achievement are stronger in organizations practicing Total Quality Management (Gore, 1999). It follows that the implementation of a Total Quality Management system in Greek Science and Technology Parks could additionally contribute to the enhancement of an organization's efficiency and effectiveness.

It is also important to point out that changing an organization's culture is a long-term endeavour. During this process, communication with all employees and stakeholders plays important role. Al-lowing employees to participate and get involved in making the changes in the culture may facilitate change. We also believe that relevant regional and sectoral studies need to be elaborated to determine and suggest even more specific and appropriate policy measures that take advantage, transform or restructure if necessary existing business policies and practices towards, goal orientation, customer driven functions, modern team working and effective culture unity, within each park and even within each spin-off, if possible.

REFERENCES

Antonelli, C. (Ed.). (1988). *New Information Technology and Industrial Change: The Italian Case*. London: Kluwer.

Cameron, K. S., & Freeman, S. J. (1991). Cultural Congruence, Strength, and Type: Relationships to Effectiveness. *Research in Organizational Change and Development*, *5*, 23–58.

Coulon, F. (2003). *Regional Systems of Innovation: A Case Study of four Science Parks in Belgium and Sweden*. University of Linkoping, Sweden. Retrieved from http://www.esst.uio.no

Crocker, O., Charney, C., & Chiu, J. (1984). *Quality Circles*. New York: Methuen.

Deal, T. E., & Kennedy, A. A. (1982). *Corporate Cultures*. Reading, MA: Addison-Wesley.

Deming, W. E. (1986). *Out of the Crisis*. Cambridge, MA: Cambridge University Press.

Enright, M. (2000). *Survey of Characterization of Regional Clusters*. University of Hong Kong working paper.

Gore, E. (1999). Organizational Culture, TQM and Business Process Reengineering. *Team Performance Management: An International Journal*, *5*(5), 164–170. doi:10.1108/13527599910288993

Hall, P., & Markusen, A. (Eds.). (1988). *Silicon Landscapes*. Boston: Allen and Unwin Inc.

Hofstede, G. (1980). *Culture's Consequences*. Beverly Hills, CA: Sage.

Kotter, J. P., & Heskett, J. L. (1992). *Corporate Culture and Performance*. New York: Macmillan.

Lim, B. (1995). Examining the Organizational Culture and Organizational Performance Link. *Leadership and Organization Development Journal, 16*(5), 16–21. doi:10.1108/01437739510088491

Lund, D. (2003). Organizational Culture and Job Satisfaction. *Journal of Business and Industrial Marketing, 18*(3), 219–236. doi:10.1108/08858620310473 13

Ouchi, W. G. (1981). *Theory Z*. Reading, MA: Addison-Wesley.

Peters, T. J., & Waterman, R. H. (1982). *In Search of Excellence*. New York: Harper & Row.

Piore, M., & Sabel, C. (1984). *The Second Industrial Divide*. New York: Basic Books.

Sadri, G., & Lees, B. (2001). Developing Corporate Culture as a Competitive Advantage. *Journal of Management Development, 20*(10), 853–859. doi:10.1108/02621710110410851

Sashkin, M. (1996). *Organizational Culture Assessment Questionnaire*.

Schein, E. (1990). Organizational Culture. *The American Psychologist, 45*(2), 10–19. doi:10.1037/0003-066X.45.2.109

The British Council. (1999 October). *Science Parks, Briefing Sheet 7, UK Partnerships*. Retrieved from http://www.ukspa.org.uk

Uttal, B. (1983). The Corporate Culture Vultures. *Fortune, 108*(8), 66–79.

Verespej, M. (1990). When you Put the Team in Charge. *Industry Week*, 30–33.

Whiteley, R. (1991). *The Customer Driven Company*. Reading, MA: Addison-Wesley.

Williams, A., Dobson, P., & Walters, M. (1993). *Changing Culture: New Organisational Approaches*. London: Institute of Personnel Management.

ENDNOTES

[1] Thessaloniki Technology Park was established in 1988, to meet the need for greater exchange of ideas, people and facilities between universities and industry. In 1994, the Thessaloniki Technology Park Management and Development Corporation (TTP/MDC S.A.), a separate company, was created with the participation of FORTH/CPERI and major industries of central Macedonia. The company promoted and enhanced the activities of the Thessaloniki's Technology Park in close co-operation with the Association of industries of Northern Greece, and with the University of Thessaloniki.

"The Center for Research and Technology Hellas" promotes activities, which contribute to the increase of competitiveness of Greek industry with special emphasis on Chemical Technology (specialised software for polyethylene and propylene production facilities, environmental friendly catalyst for production of fuel etc), Food & Beverage, Textiles and Energy and Environment. Furthermore, TTP/MDC identifies present, future and latent industry needs within Northern Greece and links them with technological innovation. It promotes technology transfer among Greece, the EU, the USA, Eastern Europe and the Balkans and co-ordinates the Greek-American initiative for technology co-operation with the Balkans. This is being accomplished through organisation, implementation and participation in national and European training programmes and workshops on the use of technologies.[1] It also serves as Industry – Research Liaison, performs partner searches, executes assessment and exploitation of research results, assists with RTD proposal preparation, submission and project management. Furthermore, it ensures information dissemination concerning research results, technological developments and the emergence of new technologies. Technology brokerage, technology search & assessment, assistance for technology implementation are also provided. Finally measurements and testing quality control through promotion of analytical services are also undertaken.

[2] The Science and Technology Park of Crete established in 1993, it was inspired to promote the creation of a third thrust of development on the island, in addition to the agriculture and tourism industry. The EU as well as the local and central government funds supported the development of the Park during the early 90's. The Managing Company of STEP-C (EDAP S.A) was established in December 1993 with FORTH as its main shareholder (35%). STEP-C gears itself to become an ever increasing attraction as an incubator, nurturing spin-offs and small innovative companies in the areas of Medical Equipment, Biotechnology, Telecommunications, Telematics and Teleworking, Microelectronics and Laser Applications, Polymers and Applied Mathematics, which are key strength areas of FORTH and the UoC. The park focuses on technology transfer, incubation facilities and promotion of the park products. One of the key objectives of STEP-C is the transfer of deliverables of research and other activities to the industry. STEP-C has developed incubation facilities through various projects financed by the Greek Ministry of Development. Today there are 25 companies, which reside within the park premises in the areas of Information Technology, Biotechnology, Environmental Technology, Laser Applications, Biomedical Technology and Services. The Park also developed co-operation and bilateral relations with the main local actors in the field of Education, Science and Technology and Business as well as with the Regional Authorities. The Science and Technology Park of Crete, known to many by one of its key activities as the Heraklion Incubator, is today the leading Park in the country, with promising perspectives.

[3] Patra's Science Park, mainly still under construction, was founded in 1989. It is interested in Business Exploitation of R&D results, with emphasis on new innovative technology based companies. In addition, it concentrates on R&D – Production liaison, promotion of Innovation, linking of finance innovation and also activities outside the park aiming at: enhancement of competitiveness and construction of an environment favoring innovative developments in the area.

[4] The technological park of Volos (Thessaly) was founded in November 2001. Taking advantage of the Volos' industrial area, the aim of the technological park is to provide facilities to knowledge-based enterprises that are located in the greater Thessaly region, to connect them with the Polytechnic University of Volos and to give birth to new spin-offs in industrial sectors and fields. The "parks is a S.A. and its among shareholders are 39 modern firms, the University of Thessaly and the local authorities.

APPENDIX

Frequency Tables

CHANGE

		Frequency	Percent	Valid Percent	Cumulative Percent
Valid	12,00	4	12,1	12,1	12,1
	13,00	1	3,0	3,0	15,2
	14,00	3	9,1	9,1	24,2
	15,00	5	15,2	15,2	39,4
	16,00	8	24,2	24,2	63,6
	17,00	8	24,2	24,2	87,9
	19,00	1	3,0	3,0	90,9
	20,00	2	6,1	6,1	97,0
	21,00	1	3,0	3,0	100,0
	Total	33	100,0	100,0	

GOALS

		Frequency	Percent	Valid Percent	Cumulative Percent
Valid	10,00	1	3,0	3,0	3,0
	12,00	4	12,1	12,1	15,2
	13,00	3	9,1	9,1	24,2
	14,00	6	18,2	18,2	42,4
	15,00	7	21,2	21,2	63,6
	16,00	5	15,2	15,2	78,8
	17,00	2	6,1	6,1	84,8
	18,00	3	9,1	9,1	93,9
	19,00	1	3,0	3,0	97,0
	23,00	1	3,0	3,0	100,0
	Total	33	100,0	100,0	

TEAMWORK

		Frequency	Percent	Valid Percent	Cumulative Percent
Valid	9,00	1	3,0	3,0	3,0
	10,00	2	6,1	6,1	9,1
	11,00	3	9,1	9,1	18,2
	12,00	2	6,1	6,1	24,2
	13,00	11	33,3	33,3	57,6
	14,00	4	12,1	12,1	69,7
	15,00	3	9,1	9,1	78,8
	16,00	2	6,1	6,1	84,8
	17,00	3	9,1	9,1	93,9
	21,00	1	3,0	3,0	97,0
	27,00	1	3,0	3,0	100,0
	Total	33	100,0	100,0	

CUSTOMER

		Frequency	Percent	Valid Percent	Cumulative Percent
Valid	9,00	1	3,0	3,0	3,0
	10,00	1	3,0	3,0	6,1
	11,00	4	12,1	12,1	18,2
	12,00	9	27,3	27,3	45,5
	13,00	5	15,2	15,2	60,6
	14,00	3	9,1	9,1	69,7
	15,00	4	12,1	12,1	81,8
	16,00	3	9,1	9,1	90,9
	18,00	1	3,0	3,0	93,9
	19,00	1	3,0	3,0	97,0
	23,00	1	3,0	3,0	100,0
	Total	33	100,0	100,0	

CULTURE STRENGTH

		Frequency	Percent	Valid Percent	Cumulative Percent
Valid	8,00	2	6,1	6,1	6,1
	9,00	2	6,1	6,1	12,1
	10,00	2	6,1	6,1	18,2
	11,00	3	9,1	9,1	27,3
	12,00	2	6,1	6,1	33,3
	13,00	4	12,1	12,1	45,5
	14,00	3	9,1	9,1	54,5
	15,00	9	27,3	27,3	81,8
	16,00	2	6,1	6,1	87,9
	18,00	2	6,1	6,1	93,9
	19,00	1	3,0	3,0	97,0
	24,00	1	3,0	3,0	100,0
	Total	33	100,0	100,0	

Chapter 9
The Emerging Value of Social Computing in Business Model Innovation

Peter Knol
Deloitte Consulting, The Netherlands

Marco Spruit
Utrecht University, The Netherlands

Wim Scheper
Utrecht University, The Netherlands

ABSTRACT

The value of Social Computing and its application in business has largely remained unclear until now. However, this chapter reveals that Social Computing principles may have important business value, as they can help lower transaction costs. This makes the Social Computing development here to stay, instead of another hype. This chapter describes Social Computing with nine technological and social principles, obtained by comparing both Internet and academic sources in this field, being Open Platform, Lightweight Models, Enabling Services, Intuitive Usability, Long Tail, Unbounded Collaboration, Collective Intelligence, Network Effects, and User Generated Content. The results show that Social Computing provides most support in those aspects of business where connections with the environment exist; the relations with partners and customers. This chapter will explain what Social Computing is, and how one can use it to increase business value.

INTRODUCTION: SOCIAL COMPUTING AND BUSINESS MODELS

Around the millennium the hype around the Internet reached its top and we found the Internet was highly overrated. The bubble popped. Currently too, a certain euphoria exists on seemingly unbounded possibilities coming with what has been labeled Web 2.0[1]. From around 2005, developments on the Internet do sometimes draw comparisons to the Internet hype around the millennium. The impact of Social Computing is not restricted to circles of technology adepts,

DOI: 10.4018/978-1-61520-623-0.ch009

but expands to the business world as well. Consider the amount of start-ups and acquisitions in the field of e-business, often in combination with astronomical sums of money. Apparently, corporations do not want to stay behind in these developments. More than half of the North American and European corporations consider Social Computing to be a priority in 2008 (Forrester, 2008). Those investing in Internet technologies in the last five years are very satisfied with the results (McKinsey, 2007). Many corporation are already rethinking their business models and say they have to make fundamental changes in their businesses. "*Business model innovation matters. Competitive pressures have pushed business model innovation much higher than expected on CEOs' priority lists*" (IBM, 2006). The same research shows that outperformers in industry did place higher priority on business model innovation than underperformers did.

But are these developments another hype? Or is there something more happening, and are we part of a revolution? More and more indications appear, which suggest that Social Computing might be of lasting value. But there are hardly any studies on why Social Computing is valuable. History provides interesting insights on technological developments, or even revolutions, like the Internet and Social Computing. With these insights we might be able to value the Social Computing developments that are happening currently. Moreover, limited research is available on how to apply Social Computing ideas in business. Both these aspects will be examined in this chapter, guided by the idea that Social Computing developments as emerging IT innovation enablers demand new management and business models.

This chapter will perform an explorative and qualitative search towards Social Computing, since the field of Social Computing is new, and not much scientific literature is available yet. Next, this chapter will describe how Social Computing can be of value in business. The subsequent sections each elaborate on a different topic related to this subject. Section 2 revisits technological revolutions in recent history and describes the role of standards, to provide analogies for the technologies under discussion in Internet and Social Computing. Section 3 gives a more thorough description of what Social Computing is. Section 4 elaborates on business models and their role in an organization. Section 5 describes how Social Computing can be used in business by relating it to business models. Section 6 gives conclusions and discussion.

STANDARDS AND TRANSACTION COSTS ECONOMICS

Looking back in time, we can find some illustrative examples explaining the role of standards in technological revolutions. Around 1778, a French gunsmith Honoré Blanc pioneered in developing muskets from parts which were exactly the same for each musket; interchangeable parts. He created some muskets, disbanded them into separate bins and then reassembled the muskets from picking parts at random from each bin. Around 1800, Henry Maudslay pioneered by developing screw thread on interchangeable bolts and nuts, which became a practical commodity. It was a major advance in workshop technology. Not only because they were interchangeable parts themselves, but also because they boosted modularity, since they act as connectors. In the late 1880s, the invention and standardization of electric current caused the so-called 'War of the Currents'. The feud between alternating current (AC), promoted by George Westinghouse, and direct current (DC), promoted by Thomas Edison involved demonstrations including the electrocution of an elephant and the invention of the electric chair. Only since the wide acceptance of the AC standard, mass usage of electricity, and its commoditizing, ran off. What we can learn from these cases is that standards in an industry support interchangeability, and interchangeability decreases complexness (Christensen & Raynor, 2003).

The aforementioned analogies can be transposed to the Internet as well. The success of the World Wide Web arguably depended mainly on open standards and interchangeability (Berners-Lee, 2007). Therefore, "*t*he Internet creates value by reducing the costs of transmitting information. (…) [It] is a terrific advance in lowering the cost of information" (Liebowitz, 2002, p. 9). This can be achieved, because standards lead to better interchangeability between products and services, much like the historical cases described above. In terms of ICT, standards lead to higher compatibility.

Low compatibility leads to an unequal distribution of information between parties. This links us to the transaction costs economics; the value of transaction cost economics lies in the increase of efficiently managing uncertainty or complexity, leading to more equally distributed information, thus decreasing the transaction costs (Cordella, 2001). In his influential work *The Nature of the Firm*, Coase (1937) mentions "*the costs of the price mechanism*", referring to transaction costs. Williamson extends with "*the economic equivalent of friction in physical systems*" (Williamson, 1985, p. 17). In other words, transaction costs are the costs of making an economic exchange. With that in mind, and looking again to the Internet, we can conclude that the value of the Internet may be related to the decrease of transaction costs. But how does Social Computing fit in this picture?

When the World Wide Web increasingly became more common during the '90s, its primary use by companies was to represent themselves online, and by consumers to find information about these companies, or other consumers. Instead of using the new technology as a new concept, with all of its new possibilities, it was used like an old concept, similar pressed media. This is a commonly observed behavior with respect to new technologies (McLuhan, 1964). Compare it to the development of vehicles, from stage coaches to cars. The first cars looked just like stage coaches; wheels with spokes, its appearance, and so on. But

instead of horses they were driven by engines. Later, people found there were better shapes for vehicles with an engine. Then, the use of the new technology adjusted to the new possibilities of this technology.

The same holds for the Internet; a new technology (the World Wide Web) was used for old concepts (brochures, newspapers, catalogs, business cards, etc.). In the second era (which started approximately in 2001), the Internet is used in a different way, more adjusted to the possibilities of the Internet (Tapscott & Williams, 2007). So the value of The Internet as a whole, and Social Computing specifically, lies in the lowering of information transaction costs. This is not a hype, but valuable to everyone using the Internet for information transaction. Who is not? Time to take a closer look to what Social Computing actually is.

DEFINING SOCIAL COMPUTING

More and more is written and heard about Social Computing. It has become a marketing buzzword and without you or your product being marked 2.0, as in Web 2.0, you seem out to be of the market. Even though many of those using the term don't even know what it really is. The opinions on Web 2.0 rather differ from evangelists (IBM, 2006; Hinchcliffe, 2006; Leadbeater, 2007) to antagonists (Boutin, 2006; Keen, 2007). This section will give the floor to both evangelists and antagonists. Also the definition varies from study to study and from blog to blog, which could explain the disputes among bloggers, trend watchers and scientists about a proper definition. It took a while to even find a common perspective since the first definition attempt of O'Reilly and Graham in 2004, varying from just graphical elements, technologies and design patterns, to more abstract attitudes and philosophies (O'Reilly, 2005; Hoegg, Martignoni, Meckel, & Stanoevska-Slabeva, 2006). Maybe a combination of one or more of these abstraction levels should be incorporated when defining Social Computing.

All these aspects are due to the newness of the subject of Social Computing. Every opinion and study contributes to the crystallization of the concept. Therefore many of these opinions, writings, studies, and researches will be presented to find some common ground in the currently forming field of Social Computing. That will be the start of the description of Social Computing used in this chapter. It is interesting to focus on what can be learned from current developments. Therefore the quest will reach out to principles underlying Social Computing, at a higher level of abstraction then just bare examples or cases. A principle is an initial concept, a fundamental idea, a basic rule. The principles should be applicable in other situations on the Internet. This section will use examples, mention technologies, services, and so on, to define Social Computing.

Nine Social Computing Principles

The previous section has positioned Social Computing in a context. In this section some more focus will be placed on what Social Computing is. In the attempt to define Social Computing, many examples will be used to clarify the definition. Some different existing views will be posed as well. This way a common ground will be established out of all cited opinions on the subject and the discovered similarities point to the principles of Social Computing.

When exploring the field of Social Computing, we used both Internet sources, since it is the platform presenting the newest opinions and discussions in this field, which makes it a necessary source for up to date information, as well as scientific sources, if any. Several more or less substantiated definitions, descriptions, principles, and design patterns came by. All used sources do attempt to define Social Computing in a way. O'Reilly seeks principles (O'Reilly, 2005), Hinchcliffe goes for key aspects (Hinchcliffe, 2005),

Hoegg et al look for fundamentals (Hoegg, Martignoni, Meckel, & Stanoevska-Slabeva, 2006), McAfee finds ground rules (McAfee, 2006a), and Vossen and Hagemann stick to essences (Vossen & Hagemann, 2007). All found definitions or descriptions exist out of one or more elements. For comparison, these elements are put together in Table 1. The column header contains the author of the definition or description placed in that column. Each cell in that column contains elements of the author's definition or description. Elements that look similar between different definitions or descriptions are placed at the same row level. This way an extensive overview of different elements of Social Computing definitions and descriptions is presented, as found in Internet and academic sources. Different definitions are compared to each other on the same row level. The first column presents the defined principles based on the definitions from the other columns at that row level. The cells in the first column therefore contain elements of defining Social Computing of the researched sources. The remainder of this section will elaborate on these principles as mentioned in the first column of Table 1.

Open Platform

O'Reilly (O'Reilly, 2005) is an often cited source when talking about Web 2.0, which is why this chapter cannot ignore his views on the subject. O'Reilly shortly defines Web 2.0 as "*the business revolution in the computer industry caused by the move to the Internet as platform, and an attempt to understand the rules for success on that new platform*" (O'Reilly, 2006). The key element in this definition is the Internet as a platform, which means that the Internet is the computer and the operating system on which services should be offered, instead of a desktop computer running software. Although the Internet is already often used to ship new software versions to customers, the idea of the Internet as a platform goes one step further, according to O'Reilly. It means that

Table 1. Comparison of social computing definition elements

Social Computing principles	O'Reilly (2005) principles	Hinchcliffe (2005) key aspects	Hoegg et al. (2006) fundamentals	McAfee (2006a) ground rules	Vossen and Hagemann (2007) essences
User generated content	Data is the core	Data consumption and remixing from all sources, particularly user generated data	Information enrichment		Ways to utilize and combine data and data streams
Network effects	Network effects as more people participate	Architecture of participation that encourages user contribution	Mutually maximize collective intelligence	Network effects	A socialization of the Web, where a user makes personal entries available to the general public, and where this often leads to an improvement of the underlying platform
Collective intelligence	Harnessing collective intelligence			Support emerging of knowledge	
Unbounded collaboration	Cooperate with users as co-developers		Creating and sharing of information		
Leverage the long tail	Leverage the long tail				
Intuitive usability	Lightweight and rich user interfaces	Rich and interactive user interfaces		Easy to use offerings	Functionality- as well as service-oriented approaches to build new applications as a composition of other, and in order to enrich user experiences
Enabling services	Cost-effective scalable services instead of software		Dynamic services	Technologies that let users build structure over time can coexist peacefully with those that define it up front	
Lightweight models	Perpetual beta	Continuous and seamless update of software and data, often very rapidly			
	Lightweight programming models and business models				
Open platform	Software above the level of a single device	The Web and all its connected devices as one global platform of reusable services and data	Formalized interaction	Online platform with a constantly changing structure build by distributed, autonomous and largely self-interested peers	
	Web as platform				

the browser is your only local tool, which gives you access to everything else you want to do, since everything you do happens on the Internet (O'Reilly, 2005).

Andrew McAfee puts it a little bit different, noting that "most current platforms, such as knowledge management systems, information portals, intranets and workflow applications, are highly structured from the start, and users have little opportunity to influence this structure" (McAfee, 2006a). It is not that the Internet should be the platform per se, but that most current platforms, like desktops, are too structured, preconceived, or imposed. The platform should be open, blank, in

a way unstructured but able to emerge: "Instead, they [should be] building tools that let these aspects of knowledge work emerge" (McAfee, 2006a). At this moment the Internet is an example of such a platform. This idea corresponds with that of Berners-Lee, which we saw in the chapter on standardization: "The lesson from the proliferation of new applications and services on top of the Web infrastructure is that innovation will happen provided it has a platform of open technical standards, a flexible, scalable architecture, and access to these standards on royalty-free ($0 fee patent licenses) terms" (Berners-Lee, 2007, p. 4). Tapscott mentions 'being open' or 'transparency' as a new idea in the current Internet era, in his book Wikinomics (2007). Being open also increases trust, according to Tapscott. Next, a global platform for collaboration will open many new possibilities in many fields (Tapscott & Williams, 2007).

On the other hand, McAfee does not promote one platform like the Internet, but suggests building and adding upon existing platforms, an opinion in which he shares the side of Microsoft, as we can see in the example in the sidebar. He gives as ground rule to create an "... online platform with a constantly changing structure build by distributed, autonomous and largely self-interested peers" (McAfee, 2006a, p. 26). McAfee describes how these platforms should be used in a business environment: "*Simple, Free Platforms for Self-Expression; Emergent Structures, Rather than Imposed Ones; Order from Chaos.* (...) They're meant instead to illustrate how technologists have done a brilliant job at three tasks: building platforms to let lots of users express themselves, letting the structure of these platforms emerge over time instead of imposing it up front, and helping users deal with the resulting flood of content" (McAfee, 2006a; McAfee, 2006b). These remarks already entails many elements considered in the next subsections, but again an open, simple, and even free platform is mentioned.

Trend watcher Dion Hinchcliffe says about the platform: "*The Web and all its connected devices as one global platform of reusable services and data*" (Hinchcliffe, 2006). He, in a way, extends on what McAfee said, by noting that the platform is not just the Internet, but all connected devices, like the Internet, but more. That is why this element is called *Open* Platform, leaving it open which system this platform should contain. One could for instance think of the increasing developments in the field of mobile telephony and its synergy with the Internet. O'Reilly too, mentions different devices as an element of Web 2.0, but in relation to software (O'Reilly, 2005). An example of the synergy between different devices is the combina-

tion of iTunes, which makes use of the Internet as music database, iTunes as local software client to play and buy music, and the possibility to copy music to an iPod to listen to the music.

This does not mean that existing platforms, like local desktop PC's, or organization computer systems, should be replaced by the Internet straight away. Why let go the advantages of a well built history and switch solely to the Internet? That is not what is suggested. Instead, try to use the good of the two worlds and integrate openness onto your existing platform. Compatibility is a keyword in such an approach, and everyone should be able to add, edit and build upon this platform. Authoring doesn't have to be as big a problem as will be discussed in the subsection about User Generated Content.

Why an open platform lowers transaction costs is not difficult; when an open, accessible, maybe free, platform exists to build your information systems upon, users are easily able to switch services, or edit them. They do not have to worry about local hardware as much as they used to do, since only a desktop PC with a browser will be necessary. The users save costs.

The Open Platform is the fundament on which many of the next principles are building, as we will see in the next subsections, which is why this principle is handled first.

Lightweight Models

O'Reilly calls lightweight programming models and business models one of the core competences of Web 2.0. With this he means to aim at several strategies. First, the programming and business models should allow for loosely coupled systems. Next, syndication is more important than coordination of information. Finally, one should design for hackability and remixability (O'Reilly, 2005). These strategies should assure flexible businesses that can easily anticipate on a changing environment. Since the environment in which we do business today is changing faster and faster, these strategies help making an organization, or web service, lean and agile. In the development of a product one should already take into account the possibilities for re-use by third parties, or possibilities to easily extend on that product.

The idea of Lightweight Models is very superficially shown sometimes by sites, like Google's Gmail, containing the term 'beta' in their logo or header. The reasoning is to suggest that the service is still in development, while, in the mean time, it is already in use. By suggesting that the service is not yet complete, Google suggests to improve the service soon, just like one would do after releasing beta versions of a software packet. But the term beta remains in the logo, which suggests Google will always be working on improving the service. This phenomenon is called 'perpetual beta'. Updating with such fast subsequences requires an agile business model which can handle such a fast update rate. Instead of revising every year or month, like traditional software companies do with their products, web services implement new versions up to a few times a day. The required agility to be able to do so is the basis for an enabling service, the subject of next subsection.

Agility also has to do with not creating structures and limits to a service up front. McAfee mentions "Technologies that let users build structure over time can coexist peacefully with those that define it up front" (McAfee, 2006a). He suggests letting structures emerge over time, by the use of a tool or service, see the subsection on Network Effects. This is something a development model should take into account and extends the openness of the platform of the previous subsection. Again, compatibility is an important issue. Tapscott calls for removing insulation to open the way for 'acting globally' (Tapscott & Williams, 2007, p. 30).

Aiming for Lightweight Models also lowers transaction costs. Changing an organization costs a lot in terms of energy and investments. But developing a business in an agile and lean way

from the start, makes anticipating on a changing environment take less effort.

Enabling Services

This subsection wants to compare services with regular software. Online services, or software brought to you as a service, are often promoted with the term 'SaaS'. Examples of online services are Gmail, an email service, salesforce.com or Sugar-CRM, both CRM services, or osCommerce, a web shop service. These are online offered services, with or without paid membership, sometimes open source, otherwise offered by a commercial company. These services compete with software packages like Outlook for mail and SAP for CRM.

There are many advantages of online services above local software. First, there is the advantage of the maintenance of the package, which becomes part of the service provider, instead of the user. Next, updates can be implemented right away, since every user is using the online product, which discards the need for users to achieve updates, which saves costs. Updating is far easier on an Open Platform with lightweight development and business models since every user uses the online version. Furthermore, since the services run on the deliverer's server, the delivering company has the possibility to update whenever they feel to, immediately assuring every user uses this updated version. Next, there is a logistic advantage; products delivered as a service through the Internet don't need shipping and will therefore be delivered faster and cheaper. Next, data storage is managed online. In relation to this, the content resulting from services, for example, a document from Google Documents, is easier to share through the Internet, since the results already are stored online. This holds for backups too.

These services should not only be flexible, but enabling. This means, it should be easy to interact between services. Services, or parts of them, should ask to be interchanged with other services, to create mash-ups. Vossen & Hagemann mention "functionality- as well as service-oriented approaches to build new applications as a composition of other, and in order to enrich user experiences" as a core aspect of Social Computing (Vossen & Hagemann, 2007, p. 67). Elements of this refer already to the next subsection, Intuitive Usability, but they also mention mash-ups and remixability when they mention the aim to build new applications as a composition of others. Also Hoegg et al. assure that "Web 2.0 services are highly dynamic, which is why this context has to be understood as an interactive development process" (Hoegg, Martignoni, Meckel, & Stanoevska-Slabeva, 2006, p. 13). The last part of this citation refers back to the previous subsection.

One condition is that the service must be scalable, preferably cost effective (O'Reilly, 2005). Since every software or service is a tool to manage content, or data, may it be documents, music, movies, financial administration, or whatever, the service must be scaled with the amount of data it handles, often related to the amount of users.

Enabling Services too lower transaction costs; one does not need local resources as much as with local software. Interchangeability enables the re-use of pieces of services and with some creativity supports innovation. There is less need for distribution, so efficiency increases. Storing the results of online services make those results better distributable to or accessible for colleagues for instance.

Intuitive Usability

Many of the researched resources mention something about usability or functionality. According to O'Reilly, user experiences should be rich (O'Reilly, 2005). To Hinchcliffe, user interfaces should be rich and interactive (Hinchcliffe, 2005). To McAfee, offerings should be easy to use (McAfee, 2006a). And to Vossen & Hageman functionality should enrich user experiences (Vossen & Hagemann, 2007). Usability is about the ease of use of a user interface, usability guru

Jakob Nielsen explains. This breaks down to five elements; learnability, how easy is it to accomplish tasks; efficiency, how quickly can tasks be performed when learned; memorability, ease of reestablished proficiency; errors, how severe and recoverable when made; and satisfaction, how pleasant to use the design (Nielsen, 1993).

Intuitive in the current context means that the user should not have any concern about how to use a service. The *walk up 'n'use* idea in usability jargon explains the idea. It goes one step further then the ease of learning aspect of usability. The intuitivity should ensure both experienced and non-experienced users are able to use a service. This needs a design for experienced users, who want to find enough features or personalization options in the service, to remain being of interest. On the other hand, it needs a design for non-experienced users, who want to be able to immediately know how to use the service without being discouraged by the amount of features. This is one of the preconditions for the Long Tail principle, further elaborated upon in the next subsection.

McAfee suggest replacing the WIMP components (windows, icons, menus and pointers), often used for interface design up to date, with SLATES (search, links, authoring, tags, extensions and signals) (McAfee, 2006a):

- **Search:** let users search themselves instead of preconceived notions brought up through page layout and navigation structures by editors or professional staff.
- **Links:** let (intra)nets be built by large groups so a dense link network can evolve containing information on relevance and interest.
- **Authoring:** many people can add value to a service, authoring should support the elicitation of these contributions. Wikipedia proofs that these contribution emerge to convergent, high quality content (Giles, 2005).

- **Tags:** a categorization system that emerges over time due to users' actions. This is called a folksonomy, versus a taxonomy which imposes a categorization up front.
- **Extensions:** recommendation systems or algorithms that reason by extension to offer users things they might be interested in.
- **Signals:** when new content of interest appears, users are notified, compare syndication or RSS feeds.

Many of the underlying ideas of these components come back in the subsections about Collective Intelligence and Network Effects, but the goal is clear; make the use of a service as easy as possible, and don't concern the user with difficulties the service can do smartly by itself. Instead, advance the user with offerings or help with information gathered in the background.

Macromedia coined the term Rich Internet Applications (RIA) to focus more on the GUI style applications that could be build with Flash. But when Google introduced AJAX technologies to create their services like Gmail, the web-based applications really got the look and feel of PC-based applications without losing their web advantages (O'Reilly, 2005). Ruby on Rails, from David Heinemeier Hansson, is another language in development and often used in recent designs. In their Web 2.0 discussion, Hinchcliffe and others called aforementioned technologies and languages, a lightweight version of SOA (Service Oriented Applications), or WOA (Web based Oriented Applications). It needs to be expressed that the specific mentioned languages are not Social Computing in itself, but programming languages in their broadest form do enable intuitive design and therefore usability. Mentioned languages are examples of enabling technologies.

That Intuitive Usability lowers transaction costs is straight forward. Ease of use increases efficiency, lowers search costs, and lowers the costs of learning a tool or service. The four principles mentioned so far are the basis for the remaining

principles. They are more technological, and closely related to each other. These principles trigger lower transaction costs. The following principles tend to be more social. Those principles are a result of lower transaction costs.

Long Tail Focus

The 0 is the only principle mentioned by just one source as a core element in Web 2.0. Still, it is included in the model. This is been done, first, because also the other sources mentioned Long Tail, though not in their definition (Hinchcliffe, 2005; Vossen & Hagemann, 2007). Next, this is been done because also not listed sources have mentioned it (Forrester, 2008). The Long Tail is an old concept, but in relation to the Internet developments popularized by Chris Anderson in his book *The Long Tail* (Anderson, 2007). Take a power law distribution, or a Pareto distribution, as in Figure 1. The horizontal axis depicts for instance an amount of clients, the vertical axis depicts for instance an amount of profit. The curve depicts the profit gained from those specific clients. As we see in the figure, there is a small amount of clients who each generate a large amount of profit, called the short neck, often about 20% of the Pareto principle. Next, we see there is a large amount of clients who each generates a small amount of profit, called the long tail, often 80% of the Pareto principle. Obviously is seems most interesting to target those clients who generate high profits. But the idea of the Long Tail is that a large amount of clients, who generate only a small profit, total for a high amount of profit as well.

The focus on the Long Tail is made possible since a decrease of, for instance, stocking and distribution costs make it more attractive to also serve niche clients. Another trend is that lower transaction costs for clients, make it more attractive for them to find other providers, which makes self-service possible. In that case it is not a provider who actively searches for clients, but a client searching for a provider, with the provider

Figure 1. A power law distribution

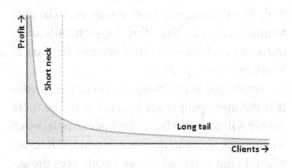

just enabling and facilitating these searching clients.

The idea of the Long Tail is applicable in many fields. For instance, auction sites and market places on the Internet. Or online book stores like Amazon as described by Brynjolfsson et al. (Brynjolfsson, Hu, & Simester, 2007), where they describe how a large proportion of the sales of Amazon comes from niche products often not available in normal book stores. In another article they describe how lower search costs can increase the distribution of sales (Brynjolfsson, Hu, & Smith, 2003). This shows how the decrease of transaction costs makes it possible to leverage the Long Tail.

Unbounded Collaboration

Collaboration might be the main goal where the enabling role of the Internet becomes apparent. The recent Social Computing developments really add to this goal. Services and programs can cooperate, like shown in the subsection of Enabling Services. In this subsection will be focused on collaboration between people, organizations, or both.

O'Reilly mentions that respecting users as co-developers is one of the core competencies of Web 2.0 companies and acknowledges there is need for trust do to so (O'Reilly, 2005). Hoegg et al. mention the need for creating and sharing information (Hoegg, Martignoni, Meckel, & Stanoevska-Slabeva, 2006), which also points already to the next subsections. Vossen & Hage-

man also make statements in this direction, but generalize by saying that personal contributions are made available to the general public (Vossen & Hagemann, 2007, p. 67). The idea of them all is clear: users add value. Or as McAfee puts it, "... most people have something to contribute, whether it's knowledge, insight, experience, a comment, a fact, an edit, a link, and so on, and authorship is a way to elicit these contributions" (McAfee, 2006a).

With collaboration that is unbounded, we mean that collaboration is less and less dependent of place and time. When the Internet is used as a platform, offering intuitively usable enabling services, collaboration around the globe becomes very easy. Not only involving customers in the development of a new product, which is more the area of the next subsection on Collective Intelligence, but really collaboration initiated from both, or more, sides, like in the development of open source software. This new form of organization is called *peering* by Tapscott, and, according to him, also refers to a more horizontal organization (Tapscott & Williams, 2007, p. 23).

Users often meet in communities, dealing with a certain subject, task, or interest. When collaboration is a goal enabled by the Internet, then communities could be seen as the socialization of the Internet, or, broader, the socialization of computing. User contributions, in their broadest form, are often valuable to other users or to organizations. Those contributions lead to content enrichment and the improvement of the services dealing with this content. This enrichment and improvement will emerge over time. This is the relation between the last four subsections.

Just as leveraging the Long Tail is becoming attractive because of lower transaction costs, also Unbounded Collaboration is made possible due to lower transaction costs of working together. The Open Platform forms a perfect basis to collaborate on, using the services, usability, and resources of this platform.

Collective Intelligence

Unbounded Collaboration focused on collaboration of different parties, initiated from different sides, with the goal to together develop something. Collective Intelligence is more about individuals who do not per se have the goal to develop something collectively, but who individually work on the Open Platform, and, as a result, are developing something of value. Therefore this is also called co-creation (Prahalad & Ramaswamy, 2004).

According to Hoegg et al. Web 2.0 is *"the philosophy of mutually maximizing collective intelligence and added value for each participant by formalized and dynamic information sharing and creation"* (Hoegg, Martignoni, Meckel, & Stanoevska-Slabeva, 2006). This definition includes different elements. Dynamic services are mentioned again, as in the subsection about Enabling Services. Another element is to mutually maximize collective intelligence. Collective Intelligence is also a core competence according to O'Reilly (O'Reilly, 2005). Users can add value in different ways, we already saw in the previous subsection, and will do so if you harness it.

The term 'collective intelligence' is actually a fallacy of wrong level, since a collective cannot have intelligence. The term refers more to the process of eliciting intelligence of a lot of individuals. Collective Intelligence is the knowledge of the mass, the knowledge and competences of the total of a collection of users, on the Internet, in a community, and so on. This is also called 'the wisdom of crowds', a subject James Surowiecki wrote a book about; he explains: *"Large groups of people are smarter than an elite few, no matter how brilliant the elite few may be. The wisdom of crowds is better at solving problems, fostering innovation, coming to wise decisions, and even predicting the future"* (Surowiecki, 2004). This has been researched in the case of Wikipedia, the online encyclopedia created by Internet users. The results show that Wikipedia is almost as accurate in scientific articles as the Encyclopedia Britan-

nica (Giles, 2005). But users do need to share their intelligence, whatever it may be, to be able to make use of it. Therefore Tapscott calls *sharing* as a new idea in the Internet era (Tapscott & Williams, 2007, p. 26).

The crowd is an emergent entity. This means that the more people act in some way, the more people will copy that behavior. For example, when someone is about to drown in a pond, witnesses often do not react, while everybody sees the accident happening. In such a case people are like a colony of ants, a herd of sheep, or a school of fishes. These are also called boids. Central decision making is very difficult in such a situation, since there is no common point to address, no one you can speak to in particular to reach the entire group. This phenomenon is extensively elaborated upon by Rod Beckström, in his book *The Starfish and the Spider* (Beckstrom & Brafman, 2006). He describes the decentralization of the Internet and explains the need for trust, as O'Reilly did in the previous subsection, since decentralization lacks control. One can create a social environment, like a community, not per se restricted to the Internet, with some structures, or facilities, where a community can and may emerge. This emerging is an organic process, which can be steered by the service providers through the identity, visibility, conversation, relation, sharing, reputation, authoring, and so on, of users. The theory of bounded rationality gives more insights in these issues (Simon, 1991).

A remark that needs to be placed is the phenomenon of the 'one percent rule'. This rule explains that in a community, just one percent of the visitors will contribute to the community, only ten percent will react in some way, but the majority of 90% just lurks, which means, read, consumes, uses, but does not add anything of value to the community. This is a common habit in newsgroups, for example, but also on social network sites like Facebook, or initiatives like SecondLife. A possible solution for this is presented in the next subsection.

The increased possibilities for knowledge elicitation from many individuals are also made possible by lower transaction costs for those individuals to share their intelligence.

Network Effects

Instead of Unbounded collaboration, or Collective Intelligence, which implies purposeful interaction, users also can be unaware of their contributions, when just using a service. An example of this phenomenon is the Amazon suggestions: *"If you like this book, you'll probably also like this one."* Amazon can do these suggestions based on browsing and buying information of other users. This is called a 'network effect'. Robert Metcalfe introduced the term around his network law, based on the use of the Ethernet card in the 1980s (Metcalfe, 1980). This law relates the value of a network to the amount of cards in that network. The value of one card increases exponentially when more users with a card join the network. Another example is that of a telephone; when you are the only one in possession of a telephone, it would be useless. But the more people obtain a telephone, the more people you can connect to, the more valuable you telephone will become. The same idea holds for services on the Internet where Network Effects are used. Network Effects are also known as network externalities (Katz & Shapiro, 1985).

Hincliffe calls Network Effects *"the real secret sauce of Web 2.0"*, emphasizing this phenomenon is becoming really visible and used in recent Internet developments This is because the appliance to a service has been made easy through other developments, like sharing and feedback loops (Hinchcliffe, 2006). The more users use a service, the more valuable the service becomes. Examples are countless: Wikipedia; the more users contribute and edit articles, the more accurate information on it will become, and the more users will come to use Wikipedia. Del.ici.ous; the more users add tags to their bookmarks, the better these tags describe the content behind the bookmark, the more findable they become. Flickr; the more users add tags to a picture, the better the content on this picture is described, the better findable it becomes.

To leverage the value of Network Effects, a certain amount of users, contributors, editors, and so on is needed. This amount is called the critical mass. Depicted in a usage curve, when the critical mass is reached, the usage of the service will increase steep at once, whereas before that point the usage did increase slowly. This point in the curve is called the 'tipping point' (Gladwell, 2000). How to reach this point has been described by Moore in his book *Crossing the Chasm* (Moore, 1991). This, again, has relations to the adoption phases in the diffusion of innovations theory of Rogers (Rogers, 1962).

To make use of the Network Effects, and to overcome the problem of the one percent rule of the previous subsection, the aim is to let the Network Effects happen automatically. "Only a small percentage of users will go through the trouble of adding value to your application. Therefore: Set inclusive defaults for aggregating user data as a side-effect of their use of the application" (O'Reilly, 2005). This way, users contribute to building applications getting better the more it's been used. One of the first success stories relying on this phenomenon was Napster, since Napster was configured to share downloaded music by default, which automatically increased the size of the music database. This architectural trick uses the 'selfish' pursue of users to collectively build value as an automatically byproduct, explains O'Reilly.

McAfee calls this phenomenon 'extensions', meaning "… automating some of the work of categorization and pattern matching", as we already saw in the subsection on Intuitive Usability (McAfee, 2006a). Vossen & Hagemann mention that the socialization of the web often leads to improvement of the underlying platform (Vossen & Hagemann, 2007, p. 67). Again, this is something reached with a service developed to make use of those improvements.

In relation to the Network Effects stands the phenomenon of cumulative advantage, or the Matthew-effect, from the parable of the talents in the Bible in the book of Matthew. Robert K. Merton described this effect already in 1968 (Merton, 1968). The theory learns that the rich get richer or he that has much will get more, and he that has few, even what he has will be taken. Take again the tipping point in the usage of a service from the previous subsection. When a service reaches the tipping point in usage, its usage will highly increase. Therefore the Network Effects become more usable to the service, resulting in even more value. Also called a waterfall effect or increasing returns.

Because of these increasing returns, some argued that being first to a market will result in first-mover-wins, or winner-take-all principles. According to them, lock-in should guarantee corporations to ultimately make profit from the Network Effects. But, as Liebowitz explains, the opposite is true on the Internet, whereas the Social Computing developments even more undermine these thoughts. Because of lower transaction costs, it will be easier for users to switch from providers, so lock-in will not hold (Liebowitz, 2002, pp. 20, 21). Section 2 already showed how lower transaction costs help coordination barriers from switching to other providers. Social Computing highly extends to lower transaction costs and coordination, thus decreasing lock-in possibilities even more.

This does not mean the Network Effects will decrease in the Internet era, they will not. But using Network Effects for first-mover-wins, or winner-takes-all principles, thus aiming at lock-in is not truer on the Internet then it is in the off-line world. Social Computing doesn't change that, or undermines it. A research from McAfee and Brynjolfsson revealed that winners might win big and fast, but not necessarily very long (McAfee & Brynjolfsson, 2008). Remember how quick Yahoo! replaced AltaVista, and how quick Google replaced Yahoo!. They conclude, therefore, that competition gets nastier.

User Generated Content

All the previous subsections were about how to approach a platform, build services, deal with users and their contributions. But O'Reilly is right, when he says, in the end it's actually all about data (O'Reilly, 2005). Hinchcliffe calls data consumption and remixing a key aspect of Web 2.0 (Hinchcliffe, 2006). Also McAfee and Vossen & Hagemann mention the central role of data or information and its enrichment and utilization. In sketching the trends of the Web for the future, Berners-Lee sees that "*... the Web will become one big database*" as one trend (Berners-Lee, 2007, p. 5).

O'Reilly stimulates to seek for hard to recreate data for competitive advantage. Good examples of valuable data owning companies are NavTeq and TeleAtlas, who create geographical maps. Both companies were bought in 2008 for more than ten times the turnover they made in 2006, NavTeq by Nokia and TeleAtlas by TomTom. What's more, TeleAtlas did not even had one year of profit in its existence. Many companies rely on their data, as do some organizations on the Internet as well; MapQuest, Yahoo Maps, MSN Maps, Google Maps and Google Earth.

This data can be news, information on books, events, weather, market places, stock and market prices, and so on. Many websites rely on only a few data sources. Advantages are sought for in reusing and smartly enriching data, or offering tools to do so. The owner of the data is key. Ownership is important, but also in this area things are changing. For example the authorship rights on the Internet are very difficult to restrain. On the Internet, especially in recent developments, combining, sharing, enriching content is of value, as we have seen so far. So by claiming too much rights and protecting data, one blocks the value adding possibilities. This not only is a missed chance for the community, but also puts the author out of the picture, since it is hard to use content which is not accessible. A corporation doesn't make money with content, but because of content. Graham puts it this way: "*Experts have given Wikipedia middling reviews, but they miss the critical point: it's good enough. And it's free, which means people actually read it. On the web, articles you have to pay for might as well not exist. Even if you were willing to pay to read them yourself, you can't link to them. They're not part of the conversation*" (Graham, 2005). Therefore some new initiatives rise around this subject, like the Creative Commons, which is a method for describing the authority of created content.

Content may be the core in Social Computing, there are also drawbacks to opening up content, and working and storing your work online. First, there is the concern of often heard suspicion on privacy issues. When using Gmail as your email service, its contact list as your address book, Google Docs to create and share your work, and Google Blogger to write about your personal interest, imagine the amount of personal and professional information Google gathers about you.

Another, relating issue is that of authoring; what about security of what you create online? Microsoft assures that a platform like Windows on a local desktop PC is necessary to guarantee the right application of these issues. This is not necessarily the case. Again, it is about trust. If Google would be transparent enough to its users, by showing how they deal with these issues, it is possible for the user to decide whether that is sufficient. Then, the user will remain using the services of Google. Or whether that is not sufficient enough. Then, the user than can switch to an organization that offers privacy and security according his or her wishes. It therefore is the user who decides who to trust and who not. This aspect is in such a situation just a part of the business model of the organization, an added value of an online corporation. As for privacy issues, the dis-

cussion will presumably change from protection by authorities, to self protection, or openness, from users. So these aspects do, in fact, have nothing to do with the platform. But now we are already too much into the next sections, where business models make their entry.

The Nine Social Computing Principles

We have elaborated upon the nine Social Computing Principles. The first four principles are technological and lower transaction costs, since searching, editing, and reaching of content and services becomes more easy, more accessible, increasingly efficient, or cheaper The last five principles are social and emerge due to lower transaction costs. The principles are depicted in Figure 2, in a more structured way, with technical enabling principles at the bottom, to more social resulting principles at the top. In previous research we would refer to Social Computing based on these principles as a development where technologies enable empowerment of individuals, or groups of individuals, to express themselves in a more natural way, leading to easier creation, enriching, sharing, and finding of content (Knol, Spruit, & Scheper, 2008).

BUSINESS MODELS

To see where in business Social Computing can be supportive, we will relate them to a business model. A generic business model is a tangible tool to point out which aspects of an organization can be supported with the Social Computing principles. The increasing impact of Social Computing on business "should (…) not be neglected from an academic perspective. New business models arise and existing business models are highly affected by Web 2.0 communities" (Hoegg, Martignoni, Meckel, & Stanoevska-Slabeva, 2006).

Figure 2. The nine principles of social computing, of which the bottom darker four are technology oriented and the upper lighter five are socially oriented (Knol, Spruit, & Scheper, 2008)

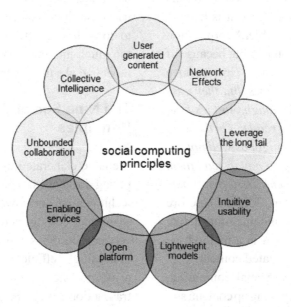

Although the term 'business model' gained growing reputation in the last two decades (Osterwalder, Pigneur, & Tucci, 2005, p. 3), the basis of its definition comes from Andrews' classic definition of the strategy of a business (Chesbrough & Rosenbloom, 2002, p. 7). This definition states business strategy as "*the determination of how a company will compete in a given business and position itself among its competitors*" (Andrews, 1971, p. 12). Chesbrough, stresses that the strategy of a corporation is at several points somewhat else than a business model; first, a business model focuses on value creation, while a business strategy focuses on how value will be captured; next a business model seeks to create value for the organization, while a business strategy seeks to create value for an organization's shareholders; and finally, a business model needs less environmental knowledge, whereas a business strategy needs more complex information, also about the environment (Chesbrough & Rosenbloom, 2002, p. 535).

In his book *Open Innovation*, Chesbrough elaborates on business models in the context of innovation within a corporation, based on both scientific and business cases. He defines a business model as a method to convert a new technology into economic value (Chesbrough, 2003, p. 63). That places a business model in a bigger picture.

Chesbrough stresses the need of a business model by explaining that the commercializing of an innovation does not exists in the product or service using the new technology, but in the business model which underlies that product or service (Chesbrough, 2003). Osterwalder did a thorough research to the origins and developments of the business model, and gives a useful representation of most recent literature on this topic. He defines a business model as: "*... a conceptual tool that contains a set of elements and their relationships and allows expressing the business logic of a specific firm*" (Osterwalder, Pigneur, & Tucci, 2005). His generic business model is depicted in Figure 3.

Business Model Building Blocks

From the point of view of Chesbrough, a new innovation, the Value Proposition is held in the new technology. More abstract, the Value Proposition

Figure 3. The business model and its building blocks (Osterwalder, 2005)

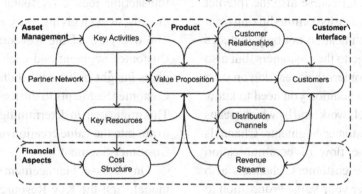

is what you as corporation offer to a market or a customer (which also might be the next link in the value chain), that satisfies in a specific need of that market or customer. It might be the solution to a problem which that customer has. The value of your offered solution is determined by a few aspects, including how big the problem is to your customer, the acuteness of the need for a solution, and the benefit of the solution to the customer. These all add to the perceived value of your offer to the customer.

The customer, obviously, is of importance in the determination of your Value Proposition. Therefore the next step in business modeling is to determine your customers, how you communicate with them and distribute your Value Proposition to them and what kind of relationships you maintain with them. But the Value Proposition is composed by other elements; your Partner Network, the configuration of you key activities, your key Resources and Competencies, and of course the costs you have to make to achieve aforementioned three elements. Those will be the last steps of the business model design. This building block is closely related to the value discipline 'Product Leadership' of Treacy & Wiersema in that it focuses on an innovative, excellent product (Treacy & Wiersema, 1995). Porter defines competing on 'differentiation' as one way of sustaining competitive advantage against your competitors (Porter, 1985).

As mentioned in the previous section, the Value Proposition and the customer, or market, segments are closely related. A segment is a group of customers with the same characteristics. The Value Proposition is determined for each Customer Segment, or the other way around, the Customer Segments are determined for the different Value Propositions of an organization. Sometimes it might be better first to determine the Customer Segments and next find proper Value Propositions for each segment. The satisfaction of a customer's need should be turned in to a Revenue Stream. You need to know the customer in order to know what value you should create for him or her and where you should focus your activities in order to create or capture these values. Therefore it might be that, with the same technology but a different customer, a different value should be created. Famous is the case of Canon entering the printing market, which up till then was dominated by Xerox. Canon targeted the small businesses and home consumers, and took a fair bit of the market share from Xerox, which in turn had always targeted the big corporations (Chesbrough, 2003, p. 74). A smart business model made the low-end focus of Canon successful, in this seemingly impenetrable industry.

Once the Customer Segments are mapped, you need to determine how you are going to communicate with your customers. This can be by advertising, promotion teams, websites, phone inquiries, and so on. Of course also the Internet plays a growing role since its commoditizing from around 1995. Communication not only includes sending your message to the customers, but also to hear from the customers their reaction on your Value Proposition. In addition you need to know how well your channels work, and by which means you reach which Customer Segments. Channels not only include the flow of communication between you and the customers, channels also include how you offer your Value Proposition to them. You should determine the best distribution channel for each of your offerings. This, of course, heavily depends on what this Value Proposition is. Be it an online service, then the Internet will be your channel, which results in low costs. Be it a tangible product, then it might be delivered through a retail shop with additional transport aspects. Or you might use both channels for the deliverance of your tangible product and for the after sale services.

Customer Relationships include the type of relation you maintain with each Customer Segment for each Value Proposition. Important is the expectation you create with your customer. Different customers expect different relationships, for example customers paying more expect more. Customer Relationships has great overlap with Customer Relationship Management (CRM), which also is about how you create an appealing environment in which the customer wants to identify himself and what a customer is willing to pay for that. Closely related to the Customer Interface of the business model is the value discipline 'Customer Intimacy' of Treacy & Wiersema (Treacy & Wiersema, 1995).

The Customer Interface for a certain Value Proposition is now described. But for the Value Proposition you offer to the customer, you want something in return. That is called the Revenue Stream. The Customer Interface of the business model needs to convert your offered Value Proposition into revenue. Those Revenue Streams might be the profits of selling products, renting products, transaction fees, advertising fees, subscription models, or even giving away a Value Proposition. The overview of the Revenue Stream for each Customer Segment and each Value Proposition gives insight in the contribution of the different Customer Segments to the total Revenue Stream. This might help in determining the effort you want to put into the value creation or capturing for each Customer Segment.

On the Asset Management side of the business model, first the Key Resources and Competencies block shows up. Here you need to describe which resource your corporation has internally, like human resources, building materials, and capital. They also might be your competences, like knowledge, data, or IT infrastructure. Some of these core capabilities might be increasingly difficult to measure, like your brand equity or expertise. You should ask yourself whether each resource is needed to create the Value Proposition you deliver. Your Key Resources and Competencies are highly accountable for how your corporation will sustain competitive advantage in how you gain differential access to these resources (Wernerfelt, 1984).

The Configuration of Key Activities is a highly accountable building block for sustaining competitive advantage in how you design your internal processes to create value for the customer, when they are difficult to imitate (Wernerfelt, 1984). This block determines the configuration of your Key Resources and Competencies mentioned in the previous building block. Having the right resources and competencies is one thing, but how to apply them to create a Value Proposition is another one.

Your Partner Network is the last building block on the infrastructure management side of the business model. This block determines who the partners and suppliers are that you work with to create your offered value. Therefore this block sometimes is called value network. This block gains importance since networks are increasingly important in today's economy, a network economy.

Also, the value chain is more and more becoming a value network, where the customer also might be someone helping on new product design. This block also determines which activities the corporation does by itself, and which activities should be in-sourced, or out-sourced to obtain the required resources for your Value Proposition. Finally the relation of your Value Proposition and that of other corporations is determined here, for example by finding complementary products that increase the value of your proposition. The Asset Management side of the business model is closely related with the value discipline 'Operational Excellence' of Treacy & Wiersema (Treacy & Wiersema, 1995). Not the partners themselves are part of the operations, but the ability to incorporate the necessary input of partners into your operations.

The costs of the running a business according to your business model is determined in the Cost Structure building block. Here, you can specialize the costs by sorting them in high to low order, and by referring them to other building blocks, like resources or Customer Segments. This way the profitability of a value offering can be determined. The Cost Structure also gives insight in the demanded prices of your offerings and the justification of target margins. Competing on 'costs' is another way defined by Porter in sustaining competitive advantage against your competitors (Porter, 1985). Notice that the financial result of your business is determined by the results of the Revenue Streams minus the results of the Cost Structure.

RELATING SOCIAL COMPUTING TO BUSINESS MODELS

This section will now extend upon the previous chapters. The idea is to look again to business models, only now with the Social Computing principles in mind. The aim of this section is to

see how Social Computing supports the different business model building blocks. Although the application of Social Computing in an organization often is referred to as Enterprise 2.0, according to McAfee (McAfee, 2006a), the school of Enterprise 2.0 limits itself to the intranet of the company. This chapter takes a broader perspective and examines both the internal and external environment of an organization, including both intranet and the Internet. This chapter therefore proposes to broaden the term Enterprise 2.0 accordingly.

Knol, Spruit and Scheper (2008) analyze a series of thirteen expert interviews to obtain more insight into the relationships between Social Computing principles and business model building blocks. Therefore, they asked experts to mark relations between them. Next, they analyzed these relations, clustered them in three groups and labeled those groups Open Collaboration, Lean Configuration, and User Value. Open Collaboration contains the Social Computing principles covering openness, accessibility, remixability, and interchangeability, as basis for collaboration without boundaries. Lean Configuration contains Social Computing principles relating to flexibility, scalability, and focus on all users. Finally, User Value contains Social Computing principles focusing on the users and how and what they contribute. They find which building blocks are most strongest related to the principles in each cluster. The first cluster highly supports both Customer Relationships and Partner Network. The next cluster mostly supports Customer Segments, Communication and Distribution Channels, and Configuration of Key Activities. The third cluster mostly supports Value Proposition, Customer Relationships, and Partner Network, considering the user might also be a partner. The three clusters reveal where the Social Computing principles most support the business model, see Figure 4. At these places most possibilities exist for business model innovation supported by Social Computing principles.

Figure 4. Social computing support for an organization mapped on a business model

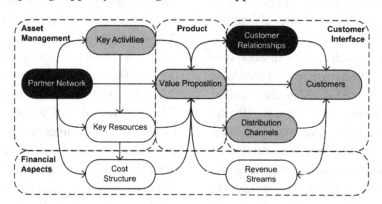

Application

Following Osterwalder (2005) we will use the music industry as a case to apply the Social Computing principles in business. The Value Proposition in the music industry can very well be created by the customer. When thinking of User Generated Content, it is the user himself who is enabled to create and share music. He is enabled to express himself online and share those expressions on open accessible platforms like MySpace, YouTube, and AmieStreet. The Intuitive Usability of these services makes them highly used. More Value Propositions will be invented, because of the ease of combining them; creating mash-ups. Since the music can be copied in a wink at hardly any costs, value goes to more one-of-a-kind experiences, which cannot be copied.

Next, it is also the user who selects the music he wants to hear. This can be very niche, since there are enough sources and access is easy. Customers are to be found in the Long Tail, small groups, or even individuals, with very diverse music tastes. Size is no restriction, there is enough supply. The musician can link to his work, his Value Proposition, share it, give it away, and so on. Many bands already did this: Radiohead puts their newest album online for free and just asks for a tip. Prince gave its new album away through a magazine. And there are more examples. The

Communication and Distribution Channels change from pushed distribution, to pulled discovery channels. Searching and finding is important. The availability of accessible work makes an artist better known, yielding more demand, so Network Effects appear. Distribution costs almost nothing.

The relationship between a musician and a customer becomes more individual. Customers become ambassadors of their favorite artist. Relationships occur in social networks. Because User Generated Content supports Customer Relationships, customers are involved in the music creation. The Collective Intelligence of customers is input for the artist. These sources can be approached since it becomes easy to contribute. Intuitive Usability is the basis for reaching those inputs. The Revenue Streams per song go down fast. Profit needs to be found on other aspects, adjacent stages of a music song. These stages probably will be more focused on experience, live concerts, merchandising, and other aspects of music which remain scarce. Music itself tends to be free, the transaction costs for it are too low to charge for it: Music becomes a commodity, because of an infinite supply and an infinite demand, and since barriers in transaction are taken away.

The artist will use other Key Resources to create his music. Not only his talent, but also his ability to use someone else's input becomes important. Other musicians and customers become important resources. An artist doesn't need a label anymore. He himself can aim on discovery by being active in proper networks. This becomes a Key Activity for an artist. Customers like personal experience. So the artist needs to be active in Open Platforms ensuring discovery. On these platforms the Partner Network can be found too, often being customers. They together have Collective Intelligence to help an artist create the proper Value Propositions. These platforms are the places where the Unbounded Collaboration occurs.

Because of his highly Lightweight Models, the artist isn't left behind with high costs. The needed infrastructural assets are easily achieved by subscription. For instance, Amazon S3 supplies him with hardware needed to store his musical works, online, easily accessible, easy to share, maintained by the provider. When not needed anymore, he just stops the subscription and doesn't stay with the hardware. Most of his costs become variable, making his business scalable.

Where does that leave the music labels? Some think new opportunities exist in full-servicing musicians. Not only finding talent and commercialize their work on CD's. But also taking care of the concerts, the merchandizing, the promotion, video's, producing, recording, and so on. Everything an artist needs should be covered by one company. Another option would be to seek new-markets. Most likely those markets will concern some experience, wanted by customers, and that cannot be copied.

CONCLUSION AND DISCUSSION

This chapter walked through a few steps. First, we showed that standards increase efficiency and interchangeability. Because of this efficiency, transaction costs, like searching and negotiating, will become lower, making it easier to share, create, and locate transactions containing a certain Value Proposition. Lower transaction costs therefore

are a main driver in the value of the Internet as a whole and Social Computing in particular.

Next, based on literature the main principles that underlie Social Computing were found. These principles first exist of technologically oriented ones, being Open Platform, Lightweight Models, Enabling Services, and Intuitive Usability. Next, social or user oriented principles are the Long Tail, Unbounded Collaboration, Collective Intelligence, Network Effects, and User Generated Content. These principles were validated in the interviews with Social Computing experts. Based on these findings Social Computing has been defined by this research as referring to a development where technologies enable empowerment of individuals, or groups of individuals, to express themselves in a more natural way, leading to easier creation, enriching, or finding of content.

Third, a business model was shortly described, based on recent literature, as a conceptual tool that contains a set of elements and relationships, and allows expressing the business logic of a specific firm. The different building blocks gave insight in how a business model can be designed and applied, with respect to a Value Proposition, the Customer Interface, the Asset Management, and the Financial Aspects. The business model was introduced to find a way to relate the found Social Computing principles to a tangible model representing the way of doing business.

Next, this chapter showed that the parts which are best supported by Social Computing are Customer Relationship and Partner Network. But also Value Proposition, Communication and Distribution Channels, and Configuration of Key Activities can be supportive in business. Many of those building blocks with a strong relation to Social Computing, connect the business to its environment, which is assumed to be the main reason why actually these building blocks can be supported with Social Computing. Recent developments show a standardization and commoditizing of ICT and its tools which will lead to lower transaction costs in the area of information transactions.

Most of these transactions take place between a company and its partners and customers, in the transformation from input to throughput, and from throughput and output of an organization. Next, partners, including customers, also can be of high value in co-creating a value proposition. This is because standardization and commoditizing make information sharing, finding, and enriching more accessible to individuals. Therefore, organizations should focus on those areas, for as Social Computing is most supportive there. It does need an adjustment of the key activities of a company, and an adjustment of the channels to reach the customers which can be assumed to be the main reason why those building blocks are affected as well by Social Computing. These building blocks especially do need thorough consideration for Social Computing support in a business model innovation process.

REFERENCES

Anderson, C. (2007). *The Long Tail, Why the Future of Business Is Selling Less of More*. New York: Hyperion Books.

Andrews, K. (1971). *The Concept of Corporate Strategy*. Homewood, IL: Dow Jones-Irwin, Inc.

Beckstrom, R., & Brafman, O. (2006). *The Starfish and the Spider, The Unstoppable Power of Leaderless Organizations*. London: Penguin Books.

Berners-Lee, T. (2007, March 1). The Future of the World Wide Web. *Hearing on the Digital Future of the United States before the United States House of Representatives Commitee on Energy and Commerce Subcommittee on Telecommunications and the Internet*. Cambridge, MA: Massachusetts Institute of Technology.

Boutin, P. (2006, March 29). Web 2.0 - The new Internet boom doesn't live up to its name. *Slate*. Retrieved January 15, 2008, from http://www.slate.com/id/2138951/

Brynjolfsson, E., Hu, Y. J., & Simester, D. (2007, November). Goodbye Pareto Principle, Hello Long Tail: The Effect of Search Costs on the Concentration of Product Sales. *SSRN*. Retrieved from http://ssrn.corn/abstract=953587

Brynjolfsson, E., Hu, Y. J., & Smith, M. D. (2003). Consumer Surplus in the Digital Economy: Estimating the Value of Increased Poduct Variety at Online Bookstores. *Managment Science, 49*(11).

Chesbrough, H. (2003). *Open Innovation: The New Imperative for Creating and Profiting from Technology*. Watertown, MA: Harvard Business School Press.

Chesbrough, H., & Rosenbloom, R. S. (2002). The Role of the Business Model in Capturing Value from Innovation: Evidence from Xerox Corporation's Technology Spin-off Companies. *Industrial and Corporate Change, 11*(3), 529–555. doi:10.1093/icc/11.3.529

Christensen, C., & Raynor, M. (2003). *The Innovator's Solution - Creating and Sustaining Successful Growth*. Boston: Harvard Business School Press.

Coase, R. H. (1937). The Nature of the Firm. *Economica, 4*(16), 386–405. doi:10.1111/j.1468-0335.1937.tb00002.x

Cordella, A. (2001). Does Information Technology Always Lead to Lower Transaction Costs? In *Proceedings of ECIS*, Bled, Slovenia.

Forrester. (2008). *Global Enterprise Web 2.0 Market Forecast - 2007-2013*.

Giles, J. (2005, December 15). Internet encyclopaedias go head to head. *Nature - International weekly journal of science*. Retrieved January 23, 2008, from http://www.nature.com/nature/journal/v438/n7070/full/438900a.html

Gladwell, M. (2000). *The Tipping Point: How Little Things can make a Big Difference*. Boston: Little, Brown and Company.

Graham, P. (2005, November). *Web 2.0.* Retrieved January 7, 2008, from http://www.paulgraham.com/web20.html

Hinchcliffe, D. (2005, September 24). The Web 2.0 Is Here. *Dion Hinchcliffe's Web 2.0 Blog.* Retrieved January 15, 2008, from http://web2.socialcomputingmagazine.com/web2ishere.htm

Hinchcliffe, D. (2006, April 2). The State of Web 2.0. *Dion Hinchcliffe's Web 2.0 Blog.* Retrieved November 12, 2007, from http://web2.socialcomputingmagazine.com/the_state_of_web_20.htm

Hinchcliffe, D. (2006, July 15). Web 2.0's Real Secret Sauce: Network Effects. *Dion Hinchcliffe's Web 2.0 Blog.* Retrieved January 23, 2008, from http://web2.socialcomputingmagazine.com/web_20s_real_secret_sauce_network_effects.htm

Hoegg, R., Martignoni, R., Meckel, M., & Stanoevska-Slabeva, K. (2006). Overview of business models for Web 2.0 communities. In [Dresden, Germany: Universität St. Gallen, Institute of Media and Communication Management.]. *Proceedings of GeNeMe, 2006,* 23–37.

IBM. (2006). Expanding the Innovation Horizon - The Global CEO Study 2006.

Katz, M. L., & Shapiro, C. (1985). Network Externalities, Competition, and Compatibility. *Teh American Economic Review, 75*(3), 424–440.

Keen, A. (2007). *The Cult of the Amateur: How Today's Internet is Killing Our Culture.* New York: Currency.

Knol, P., Spruit, M., & Scheper, W. (2008). Web 2.0 Revealed. In *Proceedings of the Seventh AIS SIGeBIZ Workshop on e-business (WeB 2008),* Paris.

Leadbeater, C. (2007). *We-Think: the power of mass creativity.* Retrieved from http://www.wethinkthebook.net.

Liebowitz, S. (2002). *Re-Thinking the Network Economy - The True Forces that Drive the Digital Marketplace.* New York: Amacom.

McAfee, A. (2006a). Enterprise 2.0: The Dawn of Emergent Collaboration. *MIT Sloan Management Review, 47*(3), 21–28.

McAfee, A. (2006b, March 24). The Trends Underlying Enterprise 2.0. *The Impact of Information Technology (IT) on Businesses and their Leaders.* Retrieved January 17, 2008, from http://blog.hbs.edu/faculty/amcafee/index.php/faculty_amcafee_v3/the_three_trends_underlying_enterprise_20/

McAfee, A., & Brynjolfsson, E. (2008, July/August). Investing in the IT That Makes a Competitive Difference. *Harvard Business Review.*

McKinsey. (2007). *How Business are using Web 2.0.*

McLuhan, M. (1964). *Understanding Media: The Extensions of Man.* New York: McGraw Hill.

Merton, R. K. (1968). The Matthew Effect in Science. *Science, 159*(3810), 56–63. doi:10.1126/science.159.3810.56

Metcalfe, R. (1980). Pup: An Internetwork Architecture. *IEEE Transactions on Communications, 28*(4), 612–624. doi:10.1109/TCOM.1980.1094684

Moore, G. A. (1991). *Crossing the Chasm: Marketing and Selling High-Tech Products to Mainstream Customers.* New York: Harper Business Essentials.

Nielsen, J. (1993). *Usability Engineering.* San Diego, CA: Academic Press.

O'Reilly, T. (2005, September 30). What is Web 2.0. *O'Reilly Media.* Retrieved July 4, 2007, from http://www.oreillynet.com/pub/a/oreilly/tim/news/2005/09/30/what-is-web-20.html

O'Reilly, T. (2006, December 10). Web 2.0 Compact Definition: Trying Again. *O'Reilly Radar.* Retrieved January 9, 2008, from http://radar.oreilly.com/archives/2006/12/web_20_compact.html

Osterwalder, A., Pigneur, Y., & Tucci, C. L. (2005). Clarifying Business Models: Origins, Present, and Future of the Concept. *Communications of the Association for Information Systems, 16,* 1–25.

Porter, M. (1985). *Competitive Advantage.* New York: Free Press.

Prahalad, C., & Ramaswamy, V. (2004). *The Future of Competition: Co-Creating Unique Value with Customers.* Boston, MA: Harvard Business School Press.

Rogers, E. M. (1962). *Diffusion of Innovations.* New York: Free Press.

Simon, H. (1991). Bounded Rationality and Organizational Learning. *Organization Science, 2*(1), 125–134. doi:10.1287/orsc.2.1.125

Surowiecki, J. (2004). *The Wisdom of the Crowds - Why the Many Are Smarter Than the Few and How Collective Wisdom Shapes Business, Economies Societies and Nations.* New York: Doubleday.

Tapscott, D., & Williams, A. D. (2007). *Wikinomics: How Mass Collaboration Changes Everything.* New York: Penguin.

Treacy, M., & Wiersema, F. (1995). *The Discipline of Market Leaders.* Reading, MA: Addison-Wesley.

Vossen, G., & Hagemann, S. (2007). *Unleashing Web 2.0, From Concepts to Creativity.* Burlington, MA: Morgan Kaufman Publishers.

Wernerfelt, B. (1984). A Resource-Based View of the Firm. *Strategic Management Journal, 5*(2), 171–180. doi:10.1002/smj.4250050207

Williamson, O. E. (1985). *The Economic Institutions of Capitalism - Firms, Markets, Relational Contracting.* New York: Free Press.

ENDNOTE

[1] We use the term *Social Computing* in this paper, since it covers both the technological and social aspects of the developments under discussion. Web 2.0 is popular, but rather biased, and strictly speaking not accurate; the developments we are talking about occur on Internet as a whole, and are thus broader than just the Web.

Chapter 10
Pricing Model Dynamics in the Chinese Online Game Market

Qun Ren
Bournemouth University, UK

Philip Hardwick
Bournemouth University, UK

ABSTRACT

This chapter examines how incumbent firms respond to the industrial pricing dynamics with the adjustment of their own pricing strategies so as to create and sustain their market share dominance. The empirical context of this chapter is the strategic behavior of online game operators (i.e. the companies who operate online games) in the Chinese online game market, one of the most active markets in the world with strong network effects. This chapter introduces Velu's business model theory in the market with strong networks. Further, in this research, the authors extend Velu's research by challenging some of his propositions by a careful observation of pricing dynamics in the Chinese online game industry since 2000 and how dominant and non-dominant incumbent firms adjust their pricing strategy. In the Findings Part, this paper explains why acquisition is regarded by main dominant game operators as the most effective way to complement their pricing model revolution.

INTRODUCTION

Background of the Research Problem

Pricing is generally recognized at the root of company philosophy and a company can be either as a price taker or price maker whose attitude to pricing may be passive or active (Winkler, 1983,

DOI: 10.4018/978-1-61520-623-0.ch010

Gabor, 1988). In the discipline of marketing, Product, Price, Promotion and Place (i.e.4Ps) are often referred to as the key elements of marketing mix. It is generally recognized that among the 4Ps, only price generate income while the rest involves cost (Fletcher & Russell-Jones, 1997). That is why in the competitions for customers, companies always utilise price as a tactical weapon since the effects of price are 'more immediate and direct, and appeals based on price are the easiest to communicate' (Rao, 1984, p. 39). Meanwhile, more and more academic and industrial professionals agree that 'price is a dangerously explosive and complex variable' (Oxenfeldt, 1973, p. 49). If the price is not right (i.e. too cheap or too dear), all the merchandising effort might be wasted, bring in new-product failure or even decrease the entire industry's profitability (Gabor, 1988, p.3, Simon, 1992). If prices are too cheap, sales are not problems any more, but the producer will worry how to accrue the profit. If they are too dear, sales will almost certainly suffer, and profits will fall as well (Fletche & Russell-Jones, N., 1997). In terms of this, more and more firms realize that 'price is a dangerously explosive and complex variable' and its sufficient importance and complexity merit strategic attention (Oxenfeldt, 1973, p. 49; Dutta et al., 2003).

Apart from the importance of price setting, pricing decisions are the most difficult ones to make in marketing as the company may be (1) subject to government regulations, (2) controlled by a price leader or (3) in the case of a distributor (4) lack kinds of resources needed. All above reasons and other uncertain variables are interrelated and constrained with each other, and even can vary between different pricing situations within the same company (Dorward, 1987, p.1). In addition, environmental pressures such as technology advancement, customers' increasingly unexpected demand for services and changes in legal and marketing context manifest the delicacy, complexity and importance of pricing.

Previous studies indicate that much academic research attention has been given to the issues of company pricing policy which concentrated on: how customers exchange value for benefit, pricing decision process and analysis of price variable natures and oligopoly pricing (Thaler, 1985; Farley et al., 1980; Monroe & Della Bitta, 1978; Rothschild, 1947). However, few academic attentions were paid to the pricing in managerial practice from the marketing point of view. Oxenfeldt (1973) regarded it as a 'gap between pricing literature and practice." Bonoma et al., (1988, p.359) pointed out that scholars failed to identify the complexity of price during the previous pricing study, and used to consider it as a single number. Besides, the dearth of published work of empirical study of pricing (Silberston, 1970) failed to win the recognition in practice and did not manage to offer enough advice to practitioners (Simon, 1982, p.23).

Three decades earlier, Monroe and Della Bitta (1978, p.413) stated that " a lack of descriptive research on pricing practice" can partly explain " the lack of creative development of new approaches to solve marketing problems". They then called for more qualitative research and more descriptive case studies for pricing study, which gained support from Ingenbleek (2002, pp. 161-162).

Diamantopoulos et al attributed the limited progress of pricing study to the misdirection of conventional price theory which "stimulated a search for end-state, universalistic and categorical explanations rather than contextual factors in an attempt to identify and explain variations in practices" (1991, p.137), while the company policy problems should have to resort to the study of inter-firm and inter-firm variations in pricing with the analysis of data collected at multiple organizational levels.

With the aim to turning theoretical pricing into more complex and more realistic, Dutta et al (2003) made efforts to overcome the above limitations. Their main contribution is the development of a resource-based perspective of the process by which prices in companies are determined. They suggest that pricing is a capability "which involves both capturing value and balancing competing interests within the firm". Their conclusion is that value creating resources firms should compete by investing in value-capturing resources. Following this resource-advantage theory, Ingenbleek (2002, p. 151) also explored how firms can develop successful pricing practice. He deducted that "value extraction is rooted in value creation except in markets with high demand uncertainty. In these markets capturing value is rooted in customer orientation."

Scope of the Research

The significance of pricing study is not only rooted in the general company philosophy but applies very well in the online game market, the increasingly popular Internet-based entertainment and service sector.

Early text-based or simply animated Virtual Worlds started with the emergence of first multi-user Dungeon (MUD) in the late 1970s. During the past few years, improvements in software and hardware, especially the internet-based technology speeded up the emergence of a number of highly sophisticated virtual worlds. Massively multiplayer online games (MMOGs) have been working as the pioneers in offering the millions of users the opportunities for entertainment, communication, collation and cooperation.

Right Time for Pricing Study in the Chinese Online Game Market

Pricing is the setting of a price for goods and services to be supplied to a third party. The types of organization that set prices include: manufacturers; service providers; intermediaries (e. g.: wholesalers); the public sector; and retailers (Fletcher & Russell-Jones, 1997). This study is intended to synthesise limited existing knowledge concerning the pricing model innovation of the Chinese online game industry, and specifically to develop a framework which demonstrates the dynamic nature of the pricing models. This research comes at a timely moment as:

1. Broadband has gained widespread penetration and the Internet is steadily growing as an entertainment medium in the world. In terms of this, the online game market, the young and robust interactive entertainment market is changing at a rapid pace throughout the world. COMSCORE, Inc., a global leader in measuring the global digital market released in July 2007 that 217[1] million people world-

wide (i.e., 28 per cent of all internet users) play online games. The study considered all sites that provide online or downloadable games but excluded gambling sites.

2. The Chinese online game industry has grown strongly over the past decade. The Asian online game market totalled around US$ 3 billion in 2006 and 33 per cent was from China.

3. The global online game industry is limited into two pricing models. In addition, and this industry is under the pricing model evaluation with the purpose to know whether the predominant pricing models can work appropriately and possess the capabilities to secure the revenue streams to sustain in the industry's future growth.

Online Game Operators' Approaches to Access the Game Sources

Presently, three different approaches to access the game sources are used by Chinese online game operators, i.e. self developing &operating approach; licensing, localizing and operating approach; self developing & licensing approaches that run parallel.

Self Developing-Operating Approach

1. Successful self-developing games can create healthy margins because the game operators do not need to pay upfront licensing fees. With the intellectual property under control, the online game operators can update the content and release the expanding packs quickly which are important components of a successful game's lifespan. NetEase is the pre-eminent example of this model in China.

2. Licensing-Localizing-Operating approach: Many game operators lack the R&D capability to develop their own games, so they count upon licensing-localizing-operating

approach as a key strategy for market entry and future competition. China's The9 is an example. The9 imported game titles with proven track records abroad. By comparison, even with little R&D cost to bear, the licensing fee is quite high and the margins are lower than those obtained by NetEase.

3. Self developing & licensing approach: Different from the above two approaches and represented by Shanda, the third approach is to use the combination of self developing and licensing. The approach aims at minimising the possible loss by some unprofitable games and trying to maintain the high margins.

Two Main Pricing Models in the Chinese Online Game Market

The pricing models in the Chinese online game market comprises of: traditional purchase fee models, subscription model, come-stay-play model (or: free-to-play model) which became prevailing since 2006 and in-game advertising model. As to the in-game advertising model, it is still in its initial stage and not widely used whose revenue is generated from the embedded-advertisements. Here I will introduce the two main pricing models in the Chinese Online Game Market.

1) Time-based pricing model

Chinese online game industry began to take off in 2001. Till 2005, the top two Chinese online game companies, Internet portal NetEase.com Inc and Shanda Interactive Entertainment Ltd, dominated 57 percent of the -market share and shaping the Chinese online game industry (Morgan Stanley, 2005). Prior to 2005, nearly all MMORPGs were under a pay-to-play model, which is also called "time-based pricing" or subscription-based model. Under this model, game players purchase pre-paid cards to play for a fixed number of hours or for an unlimited amount of time within a specified number of days. The pioneer of the Chinese online game industry, Shanda developed this pre-paid

card (or called Point card) which was hard to duplicate and became the first Chinese online game operator who successfully adopted this subscription-based model and was followed by other Chinese online game operators.

2) Item-based pricing model

17 Games, a business unit of CDC Corporation (NASDAQ: CHINA) is the first fiPM in China to adopt another pricing model, "free-to-play, pay-for-merchandise" model when operating a gamed named Yulgang in China in July 2005. Currently, this model is also called "Free-of-charge model", "virtual item sales model" or "item-based pricing model". Shanda prefers to call it "Come-Stay-Pay", or CSP, pricing model. Under the Free-to-Play model, users are able to play the basic functions of an MMORPG for free and may choose to purchase in-game value-added services, including certain in-game items and premium features, which enhance the game experience.

In this paper, the authors regard these two models as "time-based pricing model" and "item-based pricing model" respectively.

Starting from 2006, the China online game market kept transforming from the exclusively time-based pricing model to the item-based model. It is the second time that Shanda acts as the most influential driver in the Chinese online game market for the business model innovation. An increasing number of online game operators have followed suit and announced to operate their games under the item-based model. According to statistics from IDC[2] China, over 80 percent of online games on the Chinese market have adopted the free-to-play model, relying on virtual item sales to generate money[3]. It is also revealed that only 13 percent of game players play time-based billing games[4].

2007 was a landmark for the Chinese online game industry and in this year, 4 online game companies in China were listed in HKSE, NASDAQ and NYSE. Several other online game companies such as 9You, Netdragon and Suzhou Snail are on their way for getting listed abroad. Shi Yuzhu, CEO of Giant summarized that whole industry market revenue increased by 70 percent annually during the past three years, which was due to the successful transformation of the pricing model. The shift of business model not only strengthened the mature game operators, but speeded up the growth of the new operators.

In middle 2007 and early 2008, NetEase and The9, who had stuck with the use of time-based pricing model, began to apply item-based pricing model into their new games.

LITERATURE REVIEW

Traditional Pricing under Different Forms of Competition

Economists have long been investigating the issue of price determination by firms. For many years, profit maximization was traditionally assumed to be the single goal of the firm, and scholar of economics concentrated their pricing study on the type of market in which the firm operates. According to the traditional economies, the decisions about the quantity to produce and the price to charge are under different forms of competition. Perfect competition, monopolistic competition, oligopoly all confronts the firm with their special problems. (Parkin, Powell & Matthews, P.202). As a result, a certain number of different models, especially those aiming at investigating the interactions in the context of game theory, have been put forward, (Skouras et al., 2005). Though the above market structure theories are well recognized and widely collected in the textbooks of the discipline of economics, Harvard Law Review (2001) point out that this empirical market structure theory is only applicable to the traditional manufacturing.

Based on the economic competition theory, following Marshall (1920), lots of economist from the branch of industrial economics focus their

research contribution on investigating economies of scales, barriers to entry or exit from a market, governmental intervention through prices and other factor controls, product differentiation (Chamberlin, 1933; Mason, 1939; Bain 1956; Bain 1959; McGee, 1988; Scherer, 1980; Tirole, 1989). However, the traditional economy theory seems doesn't work very well in the Internet-based new economy in general and in online game sector in particular.

Limitations of Traditional Economy Theory

1. Zero Marginal Cost in New Economy

Atkinson (2002) put forward the definition of New Economy", which has the similar meaning with. New Economy is referred to "a combination of technological developments- powerful personal computers, high-speed telecommunications, and the Internet – which has created a new market environment.

As a disruptive technology, Internet has threatened the basis of companies in the traditional economy and brought big changes in the links of their value chain (such as: service and distribution channels). According to Harvard Law Review (2001), nothing is newer than the existence of information goods. "The technological revolution impacts the cost and distribution of such goods in a way that fundamentally alter how their purveyors must operate." Detailed difference lies in the concept divergence between new economy and traditional economy, such as the concept of "returns" and "marginal cost".

The traditional understanding of the market economy was based largely upon the assumptions of diminishing returns (Harvard Law Review, 2001, p. 1623). That is to say, "Products or companies that get ahead in a market eventually run into limitations, so that a predicable equilibrium of prices and market shares is reached. (Arthur, 1998)". Contrary to traditional goods, the costs of innovation and product development in new economy are extremely high. However, what usually follow the high initial fixed costs are the negligible marginal costs associated with mass-production. For example, it is normal to take millions of dollars to produce a DVD, while the digital reproduction and DVD distribution cost virtually nothing. Another example is, it normally took a software developer millions of dollars to develop a software application while the copy selling to customers is almost zero because this software is posted on the web free for customers to download.

The cost structure in new economy has made the traditional understanding of market eroded because firms can enjoy increasing rather than diminishing returns. Increasing returns and low unit cost create the potential for vast economies of scale, which give larger firms a market advantage and make new entrants harder to compete.

2.   Cost-Based Pricing vs. Value-Based Pricing

Historically, cost-plus pricing is the most common pricing procedure because it is achieved by pricing every product or service to yield a return over all costs (Nagel & Holden, 2002). With respect to the traditional pricing, its price setting often is based on a percentage mark-up form the marginal cost. However, the financial prudence of the traditional cost-plus pricing is ineffective to information goods, because the marginal cost per unit is close to zero. Value-based pricing emphasizes the customer value and its role in pricing strategy. Also, if a company is going to set prices based on value, it has to decide whether it chooses to serve only customers willing to pay or will it try to serve multiple segments at different price points?

3.   Increasing Free Services in New Economy

Apart from the zero marginal cost of digital manufacturing, distribution – one of the main scarcities of traditional economics is always offered free. Besides, everything that web technology touches comes closer to free. YouTube is free; search engines of Google, Yahoo and MSN are free; Web-based mail accounts of GoogleMail, Yahoo! are free. Virtual goods have lots of differences with the physical products in the physical world due to the unique properties of the Internet. Internet has the capability to eliminate geographic distance and deliver information and content to the customer instantaneously. A person can play games with friends and relatives or anyone from thousands miles away. Distance is no longer a drawback to belonging to a community. The time moderator also suggests that groups do not have to meet at the same time.

Milton Friedman pointed out quite often "There is no such thing as a free lunch." Echoing Friedman's conclusion, Anderson (2008) clarified that free product doesn't mean that someone is not earning money." In his opinion, the basic view of market concerns two parties-buyers and sellers. However, "the most common of economies built around free is the three-party system". This is why traditional economy theory cannot be used to explain the free services offered by web technology. Further, he uses the example of the newspapers to explain the "three-party market". The publishers do not charge readers anything for paying back the actual cost of creating, printing and distributing. Rather, they are selling readers to advertisers. Afuah and Tucci (2001) stated, "Most media/content suppliers have been satisfied to give away their content for free, raise the number of 'eyeballs (the number of unique viewers) and pin their hopes on an advertising model. Some sell complementary goods and make money from that rather than the content."

Empirical Academic Achievement Presented in the Online Game Context

MacInnes (2005) designed a four-stage dynamic business model framework for the Chinese online game industry and he summarized factors that affected a company's business model at its different stages. But it should be noticed that what he concerns about is not pricing strategy dynamics but product innovations.

Little empirical research on the pricing strategy dynamicss in game industry was available until the arrival of **DiGRA 2007: Situated Play Conference** in Tokyo in 2007 (Nojima, 2007; Lin & Sun, 2007; Ström, & Ernkvist, 2007). However, most of their discussions are related to discuss the relationship between pricing models and game player motions.

How to make a rational pricing model option is a challenging task that companies with different market dominance in the Chinese online game market have to confront. A widely held view is that "dominance and profits maintain a static relationship and dominant incumbents are less innovative than non-dominant incumbents because of the need to protect their traditional business model" (Conner, 1988; Dasgrupta, & Stiglize, 1980, Nault, et al., 1996). Velu verified that "The dominant firm is more innovative and the power to influence the success of a new business model from the strong network effects of the installed customer base makes the dominant firm commit to a particular narrow investment." He further proposed that less dominant firms tended to diversify their investments due to the threat of lock-out as a result of their weaker ability to influence the success of the investment. All his propositions are supported by the investment strategies of the incumbent dealer banks in the US fixed income market in the years 1995-2000, another industry with strong network effects.

Here, the authors aim to extend Velu's research by challenging some of his propositions and the research targets are the Chinese online game operators with different market dominance levels.

RESEARCH QUESTIONS

This research is intended to investigate the drivers of pricing strategy dynamics in the Chinese online game market and to explain the relationship between the companies' market dominance, the timing and the way they innovate their pricing models. And the authorswill explore the determinants of pricing strategy dynamics from perspectives of Chinese online game companies with different market dominance.

RESEARCH METHODS

Data are collected through multiple methods in this study. Secondary quantitative data are from online games' annually and quarterly financial reports while qualitative measurement keeps the original quality of the data. Dozens of semi-structured face-to-face interviews with sampled Chinese online game operators were held in Phase 2 with CEOs, professional game developers and marketing managers. The specific characteristic of "to be operated online" indicates that some related information may be available from each company's website.

FINDINGS

It seems that item-based billing become prevailing and time-based pricing model are obsolete according to the introduction in 1.2.3. However, some dominant game operators began to adopt the time-based pricing model in 2008. According to the official secondary data, the innovation trend in the Chinese online game market can be summarized into the following two points (See Table 1).

Relationship between Market Dominance and Pricing Strategy Dynamics

According to the data collected by questionnaire survey and official secondary data, the innovation trend in the Chinese online game market can be summarized into the following two points.

Stage 1 (2004- early 2008): Revolutionary pricing strategy (shifting from time-based model to item-based model). Revolutionary pricing strategy emerged with the adoption of item-based billing by three less dominant operators firstly. However, their pricing model revolution was not influential until dominant operator Shanda applied this model into its three games in the end of 2004 and took the lead in the whole country. With the announcement of NetEase to adopt item-based billing in 2008, no game operator in China regards time-based billing as its only pricing model.

Stage 2 (2008-): Emergence of diversifying pricing models. Since the beginning of 2008, several game operators announced to combine time-based billing as one of their pricing models. Except iyoyo.com, other operators such as Shanda, Giant, Perfect World and Kingsoft are all dominant operators in terms of their yearly revenue in 2007. It should be noticed they all innovated their item-based pricing model more or less so as to make this pricing model more efficient. In addition, Kingsoft put forward the credit-based pricing model. Another pricing model, Internal-game advertisement (IGA) has aroused the interest of many companies. Presently, both credit-based model and IGA model are still in their initial stages. Here are the detailed measures:

- In April 2008, Perfect world announced to offer a totally free game Hot Dance Party with the intention to "pay back the support of its game players."
- In May 2008, Kingsoft tried credit-based purchasing system for The First Myth 2 in May for its open-beta testing and Kingsoft will utilize time-based pricing model for its forthcoming Sword Online III at the end of 2008.
- In July 2008, Shanda announced to adopt time-based pricing model for its new game Chang Chun;
- In July 2008, Giant announced to apply three versions of its game ZT online. One version is item-based, one is time-based

Table 1. Relationships between market dominance & pricing strategy dynamics

	Pricing model changes	Pricing model Change Procedures
Stage 1: (2004-early 2008) Revolutionary pricing strategy dynamics	Time-based pricing model (TBPM) ↓ Item-based pricing model (IBPM)	Period 1: IBPM was Adopted by 3 less dominant companies without much notice. o Gamania (Game:Jushang), Sept 01, 2004; o Happydigi (Game:Tantra), Dec 15, 2004; o CDC (Game: Yulgang), May 13, 2005
		Period 2: Top 1 company Shanda adopted IBPM for its 3 games in Nov 2005, and followed by most less dominant game companies (2006-2007); No.3 company, Giant Interactive, founded in November 2004, is the company who benefited most from the item-based pricing model. By operating its own developed item-based game ZT Online in January 2006, it became the 3rd largest game company in China and successfully publicly listed in New York Stock Exchange in November 2007.
		Period 3: The last 2 dominant companies who adopted IBPM o The9 (one of the Top 5), May 2007; o NetEase (No.2 company), Early 2008
Stage 2:(early 2008-p resent) Evolutionary pricing strategy dynamics	Mixed pricing models (TBPM+ +IBPM + possible other models)	Top 10 dominant companies who adopted MPM o Perfect World (one of the Top 5 companies) (April, 2008); o KingSoft (one of the Top 10 companies) (May 2008); o Shanda (July 2008); o Giant (July 2008); Less dominant company who adopted DPM o Iyoyo.com(out of the top 10 companies) (July 2007)

and one is item-based pricing model with a big evolution.

- Iyoyo.com announced its game SANGO would combine four pricing models in the same game in the summer 2008. (Such as: item-based area, time-based area, PK area and the strength competition area).

The above phenomena indicate that Velu's theory doesn't apply very well in the Chinese online game market.

What Dominant Game Operators have Done for Acquiring R&D Capabilities?

In January 2009, Giant Interactive announced the launch of a "Win@Giant" incubation program aimed at attracting talents in areas including game design, project management, programming and art. Company chairman and CEO Shi Yuzhu said that the platform will offer participants capital, technical and operational support, as well as additional staff, nationwide promotions and 20% of profit if their games are successful, Mr. Shi set the plan and would like to contact teams and exchange ideas face to face when necessary.

In 2007, Shanda launched its "Feng Yun Plan" and "18 Plan" with the capital scale of PMB 2 billion (US$263.09 million) for acquiring game-development talents to reinforce the company's capability to develop new games.

In 2008, The9 Ltd planned to use its cash in hand nearly USD 300 million cash for investments and acquisitions of R&D firms within one year so as to shift into a research-oriented company from cyber game agency.

In 2008, TQ Digital, expressed a preference for acquisitions, and planned to use 49% of capital financed by the stock market for acquisitions and cooperation with other firms.

Following its significant shareholding increase in 17game to 100% in 2005, CDC in 2007 acquired OPTIC's Shanghai Division which has highly synergistic products and delivery capabilities.

Perfect World spent $3 million for a minority stake in online game developer Chengdu Seasky Digital Entertainment Co., Ltd in April 2008. In May 2007, Kingsoft invested RMB 10 million in a joint venture project with online game research and development studio Lianking and acquired a Dalian-based game company for RMB 30.30 million on May 27, 2008.

Dominant Operators' New Hot Acquisition Targets

Established in 2004, Giant listed successfully in NYSE in 2007 with the operation of its only self-developed game ZT online and its market dominance ranks No.3 in the Chinese online game market. CEO of Giant, Shi Yuzhu, has his unique opinion on the two types of acquisition targets: online game companies that have reputed strengths, or community Web sites that are able to help Giant Interactive carry out online game communalization. In July 2008, Giant paid $ 51 million to buy 25% stake in blog community 51.com. 51.com is China's largest independent social network website with total users of around 120 million as of June 15 2008. Further more, Giant plans to invest $ 800 million for future acquisitions. Giant's stake purchase in 51.com is expected to bring along a convergence between online game s and social network communities and Giant is at the forefront of the trend.

Strategic Alliances with Different Platforms

Comparing with dominant game operators, less dominant ones usually do not have their own platforms. Their capabilities in game operating and the channel exploration for game distributing are comparatively weak. Instead of waiting for being acquired or swallowed by big game operators, Chengdu's Dreamworks set up strategic alliances with Baidu and Shanda. Dreamworks offer self-developed game, maintenance and customer service. Baidu and Shanda are responsible for operating the games and exploring the distribution channels. The strategic alliance enabled the profit of Dreamworks over RMB 60 million in 2007. Its revenues in 2008 are expected to exceed RMB 0.1 billion. In summary, the success of Dreamworks indicates the feasibility and validity for less dominant game operators to cooperate with dominant ones.

CONCLUSION AND RECOMMENDATIONS

One of the hottest topics discussed by the Chinese online game industry is whether should each company change company's pricing strategy, when and how to change within the constant changing context of constant industrial pricing dynamics. Changes are unavoidable since the tastes of game players tend to change constantly and unexpectedly. They always try to satisfy themselves by exiting one game and joining another which is more attractive, which explains why each company has to what is the most efficient pricing strategy: i.e. whether to innovate an existing pricing model radically or making the existing pricing models more efficient. In addition, companies with different market dominance are busy in using different strategies in terms of their unique features. By comparison, dominant companies with rich cash flows prefer to use acquisitions as the quickest way to acquire game-development talents to reinforce the company's capability to develop new games. It is not hard to find out that all above efforts aim to extend the life cycles of their games, capture more players who are willing to pay. In one word, the suitable way is customer-oriented and manages to give what customers want. If there is something that can make game players enjoy, they will eventually pay for it. Authors believe that who can get the technology and talents ear-

lier will hold more opportunities in the competition. The authors also agree that game operators should try to explore customer segmentation so as to guarantee its game product segmentation. Games without value in design differentiation or companies without operation differentiation will be eliminated.

REFERENCES

Afuah, A., & Tucci, C. (2001). *Internet Business Models and Strategies, text and cases*. New York: McGraw-Hill/Irwin.

Anderson, C. (2008). *Free! Why $0.00 is the Future of Business*. Retrieved from http://www.wired.com/techbiz/it/magazine/16-03/ff_free

Arthur, W. B. (1998). Increasing Returns and the New World of Business. *The Knowledge Economy*, 75.

Atkinson, R. D. (2002). *The 2002 State New Economy Index-Benchmarking Economic Transformation in the States*. Retrieved from http://www.neweconomyindex.org/states/2002

Bain, J. S. (1956). *Barriers to New Competition*. Cambridge, MA: Harvard University Press.

Bain, J. S. (1959). *Industrial Organization*. New York: John Wiley & Sons.

Bonoma, T. V., Crittenden, V. L., & Dolan, R. J. (1988). Can the authors have Rigor and Relevance in Pricing Resarch? In Devinney, T. M. (Ed.), *Issues in Pricing: theory and research* (pp. 337–359). Toronto, Canada: Lexington Books.

Chamberlin, E. H. (1933). *Theory of Monopolistic Competition*. Boston, MA: Harvard University Press.

Conner, K. R. (1988). Strategies for product cannibalism. *Strategic Management Journal*, 9, 9–26. doi:10.1002/smj.4250090704

Conner, K. R. (1988). Strategies for product cannibalism. *Strategic Management Journal, 9*, 9–26. doi:10.1002/smj.4250090704

Dasgrupta, P., & Stiglize, J. (1980). Uncertainty, industrial structure and speed of R&D. *The Bell Journal of Economics, 11*(1), 1–28. doi:10.2307/3003398

Dorward, N. (1987). *The Pricing Decision: economic theory and business practice*. London: Harper & Row.

Dutta, S., Abaracki, M. J., & Bergen, M. (2003). Pricing Process as a Capability: a resource-based perspective. *Strategic Management Journal, 24*(7), 615–630. doi:10.1002/smj.323

Farley, J. U., Hulbert, J. M., & Weinstein, D. (1980). Price Setting and Volume Planning by two European Industrial Companies: a study and comparison of decision processes. *Journal of Marketing, 44*(1), 46–54. doi:10.2307/1250033

Flecther, T., & Russell-Jones, N. (1997). *Value Pricing: How to maximize profits through effective pricing policies*. London: Kogan Page.

Gabor, A. (1988). *Pricing: Concepts and Methods for Effective Pricing*. Aldershot, UK: Gower.

Ingenbleek, P. (2002). *Money for Value: pricing from a resource-advantage perspective*. PhD Tilburg University.

Lin, H., & Sun, C. (2007). Cash Trade within the Magic Circle: Free-to-Play Game Challenges and Massively Multiplayer Online Game Player Responses. In *Proceedings of DiGRA 2007: Situated Play*, The University of Tokyo, September, 2007 (pp. 335-343).

MacInnes, I. (2005). Dynamic Business Model Framework for Emerging Technologies. *International Journal of Services Technology and Management, 6*(1). doi:10.1504/IJSTM.2005.006541

Marshall, A. (1920). *Industry and Trade*. London: Macmillan.

Mason, E. S. (1939, March). Price and production policies of large-scale enterprise. *The American Economic Review, 29*, 61–74.

McGee, J. S. (1988). *Industrial Organization*. New York: Prentice-Hall.

Monroe, K. B., & Della Bitta, A. J. (1978). Models for Pricing Decisions. *JMR, Journal of Marketing Research, 15*(3), 413–428. doi:10.2307/3150590

Nagle, T., & Holden, R. (2002). *The strategy and Tactics of Pricing: a guide to Profitable Decision Making* (3rd ed.). Upper Saddle River, NJ: Prentice Hall.

Nault, B. R., & Vandenbosch, M. B. (1996). Eating your own lunch: protection through preemption. *Organization Science, 7*(3), 342–358. doi:10.1287/orsc.7.3.342

Nojima, M. (2007). Pricing models and Motivations for MMO play. In *Proceedings of DiGRA 2007: Situated Play*, The University of Tokyo, September, 2007 (pp. 672-681).

Oxenfeldt, A. R. (1973). A Decision-making Structure for Price Decisions. *Journal of Marketing, 37*(1), 48–53. doi:10.2307/1250774

Parkin, M., Powell, M., & Matthews, K. (2002). *Economics* (6th ed.). Harlow, UK: Pearson Education Ltd.

Rao, V. R. (1984). Pricing Research in Marketing: the State of the art. *The Journal of Business, 57*(1), 39–60. doi:10.1086/296235

Review, H. L. (2001). Antitrust and the Information age, Section 2: Monopolization. *Analyses in the New Economy, 114*, 1623–1646.

Rothschild, K. W. (1947). Price Theory and Oligopoly. *The Economic Journal, 57*(227), 299–320. doi:10.2307/2225674

Silberston, A. (1951). The Pricing of Manufactured Products: a comment. *The Economic Journal*, *61*(242), 426–429. doi:10.2307/2226968

Skouras, T., Avlonitis, G. F., & Indounas, K. (2005). Economics and Marketing: How and Why Do They Differ? *Journal of Product and Brand Management*, *14*(6), 362–374. doi:10.1108/10610420510624512

Stanley, M. (2005). *China Internet - Creating Consumer Value in Digital China*. Retrieved from http://www.morganstanley.com/institutional/techresearch /pdfs/China_Internet_091205.pdf

Ström, P., & Ernkvist, M. (2007). The unbound network of product and service interaction of the MMOG industry: with a case study of China. In *Proceedings of DiGRA 2007: Situated Play*, The University of Tokyo, September, 2007 (pp. 639-649).

Thaler, R. (1985). Mental Accounting and Consumer Choice. *Marketing Science*, *4*(3), 199–214. doi:10.1287/mksc.4.3.199

Tirole, J. (1989). *The Theory of Industrial Organization*. Cambridge, MA: MIT Press.

Velu, C. (2005). *Business Model Innovation in Network Markets*. Cambridge, MA: Cambridge University.

ENDNOTES

[1] The data is available from: http://www.comscore.com/press/release.asp?press=1521, Worldwide Online Gaming Community Reaches 217 Million People, Andrew Lipsman, July 2007

[2] IDC is the premier global provider of market intelligence, advisory services, and events for the information technology, telecommunications, and consumer technology markets. IDC helps IT professionals, business executives, and the investment community make fact-based decisions on technology purchases and business strategy. More than 900 IDC analysts provide global, regional, and local expertise on technology and industry opportunities and trends in over 90 countries worldwide. For more than 43 years, IDC has provided strategic insights to help our clients achieve their key business objectives.

[3] The data is available from: The data is available from: http://tech.sina.com.cn/i/2007-12-14/15431914192.shtml

[4] The data is available from: http://game.zol.com.cn/96/967321.html

Chapter 11
Impact of Classroom Technologies on Individual Learner Attitude:
A Case Based Analysis of Introducing IT within the Qatari Education Sector

Salaheldin Ismail Salaheldin
Qatar University, Qatar

Khurram Sharif
Qatar University, Qatar

ABSTRACT

The study aims to uncover the influence of classroom technologies (i.e. a variety of audio-visual and online equipment) on an individual's (i.e. student's) learning attitude. The antecedents that were considered relevant in the early post implementation phase were: (1) experience with Information and Communication Technologies, (2) enhanced communications, (3) learner independence and (4) ease of technology use. The original concept for the research was derived from Technology Acceptance Model (TAM) which has been a source of numerous studies exploring user attitude towards technology. The outcome indicated a positive and significant relationship between learner independence and individual learner attitude; enhanced communications and individual learner attitude and ease of technology use and individual learner attitude. However the relationship between ICTs experience and individual learner attitude was non-significant. The study outcome implicated that use of classroom technologies, in the introduction stage, does increase with the degree of perceived and encountered ease of use and extended capacity for self-directed learning.

DOI: 10.4018/978-1-61520-623-0.ch011

RESEARCH BACKGROUND

State of Qatar has grown exponentially economically and technologically. A particular and vigorous emphasis has been placed on Information Technology (IT) developments especially within the domain of infrastructure improvements. The Qatari government sector has been proactive in bringing IT based initiatives and IT driven changes which are permeating numerous public and private areas. Prime example is the establishment of *Hakoomi* (an Internet platform) which contains information related to ministries, councils and authorities; it contains economic data about businesses and enterprises; it has channels for paying utility bills and traffic violations; it has facility to apply for online visa and may other similar initiatives. *Hakoomi* is often labeled as virtual government as it provides a number of federal and public services. Another area receiving considerable attention is education. A distinct example of these efforts is establishment of *education city* where world renowned universities (such as Weill Cornell Medical College, Carnegie Mellon University, Texas A & M University, Georgetown University) have set-up their branch campuses. These universities display some of the most advance and cutting edge educational technologies in the world. However within this rapid pace of IT developments, the impact of this change on the user has been seldom evaluated. Key questions such as ease of technology use, frequency of use, quality of experience, degree of independence, nature and level of post implementation support service have been somewhat ignored. Within the presented case study, the emphasis will be on educational technology (especially smart classrooms) and how it is perceived and received by the users. Our specific area of study will be the Qatari public education sector as it is being transformed by the introduction and application of up-to-date and modern technology with the prime aim of giving more control, and choices to the users which will help them to enhance and enrich their learning

experiences. Is this really the case is what we will endeavor to explore in this study.

In today's teaching (and learning) age, an instructor equipped with a textbook and a blackboard is no longer the sole source of educational experience. In particular, technological advancements made post 2000 provided educators and learners with new tools to support in-class instruction and coursework. Hence integrating technology into classrooms is a growing initiative that is becoming an important part of educational culture and university life (Bratina, 2002; Wiley 2001). For instance, California's educational budget provided a total of $433 million in 2003 to increase the use of technology in schools and universities. In 2008 United States provided $273 million funding to secondary and high schools to support the deployment and integration of educational technology into classroom instruction. Classroom Technology is the collection of software, hardware and processes which facilitate learning (and teaching) and thus impact (mostly positively) learner's attitude and performance (Govindasamy 2002; Khan 2000). Similarly, learner attitude is defined as the impact or influence of classroom technology on student's disposition towards learning and this can be positive, negative or neutral (meaning no change).

From September 2007 to September 2008, a public University in Qatar was fitted with classroom technology with the prime aim of creating an interactive and conducive learning environment. Within this context the issues that were considered pertinent in initial post-implementation stage, as far as learner attitude was concerned, were:

- experience with basic Information and Communications Technologies ICTs) and their effect on learner (Liaw et al., 2007).
- broadening of classroom technology initiated communications channels and its impact on learning and absorbing abilities of students (Urden & Weggen, 2000).

- level of learning independence created through use of classroom technologies (Cuban, 1993).
- level of difficulty related to both the operational (know how to use) and situational (in working order) aspects of classroom technologies (Bannan-Ritland et al., 2000; Singh, 2000).

Consequently the prime focus of this study is on introduction of an assortment of classroom technologies (i.e. a combination of audio-visual equipment and online systems) within a university (i.e. higher education) and their impact on the learner attitude. According to a number of academics in the educational technologies field through the implementation of educational technology, student attitude tends to improve and they are also better prepared to enter and succeed in the digital workplace (Chen et al., 2005; Liaw, 2004). Similarly, many collaborative learning theories

Table 1. Perception of learners regarding classroom technologies and their impact on learning

Statements	% respondents
Ehances visual and verbal experience	54
Clarity in teacher's explanation	35
Creates a virtual student	28
Integration of multiple learning sources	22
Helps with illustration of complex examples	20
Students can work at their own pace	17
Improves level of interest in the subject	13
Students can prepare lesson in advance and do extra research	9
Helps students to express themselves more clearly in presentations	7
Helps create an interactive learning environment	4
Helps concentration as lecturer is not writing and speaking at the same time	3
Lecturer's body language becomes more expressive	3

Note: The % respondents does not add up to 100%

argue that human interaction is a vital ingredient to learning and classroom technologies tend to increase the bandwidth of face-to-face (especially written and gestural) communication avenues which creates an exchange environment where information is shared and enriched through application of classroom technologies (Liaw & Huang, 2003; Bharati, 2003). These views raise a number of questions namely: Do classroom technologies create a platform for enhanced communications? Do classroom technologies provide new channels for information acquisition and exchange? Do classroom technologies help learner with self-directed learning by accessing relevant materials on their own? With these questions in sight and forming the research objective, the investigation examined the impact of classroom technologies (which included a combination of laptop, overhead projector, document camera, DVD player, speakers, video-conferencing facility and in-class wireless internet access) on learner attitude.

As exploratory research, two focus groups (one for male and one for female students) were conducted to identify the key variables of classroom technology-related learner attitude (see Table 1). This helped with the selection of key antecedents (i.e. ICT experience, Learner Independence, Enhanced Communications and Ease of technology use) and consequence (Individual learner attitude) that constituted the research model (see Figure 1).

LITERATURE REVIEW

Classroom learning within higher education involves different instruction contexts, practical activities, and variety of course assessments coupled with guidance and direction in the form of mentoring and teaching. Within this specific learning context, simulated and virtual environments (partly based on and driven by classroom technologies) provide the capability and means to create problem-solving groups and communities in which participants can gain knowledge and

Figure 1. Research model

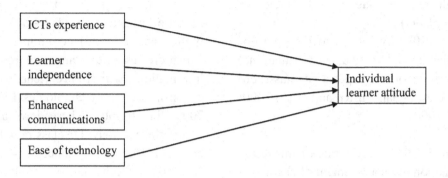

skills through interacting with other participants and different sources of relevant information. The use of classroom technologies tend to improve the quality of learning by involving learners in virtual and face-to-face exchange environments and by facilitating better access to educational resources such as internet and electronic library (Saade & Bahli, 2005). Hence university learning in digital space (and classroom technologies are part of it) can lead to enhanced learning experience largely due to opening up of student's environment (Mun & Hwang, 2003).

Among many factors that can influence the extent of individual learning include factors such as student learning style (independent or dependent), learner channels of information acquisition and exchange, familiarity with information technology and learner motivation (Stokes, 2001). Classroom technology can offer focused and clear instruction and hence can target specific needs of the learner. Furthermore, positive user attitude and user acceptance (based on previous experience of and indulgence with ICTs) have been considered as critical factors that contribute to the successful application and implementation of classroom technologies (Venkatesh et al., 2002). In addition, educational research argue that classroom technologies provides learners with elaborate and faster access to information, allows for more individualized and personalized instruction, and accommodates different learning styles. It is also

reported that classroom technologies not only promotes greater student involvement in learning but also generates more individual responsibility for learning (Wang, 2003).

Appropriately used, classroom technology can help students acquire the skills they need to flourish and develop in complex and increasingly technical and knowledge-based economies. Effective technology integration, into the classroom, should happen across the curriculum in such a way that it deepens and enhances the learning process. In particular, it should support three key components of learning: active engagement, participation in groups and frequent interaction and feedback (Rosenberg, 2001). Effective technology integration is achieved when the use of technology is routine and transparent and when technology supports course objectives. For instance learning through field projects while equipped with technology (such as a laptop, loaded with SPSS, for data collection and analysis) allows students to be intellectually challenged while providing them with a realistic experience and a snapshot of what the modern workplace looks like where most students will end up eventually.

Hence a primary goal in utilizing a new medium of communication for educational delivery should be the identification of its impact on learning. A number of theorists (to include Hemlo, 1993; Brown et al., 1989; Bostrom et al., 1990) have argued that the structure of typical traditional classrooms discourages the kinds of learning necessary for the 21st century. It is time to reengineer the educational field by adopting new and innovative ways of creating effective and efficient teaching and learning atmospheres that will better prepare the human resource to enter the professional arena of the 3rd millennium. To achieve this transformation, a growing number of courses in higher and further education are being delivered using a variety of educational technology. These progressive approaches are found to be effective in positively impacting an increasing numbers of learners (Chang, 2001).

Another important reason for doing this research was perceived scarcity of research focusing on learner's attitude when dealing with new and sometimes unknown classroom technology. This research investigates issues (mainly technobehavioral) that are likely to influence learner's disposition towards introduced classroom technologies.

RESEARCH MODEL AND HYPOTHESES

In this section, we will first describe the research model followed by the hypotheses. Two focus groups, one including 10 male students and one including 10 female students, were conducted to collect the perceptions of learners as far as initial utilization of classroom technologies and its impact on their learning attitude was concerned (see Table 1). Consequently a model was conceptualized (from the key perceptions collected during the focus groups) that had four antecedents and one consequence. The research model is partially grounded in and reflects some components (i.e. ease of technology use and learner's attitude towards technology) of Technology Acceptance Model, TAM, (Davis et al., 1989) which has been widely utilized to explain technology adoption within education (Jong-Ae, 2005). Especially TAM has been widely used in surveying user attitudes related to information technologies which include classroom and educational technologies (Ma & Liu, 2004; Saga & Zmud, 1994).

H1: *There is a positive relationship between ICTs Experience and Individual Learner Attitude.*

(ICTs Experience is defined as frequency and depth of interaction with basic software such as MS Office and internet search engines such as Google and Yahoo used for surfing and web browsing. Technology-driven individual learning is defined as the impact and influence of utilization of classroom technologies on student's attitude).

H2: *There is a positive relationship between Learner Independence and Individual Learner Attitude.*

(Independence is defined as self-management of studies by working on own initiative).

H3: *There is a positive relationship between Enhanced Communications and Individual Learner Attitude.*

(Enhanced communications is defined as widened scope of information exchange through various IT based and personal channels such as use of video and audio equipment, increased use of body language by instructor, face-to-face communication by the instructor by using voice projection and improved eye contact).

H4: *There is a positive relationship between ease of technology use and Individual Learner Attitude.*

(In using the classroom technology, 'operational' difficulty relates to know-how in terms of using the technology whereas 'situational' difficulty relates to the 'fitness status' (i.e. ready for use/in working order) of the equipment.

RESEARCH METHODOLOGY

Reliability, Validity and Regression Analysis

Prior to being used for final data collection, all the measures were reliability and validity tested. Refer to Tables 3 (Descriptive statistics and reliability analysis), 4 (Correlation matrix) and 5 (Exploratory Factor Analysis). In addition regression analysis (Table 6) was performed to evaluate the model pathways (i.e. proposed hypotheses). The regression analysis indicated a stable model with acceptable goodness of fit. All the items were based on 5-point Likert scales. The research model was tested using a self-completion questionnaire in English and Arabic.

Sample

Sample was based on the QU students, both male and female, from different colleges and departments. The questionnaire was broadcasted, using the university e-mail network, to the students. Eight hundred (800) questionnaires were sent out for self-completion with clear instructions. A total of 178 questionnaires were returned. This represented a response rate of about 22% which is comparable to similar studies (Klass *et al.*, 2002).

After taking out the unusable questionnaires, a total of 161 questionnaires were deemed suitable for further analysis. The test of non-response bias (i.e. comparing early and late respondents) was not necessary as all the data was collected in one phase.

Table 2. Measures and items details

Measure	Items
ICTs Experience	Item 1- Knowledge and ability of the learner to use basic ICTs Item 2 – Use of internet and e-mails to supplement learning
Learner Independence	Item 3 - Proactive course involvement of learner as a result of utilizing classroom technologies Item 4 - Classroom technologies aiding learner with lesson preparation Item 7 - Classroom technologies helping learner to do more work on its own Item 8 - Classroom technologies helping learner to control its pace and speed of learning
Enhanced Communications	Item 9 - Classroom technologies are further stimulating learner's problem solving ability through enhancement of visual (image based) communication Item 10 - Classroom technologies are further stimulating learner's problem solving skills through enhancement of audible (sound based) communication Item 12 - Learner becomes more involved and interactive, during sessions, when classroom technologies are used
Individual Learner Attitude	Item 5 - Classroom technologies help learner understand course materials through multiple sources Item 6 - Classroom technologies help (lecturers/teachers) with clear explaining of the subject materials through different forms of communication (verbal, written and non-verbal i.e. body language becoming more expressive) Item 11 - Classroom technologies improve the learning process of the individual through multiple sources of stimulation Item 13 - Classroom technologies create an effective classroom environment through which concepts and ideas can be grasped and exchanged more effectively and easily
Ease of technology use	Item 14 – I have no problem in operating the class room technologies Item 15 – If there is something wrong with the equipment than technical support is immediately available Item 16 – I do not need any training to teach me how to use the classroom technologies Item 17 – I find classroom technologies in full working order whenever I want to use them

Measures

Table 2 lists all the items (thirteen in total) that formed the antecedents and consequence used in the research model.

From the information presented in Table 3 we can see that the Cronbach's α value for all constructs is above 0.60 which is considered as a threshold value indicating acceptable reliability (Fornell & Larcker, 1981; Hair et al., 1998). The bivariate correlations (i.e. correlation matrix) of the constructs are presented in Table 4. The fact that none of the correlations approached the reliability values of the constructs is an indication of the discriminant validity. On the strength of the above evidence we are satisfied with the overall validity and reliability of the measures.

RESULTS

Demographics

Demographics related to the study included the gender, age, and college split are given in Table 6.

Table 6 clearly indicates that there were far more female respondents than male respondents (i.e. ratio of almost 2:1). Similarly most of the respondents belonged to 17 – 25 years old age group, displaying a rather young population. In terms of the college representation, a majority of the respondents came from College of Business and Economics followed by Engineering and Arts and Sciences.

Frequencies

The data related to frequencies of use are given in Figures 2, 3 and 4.

Table 3. Descriptive statistics and reliability analysis

Construct	Mean	SD	Cronbach's α
IT Experience	3.71	0.965	0.631
Learner Independence	3.70	1.020	0.803
Enhanced Communications	3.69	1.000	0.746
Individual Learning Attitude	3.98	0.939	0.791
Ease of classroom technology use	3.86	0.923	0.815

Table 4. Correlation matrix

Construct	Individual Learning Behavior	IT Experience	Learner Independence	Enhanced Communications	Ease of classroom technology use
Individual Learning Behavior	1				
IT Experience	0.218	1			
Learner Independence	0.599**	0.352**	1		
Enhanced Communications	0.716**	0.317*	0.578**	1	
Ease of classroom technology use	0.621**	0.458**	0.598**	0.361*	1

Table 5. Exploratory factor analysis

	Components				
	1	2	3	4	5
Item 1	.275	**.491**	.660	.008	.772
Item 2	.472	**.540**	.383	.330	.136
Item 3	.714	-.026	**-.124**	.407	.698
Item 4	.642	.151	**-.293**	.283	.251
Item 5	**.664**	-.472	-.090	.217	.639
Item 6	**.672**	-.537	.069	-.042	-.352
Item 7	.648	.332	**-.262**	.214	-.264
Item 8	.719	.244	**-.333**	.074	.129
Item 9	.660	.246	-.144	**-.547**	.224
Item 10	.663	.245	-.060	**-.418**	-.119
Item 11	**.721**	.063	-.077	-.315	.308
Item 12	.761	-.373	.318	**-.153**	.672
Item 13	**.709**	-.381	.403	.062	.280
Item 14	.296	-.451	-.437	.063	**.526**
Item 15	.340	.596	.706	.213	**.481**
Item 16	.197	.453	.138	.459	**.572**
Item 17	.390	.112	.281	.127	**.502**

Component 1: Individual Learner Attitude
Component 2: ICTs Experience
Component 3: Learner Independence
Component 4: Enhanced Communications
Component 5: Ease of classroom technology use

Table 6. Sample breakdown

Gender split	Female: 103 Male: 58
Age split	71 (17-20 years); 87 (21-25 years); 3 (26-30 years)
College split	Business & Economics 87; Engineering 44; Arts and Sciences 21; Sharia and Islamic Studies 6; Pharmacy 3

(n=161)

Figure 2. Classroom technologies used by faculty

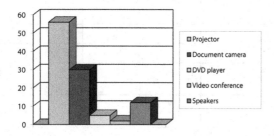

Figure 3. Student perception of usefulness of classroom technologies

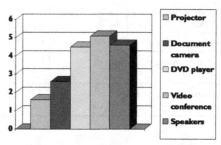

1=most useful in learning; 6=least useful in learning

A common thread related to usage (both by faculty and students) and usefulness (students perception) seems to be that projector and document camera (basic technologies) are predominantly used with higher perceived usefulness whereas DVD and Video Conferencing are less frequently used and considered to be less useful.

Hypotheses Testing and Pathway Analysis

The outcome of the regression analysis is presents in Table 7.

Dependent Variable: Individual Learner Attitude

The research model was subjected to Multiple Regression Analysis (MRA) using SPSS 15. R-Square value (Co-efficient of variance) was .567 which implied that 56.7% of the model variation was explained by the three independent variables (i.e. ICTs experience, Learner Independence and Enhanced Communications). In terms of the studied pathways, the MMR showed significant and positive relationships between Learning Independence, Enhanced Communications and Ease of classroom technology use (t-values of 2.759, 5.381 and 4.973 respectively) and Individual Learner Attitude. However the association between ICTs Experience and Individual Learning

Figure 4. Classroom technology use by students

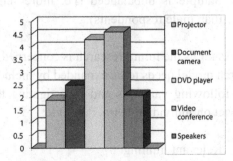

1=Daily; 2=Every other day; 3= Once a week; 4=Once every two weeks; 5=Once a month

Attitude was non-significant (t-value = -.713). With this outcome, in terms of the 'Outcome of the hypotheses' (Table 8), following can be concluded.

DISCUSSION

The major contribution of the study is that it is the first attempt to investigate the impact of classroom technologies in the initial phase of their implementation. This type of early analysis can help identify the developing attitudes of users which can be an important finding as far as the future utilization of the classroom technologies is concerned.

The study outcome implicated that use of classroom technologies, in the initial stages of introduction, does increase the capacity for self-directed learning through the availability, and creation, of further interaction and communications channels. However, prior ICTs experience seemed to have no impact on use of classroom technologies.

As instructors cannot always accommodate each student's need, it is important that several learning opportunities are provided. In this respect classroom technologies do present additional avenues through which learning can be generated and exchanged (e.g. accessing electronic library through laptop via wireless network anywhere and anytime, retrieving and placing learning materials on Black Board etc). Furthermore, it is expected that when the learning experience is

Table 7. Regression analysis

Model	t-value	Sig.
(Constant)	3.538	.001
ICTs Experience	-.713	.479
Learner Independence	2.759	.008
Enhanced Communications	5.381	.000
Ease of classroom technology use	4.973	.000

Table 8. Outcome of the hypotheses

Proposed Hypotheses	Statistical Outcome	Hypotheses Status
IT Experience → Individual Learning Attitude (+)	Non-significant	Rejected
Learner independence → Individual Learning Attitude (+)	Significant and positive	Retained
Enhanced Communications → Individual Learning Attitude (+)	Significant and positive	Retained
Ease of classroom technology use → Individual Learning Attitude (+)	Significant and positive	Retained

more relevant to the student, an increased level of individual user acceptance of information systems will result. Therefore, independence in learning (i.e. increased efficacy towards self managed and self-directed learning) is likely to occur (Compeaux & Higgins, 1999).

In terms of enhancements of communications, it is likely to be enhanced (partly) due to the projection and display of information (mostly typed or written) by the classroom technologies (such as overhead projector, document camera, speakers and DVD player). When this support is provided by the technology, teacher has more time to concentrate on explaining and clarifying the material through gestures, eye contact and such other body language displays). When interaction with peer groups, teachers and online sources is improved it opens up the learner communication (at individual and group level) which facilitates opportunities for independent learning.

Ease of use in terms of equipment in a ready state of fitness during the class time affects the learner's attitude positively (Moon & Kim, 2001). If learner is unable to operate the equipment (whether it is due to lack of operational knowledge or unavailability of timely technical support) the likely attitude towards classroom technology use will be negative.

It seems that previous experience with general ICTs does not impact uptake and utilization of classroom technologies for educational purposes. The probable reason for this (also supported by Passerini & Granger, 2000) could be interest and motivation as a fundamental condition for

technology-based learning rather than experience with ICTs.

PRACTICAL IMPLICATIONS, LIMITATIONS & FUTURE RESEARCH

Training should be organized for the students to bring them to the same level of competence. It is quite probable that some students may be encountering difficulty in using the new classroom technology or technologies.

Technical support should be prompt and comprehensive especially during the early stages of classroom technology implementation as most of the problems are likely to occur during the introduction of new technology.

In terms of limitations:

- Study is restricted to one institution therefore results should not be generalized.
- Quantitative research design may have created information gaps through which some of the relevant information may have slipped.
- Sample is unbalanced (i.e. more female than male respondents).

As far as the future research is concerned, research model needs to be expanded by including the following variables and investigating their impact on individual learner attitude:

- Relevant training
- Technical and maintenance support

Group analysis should be performed by cutting the data using the following variables:

- Gender of the learner
- College/department of the learner
- Age of the learner

Study should be repeat study in a different learning environment to give it more validity.

REFERENCES

Bannan-Ritland, B., Dabbagh, N., & Murphy, K. (2000). Learning object systems as constructivist learning environments: related assumptions, theories, and applications. In D. A. Wiley (Ed.), *The Instructional use of learning objects: online version.* Retrieved June 18, 2005, from http://www.reusability.org/read/chapters/bannan-ritland.doc

Bharati, P. (2003). People and information matter: task support satisfaction from the other side. *Journal of Computer Information Systems, 43*(2), 93–102.

Bratina, T. A., Hayes, D., & Blumsack, S. L. (2002). *Preparing teachers to use learning objects.* Retrieved January 12, 2002, from http://technologysource.org/article/preparing_teachers_to_use_learning_objects/

Chen, C. M., Lee, H. M., & Chen, Y. H. (2005). Personalized e-learning system using Item Response Theory. *Computers & Education, 44,* 237–255. doi:10.1016/j.compedu.2004.01.006

Compeau, D. R., Higgins, C. A., & Huff, S. (1999). Social cognitive theory and individuals reactions to computing technology: a longitudinal study. *Management Information Systems Quarterly, 23*(2), 145–158. doi:10.2307/249749

Cuban, L. (1993). Computers meet classroom: Classroom wins. *Teachers College Record, 95*(2), 185–210.

Davis, F. D., Bagozzi, R. P., & Warsaw, P. R. (1989). User acceptance of computer technology: a comparison of two theoretical models. *Management Science, 35*(8), 983–1003. doi:10.1287/mnsc.35.8.982

Fornell, C., & Larcker, D. F. (1981). Evaluating Structural Equation Models with Unobservable Variable and Measurement Error. *JMR, Journal of Marketing Research, 18*(1), 39–50. doi:10.2307/3151312

Govindasamy, T. (2002). Successful implementation of e-learning pedagogical considerations. *The Internet and Higher Education, 4,* 287–299. doi:10.1016/S1096-7516(01)00071-9

Hair, J. R., Anderson, R., Tatham, R., & Black, W. (1998). *Multivariate Data Analysis* (5th ed.). Upper Saddle River, NJ: Prentice Hall Inc.

Jong-Ae, K. (2005). *User acceptance of web-based subscription databases: extending the technology acceptance model.* Unpublished Doctoral Dissertation, Florida State University, Tallahassee, Florida.

Khan, B. H. (2000). *A framework for web-based learning.* Englewood Cliffs, NJ: Educational Technology Publications.

Klass, B. S., McClendon, J., & Gainey, T. W. (2002). Trust and Role of Professional Employer Organisations: Managing HR in Small and Medium Enterprises. *Journal of Managerial Issues, 14*(1), 31–48.

Liaw, S. S. (2004). Considerations for developing constructivist Web-based learning. *International Journal of Instructional Media, 31*(3), 309–321.

Liaw, S. S., & Huang, H. M. (2003). An investigation of users attitudes towards search engines as an information retrieval tool. *Computers in Human Behavior, 19*(6), 751–765. doi:10.1016/S0747-5632(03)00009-8

Liaw, S. S., Huang, H. M., & Chen, G. D. (2007). Surveying instructor and learner attitudes towards e-learning. *Computers & Education, 49,* 1066–1080. doi:10.1016/j.compedu.2006.01.001

Ma, Q., & Liu, L. (2004). The technology acceptance model: A meta analysis of empirical findings. *Journal of Organizational and End User Computing, 16*(1), 59–72.

Moon, J. W., & Kim, Y. G. (2001). Extending the TAM for a World-Wide-Web context. *Information & Management, 38,* 217–230. doi:10.1016/S0378-7206(00)00061-6

Mun, Y. Y., & Hwang, Y. (2003). Predicting the use of web-based information systems: self-efficacy, enjoyment, learning goal orientation, and the technology acceptance model. *International Journal of Human-Computer Studies, 59,* 431–449. doi:10.1016/S1071-5819(03)00114-9

Passerini, K., & Granger, M. J. (2000). A development model for distance learning using the Internet. *Computers & Education, 34,* 1–15. doi:10.1016/S0360-1315(99)00024-X

Rosenberg, M. J. (2001). *E-learning, strategies for delivering knowledge in the digital age.* New York: McGraw Hill.

Saade, R., & Bahli, B. (2005). The impact of cognitive absorption on perceived usefulness and perceived ease of use in on-line learning: an extension of the technology acceptance model. *Information & Management, 42*(2), 317–327. doi:10.1016/j.im.2003.12.013

Saga, V., & Zmud, R. (1994). The nature and determinants of IT acceptance, routinization, and infusion. *IFIP Transactions A (Computer Science and Technology, A*(45), 67-86.

Singh, H. (2000). *Achieving interoperability in e-learning.* Retrieved October 21, 2002, from http://www.learningcircuits.org/2000/mar2000/singh.html

Urden, T. A., & Weggen, C. C. (2000). *Corporate E-learning: Exploring a new frontier.* W. R. Hambrecht and Company Equity Research Report.

Venkatesh, V., Speicer, C., & Morris, M. G. (2002). User acceptance enablers in individual decision making about technology: towards an integrated model. *Decision Sciences, 33*(2), 297–316. doi:10.1111/j.1540-5915.2002.tb01646.x

Wang, Y. S. (2003). Assessment of learner satisfaction with asynchronous electronic learning systems. *Information & Management, 41,* 75–86. doi:10.1016/S0378-7206(03)00028-4

Wiley, D. (2001). *Peer –to-peer and learning objects: the new potential for collaborative constructivist learning online.* Paper presented at the Proceedings of the IEEE International Conference on Advanced Learning Technology.

Chapter 12
The 'Perfect Technology Syndrome':
How to Solve the Technology Dominance in Technology-Program Projects

Seppo J. Hänninen
Helsinki University of Technology, Finland

ABSTRACT

Recent research literature in product innovation has paid attention to the fact that technological discipline can lead to dominance by a knowledge base. Technology-intensive development is often partially and publicly supported and problems in finding a proper balance in technology development are in common interest. The objective of this study is to deepen the understanding of the dominance by technological knowledge base with reference to the sources, consequences and solutions of this overemphasis. Finnish publicly supported technology-intensive product innovation projects are studied. In the case studies, examples of the 'perfect technology syndrome' are identified and their sources are analyzed. This syndrome describes the intention to achieve the ultimate level in the technology development. Solutions proposed to the unfavorable consequences included alliances with organizations having complementary resources, careful pretesting of products with key partners and developing the technological products to specific target groups.

INTRODUCTION

Technology has kept its position as a key factor in technology-intensive product innovation. The prize of the first-mover advantage is a unique position in the market without competition and a wide time margin to exploit the technological breakthrough (Lieberman &Montgomery, 1988).

DOI: 10.4018/978-1-61520-623-0.ch012

Where the pioneer position is no longer available, one alternative policy is to aim for the ultimatum reach in the technology – to attain the perfect technology.

Technology challenges, developers try to and overcome all perceived technological limitations, without necessarily paying adequate attention to the commercial demands of user-friendliness, branding or customer preferences (Ernst &Soll, 2003). Aspirations towards 'perfect technology' are inherent to publicly supported technology development but common also in privately financed technology-intensive product innovation. Typically, public financing is directed solely to facilitate the development of the technology and addressing technological problems; funding the solutions to all other challenges is assumed to be the developer's own responsibility. One possible consequence of such public financing is that it is only the technological challenges that simulate the developers. Technology-intensive development is often partially and publicly supported, and problems in finding a proper balance in technology development are in common interest.

This study uses 'perfect technology syndrome' to describe the intention to achieve the ultimate level in the development of the technology. 'Technology dominance' is used in the literature to describe overemphasis of technological resources (Kim & Mauborgne, 1997). The dominance of technology has been discussed in many outstanding papers and books. Burns and Stalker (1961) observed technology development projects in Great Britain in the 1940s. In them an intensive publicly supported technology development phase was followed by strong technological orientation when the products developed were brought to consumer markets. Cooper (1975) listed a strong technology orientation as a key barrier to the commercialization of innovations. Ettlie (1982) compared radical and incremental innovations developed in public organizations. He noticed that a strong technological orientation had serious negative consequences. However, despite these critical reports, the observations indicate that the dominance of technological knowledge base has persisted with an alarming extent, in technological product innovation projects.

The objective of this study is to deepen the understanding of the dominance by technological knowledge base with reference to solutions of this overemphasis. This study will start with a discussion of knowledge bases of product innovation. Then, the 'perfect technology syndrome' is described. The underlying motives for one-sided technology development orientation will be discussed, as well as the associated risks and challenges of such orientation. More specifically, the traps associated with overdeveloped technological enthusiasm will be described. Then, three solutions used by successful technology-oriented industrial organizations are identified. Finally, guidelines for implementing these solutions in other organizations are given. In course of time, the development of the innovation process and the knowledge-related, resource-based dependence change the context of the knowledge utilization, and adaptations to the development process may be necessary.

THEORY ON KNOWLEDGE BASES OF INNOVATION

Features of a Knowledge Base

The concept of a knowledge base refers to the managerial and organizational cognition and concepts about the development project and its environment, and the relationships between these. In contrast to a database, the knowledge base also includes tacit knowledge, such as values, routines and stories. Cohen and Levinthal (1990) have discussed some key features of a knowledge base, which explain how one knowledge base can dominate the other knowledge bases. Typical features of a knowledge base are the demand for prior knowledge, cumulative nature of knowledge development, filtering of knowledge and knowledge-base-specific language.

Demand for prior knowledge: for any knowledge to be focused and to be of interest, there must be some prior knowledge. New knowledge cannot ring the alarm bells in the organization if there is no knowledge base where the new knowledge can be received. Some of the prior knowledge needed can be recruited with new professional personnel, and some of it is related in an evolutionary way to experience, especially dramatic experience within the organization.

Cumulative nature of knowledge development: once a knowledge base has been established, it becomes deepened through the addition of further new knowledge. Each knowledge base consists of both explicit knowledge and tacit knowledge, which is stored in organizational routines, stories and files. The knowledge is created through the interaction of organization members and through practicing skills relevant to the organization's objectives.

Filtering of knowledge: a part of the knowledge development process is that only knowledge supporting the prior knowledge can be accepted. The other knowledge will be rejected. This filter is based on the values formed by management and specialist personnel, on the grounds of their previous experiences. For example, anyone studying a new skill knows how difficult it is to accept new differing viewpoints.

A knowledge-base-specific language: one part of the filtering process is that the knowledge base needs a specific language. Specialists communicate through shared mental models and consensual concepts, which constitute large-scale concentrates of multidimensional information. Similarly, there are also project-specific and industry-specific 'languages'.

THE FOUR KNOWLEDGE BASES OF PRODUCT INNOVATION

The 'perfect technology syndrome' should be analyzed by considering the role of knowledge bases in product innovation. The role of knowledge bases in product innovation is a major topic in the innovation management literature (Cohen & Levinthal, 1990; Leonard-Barton, 1992; Tushman & Anderson, 1986; Walsh, 1995). This discussion has mainly either focused on the technological knowledge base or the content of the knowledge base has been left undefined. The present model makes use of four knowledge bases: the technological knowledge base, the end-user knowledge base, the brand knowledge base and the business-logic knowledge base. The total contribution of the four knowledge bases is more than the sum of the four when each knowledge base would be considered separately.

All four knowledge bases can be shown to exist during the product innovation process, but they may remain latent. Such latency is supported, for example, by the dominance of one knowledge base. Usually any organization has at least a passive consciousness of all four knowledge bases. The view of the present paper is that the knowledge bases are related to each other like networked computers, developing the information into knowledge.

The Technological Knowledge Base

The 'technological' knowledge base refers to the specific phase of technological development in which an innovation takes place, and to the potential opportunities, which that technology offers. Alongside a dominant technology, new alternative technologies may develop, which may lead to a new division of the market (Bower & Christensen, 1995). Companies need research to expand their technological knowledge and operations to exploit it (March, 1991). The technological environment, in which any innovation is developed, is regulated by standards and patents. An important task of product innovation is to ensure the alliance of an innovation with those technological solutions, which will best ensure its commercial success.

The advancement of technology, like that of scientific paradigms, occurs through both evolutionary processes and breakthroughs (Dosi, 1982). Technological breakthroughs may lead to the promotion, or to the collapse, of a company's previous knowledge base (Henderson & Clark, 1990; Tushman & Anderson, 1986). The future of technology can to some extent be predicted by means of technology roadmaps, which are a tool for forecasting probable future developments (Kappel, 2001). New developments in semiconductor technology and power battery technology, for example, are likely to have a significant impact on product innovation in high-technology industries in the foreseeable future. A roadmap can be used in ensuring that a new product innovation utilizes the optimum technology both at the time when the technology is launched in the market and for as long as possible thereafter.

A significant proportion of technological knowledge can be expressed explicitly, by means of mathematical formulas or diagrams, for instance. This is one reason for the finding that the technological dimension easily becomes overemphasized among different knowledge bases for technological product innovations (Leonard-Barton, 1992). It is common in product innovation to devote more financial resources to promoting technological development than to marketing (Cooper, 1975).

The function of the technology in product innovation, however, is to offer a solution to an explicit problem or a latent problem experienced by the end-user. The broader the scope, within which the technology is innovative, the lesser overt the needs of the end-users will be. The useful life of a product innovation will therefore be extended if several technological options can be incorporated into it. Technological options can include latent innovative features, including features, which yet cannot be used at the market launch of the product, for example, because the available infrastructure does not yet support them.

The End-User Knowledge Base

The 'end-user' knowledge base refers to the ways in which a product innovation may be able to solve problems, whether explicit or latent, faced by the end-users. End-users have two roles in relation to innovation: as prospective purchasers, and as prospective users. How much influence the end-user may have on the actual purchase itself will depend on the specifics of the purchasing process. Consumer goods are typically bought by the consumer. In corporate purchasing, the end-users' role is usually limited to influence the choice, but not to create the actual act of buying.

In the end-user knowledge base, what matters about a product innovation is that it should be user-friendly and should enrich experience – in other words, it should have what the end-users will perceive as added value. User-friendliness impacts on users' willingness to accept and adopt innovations, but for a product innovation to gain users' commitment, it needs to have as many features as possible, which will extend their experience (Prahalad & Ramaswamy, 2003). User-friendliness and experience-enrichment are complementary, not mutually exclusive features.

Lead users are those who take advantage of new products and themselves develop them further to better fulfill their own needs. Software products can be enhanced with features, which facilitate this kind of product development by the user (France & von Hippel, 2003). Corporate personnel may well be enthusiastic to take part in product innovation development process as users, not merely as a part of the product development machine.

The end-users knowledge base is constructed through a variety of channels. Such are, for example, feedback from clients, case stories, usability surveys and market research.

The Brand Knowledge Base

The 'brand' knowledge base was presented and discussed in an editorial article by Tauber (1983). The 'brand' knowledge base describes how an innovation relates to the company's brand equity (Aaker, 1991). Brand equity is constituted not merely by a range of products, but by the project's total systematic mode of operations, irrespective of the company's size. Even open-source software products have a brand identity, one purpose of which is to identify the copyright holder (O'Mahony, 2003).

The company's brand does not exist independently of its products; at the heart of the concept of a brand are product innovation and the added value, which the innovation creates for the end-users (Aaker, 1991). Brand can also relate to technological added value. The slogan 'Intel inside', for instance, tells us nothing about the technology deployed, but rather, promises value to the personal computer user (Ward et al., 1999).

A product needs to share the same idiom with the rest of its brand. The design needs to be consistent and coherent throughout, from the innovation itself to the product's entire mode of operations. Consistency reduces costs, and concentrates the message on a coherent set of values. The construction of a brand knowledge base may well begin with the graphic design of the brand and the industrial design of the product (Schmitt et al., 1995). Development of a brand and of brand equity is, however, very much time-consuming operations (Aaker, 1991).

The Business-Logic Knowledge Base

The 'business-logic' knowledge base describes the status and function of an innovation within the overall context of the project's business operations. The term 'business logic' is used to describe the dominant mode of operation within a specific company or branch of business, which is constituted by the various logics of value creation within this environment and which supports commercial success. Other closely related terms and concepts include 'dominant logic' (Prahalad & Bettis, 1986) and 'strategic logic' (Kim & Mauborgne, 1997). Understanding the dominant business logic is particularly important both for radical product innovation and in mature business sectors.

Typically, a new product innovation is intended to replace or displace alternative substitute products from the market. Even if none of the substitute products is strictly speaking in immediate competition with the new product, all substitutes are effectively in competition for parallel roles for the end-users and for business operations (Porter, 1980). To avert a situation of

direct competition, companies need to develop innovations, which will be capable of changing the dominant business logic (Kim & Mauborgne, 1997). Companies, which cannot alter the prevailing rules of the market, must make their products comply with the dominant logic. To challenge and alter the dominant logic is in fact one of the ways in which it is possible to challenge the status of the current market leader (Kim & Mauborgne, 1997). If a company is not thoroughly familiar with the particular field of business, it may delegate the marketing of an innovation to another company, which does know the field and is capable of carrying the financial risk (Mitchell, Singh, 1996). This is a strategy very typical of small start-up companies. These four knowledge bases of the product innovation are presented in Figure 1.

Initially, the development of the knowledge bases relating to product innovation started with technological knowledge, but the understanding of product innovation has steadily expanded and these other knowledge bases relating to end-users, brands and business logic have been included. The relatively important shifts of the various knowledge bases in relation to product innovation development also imply shifts within corporate

Figure 1. The 'four knowledge bases approach' in product innovation

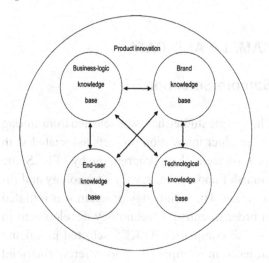

power structures (Henderson & Clark, 1990; Normann, 1971). A recurrent weakness relating to knowledge bases is that, for example, the branding tasks in large companies are often short-term training positions for other functions (Tauber, 1983). This means that all the tacit knowledge learned is lost when the person moves to new challenges.

Generally speaking, the different knowledge bases are not perceived as factors all making for change, but it is assumed that one or more of them will hold constant, and that only one of them – the technology, for instance – will change (Hänninen, 2007). In reality, however, each of these knowledge bases constitutes a potential platform for change. Both on the operative and the strategic level, projects need to explore the potential implications for a particular innovation of each knowledge base, without imposing constraining parameters (Hänninen & Kauranen, 2007).

Using the 'four knowledge bases approach' in product innovation favors cross-functional cooperation. The approach also suggests that problems related to the product innovation process are often caused by the relationships between knowledge bases and encountered in the exploration and exploitation of knowledge bases. Some of the most typical problems are caused by the dominance of the technological knowledge base, which is particularly common in product innovation.

SAMPLE AND DATA

Sample Selection

The sample studied here was selected from among the product innovation projects associated with the Usix technology program run by TEKES, the Finnish Funding Agency for Technology and Innovation. The technology program was initiated in order to enhance technology development in Finnish companies. TEKES selected promising projects in companies, and offered financial

support and expertise to the selected projects. In the Usix program the focus was on innovative software development. Technologies represented are telecommunications, the internet and GPS navigation systems. The sample was limited to eight cases. The cases represented different sizes of companies. Two of the product innovation projects were conducted in large companies, one in a medium-sized company and five in small companies. All the product innovation projects had received public funding. This study is somewhat hampered by the fact that at the time when the interviews were carried out, many key persons had recently changed their employment. This is in part, a consequence of the boom in information technology, and the resulting economic turbulence. The cases were selected through literal replication logic, that is, on the prediction that they would support the a priori framework (cf. Yin, 1989). The selected cases represent both successful and unsuccessful product innovations.

Data Collection

The material was collected by means of personal interviews with the project liaison officer or with the project's technology or research manager. In each case, the interview subject considered that he or she was quite familiar with the project than anyone else in the company. In the interviews, open-ended questions were used. The interviews were recorded and the responses were then content-analyzed for investigation. The interview data were supplemented by information obtained for example through the internet, or from written sources.

THE 'PERFECT TECHNOLOGY SYNDROME' IN COMPANY X

Technology development in product innovation encourages developers to aim for the ultimate frontiers. This aim can lead to the 'perfect technology syndrome'. This phenomenon is here discussed through a case study in some literature references.

Company X had a very promising technology development project. It was encouraged by its university partner to develop speech recognition software technology. The company management invested significant time and resources in the project, including the hiring of new specialist personnel. The objective was defined as the capacity to recognize even unclear voices, and to turn messages into digital form and commands. The company had very little interest in tailoring the technology to specific differentiated groups on the basis of thorough market and competition knowledge. The rest is typical start-up company history: fusion with another company and reformulation of the technology development project. The company was taken over by its competitor.

From the perspective of the knowledge bases, what actually had happened? The technological challenge hypnotized the management and specialist personnel. Proper attention was not paid to end-user needs, to branding or to business logic demands. Resources were invested in development based on just one knowledge base: the technology knowledge base.

The technical problems relating to the development of a new technology are huge, but more explicit than, for example, problems associated with the new business logic, which a new technology causes. That is the first factor in the robust innovation process, which can lead to dominance by the technology knowledge base.

A second factor causing dominance by technology knowledge base is overvaluing and misunderstanding the time-to-market factor. In paying the most attention to the speed of the development process, Company X ignored the development of other knowledge bases, and thus had a delayed market entrance. Contrary to plans, strong investment in development based on the technological knowledge base generated no time saving, but instead increased total time consumption.

The third factor causing dominance by technology knowledge base is a technology-oriented mode of managerial cognition and underestimating other knowledge bases. This can produce a self-confirming circle of technological knowledge.

The 'perfect technology syndrome' is consistent with some core rigidities analyzed by Leonard-Barton (1992). Of course the 'perfect technology syndrome' is not the only possible reason for market delay. For example, a telecommunications operator developed mobile video services, but because the infrastructure of third-generation telecommunication services was not yet ready, market entrance was not possible even though mobile phones available at that time had features capable of utilizing the services. In this case, technological capabilities or resource allocation had no impact on the commercialization of the technology. Even though the 'perfect technology syndrome' had disastrous consequences in Company X, the strong technology orientation itself may enhance other capabilities of the company.

SOME SOLUTIONS

In the case companies, the 'perfect technology syndrome' was solved successfully in three basic ways: by facilitating alliances with organizations having complementary capabilities, with tailored products and with close cooperation with key partners. Each of these solutions facilitates the product innovation process.

Case Sunit: Alliance with Organizations having Complementary Capabilities

Sunit Mobile (www.sunit.fi) is a Finnish software company specializing in professional drivers' knowledge management needs. The core capabilities of the company were originally developed for forest harvesters, but a similar cabin workspace is typical for many kinds of driving professions, for example, for truck drivers and taxi drivers. The cabin unit consists of a personal computer, a telecommunication module, GPS satellite positioning and backing video. The purpose of the development project was to miniaturize the processor unit to fit into the car radio slot. Earlier versions were considered clumsy by professional drivers. Sunit Mobile is innovation-development oriented, which means that new versions of the core product with new additional features are launched regularly.

Sunit Mobile's management had a vision of building an extensive international business. The company recognized a need to present its new products and corresponding skills and innovations through trade fairs. The CeBit fair in Hannover led to cooperation with Scania, which is one of the biggest European truck manufacturers. The two companies had complementary capabilities, which enabled building synergetic competitive advantages without threatening each other's core business operations. Usually alliance partners have fuzzy roles and competing interests in their cooperation. Starting this cooperation led to a learning process to achieve the skill level needed for the development objectives. Sunit had developed a special expertise in knowledge needs set by professional drivers in the cabin, and Scandia had specialized in professional driver's vehicles performance demands. By linking these two capability clusters, the partnership offered a contribution, which was by nature more than one plus one. Instead of isolation, Sunit Mobile chose sharing its knowledge and best practices in an alliance with another organization having complementary capabilities.

The advantages for Sunit Mobile were also commercial. The company gained a highly significant reference, and experience in cooperation with a major European truck manufacturer. As a consequence the customer invests in a truck, which comes already fitted with Sunit equipment. This lowers the barrier to make a decision to purchase compared with the other alternative that the customer needs to make a separate investment decision to purchase the Sunit equipment.

At the same time, the Scania truck gains added value through the Sunit unit. One additional advantage is that the Sunit solution could be made a standard in Europe.

The price of this cooperation is that Sunit has to use reasonable and transparent pricing of its products, without skimming price options. The consequences for Sunit, compared to skimming pricing, were higher absolute profits, as a consequence of design dominance and highly increased volume of sales. Furthermore, this balanced form of cooperation in the alliance led to a valuable special focus on other user groups, such as taxi drivers and security transportation services.

Case Mupe: Pretest with Key Partners

The Nokia Multi-User Publishing Environment (www.mupe.net) is an open-source software platform for mobile telecommunication services such as virtual spaces, role games and GPS satellite positioning services. The open source enables better testing for new areas such as healthcare services: the mobile services with the highest user value are then expected to survive in the market. The main target of Mupe is to facilitate software developers' projects to create commercial services for third-generation mobile telecommunication consumer markets. Mupe can also be utilized in GPRS and EDGE telecommunication networks. The main objective of Nokia Research Center was to support the growth of telecommunication service consumption and to eliminate barriers limiting the commercialization of value-added services.

The relationship with software developers is a key success factor, and indicates the growth of the critical mass of an open-source software technology. Mupe software was developed in close cooperation with the Helsinki Institute of Information Technology (HIITT). Usually open software developers are not very enthusiastic to join open-source communities, especially if more than one developer is interested. Launching the open-source platform was delayed until the number of developers who had joined the community was sufficient. The first objective was to involve five developers, but in the end 15 developers took part. The key question in the Mupe project was how to motivate 'free' software developers to utilize the Mupe technology platform in their own development work. Mupe is in many ways a win–win solution, enabling low-cost development of new mobile telecommunication services, while these new services simultaneously motivate consumers to utilize third-generation mobile phone features. Only a few developers were supported by Nokia. Mupe is a good example of feedback-based technology where solutions are pretested with key partners.

Case Suunto: Tailored Technological Products to Specific Target Groups

Suunto (www.suunto.fi) is famous for its wrist computers and GPS-based wrist products. GPS is abbreviation for Global Positioning System, which is a satellite-supported navigation system that can be linked with more highly developed information processing services, such as guided routing navigation systems.

Suunto has developed a new product platform for its GPS product group. The challenge of miniaturizing the technology solution and optimizing the antenna were, in practice, secondary problems. From the beginning of the development project, a major focus was placed on defining target groups who would appreciate the value of GPS-features. Among the first ones to be identified were sailors and golfers. Accordingly, wrist computers were produced so that they were tailored to the specific demands of each sport. In the development process, three key questions were identified. They were as follows: To whom is the positioning information valuable? Which environments are most suitable for GPS wrist products? Which sports have the

biggest sales potential? Derived products were then developed for golfers and sailors, who operate in relative large-scale, open environments. The positioning information was then refined so as to support, for example, golfers' decision making.

The Suunto approach had three advantages. Firstly, the project group was forced to keep in mind the final target group for the future product, even during the technology development phase. Secondly, the technology was evaluated against real-life demands, not the optimistic fantasies of technology specialists. Finally, the success probability of the project was higher, since the technology had a functional value to serve project objectives. All these advantages are founded on tailoring the technological products to special target groups.

DISCUSSION

The described case studies all represent publicly supported technological product innovation projects. However, the 'perfect technology syndrome' is typical of all product innovation projects, which focus on technological challenges. The emergence of the 'perfect technology syndrome' is potentially driven by two factors.

Firstly, one developer, representing technological know-how, takes on a dominant role within the product innovation project. This dominant position may be based on the priority of technical planning, since technical problems foster a straightforward approach once the product idea has been fixed.

Secondly, the product innovation diversifies the company adhere to a new business logic. Then, the challenges created by other knowledge bases are even greater to the challenges inherent to the technological knowledge base. The technological focus in this case is typically a reaction to keep everything in order. In a very profound 'new-to-the-industry' diversification, there is usually little explicit information available about the new business environment, and descriptions of the industry dynamics and business logic are, if any, fuzzy at best. The difficulty of describing the business environment in a diversified situation encourages a focus on the most explicit product parameters, which in this situation are technical.

One solution to the problems caused by the dominance by technological knowledge base is to bring about a change in the leadership role. A possible better new change will depend on the flexibility of the project members: hierarchical routines and closed organization culture tend to support the dominance of one element in the whole. One solution to such diversification challenges is delegation. In diversification, even the weakest signals are valuable. Delegation of responsibility facilitates sensing potential business environments.

Incidentally, the 'perfect technology syndrome' has an ironic counterpart in the 'no technology syndrome', which is typical of strongly market-oriented projects. Technology avoidance, however, means low capabilities to create long-term competitive advantage. The two syndromes form a U-shaped curve in their risk-intensity, and the optimal level in maximizing competitive advantage and minimizing risks is somewhere in the middle, with a combination of the best features: technology-intensity with strong understanding of end-users, the brand and the current business-logics.

The discussion of this paper has focused on innovations in turbulent environments. Technological perfection is less threatened in environments with a slower rate of change, such as steam engine machinery. These environments with a slow rate of change are becoming rarer day by day, as fewer and fewer industries are nowadays protected by governmental policy or statutory status. In this study, the a priori framework has been discussed on the basis of just eight case studies. As at this stage the results are exploratory, there is clearly a need to test the framework further with other case studies, and eventually, with a quantitative approach.

CONCLUSION AND IMPLICATIONS

The findings of this study lead us towards re-thinking the prevailing consensus about major challenges, which face us in technological product innovation projects. A one-sided focus on technical challenges leads to delays in planned product innovation launch schedules and the anticipated cut in time turns into a longer development period. Some product innovation projects, nonetheless, have overcome this one-sidedness. However, obvious the solutions presented in this study may seem, the real-life situation can mislead even experienced developers if conscious attention is not paid to finding a balance of technology orientation.

This study has five managerial implications. Firstly, a need to focus on complementary resources must be acknowledged. This often requires alliances with organizations having complementary capabilities. Secondly, the product innovation solutions should in the course of the development process be continuously pretested with key partners. Thirdly, tailored technological products should be developed to specific target groups. Fourthly, the business logic of each new product innovation should be carefully studied and deeply understood. Often as a result of the diversification inherent to a new product innovation, the company is confronted with new unfamiliar business logic. The last (but not least) implication is that all relevant knowledge bases, not just one, need to be fully deployed as early as possible, starting already from the early technology research phase.

ACKNOWLEDGMENT

The financial support of the Jenny and Antti Wihuri Foundation and the Finnish Cultural Foundation is acknowledged.

A previous version of this book chapter was published by Inderscience Published Ltd. (UK) in Int. J. of Technology Management, 39(1/2), 20-32.

REFERENCES

Aaker, D. (1991). *Managing Brand Equity: Capitalizing on the Value of a Brand Name*. New York: The Free Press.

Bower, J. L., & Christensen, C. M. (1995). Disruptive technologies: catching the wave. *Harvard Business Review, 73*(1), 43–53.

Burns, T., & Stalker, G. M. (1961). *The Management of Innovation*. London: Tavistock Publications.

Cohen, W. M., & Levinthal, D. A. (1990). Absorptive capacity: a new perspective on learning and innovation. *Administrative Science Quarterly, 35*(1), 128–152. doi:10.2307/2393553

Cooper, R. G. (1975). Why new industrial products fail. *Industrial Marketing Management, 4*(4), 315–326. doi:10.1016/0019-8501(75)90005-X

Dosi, G. (1982). Technical paradigms and technological trajectories: a suggested interpretation of the determinants and directions of technical change. *Research Policy, 11*(3), 147–162. doi:10.1016/0048-7333(82)90016-6

Ernst, H., & Soll, J. H. (2003). An integrated portfolio approach to support market-oriented R&D planning. *International Journal of Technology Management, 26*(5/6), 540–561. doi:10.1504/IJTM.2003.003422

Ettlie, J. E. (1982). The commercialization of federally sponsored technological innovations. *Research Policy, 11*(3), 173–192. doi:10.1016/0048-7333(82)90018-X

Franke, N., & von Hippel, E. (2003). Satisfying heterogeneous user needs via innovation toolkits: the case of Apache security software. *Research Policy, 32*(7), 1199–1215. doi:10.1016/S0048-7333(03)00049-0

Hänninen, S. (2007). *Innovation commercialisation process from the 'four knowledge bases' perspective*. Doctoral Dissertation Series, Development and Management in Industry. Espoo, Finland: Helsinki University of Technology.

Hänninen, S., & Kauranen, I. (2007). Product innovation as micro-strategy. *International Journal of Innovation and Learning, 4*(4), 425–443. doi:10.1504/IJIL.2007.012580

Henderson, R. M., & Clark, K. B. (1990). Architectural innovation: the reconfiguration of existing technologies and the failure of established firms. *Administrative Science Quarterly, 35*(1), 9–30. doi:10.2307/2393549

Kappel, T. A. (2001). Perspectives on roadmaps: how organizations talk about the future. *Journal of Product Innovation Management, 18*(1), 39–50. doi:10.1016/S0737-6782(00)00066-7

Kim, W. C., & Mauborgne, R. (1997). Value innovation: the strategic logic of high growth. *Harvard Business Review, 75*(1), 103–112.

Leonard-Barton, D. (1992). Core capabilities and core rigidities: a paradox in managing new product development. *Strategic Management Journal, 13*(5), 111–125. doi:10.1002/smj.4250131009

Lieberman, M. B., & Montgomery, D. B. (1988). First-mover advantages. *Strategic Management Journal, 9*, 41–58. doi:10.1002/smj.4250090706

March, J. R. (1991). Exploration and exploitation in organizational learning. *Organization Science, 2*(1), 71–87. doi:10.1287/orsc.2.1.71

Mitchell, W., & Singh, K. (1996). Survival of businesses using collaborative relationships to commercialize complex goods. *Strategic Management Journal, 17*(3), 169–195. doi:10.1002/(SICI)1097-0266(199603)17:3<169::AID-SMJ801>3.0.CO;2-#

Normann, R. (1971). Organizational innovativeness: product variation and reorientation. *Administrative Science Quarterly*, *16*(2), 203–215. doi:10.2307/2391830

O'Mahony, S. (2003). Guarding the commons: how community managed software projects protect their work. *Research Policy*, *32*(7), 1179–1198. doi:10.1016/S0048-7333(03)00048-9

Porter, M. (1980). *Competitive Strategy*. New York: The Free Press.

Prahalad, C. K., & Bettis, R. A. (1986). The dominant logic: a new linkage between diversity and performance. *Strategic Management Journal*, *7*(6), 485–501.

Prahalad, C. K., & Ramaswamy, V. (2003). The new frontier of experience innovation. *MIT Sloan Management Review*, *44*(4), 12–18.

Schmitt, B. H., Simonsen, A., & Marcus, J. (1995). Managing corporate image and identity. *Long Range Planning*, *28*(5), 82–92. doi:10.1016/0024-6301(95)00040-P

Tauber, E. M. (1983). Editorial: corporate wisdom: the need for 'the brand knowledge base. *Journal of Advertising Research*, *23*(1), 7.

Tushman, M. L., & Anderson, P. (1986). Technological discontinuities and organizational environments. *Administrative Science Quarterly*, *31*(3), 439–465. doi:10.2307/2392832

Walsh, J. P. (1995). Managerial and organizational cognition: notes from a trip down memory lane. *Organization Science*, *6*(3), 280–321. doi:10.1287/orsc.6.3.280

Ward, S., Light, L., & Goldstine, J. (1999). What high-tech managers need to know about brands. *Harvard Business Review*, *77*(4), 85–95.

Yin, R. K. (1984). *Case Study Research: Design and Methods*. Thousand Oaks, CA: Sage Publications.

Chapter 13
Comparative Evaluation of ITIL–Based Process Landscapes

Vladimir Stantchev
Berlin Institute of Technology, Germany

Martin Goernitz
Krallmann AG, Germany

ABSTRACT

The Information Technology Infrastructure Library's (ITIL) is widely used as a model for IT service processes mainly due to its general nature. A drawback of this generality is that it greatly hinders the conversion of best practices into specific implementable processes. To assess such processes for their completeness and to find and overcome possible weak-spots in the design, this work proposes an in-depth comparison with available best practice frameworks that relate to and extend the ITIL, such as the Microsoft Operations framework (MOF). The comparison and evaluation method is presented and verified exemplarily with an actual pilot-phase process implementation.

1. THE HARDSHIPS OF ASSESSING ITIL-BASED PROCESS LANDSCAPES

The Information Technology Infrastructure Library (ITIL) is the framework that most IT service providers base their service process landscapes on, making it "the most widely accepted approach to IT service management (ITSM)" (OGC 2008). The release of version 3 of ITIL (V3) in May 2007 and its quite different approach to IT services over its

predecessor version 2 (V2), attempts to resolve two known problems of ITIL V2:

1. ITIL V2's unspecific nature required a creative design of service processes that were not defined by ITIL, but merely based on it.
2. ITIL V2 did not present a complete view of all the processes required by ITSM, one example being the absence of a service life-cycle.

The wide adoption of ITIL V2 combined with the limited implementation of its two main service areas of Service Delivery and Service Support,

DOI: 10.4018/978-1-61520-623-0.ch013

as practiced at the majority of its users served to heighten the impact of these problems. The result is a continued presence of a large number of IT service process landscapes that represent free interpretations of the ITIL V2 service areas and have been enhanced by home-grown or need-driven activities and processes covering ITIL V2's missing or excluded service areas.

When planning to analyze this kind of process landscapes for optimization three – non-exclusive – approaches present themselves:

1. Transitioning to ITIL V3, by redesigning processes, basing improvements on the knowledge gained with the operation of the current processes and the improvements of the current ITIL over its previous version.
2. Optimizing or rebuilding the existing processes using a quality improvement method such as Six Sigma (for optimization, based on the current processes' failure to perform according to business requirements) or Design for Six Sigma (for redesign, based on the established business requirements).
3. Drawing on the knowledge of others and optimizing the established processes by introducing improvements derived from other companies' ITSM implementations.

As media coverage shows (representational see Dierlamm 2008, Anthes 2008), many implementers of ITIL V2 do not plan a transition to ITIL V3 (approach 1) in the near future, refraining for reasons such as contentment with the current implementation, the increase in the number of processes to implement, an ongoing V2 implementation, or the cost and effort necessary.

Quality improvement and control methods, such as Six Sigma (approach 2) are an established way to optimize processes, but they also require a high degree of knowledge of the method applied that often has to be introduced by costly external experts, as well as requiring the effort to implement organizational and cultural changes.

In addition these methods depend strongly on the availability of metrics representing the attributes of the process in focus, preferably collected over a prolonged period of time. This disqualifies them for any analysis of processes still in their concept, design, or piloting phase or having only been introduced into operation recently. Design for Six Sigma manages to solve the absence of utilizable metrics during the concept and design phase, but promotes a greenfield approach that obsoletes any established process designs. It is questionable if companies that have introduced ITIL V2 or are in the process of doing so are willing to procure the finances and personnel efforts necessary to perform such an quality improvement project for a whole process landscape, especially when ITIL V3 is still an option or the need for change is not pressing beyond certain bearable limits.

The third approach, basing improvements on the service implementation of others, relates directly to the common "I wish I knew how the others did this"-mentality, often called upon, when faced with a problem that is known to have surfaced and been resolved elsewhere. It is also reflected in the reasons, why companies hire external consultants, which lie to a high degree with the consultant's knowledge of the industry's approach to a problem or his previous experience with a similar problem at another customer (Figure 1). Two reasons hinder the practical applicability of this approach: the high costs when hiring an experienced external consultant to analyze and improve a complete ITIL-based process landscape and the protectiveness that companies show toward their process designs, especially when they are optimized to a degree that is reflected in an actual contribution to business value.

A business' decision to follow the first or the second approach depends mainly on the willingness to employ the funds and human resources to master the necessary efforts. The assets needed for the third approach to the analysis and improvement of ITIL-based process landscapes however can be reduced when applying a comparison that

Figure 1. Reasons for choosing a consultant (translated and redrawn from Welp (2007), accentuation by authors)

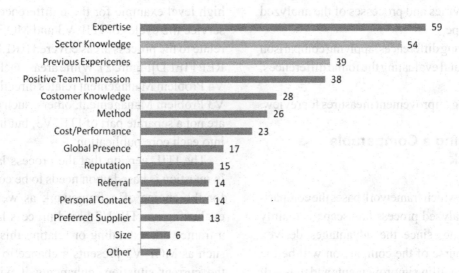

Expertise	59
Sector Knowledge	54
Previous Expericenes	39
Positive Team-Impression	38
Costomer Knowledge	28
Method	26
Cost/Performance	23
Global Presence	17
Reputation	15
Referral	14
Personal Contact	14
Preferred Supplier	13
Size	6
Other	4

is not conducted with actual processes that are implemented elsewhere, but with a process framework that extends or relates to ITIL and that is preferably based on the ITSM implementations at a specific company or at several companies. Frameworks that extend or relate to ITIL are available from a variety of Service providers, the most notable being:

- the Microsoft Operations Framework (MOF) (Microsoft Corporation 2008), that is applied at Microsoft itself, as well as a wide base of customers employing Microsoft's products, and whose version 3 (MOF V3) extends ITIL V2, whereas MOF version 4 (MOF V4) extends ITIL V3,
- the IBM Tivoli Unified Process (ITUP) (IBM 2008), that is aligned with ITIL V3 (ITUP version 7.1.3) and based on the experiences gained at IBM's customers, and
- the Application Services Library (ASL) (ASL BiSL Foundation, 2007) focuses on and relating mainly to ITIL V2 Application Management.

The realization of such a comparison is to be systematized, tested, and evaluated in the further course of this work, starting with an description of the methodic in Section 2, the verification of the method with a comparison of ITIL-based process designs currently being piloted at an international operating communication device manufacturer with the MOF in Section 3, and the evaluation of derived and expected results as well as further research activities in Section 4.

2. THE ASSESSMENT BY COMPARISON

When comparing an ITIL-based process landscape to an ITSM framework a six-step approach is proposed:

1. Choosing a comparable framework,
2. Establishing a number of comparison criteria and weighting them,
3. Mapping ITIL-based processes to the comparison framework,

4. Mapping additional process areas of the comparison framework to the corresponding activities and processes of the analyzed landscape,
5. Identifying differences, applying comparison criteria and evaluating the found differences, and
6. Deriving improvement measures for review.

2.1 Choosing a Comparable Framework

The decision, which framework bases the comparison to the analyzed process landscape is mainly a strategic one, since the advantages derived during the course of the comparison will be the first choice regarding improvements and thus will influence the future landscape considerably. The preferred choice reflects aspects of the pursued IT or business strategy, such as a framework that is published by an established vendor, that is supported by a strong and active community, that is supported by systems already acquired or planned for acquisition, or that has a firm customer base within one's own industry. As an example, the MOF might appeal to companies that operate an infrastructure that bears a strong relation to Microsoft's products, as they might profit additionally from vendor's knowledge and insight.

The availability of additional supportive products especially for vendor-published framework, such as Microsoft's System Center Operations Manager or IBM's Tivoli might also influence the decision toward one or the other. It should not be held against it though, since the software products tend to extend the framework, while the frameworks do not rely on specific software being used.

One aspect of the framework in question that should be assessed beforehand is its relation to ITIL. While frameworks, such as MOF, ITUP or ASL extend ITIL by adding areas not covered there or enhancing ITIL-covered areas by providing an action-oriented approach, their wording

and organization might differ greatly, making it harder to apply them to a process or field area. A high level example for these differences are the service life cycles of ITIL V3 and MOF V4, that relate to the process areas covered ([REMOVED REF FIELD]Figure 2). While areas, such as MOF V4 Problem Management relates directly to ITIL V3 Problem Management, others, such as Policy are not a separate part of ITIL V3, but integrated into each core publication.

The ITIL version that the process landscape in question is based upon needs to be considered for the choice of a framework as well. When evaluating an ITIL V2 based process landscape a framework extending or relating this version, such as MOF V3 presents a chance to improve the current situation, enhancing it with a life cycle and in-depth methodology and creating a kind of ITIL V2.5. Choosing an ITIL V3 related Framework might result in a high count of differences, depending on the ITSM maturity of the current processes and the degree to which the white-spots of ITIL V2 have been solved during the original design. Furthermore, this choice might enable a full-scale transition to an enhanced ITIL V3 implementation. In ITUP the process models are put into relation to both, ITIL V3 and V2, easing the efforts of such a comparison. When working with ITIL V3-based processes, up-to-date and ITIL V3 related frameworks should be favored.

2.2 Establishing and Weighting a Number of Comparison Criteria

Once a framework for comparison has been chosen, the criteria that reflect the value of a difference found during the comparison have to be established and weighted for their relevance. These attributes represent a decisional base of whether an identified difference represents an advantage of the process analyzed over the approach of the comparison framework or if the frameworks handling of a service area could present an improvement of the current situation, thus marking a weak-spot in the

Figure 2. Service life cycles and process areas of MOF V4 (redrawn from Microsoft Corporation, 2008a) and ITIL V3(redrawn from Microsoft Corporation 2008b)

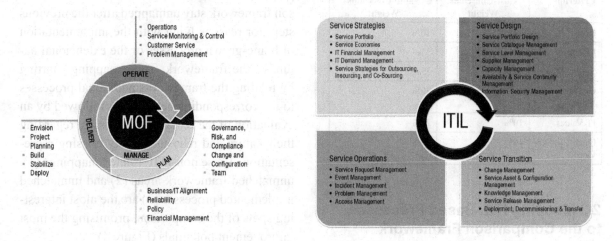

landscape that should be considered in a future implementation. The criteria listed in Table 1 are exemplary for this step.

Implementation attributes, such as Cost to Implement, should not be considered at this point, to prevent weak-spots of the current landscape to escape notice, due to the absence of a practical alternative. Their reflection is part of an evaluation process following the comparison, which is based on the possible solutions derived in step 6. This process is not a part of this work.

The weight assigned to each criterion should represent situation specific relevance to the IT strategy. Table 2 contains exemplary weighted

criteria for an IT strategy that promotes cost reduction, and for a value-focused IT.

While the decision for a specific framework is a choice that is made and stays for the complete comparison, the choice of criteria and their weight, as well as the choices made during the following steps can either be set for the comparison as a whole, or for each process area, even for each process. If they stay the same for the complete comparison, the project is a linear sequence of steps 1 through 6 (Figure 3); otherwise steps 2, 3/4 and 5 are repeated for each process (area).

Table 1. Example criteria for assessing differences derived from comparison

Criterion	Value Range	Description
a) Operation		Hard criteria relating to service operation
Cost	-10...0...10	Expected reduction in operational costs (€ p.a.) in relation to current costs (€ p.a.)
Effort	-10...0...10	Expected reduction personnel efforts (FTE) in relation to current efforts (FTE)
Skills	-10...0...10	Necessary skill profile for employees relating to current skill portfolio
b) Delivery		Soft criteria relating to the service perception
Customer Value	-10...0...10	Expected impact on service-related issues and business requirements, measured by issued solved / created
IT Value	-10...0...10	Expected impact on the IT value proposition
Quality of Service	-10...0...10	Expected change in service quality

Table 2. Weighted criteria from comparison

Criterion	Cost-Conscious Weight	Value-Conscious Weight
Cost	40%	10%
Effort	20%	5%
Skills	10%	5%
Customer Value	10%	30%
IT Value	10%	20%
Quality of Service	10%	30%

2.3 Mapping ITIL-Based Processes to the Comparison Framework

With the choice of a framework for comparison made and a set of criteria that have been weighted according to IT's goals, the next step requires the mapping of the ITIL-based processes up for analysis to their corresponding counterparts of the comparison framework. This can be done by either mapping processes at the original ITIL service level that it is based upon when using a framework that allows a direct linkage to ITIL, such as ITUP, or by basing the mapping on the process' goals linking them to the way these goals are achieved in the comparison framework. Table 3 shows a mapping of the ITIL V3 Change Management goals to the corresponding MOF V4 outcomes; Table 4 links the ITIL V3 Standard Change Processes to its counterpart in MOF V4.

2.4 Mapping Additional Process Areas of the Comparison Framework

Depending on the extend of the original ITIL implementation and the choice of framework, a certain number of processes or activities of the process landscape, as well as areas of the comparison framework stay unmapped after the previous step, for reasons lying with the implementation of home-grown processes or the extensional nature of the framework. Their mapping, starting by relating the frameworks additional processes to the corresponding activities is followed by an evaluation of the remaining activities, regarding their nature and reasons for any missing representation. These non-ITIL related mappings (1), unmatched framework areas (2) and unmatched implemented processes (3) are the most interesting spots of the comparison, promising the most improvement potentials (Figure 4).

2.5 Identifying Differences, Applying Comparison Criteria and Evaluating the Found Differences

The comparison of the mapped processes is highly depended on the quality and amount of documentation available for the processes being assessed. Whether it has been gathered from design documentation, a process portfolio documenting implemented processes, or from an observation and interview survey, several aspects have to be compared to identify the differences. A suitable starting point are high level designs, the activities generating process output from input, as well as interaction with other processes. Once differences have been identified, the criteria are applied and measured, resulting in a weighted assessment. The unmapped processes and framework areas have to be evaluated separately.

Figure 3. Linear sequenced comparison

2.6 Deriving Improvement Measures for Review

Once the differences have been evaluated they can be classified as weak-spots needing improvement, soft-spots representing adequate solutions, or hot-spots representing added value over ITIL or the comparison framework. Due to the nature of the comparison, the framework solution that is evaluated as an advantage over current practice (the weak-spot) is already mapped as a possible

improvement measure, enabling a direct transition into a conceptual evaluation phase.

3. PRACTICAL COMPARISON USING PILOT-PHASE PROCESSES

This part uses the comparison approach presented above, to evaluate actual processes in use at an international operating telecommunication manufacturer. The processes were modeled based on

Table 3. Linking ITIL V3 goals to MOF V4 process outcomes (Microsoft Corporation, 2008b)

ITIL V3 Change Management Goals	Corresponding MOF V4 Goals and Processes
Respond to the customer's changing business requirements while maximizing value and reducing incidents, disruption and re-work	Eliminate unnecessary change. Reduce unintended side effects.
Respond to the business and IT requests for change that will align the services with the business needs.	Have a predictable process for managing changes to the production environment to improve reliability and customer satisfaction.

Table 4. Mapping ITIL V3 standard change management process (OGC, 2007) to MOF V4 change and configuration SMF process (Microsoft Corporation, 2008b)

Standard Change Process	Change and Configuration Process Flow
Record the RFC / Update Change and Configuration Information in CMS	Baseline Configuration (Define the Configuration Data to Track, Audit the CMS Content) Initiate Change (Initiate an RFC)
Review RFC / Update Change and Configuration Information in CMS	Initiate Change (Check the Technical Configuration, Check the Business Process Configuration, Identify the Business Impact, Update the RFC)
Assess and Evaluate Change / Update Change and Configuration Information in CMS	Classify Change (Identify the Priority, Identify the Category, Update the RFC)
Authorize Change / Update Change and Configuration Information in CMS	Approve and Schedule Change (Route the Change to the Correct Approving Body, Approve, Reject or Seek Additional Information, Update RFC)
Plan Updates / Update Change and Configuration Information in CMS	Approve and Schedule Change (Process standard changes to release, Analyze Impact and Identify Reviewers, Update RFC) Develop and Test Change (Design the Change, Identify Configuration Dependencies)
Co-ordinate Change Implementation (including Building and Testing the Change) / Update Change and Configuration Information in CMS	Develop and Test Change (Build and Test Change, Review Change Readiness, Update the RFC) Release Change (Release Change, Stabilize the Change, Get Final Customer Approval, Document and Communicate Deployed Change, Transfer Responsibility to Operations and Support, Update the RFC)
Review and Close Change Record / Update Change and Configuration Information in CMS	Validate and Review Change (Validate Technical Success or Failure, Validate Business Success or Failure, Audit Configuration Database, Communicate and Record Change, Update and Close the RFC)

Figure 4. Intersection of processes and improvement potentials

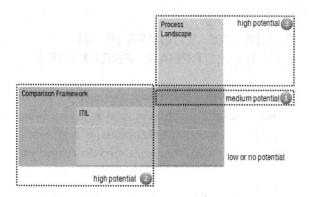

ITIL V2 and rolled out for piloting recently. Due to the early life-cycle stage they are derived from documentation, with information on practical operation results not sufficiently available. This early stage makes them perfect candidates for a comparison, with regards to the nonexistence of metrics usually needed for process optimization, for instance with Six Sigma, and the completion of the design phase, complicating the applicability of Design for Six Sigma.

The framework chosen is MOF V3, due to its relation to ITIL V2 and the fact that the customer wants to secure the investment into the ITIL V2 roll-out.

The chosen criteria (Table 1) are weighted for value (Table 2) as the IT strategy originating the ITIL implementation aimed at the reduction of defects in service delivery and the improvement of IT value.

The process in question is the Change Management Process and its goal is to ensure the use of standardized methods and procedures for efficient and prompt handling of all changes to minimize the impact of change-related incidents upon service quality and to improve the day to day operations of the organization. This goal corresponds to the MOF V3 process covered in the Change Management Service Management Function (SMF). When comparing the two, several differences become apparent (Exemplary: Table 5).

Once the differences have been established they can be evaluated by using the criteria chosen and weighted (Table 6).

The evaluation of the differences shows, that MOF V3 procedures could present improvements over the current processes regarding the differences 1, 2, and 5. These activities should be included in the review for possible process improvements. The differences 3 and 4 show an advantage over the MOF V4 and should not be considered for implementation.

Table 5. Exemplary differences between evaluated change management process and MOF V3 [10]

Evaluated Process Activity	Difference to MOF
Change Implementer Submits RFC	1. MOF includes an additional reason for an RFC: Business strategy influencing the requirements from IT. 2. MOF allows a member of IT to become change owner, if the change initiator is unfamiliar with the IT systems.
Is this an Emergency Change	3. MOF includes emergencies in the priority set by the change owner for the RFC as above a "High Priority"
Is this a Standard Change	4. MOF includes standard changes in the change category set by the change owner for the RFC
Is the RFC Valid and Complete	5. MOF first screens the RFC for completeness and appropriateness. Screening includes escalation procedures in case of delay
...	...

4. CONCLUSION AND FUTURE WORK

Assessing ITIL-based processes for optimization can either be done by classic, metrics-based optimization methods or by comparing them with frameworks that have been created to extend the ITIL with more actionable and practical procedures.

The comparison is the preferred approach when proper metrics are not available or process designs are still being tested. Its flexibility regarding the choice of framework, criteria and criteria weight ensure its orientation towards IT and business strategy. Furthermore, it enables a fast and simple early assessment at a low cost / low effort, delivering possible improvement measures as its side-product.

The exemplary test with an ITIL-based change management process that is part of most ITIL-implementations raised three improvable differences and established two process features that

can be regarded as improvements to ITIL V2 as well as MOF V3. Nevertheless, it can only provide a starting point for an optimization and does not replace a necessary in-depth review of improvements considered for implementation. Secondly, it is highly dependent on the ability to apply the comparison criteria to the concepts provided by the comparison framework.

Further development of the method currently focuses on the creation of a criteria catalogue and the extension of the framework areas included in the comparison towards role-models, tools and work products.

REFERENCES

Anthes, G. (2008, July 21). *How to get more out of ITIL with Version 3*. Retrieved July 31, 2008 from http://www.computerworld.com/action/article.do?command=viewArticleBasic&articleId=321499&source=rss_news10

Table 6. Evaluated differences

Difference Nr.	Cost	Effort	Skill	Customer Value	IT Value	QoS	Weighted Sum
1	Including changes responding to business strategy changes of the requirements might heighten efforts but adds value through better Business-IT-Alignment						
	-2 W:10	-3 W:5	-1 W:5	8 W:30	5 W:20	0 W:30	300/1000
2	Letting IT personnel become change owner might reduce the number of RFCs requiring additional work later in the process						
	-2 W:10	-5 W:5	-5 W:5	5 W:30	7 W:20	5 W:30	370/1000
3	Treating emergency changes as an additional priority might standardize the process, but leads to a delayed reaction due to the activities preceding authorization (Validation, Screening)						
	1 W:10	0 W:5	3 W:5	-2 W:30	-4 W:20	-6 W:30	-295/1000
4	Treating standard changes as an additional category might standardize the process, but leads to a delayed reaction due to the activities preceding authorization (Validation, Screening)						
	1 W:10	0 W:5	3 W:5	-2 W:30	-4 W:20	-6 W:30	-295/1000
5	Screening the RFC prior to validation and including an escalation procedure for an alternate screener if the screening falls behind on schedule might lead to a reduction in additional work necessary before approval						
	-3 W:10	-5 W:5	-5 W:5	6 W:30	5 W:20	3 W:30	290/1000

ASL BiSL Foundation. (2007, July 27). *ASL*. RetrievedJuly 31, 2008, from http://www.asl-bislfoundation.org/content/view/11/15/lang,en/

Dierlamm, J. (2008, May 28). Itil V3 - Good Practices versus gepflegtes Chaos. *Computerwoche*.

IBM. (2008, July 18). *IBM Service Management*. RetrievedJuly 31, 2008, from http://www-306.ibm.com/software/tivoli/governance/servicem-anagement/itup/tool.html

Microsoft Corporation. (2005). *MOF SMF - Change Management*. Redmond, WA: Author.

Microsoft Corporation. (2008a, April 25). *Microsoft Operations Framework 4.0*. Retrieved July 31, 2008 from http://technet.microsoft.com/en-us/library/cc506049.aspx

Microsoft Corporation. (2008b, April 25). *Change and Configuration Service Management Function*. Redmond, WA: Author. Retrieved from http://www.microsoft.com/downloads/details.aspx?FamilyId=457ED61D-27B8-49D1-BACA-B175E8F54C0C&displaylang=en

OGC - Office of Government Commerce. (2007). *Service Transition*. London: TSO.

OGC - Office of Government Commerce. (2008, June 16). *ITIL*. Retrieved July 31, 2008, from http://www.ogc.gov.uk/guidance_itil.asp

Pevzner, B. (2007, June 4). ITIL v3 – Building a successful IT service delivery organization brick by brick, with the Service Portfolio as the cornerstone! *The Boris Files*. Retrieved July 31, 2008, from http://blog.centrata.com/weblog/

Welp, C. (2007). Gefühltes Glück. *Wirtschaftswoche*, 21.

Chapter 14
Exploring E-Marketing Practises as Tool for Globalisation by Egyptian SBEs

Hatem El-Gohary
Birmingham City University, UK & Cairo University Business School, Egypt

ABSTRACT

This chapter aims to add to the accumulative knowledge in the field of E-marketing through exploring E-Marketing practises by Egyptian small business enterprises as a tool for globalisation. An organised systematic examination of the published work related to E-Marketing practises by small business enterprises is discussed and illustrated. Moreover, the chapter demonstrates that although many Egyptian small business enterprises seems to conduct E-Marketing activities, only very small number of these enterprises conduct an effective and efficient E-Marketing activities for expanding globally. The chapter illustrates an exploratory research to explore the current aspects related to E-Marketing adoption and implementation by Egyptian small business enterprises as a tool for globalisation. The main aim of conducting such exploratory study is to achieve a deep and reflective understanding of E-Marketing practises by Egyptian small business enterprises as a tool for globalisation. The results of the fieldwork research conducted by the author through survey and case studies will enable authors, entrepreneurs, policy makers, students and practitioners to build a greater understanding of E-Marketing practises by Egyptian small businesses. Moreover, the chapter will help authors and scholars in the field of E-Marketing to have a clearer view towards suitable future research studies in the field of E-Marketing that in turn will contribute to the related accumulated knowledge in the field.

DOI: 10.4018/978-1-61520-623-0.ch014

INTRODUCTION

Unquestionably Small Business Enterprises (SBE's) are one of the most important tools to achieve economic development and employment growth for any country all over the world. According to data provided by the UK Department of Trade and Industry - DTI (2008), in 2007 99.1% of all companies registered within the UK were small sized (SBE's) and provided 47.3% of the employment in the UK.

On the other hand, as a results of the rapid developments in computer science, IT, the Internet, mobile technologies and the media the way of conducting business today is changing not only dramatically but also in a very high speed given the chance for globalisation as a phenomenon and philosophy to become a reality forcing all types of organisations (regardless of its size) to think and act globally in most cases or to think globally and act locally in some other cases.

Although the phrase "think globally and act locally" was originated by Rene Dubos in 1972 as an advisor to the United Nations Conference on the Human Environment and was mainly related to the argument that global environmental problems can turn into action only by considering local surroundings (Eblen & Eblen, 1994) it is now commonly used in business practises to illustrate the importance of thinking to compete in a global market by focussing on local actions to achieve competitive advantages.

Moreover, although E-Marketing as a phenomenon and philosophy is still a relatively new concept, predominantly for small business enterprises in the light of the limited resources available for these enterprises, the concept is gaining much more interest from authors and practitioners than the last decade. From the author point of view, conducting E-marketing activities by small business enterprise can change the scope of SBE's business all over the world. In this context, E-Marketing can generate a lot of opportunities for small business enterprises which is going to enable these enterprises to eliminate its weaknesses, fight its threats and optimise its strengths. Through that, E-Marketing will enable small business enterprises to compete in global bases which in turn will maximise its competitive advantages. Consequently, there is a need to have a much clearer and deep understanding about all the aspects related to E-Marketing problems as well as its opportunities for SBE's and how E-Marketing can be used to carry out the marketing activities in a more effective and efficient way to enable small business enterprises to compete globally.

Depending on that, the chapter aims to explore the current aspects related to E-Marketing adoption and implementation by Egyptian small business enterprises as a tool for globalisation. The chapter starts with a discussion related to the current circumstances related to small business enterprises is Egypt, within this discussion a brief background about Egypt is provided to illustrate the different factors that might have an impact on the business environment for Egyptian small business enterprises. Based on this brief background a profile of the Egyptian small business enterprises and its geographical distribution, the different Egyptian institutions linked to small business enterprises in Egypt as well as the evolution of the internet in Egypt is illustrated. Afterwards, the chapter provide a complete report for the details of two exploratory studies conducted in the direction of gaining deep and reflective understanding of the phenomenon under investigation. This understanding will provide great benefits for entrepreneurs, policy makers, students, practitioners, authors, and educators though providing them with a clearer view and deep understanding for all the issues related to E-Marketing practises by Egyptian small business enterprises

BACKGROUND

Small Business Enterprises

Despite of the important role of small businesses enterprises in the economic life for any country, defining small businesses was always very hard. Unfortunately, there is a little agreement about the different definitions for small businesses. In this context, there is no single optimal definition of a small business enterprise. Since the late 1970's there have been many various attempts to standardise the definitions of small business enterprises (SBE's) by authors, practitioners and other interested parties and institutions using many variables such as: the number of employees, annual sales, annual turnover, balance sheet, the value added by the enterprise, the value of the enterprise assets and ownership. But the first two variables are most often used to delimit the category of SBE's.

Based on that, small businesses have been defined in many different ways according to national and local needs (Theng & Boon 1996; Watson & Everrett 1996). But the best description of the key characteristics of a small firm remains that used by the Bolton Committee in its 1971 Report on Small Firms. The Committee stated that a small firm is: an independent business, managed by its owner or part-owners and having a small market share (DTI, 2008).

The SBE definition currently in force in the European Community (EC) low is that one adopted by the European Commission in its Recommendation 2003/361/EC of the sixth of May 2003 (replacing Recommendation 96/280/EC) and addressed to Member states, the European Investment Bank (EIB) and the European Investment Fund (EIF) (European Commission, 2008).

The number of employees is the most often used element in determining the category of SBE's in most countries. Furthermore, in most countries (countries of the European Union, Canada – in services -, Mexico and Turkey) a SBE will be defined as an enterprise that employs less than 50 employees. Accordingly and due to the absence of a unique official definition for SBE's, the author within this chapter will use the European definition for SBE's for the purpose of conducting the current research. According to this definition an

enterprise will be considered as a small business if it employs less than 50 employees, have an a annual turnover (or global balance) that is less than 10 million Euros and not exceeding 25% of the enterprise capital or voting rights withheld by one or more companies (or public bodies) which are not themselves SME's.

Electronic Marketing

Electronic marketing can be regarded as a new business practice associated with buying and selling goods, services, information and ideas via the Internet and other electronic means. A review of relevant literature revealed that the definitions of electronic marketing vary according to author's point of view, background and specialisation, as follows:

"Achieving marketing objectives through applying digital technologies" (Smith and Chaffey, 2005. p: 11)

"The use of electronic data and applications for planning and executing the conception, distribution and pricing of ideas, goods and services to create exchanges that satisfy individual and organizational objectives" (Strauss and Frost, 2001, p: 454)

"Any use of technology to achieve marketing objectives" (McDonald and Wilson, 1999, P: 29)

"Achieving marketing objectives through use of electronic communications technology" (Chaffey, 2007, P: 339)

"The process aimed at facilitating and conducting of business communication and transactions over networks" (Reedy and Schullo, 2004, p: 16)

The author used the Strauss and Frost (2001) definition to conduct the current research since it takes into consideration all the elements of

E-marketing, all types of products and it illustrates the main objective of E-marketing which is creating the exchanges that satisfy individual and organisational needs. Moreover it is the official definition for E-marketing adopted by the American E-Marketing Association.

SMALL BUSINESS ENTERPRISES IN EGYPT

"As Small and Medium Enterprises (SME's) in Egypt represent the greatest share of the productive units of the Egyptian economy, the current national policy directions address ways and means of developing the capacities of SME's." Dr. Ahmed Nazif (Egyptian Prime Minister, SFD, 2009a)

Egypt, an Overview

Egypt is a very important Arab, Middle East and African country due to its very important and strategic: economic, political and geographical position. It stands on northern Africa occupying the northeast corner of the continent, bordering the Mediterranean Sea from the north, Libya from the west, Palestine and Red Sea from east and Sudan from the south. With a 995,450 sq km of land, a population of 76,607,237 (as in May 2009 – CAPMAS, 2009), a 28 governorates (Al-Daqahliyah, Al-Bahr-El-Ahmar, Al-Baheyra, Al-Fayum, Al-Gharbyah, Alexandria, Al-Ismailiyah, Al-Gizah, Al-Minufiyah, Al-Minya, Al-Qalyubiyah, Al-Wadi-Al-Gadid, Al-Suez, Al-Sharqiyah, Aswan, Asyut, Bani Sowaf, Port Said, Cairo, Damietta, Helwaan, Kafr-Al-Shaykh, Matruh, North Sina, Qina, South Sina, Suhaj and 6th of October) and one special self-governing city (Luxor) as the city of Luxor is not a governorate but have a special unique characteristics and for that considered as a special self-governing city which the structure and resources of a governorate.

The country is divided by the Nile valley, where most of the population are located and most of

the economic activity takes place. The Egyptian economy depends mainly on agriculture, media, Suez Canal, tourism, the transferred income of Egyptians workforces from outside the country.

In the last 30 years, the Egyptian government has started reforming the highly centralised economy from the sixties and med seventies eras into a totally market liberalisation economy. In 2005, the government reduced both personal and corporate tax rates, reduced energy subsidies, and privatised several public enterprises. The stock market grown dramatically from 2000 to 2006 and the GDP grew by nearly 5%.

But despite these achievements, the government did not succeed in raising the living standards for most of the average Egyptians, and has had to continue providing subsidies for basic necessities for a wide range of Egyptians. These subsidies as well as the deficit in the Egyptian trading balance have contributed to a growing budget deficit - more than 8% of GDP in 2005 (CAPMAS, 2009; EMI, 2009). For that and to achieve higher GDP growth the government will need to continue its aggressive pursuit of reform, especially in the export sectors.

Some of the reasons for the problems of the Egyptian economy are: the rapidly growing population (the largest in the Arab world and one of the largest in Africa), limited arable land - 2.92% of the total land space (CAPMAS, 2009) -, full dependence on the Nile in conducting agricultural activities and the world financial crises. All these factors combined continue to consume the country available resources and stress the economy. For that the government is working very hard to continue the economic reform, conduct massive investment in communications and physical infrastructure and encouraging massive development in the SBE's sector as an attempt to reduce the bad effect of the current world financial crises on Egypt as well as to improve the country economic performance.

Profile of Small Business Enterprises in Egypt

Egyptian small business enterprises have more than seven thousand years of recorded history. Ancient Egypt was among the earliest civilizations on earth that discovered and appreciated the value of work and the real meaning of entrepreneurship. That can be traced and seen obviously on the drawings on the Egyptian temples and old papyrus papers. Furthermore, Small business enterprises are expected to be the engines of economic growth in Egypt over the next several decades and are expected to create the jobs needed by its ever growing population. The main three parties responsible for the development of the SBE's sector in Egypt are: The Social Fund for Development (SFD), the Small Enterprise Development Organisation (SEDO) and the Arab Union for Small Enterprises. But despite that, till now there is no standard definition for SBE's in Egypt.

Based on the data derived from the Egyptian Labour Market Survey 1998 and Labour Force sample survey 1988 (which are the most available recent data), the number of small enterprises witnessed a clear increase during the period from 1988 to 1998. According to the Egyptian Ministry of Trade and Industry - EMTI (2008), in 1998 there was a total of 3 322 476 SBE's in Egypt most of it (2 776 031) was informal small businesses (underground economy – the SBE does not have any licences, complete procedures and/or documents). On the other hand, based on the data provided by the Egyptian Ministry of Trade and Industry (EMTI, 2008) the women entrepreneurs have a reasonable number of the total number of SBE entrepreneurs in Egypt with a total of 613896 women entrepreneurs from a total of 3322476 entrepreneurs.

One of the reasons for that is the Egyptian culture, where many women turn to start up their own enterprises or work with relatives in small businesses so that they can manage between their household duties, their work roles and support their families. The Egyptian Ministry of Trade and Industry estimates that in the future there will be an increase in the number of women working in small business enterprises. According to the Egyptian Ministry of Trade and Industry - EMTI (2008), the higher percentage of self-employed women's are in rural areas, that is mainly because it is easier for those women living in rural areas to work independently and manage between their household duties and their work roles. While the higher percentage of wage women workers are in urban areas because of the high availability of job vacancies with good salaries.

When looking to the regional distribution of small business enterprises in Egypt it is noticeable that the northern parts of the country have created more new enterprises than those in the south, highlighting the continuing disparity and widening the economic gap between the north and the south parts of Egypt. Cairo, Damietta and AL-Sharkia governorates have the greatest firm formation rates in Egypt (EMTI, 2008). Cairo, being the capital, has traditionally been the main location of large public and private investments due to its relatively better developed infrastructure, the availability of good investment opportunities and the existence of a huge market (a population of around 20 million) and for that it represents the most attractive location for new investments.

On the other hand, Damietta region is well known not only for its wood and furniture products but also for its world class food products, dominated by its small production units, with a first class world reputation that goes beyond the Egyptian and African boundaries. Al-Sharkia governorate has the largest number of new settlements in one region, providing the attraction of new industrial land, as well as having a traditional metal industry whose outputs cater mainly for the agricultural sector. At the other end of the spectrum, according to the Egyptian Ministry of Trade and Industry - EMTI (2008), the Suez and the south Sinai regions have the lowest firm formation rates. The first is dominated by large state owned heavy industries (oil refineries and chemical industries) which absorb most of the working population. While South Sinai, the only region with no recorded new firms, has a dominant tourist industry which is likely, with its related activities to have attracted many new investments.

Social Fund for Development (SFD)

The Egyptian Social Fund for Development (SFD) had been established in late 1991 as a social safety network associated with the Egyptian government agreement to undertake a wide Economic Reform and Structural Adjustment Programme (ERASP) in collaboration with the International Bank (IB) and the International Monetary Fund (IMF). Accordingly, the Fund was considered as a very necessary and critical tool to achieve a real support of the reform programme and to help in reducing the negative effects of such a programme on the Egyptian people and the Egyptian society in general. The Egyptian SFD generally works to: increase the human resources quality within the Egyptian society, enable and support a good environment for human development, develop different mechanisms for improved understanding of the impact of globalisation and mobilises efforts to minimize the risks of social exclusion, help in improving living standards for the Egyptian people, eliminate poverty and fight unemployment. In this context, The SFD work to create employment opportunities for start-up entrepreneurs and provides them with credit, technical and managerial assistance, necessary needed skills, and technological know-how from both Egyptian and international institutions to provide all the possible opportunities for success.

The SFD is managed through it board of directors which is chaired by Egyptian Prime Minister (Currently Dr. Ahmed Nazif). At the moment, the SFD board of directors composed of the following members: the Minister of International Cooperation, Minister of Trade & Industry, Minister of Information, Minister of Transport, Minister of

Manpower and Immigration, SFD Managing Director, President of the General Organisation for Investment and Free Zones, Board Chairman of Americana company, Board Chairman of Maghrabi Group, Legal Accountant and Financial Adviser and Small Enterprise Development Expert (SFD, 2009a).

Small Enterprise Development Organisation (SEDO)

Small Enterprise Development Organisation (SEDO) is a subsidiary unit of the Egyptian Social Fund for Development (SFD). SEDO had been established on the 1st of December 1999 according to the Egyptian Presidential Decree No. 434 for the year 1999 which instituted SEDO as an organisation operating under the umbrella of the SFD and specialised in the development of small enterprises (The Small Enterprise Development Organisation - SEDO, 2009).

It aims at providing all the possible assistance in every aspect to small and medium sized enterprises (SME's) within Egypt. To help the Small Enterprise Development Organisation (SEDO) in achieving its objectives, the Social Fund for Development (SFD) allocates about 50% of its available resources for the Small Enterprise Development Organisation (SFD, 2009b). The Organisation develops various funding mechanisms and many technical and managerial support systems to help small businesses through two main groups which represent the main structure of the SEDO namely:-

- The Small Enterprise Development Group.
- The Marketing and Management Group.

The Arab Union for Small Enterprises

The Arab Union for Small Enterprises (AUSE) is a relatively new established local Arabic organisation under the umbrella of The Arab League and the Council of Arab Economic Unity. The Union membership are available for institutions, organisations, agencies, funds, federations, associations, centres, public and private companies as well as non-governmental organisations (NGO's) working in the development, financing or supporting small business enterprises in the Arab world (21 countries namely: Egypt, Sudan, Libya, Tunisia, Algeria, Morocco, Mauritania, Djibouti, Somalia, Palestine, Lebanon, Syria, Kingdom of Saudi Arabia - KSA, Yemen, Jordan, Kuwait, United Arab Emirates - UAE, Qatar, Iraq, Bahrain and Oman).

The AUSE was established in the 31st of May 2004 and joined the specialised Arab unions working under the Council of Arab Economic Unity according to the Council's Decree No. 1259d/80 in 1/12/2004. The founding members of the AUSE were: Egypt, Sudan, Lebanon, Yemen, Syria, Kingdom of Saudi Arabia (KSA), Kingdom of Jordan, Tunisia, United Arab Emirates (UAE), Kuwait, and Oman. The membership of the Union has three main levels and consists of: Active members, Associate members and Observer members. Moreover, the AUSE assists its members not only in achieving their tasks and objectives but also consolidates mutual cooperation and coordination among them (AUSE, 2009).

Egypt had played a very important role in the development of the AUSE since 2004 and till now. In recognition of the Egyptian endless role and efforts to activate the AUSE, promote its objectives and expand its membership, the AUSE in its meeting held on the 29th of May 2008 elected the Egyptian SFD chairman (Hany Seif El Nasr) as AUSE Chairman for the second time (SFD, 2009b).

EGYPT AND THE INTERNET

In an attempt to develop the Egyptian economic performance full Internet services coverage started in Egypt in October 1993 through two main platforms namely the Egyptian Universities Network and the Information and Decision Support Centre (IDSC) (ISE, 2009). The main infrastructure for providing the service was provided by the Egyptian National Telecommunication Organisation (ENTO - Egypt Telecom). Although the official starting date for the Internet services in Egypt was the second half of 1993, there had been several initiatives by public and private organisations that had been taken before that date for the provision of partial Internet Services in the country. The user community was estimated at that time to be about 2000 - 3000 users (Internet Society of Egypt - ISE, 2009).

Starting from 1994, the Egyptian domain was divided into three major sub-domains:

- The academic sub-domain "eun" which stands for the Egyptian universities networks and provides the service for the universities, schools and academic institutions.
- The "sci" sub-domain which serves the scientific research institutes at the Egyptian Academy of Scientific Research
- The ".gov.eg" sub-domain which provides its services for the governmental authorities as well as to the commercial entities served via the various Internet Service Providers (ISP's).

Within only two years and starting from 1996 not only the Internet speeds increased by nearly 20 times but also the number of Internet users within the country increased to reach 20,000 users. Moreover, the government started to provide connectivity to private service providers under the ".com.eg" domain, while some providers have their own international gateways (ISE, 2009).

Current Internet Situation in Egypt

Due to the policy of market liberalisation in Egypt and the presence of a very good and advanced IT infrastructure the cost of acquiring computers and telecommunications systems has been decreasing resulting in accelerated use of these products.

Such trends have resulted in increased reliance on IT within the Egyptian economy by most of the Egyptian companies regardless of its size. Moreover, because of the successful implementation of a free Internet strategy in 2002, Egypt now has the largest Internet market in Africa with more than ten million users (10,532,400 users) in December 2008 and around half a million (427,100) broadband internet subscribers as of March 2008 (Internet World Stats – IWS, 2009a).

According to the ISE (2009b) there are around 300 Internet and data service providers in Egypt. Although Egypt is currently the first country in Africa in the number of people using the Internet, Internet penetration is still relatively low comparing to other countries in North America or Europe, and the vast majority of users are located in urban areas especially in Cairo and Alexandria.

Commercialisation of Internet in Egypt

Starting from January 1996, the Egyptian government allowed private companies working in the telecommunications fields to operate as private Internet service providers under the ".com.eg" domain. As a result of the fast growing number of internet users in Egypt as well as the good and sufficient infrastructure that the Egyptian government had provided, Egypt currently has the basic foundation for starting a strong commercial Internet usage. In this context, the Internet community in Egypt increased from around 5,500,000 users to more than 10,500,000 users distributed among three major sectors, academic, government and commercial sectors (ISE, 2009b).

There is also a positive policy to liberalise the country's value added services. The government and the Egyptian National Telecommunication Organisation (Egypt Telecom) started in developing internet backbone and gateway facility with affordable and reasonable prices to be used by the private sector Internet Service Providers (ISP). Moreover, the government announced that it will continue its motivation role to support

newly established ISP's and to establish a strong industry for value added information services in Egypt in few years time.

EGYPTIAN SMALL BUSINESS ENTERPRISES AND E-MARKETING

Small business enterprises represent a high percentage of the Egyptian registered companies within the country. Although, most of these Small business enterprises conduct its business on domestic, local or regional bases and only few of these enterprises conduct business transaction on international bases, Small business enterprises still plays a very important role in driving the Egyptian economy towards achieving high economic performance. Based on that, studying the different aspects that might have an impact over the performance of these small business enterprises is very important and will lead to a better understanding of how this performance can be improved. Keeping in mind the importance of marketing activities and its impact on the total business performance of any firm, with no hesitation the author can confirm the importance of studying and investigating E-Marketing practises by Egyptian small business enterprises as a tool for gaining global competitive advantage.

The author conducted an exploratory study to explore the different aspects related to the adoption and implementation of E-Marketing by Egyptian small business enterprises. The main motive for conducting this exploratory study is the lack of any research investigating the different factor affecting the adoption of E-Marketing by Egyptian small business enterprises as well as the impact of this adoption on the marketing performance of these enterprises. Based on the literature review, there is no single research that had been conducted to investigate the phenomenon investigated by the research on hand. Consequently, there is no information available about the adoption and implementation of E-Marketing by Egyptian small business enterprises or about similar research problems or research issues comparable to those associated with the current research that had been solved in the past. Accordingly, wide preliminary study is needed to gain knowledge and familiarity with the phenomenon investigated. This understanding will lead to better diagnoses for any problems related to E-Marketing practises by Egyptian small business enterprises which is turn will help in providing solutions for these problems.

To conduct the exploratory study, the author started by constructing a database that include Egyptian small business enterprises adopting or implementing E-Marketing to conduct its marketing activities or as a tool for globalisation. The main problem associated with the construction of such database is related to how to define small business enterprises? Although that there is a law associated with all the aspects related to small business enterprises in Egypt which is the Small Business Enterprises Development Law (Law number 141 for the year 2004) and despite that this law had provided a legal definition for small business enterprises in Egypt, there is still more than 12 different definition in use by different institution in Egypt to define small business enterprises. The main reason for having such a large number of definitions for SBE's in Egypt is that each of these institutions use its own definition for SBE's which in most cases serves its own purposes.

In this respect, according to article number one of the Small Business Enterprises Development Law (Law number 141 for the year 2004) a small business enterprise is defined as:-

"Any company or individual firm that conduct production, service or commercial economic activities with a capital no less than 50,000 Egyptian pounds and no more than one million Egyptian pounds and employs 50 employees or less"

(Law number 141 for the year 2004, article 1, p 2)

On the other hand there are another seven definitions that are commonly used to define small business enterprises, these definitions are as follows:-

Definition of the Industrial Development and Workers Bank of Egypt (IDWB):

"A small business enterprise will be that enterprise that the value of its fixed assets does not exceed 1,400,000 pounds" (Industrial Development and Workers Bank of Egypt, 2009)

Definition of Alexandria Small Business Association (ABA):

"A small business enterprise will be that enterprise that employs up to 15 employees" (Alexandria Small Business Association - ABA, 2009)

Definition of Central Agency for Public Moblisation and Statistics (CAPMAS):

"A small business enterprise will be that enterprise that employs between 50 and 100 employees" (CAPMAS, 2009)

Definition of the United States Agency for International Development (USAID):

"A small business enterprise will be that enterprise that employs less than 15 employees and its total fixed assets does not exceed 25,000 pounds" (USAID – 2009)

Definition of Egyptian Institute of National Planning (EINP):

"A small business enterprise will be that enterprise that employs between 10 and 49 employees" (Egyptian Institute of National Planning, 2009)

Definition of Federation of Egyptian Industries (FEI):

"A small business enterprise will be that enterprise that employs no more than 100 employees and its total investment does not exceed 500,000 pounds" (Federation of Egyptian Industries, 2009)

Definition of Crédit Agricole Egypt Bank (CAEB):

"A small business enterprise will be that enterprise that its total assets does not exceed 250,000 pounds" (Crédit Agricole Egypt Bank, 2009)

Table 1 illustrate the different criteria's that had been used in Egypt to define small business enterprises.

From Table 1, it is noticed that number of employees was the most common used criteria in defining small business enterprises in Egypt. Table 2 illustrate the different numbers of employees and capital (assets) values that had been used in these different definitions.

As can be seen from Table 2, there is no common used number of employees or a certain value for capital, investments or assets in defining small business enterprises in Egypt. In this respect, the number of employees as well as the value of capital, investments or assets varies in a very wide rang. Accordingly, no certain number of employees or a certain value for capital, investments or

assets can be considered to be the most common used criteria in defining small businesses in Egypt. Consequently, it is more appropriate when defining small business enterprises for the purpose of the current study to consider the Egyptian legal definition for small businesses derived from the Small Business Enterprises Development Law (Law 141 for the year 2004).

After solving the major problem of defining what is the most suitable definition for defining Egyptian small business enterprises, the author started in constructing a complete database for the Egyptian small business enterprises that adopt and implement E-Marketing to conduct its marketing activities. Based on the author experience with the nature of the Egyptian small business enterprises and the different governmental department, institutions and agencies dealing with SBE's in Egypt, the author started by investigating the Egyptian International Trade Points (EITP) as one of the most common used portals by Egyptian SBE's to conduct E-Marketing activities.

The Egyptian International Trade Points (EITP) is a subsector from the Egyptian Ministry of Trade and industry (EMTI) which is mainly concerned with promoting different Egyptian products to the world through different international information networks and creating new markets for these products, promoting and spreading the adoption and

Table 1. Different criteria's used to define small business enterprises in Egypt

Definition of	Capital (assets)	Number of employees	Both
Law number 141 for the year 2004	√	√	√
Industrial Development and Workers Bank of Egypt	√		
Alexandria Small Business Association		√	
Central Agency for Public Mobilisation and Statistics		√	
United States Agency for International Development	√	√	√
Egyptian Institute of National Planning		√	
Federation of Egyptian Industries	√	√	√
Crédit Agricole Egypt Bank	√		
Total	**5**	**6**	**3**

Source: prepared by the author

implementation of E-Commerce among Egyptian companies and provide small and medium sized enterprises with the needed data to help these enterprises in: establishing the business, producing their products and then promoting these products internationally (EITP, 2009).

On the other hand, there are 14 different international trade points in Egypt distributed all of the country. In this respect, there is three international trade points in Greater Cairo (the Egyptian trade point head office, the sixth of October city international trade point and the businessmen international trade point), six international trade points in the delta region (Alexandria international trade point, Kafr El Shiekh international trade point, Badr international trade point, 10th of Ramadan international trade point, Tanta international trade point and Mansoura international trade point), two in Suez Canal region (Ismailia International Trade Point and Port Said International Trade Point) and three in Upper Egypt region (Fayoum international trade point, BeniSuef international trade point and Assiut international trade point).

As a first step in constructing the Egyptian small business enterprises database, the author investigated all the Egyptian international trade points (a total of 14 EITP) to determine:

- how many firms are registered with each of these international trade points
- How many of these firms are small business enterprises.
- How many of these small business enterprises uses the international trade points as an E-Marketing platform.

Based on this investigation, a total of 12804 firms were registered with the 14 Egyptian international trade points. Out of these firms, 2783 enterprise were small business enterprise (according to the definition adopted by the author) and are using the international trade points as an E-Marketing platform. The distribution of these firms is illustrated in Table 3.

As a second step in constructing the Egyptian small business enterprises database, all the details of these 2783 SBE were reviewed to make sure that there is no duplication in the yielded SBE's and that these data are accurate and reliable. As a result of this review process 324 SBE's were excluded from the total number of the SBE's

Table 2. Different numbers of employees and capital (assets) values that had been used to define small business enterprises in Egypt

Definition of	Capital (assets)	Number of employees
Law number 141 for the year 2004	Capital from 50,000 to 1,000,000 LE	50 employees or less
Industrial Development and Workers Bank of Egypt	Fixed assets not exceeding 1,400,000 LE	-
Alexandria Small Business Association	-	Up to 15 employees
Central Agency for Public Mobilisation and Statistics	-	Between 50 – 100 employees
United States Agency for International Development	Fixed assets not exceeding 25,000 LE	Less than 15 employees
Egyptian Institute of National Planning	-	Between 10 – 50 employees
Federation of Egyptian Industries	Total investments not exceeding 500,000 LE	100 employees or less
Crédit Agricole Egypt Bank	Total assets not exceeding 250,000 LE	-

Source: prepared by the author

Table 3. Number of Egyptian firms and small business enterprises using EITP as an e-marketing platform as on May 2009

N	International Trade Point	Number of firms registered within the trade point	Number of Small Business enterprises using it as an E-Marketing platform
1	Egyptian Trade Point (Head Office)	8936	1973
2	Alexandria International Trade Point	156	131
3	Kafr El Shiekh International Trade Point	143	139
4	10th of Ramadan International Trade Point	1004	15
5	Mansoura International Trade Point	63	63
6	Businessmen International Trade Point	0	0
7	Ismailia International Trade Point	553	173
8	Fayoum International Trade Point	173	154
9	BeniSuef International Trade Point	89	84
10	Assiut International Trade Point	17	7
11	Badr International Trade Point	96	9
12	Tanta International Trade Point	4	4
13	Sixth of October City International Trade Point	1540	17
14	Port Said International Trade Point	30	14
Total		**12804**	**2783**

Source: prepared by the research depending on the different databases of the Egyptian International Trade Points

yielded because of duplication among different international trade points and another 152 SBE's were excluded because it is not in the business anymore or because it cannot be classified as small businesses. Then the excluded SBE's (a total of 476 SBE's) were removed from the database.

As a third step, all the contact and commercial details of the remaining SBE's (2307 SBE's) were collected (which include: the small business enterprise name, owner/main manager name, SBE address, phone number, fax number, e-mail address, SBE type/industry and the SBE website) and used to construct a complete primary database of these SBE's.

Moreover, more than one database and business directory were checked and investigated to generate more SBE's. In this respect the following databases and business directories were investigated:

- Egypt Small Business Directory
- Alibaba Business Directory
- Egypt Directory
- UK Small Business Directory – Egypt Directory
- Egypt Middle East B2B Directory

These five sources were used for the following reasons:

- It provides detailed information for the enterprises registered in it.
- It provides information about considerable numbers of enterprises
- It provides the ability to evaluate the registered enterprises to make sure that it can satisfy the essential requirement to be considered as small business enterprises.
- It is common databases and business directories among small business owners

The search in these five databases and business directories yielded a total of 382 Egyptian small business enterprises. The details of each of these SBE's were obtained and sorted in a sub-database. Thereafter, theses details were investigated and reviewed to make sure that there is no duplication in the yielded SBE's and that these data are accurate and reliable. As a result of this review process 173 SBE's were excluded from the total number of the SBE's yielded because of duplication among different databases and business directories, duplication with the international trade points database, being out of business or because it cannot be classified as small businesses. The remaining SBE's (a total of 209 SBE's) were added to the original database constructed from the SBE's using the Egyptian international trade points. As a result of this process, the total population frame consisted from 2516 Egyptian SBE's distributed all over the country.

EXPLORATORY STUDIES ADOPTED IN THE STAGE OF THE RESEARCH

For the purpose of gaining greater reliability and confidence in the research results, methodological triangulation was conducted in the exploratory research. Within this triangulation approach two main exploratory studies were conducted namely electronic survey and case studies. In this context, the author started by conducting a survey for a sample selected randomly from the population frame. Then the author employed case studies through conducting semi-structured interviews as a tool for gaining deep understanding about the adoption and implementation of E-Marketing by Egyptian small business enterprises as well as the use of E-Marketing as a tool for globalisation. The interviews were conducted with 35 Egyptian small business owners, marketing and sales managers and aimed to find out what are the current level of E-Marketing knowledge among Egyptian small business owners, marketing and sales managers,

the different factors affecting the adoption of E-Marketing by Egyptian small business enterprises and the impact of E-Marketing adoption on the marketing performance of Egyptian SBE's.

THE SURVEY

The author started the exploratory research by conduct survey to explore the different aspects related to E-Marketing practises by Egyptian small business enterprises. The survey was designed in the Arabic language and tested by group of academic researchers from Cairo University Business School and Tanat University Business School, small business owners and marketing practitioners within Greater Cairo region. As a result of the survey pilot testing and in the light of the recommendation received, the survey was adjusted to gain better results.

When determining the survey sample size, the author planned to determine the sample size according to the Aaker & Day (1986) sample size equation which is highly accepted by social science authors since it takes into account the degree of required confidence, the sample error, ratio of population characteristics available in the sample (50% in social sciences) and population size. According to Aaker & Day (1986) the sample size can be determined depending on the following equation:

$$S = Z\sqrt{\frac{p(1-p)}{n}}\sqrt{\frac{N-n}{N-1}}$$

Where:

Z = Degree of required confidence (95%)
S = Sample error (5%)
p = Ratio of population characteristics available in the sample (50%)
N = Population size
n = Sample size

The author started by calculating the sample size using the Aaker and Day (1986) sample size equation in different degrees of required confidence. Based on the equation, for achieving a 90% degree of confidence the sample size needs to be 87, a sample size of 96 SBE's will generate a degree of confidence of 95% and finally a sample size of 103 SBE's will generate a degree of confidence of 99%.

Meanwhile, many scholars within the fields of social sciences like Beck (1995), De Vaus (1996) and Eid (2003) illustrated that using a sample size of twenty percent of the total research population is highly accepted. To this point as far as this part of the study is concerned, the research sample was chosen to represent twenty percent of the research population. The sample size was chosen to represent twenty percent of the research population for the following reasons:

- This sample size exceeds the sample size required to achieve 99% degree of confidence according to the Aaker and Day (1986) sample size equation which is highly recognised among researches in the fields of social science.
- A sample size of twenty percent of the total population is accepted by most authors within the field.

Based on that and as a result of the very low response rate of mailed questionnaires in Egypt (as quoted by most author in Egypt), the author favoured to depend on electronic questionnaires to conduct the survey. The main reason for using electronic e-mailed questionnaires is that the author assumed that the sample SBE's will perceive it as a favourable form of communication based on the fact that these SBE's are using one form or another of E-Marketing and for that they are more technological oriented than other firms within the Egyptian market. Consequently, electronic questionnaires were e-mailed to 504 small business enterprises representing twenty percent of

the total population frame and randomly selected from this population frame. Out of these 504 small business enterprises and after several reminders to the SBE's owners and marketing managers via e-mails, mailed letters and phone calls only three questionnaires were filled.

The author was totally surprised of this response rate which was 0.59% (less than 1%) especially that the questionnaire was very short, highly organized, use very simple Arabic language, straightforward and the questions were simple and sorted in logical order.

CASE STUDIES

As a result of the unexpected very low response rate for the survey, the author decided to move to the second phase of the exploratory study by conducting case studies. In this context, invitation e-mails as well as an invitation letters were sent to the all the small business enterprises within the population frame resulted from the first phase of the exploratory study. Follow ups were made using e-mails, mailed letters and phone calls to the SBE's owners and marketing managers. As a result of this follow up, eleven small business enterprises agreed to participate in the research through an interview with the author.

Although the author did not expect to have the approval of eleven small business enterprises (in the light of the surprising response rate for the survey), the author tried to gain more SBE's approval to participate in this stage of the research. Based on the author experience with the Egyptian culture and the fact that most of the small business enterprises are highly connected with the Egyptian international trade points, the Egyptian international trade points is assumed to have a great impact on the small business enterprises owners. In consequence of that, the author contacted the head of the Egyptian international trade points as well as some other top officials in the Egyptian Ministry of Trade and industry (EMTI) to gain their support in convincing small business owners to participate in the second stage of the exploratory study. The head of the Egyptian international trade points as well as all the officials of the Egyptian Ministry of Trade and industry (EMTI) were very helpful, supportive and provided the author with all the possible assistance. Formal communications were sent to the small business owners registered with the Egyptian international trade points asking them to participate in the second stage of the exploratory study. As a result of that, another twenty four small business enterprises agreed to participate in the research through an interview with the author increasing the total number of SBE's that agreed to participate in the research to thirty five small business enterprises.

The author contacted the small businesses owners to discuss with them the most suitable time for conducting the interviews as will as the most suitable place for commencing these interviews. Based on that, a schedule of the planned interviews was made containing all the necessary needed information about the interviews participants. The interviews were conducted with the small business enterprises owners, marketing managers or the person responsible about implementing E-marketing activities within the small businesses. The interviews were mainly conducted as face-to-face interviews (only one interview was conducted over the phone due to the unavailability of one of the small business owners) and in Arabic language during January 2008.

On the other hand, the interviews included three main questions sections with a total of fifteen open ended questions. The first set of questions was investigating the level of E-Marketing knowledge among small business enterprises owners, marketing managers, or sales managers. The second set of questions was designed to explore the different factors that might have an impact on the adoption of E-Marketing by these small business enterprises owners, marketing managers, or sales managers. Finally, the last set of questions was designed to explore the impact of E-Marketing implementation on the marketing performance of the Egyptian small business enterprises as well as the use of E-Marketing as a tool for globalisation.

Table 4 illustrate the distribution of the research participants by their position within the small business enterprise. As can be seen from the table that while 77.1% of the participants (a total of 27 participant) were the small business owners themselves, 20% of them (7 participant) hold the position of marketing manager in their enterprise and finally 2.9% of them (only one participant) hold other positions (sales managers, etc) and were in charge of E-Marketing implementation within their enterprise.

The participating small business enterprises were distributed among the main geographical regions of Egypt and the distribution of the small business enterprises participating in the research is representative for the research population. In this context and as can be seen from Table 5 and Figure 1, the majority of small enterprises (43.3% - twelve SBE's) were located in Cairo followed by 22.9% (8 SBE's) located in the Delta, 20% (7 SBE's) in Alexandria and finally 11.4% (four SBE's) in both Upper Egypt and Suez Canal region.

Table 4. Distribution of the SBE's participants by position

		Frequency	*Percent*	*Valid Percent*
Valid	Entrepreneur	*27*	*77.1*	*77.1*
	Marketing Manager	7	20.0	20.0
	Other	1	2.9	2.9
	Total	*35*	*100.0*	*100.0*

Table 5. Distribution of the participating SBE's by location

		Frequency	Percent	Valid Percent
Valid	Cairo	12	34.3	34.3
	Alexandria	7	20.0	20.0
	Delta	8	22.9	22.9
	Upper Egypt	4	11.4	11.4
	Suez Canal region	4	11.4	11.4
	Total	*35*	*100.0*	*100.0*

Table 6. Distribution of the SBE's by number of employees

		Frequency	Percent	Valid Percent
Valid	Less than 10	0	0.00	0.00
	10 – 19	*29*	*82.9*	*82.9*
	20 – 29	*6*	*17.1*	*17.1*
	30 - 39	0	0.00	0.00
	40 - 50	0	0.00	0.00
	Total	*35*	*100.0*	*100.0*

With regards to the number of employees, as can be seen from Table 6 the majority of the participating SBE's (29 enterprises with a percentage of 82.9% of the total number of enterprises) fall into the category of enterprises that has between 10 - 19 employees. Followed by 6 enterprises in the category of enterprises that has between 20 – 29 employees (with a percentage of

17.1% of the total number of enterprises) and there were no enterprises in the other categories of number of employees (less than 10, 30-39 and 40-50 employees)

As age might be one of the factors affecting the implementation and adoption of new marketing philosophies like E-Marketing, Table 7 illustrate the distribution of the participants by age. As can be seen from the table, the majority of the research participants (57.1% - 20 participants) aged between 30 – 40 years, followed by 25.7% of the respondents (9 participants) in the category of age under 30 years, 14.3% of in the category of age between 41 – 50 years (5 participants) and 2.9% (one participants) in the category of age between 51 – 60 years. In other words, 82.8% of the research respondents were less than 41 years of age.

On the other hand with regards to the level of education of the participants, Table 8 illustrate the distribution of the respondents by level of education. As can be seen from the table, the

Figure 1. Distribution of the participating SBE's by location

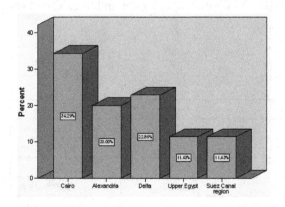

Table 7. Distribution of the participants by age

		Frequency	Percent	Valid Percent
Valid	Under 30 years	9	25.7	25.7
	30-40 years	20	57.1	57.1
	41-50 years	5	14.3	14.3
	51-60 years	1	2.9	2.9
	Over 60 years	0	0.00	0.00
	Total	*35*	*100.0*	*100.0*

Table 8. Distribution of the participants by level of education

		Frequency	Percent	Valid Percent
Valid	Collage certificate or less	20	57.1	57.1
	University graduate	14	40.0	40.0
	Postgraduate studies	1	2.9	2.9
	Total	*35*	*100.0*	*100.0*

majority of the participants (57.1% - 20 participants) had only a collage certificate or less, 40% (14 participants) were university graduates and only one participant (2.9% of the total) commenced postgraduate studies.

CASE STUDY ANALYSIS

This part of the chapter will present the details of the case study findings and will report the facts gathered about the current practice of E-Marketing by Egyptian small business enterprises with a particular emphases on exploring the different factors that might have an impact of the adoption of E-Marketing by these small business enterprises as well as the effect of this adoption on its marketing performance. The answers of the small business enterprises owners, marketing managers, or sales managers collected during the interviews were transcribed, sorted and analysed depending on content analysis. The frequency of the participants own words that had been used to answer the interviews questions were used

to identify and categorise the different aspects and relationships related to E-Marketing and to illustrate differences and similarities within the participants responses.

The case study analysis will be structured in three main sections; the first one will be devoted to evaluate the current knowledge about E-Marketing among Egyptian small business enterprises, the second section will be devoted to exploring the different factors that might have an impact of the adoption of E-Marketing by these small business enterprises and finally the third section will be devoted to explore different effects of E-Marketing adoption on the marketing performance of Egyptian small business enterprises as well as the use of E-Marketing as a tool for globalisation.

Current Knowledge about E-Marketing among Egyptian Small Business Enterprises

The author was really surprised of the findings of the case studies based on the interviews conducted with the Egyptian small business enterprises with regard to the knowledge related to E-Marketing among these SBE's. The author was expecting to find good level of knowledge about E-Marketing among the these small business enterprises based on the high level of Internet diffusion among the Egyptians (according to Internet World Stats - 2009b, Egypt is the largest African country in using the Internet with more the 10.5 million users), the good electronic infrastructure provided by the government in the IT and communications fields and the large number of small business enterprises that were found to practice one form or another of E-Marketing. In contrast with the author expectations, the findings of the case studies show a very poor knowledge about E-Marketing among Egyptian small business enterprises. As can be seen in Table 9 (which summarise the findings related to E-Marketing knowledge among Egyptian SBE's), all the 35 small business enterprises did not know what is the meaning of E-Marketing? In this context, most of these small business enterprises owners, marketing managers

and sales managers did not know anything about E-Marketing and the few of them who illustrated some knowledge about E-Marketing did not really provide any level of knowledge related to E-Marketing within the interviews.

Moreover, when asked about the different tool of E-Marketing all the 35 small business enterprises owners, marketing managers and sales managers did not know what are these tools. But when discussing with them these tools three of them (with a percentage of 9% of the total number of SBE's) had a very naive inexperienced knowledge about some of the tools used for conducting E-Marketing namely Internet Marketing and E-Mail Marketing. Within the same line; another four small business enterprises owners, marketing managers and sales managers (with a percentage of 11% of the total number of SBE's) knew about Internet Marketing, seven of them (with a percentage of 20% of the total number of SBE's) knew what is E-Mail Marketing and finally five of them (with a percentage of 14% of

Table 9. Findings related to e-marketing knowledge among Egyptian SBE's

Subject	Yes		No	
	Frequency	%	Frequency	%
Knowing what is the meaning of E-Marketing	0	0%	35	100%
Knowing what are the different tool of E-Marketing	0	0%	35	100%
Knowing any of the different tool of E-Marketing	3	9%	32	91%
Knowing any of the different forms of E-Marketing	0	0%	35	100%
Knowing what is the meaning of Internet Marketing	7	20%	28	80%
Knowing what is the meaning of E-Mail Marketing	7	20%	28	80%
Knowing what is the meaning of Mobile Marketing	5	14%	30	86%
Knowing what is the meaning of Intranet Marketing	0	0%	35	100%
Knowing what is the meaning of Extranet Marketing	0	0%	35	100%
Knowing what is the meaning of E-Commerce	5	14%	30	86%
Knowing what is the meaning of E-Business	3	9%	32	91%
Did you study marketing before	4	11%	31	89%
Did you participated in any marketing training course before	3	9%	32	91%
Do you know how to use computers	16	48%	19	52%
Do you have any access to the Internet	18	54%	17	46%
Do you use E-Marketing as a tool for globalisation	3	9%	32	91%

the total number of SBE's) knew what is Mobile Marketing but regardless of that these small business enterprises owners, marketing managers and sales managers did not know or perceive Internet Marketing, E-Mail Marketing or Mobile Marketing as one of the tools associated to E-Marketing.

On the other hand, no single small business enterprise owner, marketing manager or sales manager knew or had any kind of knowledge about Intranet Marketing, Extranet Marketing or the different E-Marketing forms. Moreover, only five of the small business enterprises owners, marketing managers and sales managers (with a percentage of 14% of the total number of SBE's) had some knowledge about E-Commerce and only three of them (with a percentage of 9% of the total number of SBE's)had some knowledge about E-Business.

With regard to normal knowledge of marketing, only four small business enterprises owners, marketing managers and sales managers (with a percentage of 11% of the total number of SBE's) studied marketing and only three of them (with a percentage of 9% of the total number of SBE's) did participate in a marketing related training course. Surprisingly and unexpectedly, only 16 of the small business enterprises owners, marketing managers and sales managers (with a percentage of 48% of the total number of SBE's) knew how to use computers! Moreover, only 18 of them (with a percentage of 54% of the total number of SBE's) had access to the Internet.

In this respect, even having an access to the Internet in meaningless because in most cases even if the small business enterprises owners, marketing managers and sales managers have an access to the Internet they will not have the needed knowledge to develop and conduct E-Marketing activities. As noted by one small business enterprise owner:

"Yes I have Internet access but I do not have the knowledge/information for developing my enterprise website or the money needed to employee someone to develop it for me...........No I do not know how much it cost to develop a website... ....I just believed that it will cost a lot, really a lot, KHARAAB BEYOUT YA ANY (as Egyptian expression - phrase - to express the very high cost of something)...........NO I do not know any information about Yahoo Small Business".

Based on the findings of the case studies and the interviews, the author can confidently accept the fact that the Egyptian small business enterprises owners, marketing managers and sales managers have a very naive and inexperienced knowledge about E-marketing as well as the different tools or forms related to E-marketing.

Different Factors Affecting the Adoption of E-Marketing by Egyptian Small Business Enterprises

Through the interviews with the Egyptian small business enterprises owners, marketing managers and sales managers to explore what could be the different factors that might have an impact on E-Marketing adoption and encouraged these SBE's to adopt E-Marketing, surprisingly only very few of these small business enterprises actually conducted professional or accepted E-Marketing activities. In this respect and as can be seen in Table 10 which summarise some of the findings related to these factors affecting the adoption of E-Marketing, only four of these SBE's (with a percentage of 11% of the total number of SBE's) had its own website, only nine SBE's (with a percentage of 26% of the total number of SBE's) depend on e-mail in conducting your marketing activities, only one small business enterprise (with a percentage of 3% of the total number of SBE's) had a contact list for its customers or perspective customers/clients. Moreover, no single small business enterprise used mobile phones, Intranets or Extranets in conducting its marketing activities.

The majority of small business enterprises depended totally on the Egyptian international trade points in conducting its marketing activities.

Table 10. Findings related to the factors affecting the adoption of e-marketing among Egyptian SBE's

Subject	Yes		No	
	Frequency	%	Frequency	%
Do you have your own website	4	11%	31	89%
Do you depend on e-mail in conducting your marketing activities	9	26%	26	74%
Do you have a contact list for your customers or perspective customers/clients	1	3%	34	97%
Do you use mobile phones to conduct your marketing activities	0	0%	35	100%
Do you use Intranets to conduct your marketing activities	0	0%	35	100%
Do you use Extranets to conduct your marketing activities	0	0%	35	100%

The international trade points had gone the extra mile for the SBE's registered in it. As a result of that and because of the nature of the international trade points which is totally devoted towards external markets to increase the value of Egyptian exports, the SBE's had only conducted partial narrow-minded E-Marketing and in most of the cases these E-Marketing activities were directed towards only external markets.

When exploring the different factors that might have an impact on E-Marketing adoption by Egyptian small business enterprises it was noticed that only few of these enterprises have a website or conduct E-Marketing in as acceptable format. When investigating the main reasons for that it was found that:

- Size of the firm,
- Type of products,
- Available resources for the SBE,
- The knowledge of the SBE owner, marketing manager or sales manager,
- Customers orientation towards E-Marketing,
- The availability of government support in the form of international trade points and finally
- The small effect of the business success

are the most important factors that might have a great impact of the decision of adopting E-marketing or at least one of its tools or forms by

Egyptian small business enterprises. As noted by some of the Egyptian small business enterprises owners, marketing managers and sales managers during the interviews:-

"I do not have a website ....I am too small to do so".

"I do not need to have a website now ....I am small and my products is not huge ... accordingly the international trade point is good enough for me ... moreover, they do it all for me I do not need to do any thing about it".

"I thought of having my own website but I did not go farther in that because I do not have enough money to pay the website developer".

"I do not how to make a website and I do not know any one who can do it for me".

"I just made the photos for my products and hand it in to the clerk in Beni Soueif international trade point and he launched the photos in the international trade point website with my details".

"YA AAM KOUL YA BASET (as Egyptian expression - phrase - to express the unavailability of something or the total dependence on luck to achieve something), I am too small for that".

"I do not know how to use the computer, how can I develop a website?".

"I do not know how to read and write....these E-Marketing related issues are too complicated from my side of things....do business in the normal traditional way is much more suitable to me....I enjoy the traditional way of conducting marketing and business".

"I did not think about using e-mails to conduct marketing activities because I do not know how to get the e-mail addresses of my prospective clients".

"My customers do not like E-Marketing tools, they do not like or trust the Internet....they need to see the goods themselves to make sure that everything is OK".

"The type of my product really does not suit the Internet.....onions and garlic.....I did try to use the international trade point because it is free and I thought that it worth trying.....Not really, I did not got that much out of using international trade point web marketing".

"Yes, I have a webpage....it is a static one, I did not update it since I developed it through using Microsoft FrontPage".

"I do not have Internet access in my small business or at my home.....I access the Internet through the local Internet Cafe in my village".

The Impact of E-Marketing Adoption on the Marketing Performance of the Egyptian Small Business Enterprises and its Usage as a Tool for Globalisation

Based on the interviews with the Egyptian small business enterprises owners, marketing managers and sales managers, the author observed that the majority of the Egyptian small business enterprises does not perceive E-Marketing as one of the effective tools in gaining competitive advantage.

Moreover, they do not find any good impact for E-Marketing on the marketing performance of their SBE's. As noted by one of small business enterprises owners:-

"I am not going to develop a website for my business or do any thing similar to that..........I tried this website thing through the international trade point website but it did not work for me".

Another small business enterprise owner noted that:-

"The type of my product really does not suit the Internet.....onions and garlic..........I did try to use the international trade point because it is free and I thought that it worth trying..........Not really, I did not got that much out of using international trade point web marketing".

Another two marketing managers noted:-

"I send a lot of e-mails to promote my products but the response to these e-mails are very small and weak".

"If the international trade point closed its services for me I am not going to do it myself.......... noted that it is worthless".

Not surprisingly (based of the level of knowledge that the Egyptian small business enterprises owners, marketing managers and sales managers have), these SBE's owners, marketing and sales managers did not find any positive impact for E-Marketing adoption on the marketing performance of their small business enterprises. In contrast, most of them (based on the findings of the interviews) perceive E-Marketing as a waste of money, effort and time which is unexpected and surprising.

Within the same line and although most of the small business enterprises were highly linked to the

Egyptian international trade points which is totally devoted towards external markets to increase the value of Egyptian exports and that these SBE's used the international trade points as a common portal to conduct E-Marketing activities, most of the SBE's had only conducted partial very narrow-minded global E-Marketing. Despite that in most of the cases these SBE's were using E-Marketing activities which were directed towards only external markets, these SBE's did not have any form of effective or efficient implementation of E-Marketing. Accordingly, it is very hard to accept that Egyptian small business enterprises uses E-Marketing as tool for globalisation of competing in the global market.

FUTURE RESEARCH DIRECTIONS

There are few studies that have investigated the international orientation of small business enterprises or the desire of such enterprises in competing globally on the adoption of new technologies, such as E-Marketing, E-commerce and E-business; consequently there is a need to conduct more research to investigate this impact in an E-marketing context in some other country and in Egypt in some other types of organisations. There is also a few numbers of studies that have researched the use of E-marketing as a tool for globalisation. Accordingly, there is a need to investigate this E-marketing usage in medium sized business enterprises as well as large companies. This will lead to a greater, deep and reflective understanding of the different factors affecting the adoption of E-marketing as well as E-Marketing implementation by small business enterprises in other types of organisations and will in turn add to the accumulated knowledge in the field of E-marketing.

CONCLUSION

Based on the results of the exploratory study with its two stages (the survey and the case studies) the author can confidently accept the following facts and findings:

1. The response rate of the Egyptian small business enterprises is extremely low (less than 1% based on the results of the exploratory survey) and does not encourage conducted electronic surveys.

2. The Egyptian small business enterprises owners, marketing managers and sales managers have a very naive and inexperienced knowledge about E-Marketing as will as the different tools or forms related to E-marketing.

3. The size of the SBE, type of products, available resources for the SBE, the knowledge of the SBE owner, marketing manager or sales manager, customers orientation towards e-marketing, the availability of government support in the form of international trade points and finally the small effect of the business success are the most important factors that might have a great impact of the decision of adopting E-marketing or at least one of its tools or forms by Egyptian small business enterprises.

4. International orientation or competing globally was not one of the factors affecting the adoption of E-Marketing by Egyptian small business enterprises.

5. Egyptian SBE's owners, marketing and sales managers did not find any positive impact for E-Marketing adoption on the marketing performance of their small business enterprises.

6. Most of the small business enterprises depended totally on the Egyptian international trade points in conducting E-Marketing

without trying to gain the needed experiences to conduct these activities independently.

7. When conducting E-Marketing activities, Egyptian small business enterprises had only conducted partial narrow-minded E-Marketing.

Based on all the above findings, it is very hard to accept that Egyptian small business enterprises uses E-Marketing as tool for globalisation of competing in the global market.

REFERENCES

Aaker, D. A., & Day, G. S. (1986). The perils of high-growth markets. *Strategic Management Journal*, 409–421.

Alexandria Small Business Association (ABA). (2009). *ABA Small business enterprises definition*. Retrieved January 15, 2009, from http://www.aba-sme.com/index.htm

AUSE. (2009). *The Arab Union for Small Enterprises*. Retrieved January 2, 2009, from http://www.sfdegypt.org/Arab_Union_e.asp

CAEB. (2009). Crédit Agricole Egypt Bank- small business enterprises definition. Retrieved January 15, 2009, from http://www.ca-egypt.com/SME/About-SME.html

CAPMAS. (2009). *The Central agency for Public Mobilisation and Statistics - Egyptian Population*. Retrieved May 5, 2009, from http://www.msrintranet.capmas.gov.eg/pls/fdl/tst12e?action=&lname=

Chaffey, D. (2007). *E-business and E-commerce Management: Strategy, Implementation and Practice*. Upper Saddle River, NJ: Financial Times/Prentice Hall.

De Vaus, D. A. (1991). *Surveys in social research*. New York: Routledge.

DTI-news-release. (2008). *National statistics, The Small Business Service (SBS), The British Department of Trade and Industry*. Retrieved October 14, 2008, from http://www.sbs.gov.uk/SBS_Gov_files/researchandstats/SMEStats2004.pdf

Eblen, R. A., & Eblen, W. (1994). *The Encyclopaedia of the Environment*. Boston: Houghton Mifflin Company.

Eid, R. (2003). *Business-to-business international internet marketing: adoption, implementation and implications, an empirical study of UK companies*. Bradford, UK: Bradford University.

EINP. (2009). *Egyptian Institute of National Planning - small business enterprises definition*. Retrieved January 25, 2009, from http://www.inplanning.gov.eg/Activities/Publication/Details.aspx

EITP. (2009). *The Egyptian International Trade Points (EITP) - About Us*. Retrieved January 5, 2009, from http://www.tpegypt.gov.eg/EITP.aspx

EMI. (2009). *Egyptian ministry of investment - Egyptian economy indicators*. Retrieved May 5, 2009, from http://www.investment.gov.eg/MOI_Portal/en-GB/Egypts+Business/Economy/

EMTI. (2008). *Ministry of Trade and Industry - Small Business Enterprises in Egypt*. Retrieved December 16, 2008, from http://www.mfti.gov.eg/English/index.htm

EUROPEAN-COMMISSION. (2006). *Small businesses definition*. Retrieved October 14, 2006, from http://ec.europa.eu/enterprise/entrepreneurship/craft/definition.htm

FEI. (2009). Federation of Egyptian Industries - small business enterprises definition. Retrieved January 14, 2009, from http://www.fei.org.eg/committees_info.asp?id=9&searchtxt=small

IDWB. (2009). *The Industrial Development and Workers Bank of Egypt (IDWB) - small business enterprises definition*. Retrieved January 25, 2009, from http://www.idbe-egypt.com/product.htm

ISE. (2009). *Internet Society of Egypt - The Internet in Egypt*. Retrieved March 5, 2009, from http://www.ise.org.eg/inegypt.htm

IWS. (2009a). *Internet World Stats - Egypt Internet and Population Statistics*. Retrieved April 15, 2009, from http://www.internetworldstats.com/africa.htm#eg

IWS. (2009b). *Internet World Stats - Africa top 10 Internet countries*. Retrieved April 15, 2009, from http://www.internetworldstats.com/stats1.htm

Law 141. (2009). Law number 141 for the year 2004, the Small Business Enterprises Development Law. In Law (Ed.), *Elmatabea Elameriah*.

Lewis-Beck, M. S. (1995). *Data analysis: An introduction*. Thousand Oaks, CA: Sage.

McDonald, M., & Wilson, H. (1999). *E-marketing Improving marketing effectiveness in a digital world*.

Reedy, J. E., Schullo, S. S., & Zimmerman, K. R. (1999). *Electronic Marketing: Integrating Electronic Resources into the Marketing Process*. Fort Worth, TX: Harcourt College Publishers.

SEDO. (2009). *The Small Enterprise Development Organisation*. Retrieved January 12, 2009, from http://www.sfdegypt.org/groups.htm#4

SFD. (2009a). *The Egyptian Social Fund for Development (SFD)*. Retrieved January 12, 2009, from http://www.sfdegypt.org/about.asp

SFD. (2009b). *The Egyptian Social Fund for Development* Retrieved March 1, 2009, from http://www.sfdegypt.org/PDF/1-12.pdf

Smith, P. R., & Chaffey, D. (2005). *E-marketing Excellence*. London: Butterworth-Heinemann.

Strauss, J., & Frost, R. (2001). *E-marketing*. Upper Saddle River, NJ: Prentice-Hall.

Theng, L. G., & Boon, J. L. W. (1996). An exploratory study of factors affecting the failure of local small and medium enterprises. *Asia Pacific Journal of Management, 13*(2), 47–61. doi:10.1007/BF01733816

United States Agency for International Development (USAID). (2009). *USAID Small business enterprises definition*. Retrieved January 25, 2009, 2009, from http://www.usaid-eg.org/display.cfm?s=USAID's_Small_and_Micro_Enterprise_%28SME%29_Development_program&pt=2&sp=2&ppc=%2BqWEgB7wUAc%3D&qs=06oENya4ZG1YS6vOLJwpLiFbgelW6za09oFkf0Q_HyPMgoQS_5rcSSiueh8dRYznz_8jvGx6IcavSpTuD8v0TKAZLvH2M0e5RsYGiYcZN49ZAeXRddZzY0OZ1T_M5oT8FwHc0z-3bu-85bIdmVrPpBK8Ose0vJs5ck21SFewZWnbZ5Ha4FZ31Dil_-5lLQ4FZG_UfGTKuFfVPd6a1ekysXYRO1hE36o,YT0z&vid=1242216953_2X04X1284826321&rpt=2&lpt=1242217007&bd=1%23600%23800%231%230%23741%2357&kt=1

Watson, J., & Everett, J. E. (1996). Do small businesses have high failure rates? *Journal of Small Business Management, 34*(4), 45–62.

Chapter 15
Engaging Learning Models with Information and Communication Technologies in Advancing Electronic Learning

Jen-Her Wu
National Sun Yat-Sen University, Taiwan

Robert D. Tennyson
University of Minnesota, USA

Tzyh-Lih Hsia
Chinese Naval Academy, Taiwan

ABSTRACT

Emerging information and communication technologies and learning models have triggered a new wave of educational innovation: electronic learning (E-learning). This study employs a hypercube innovation model to analyze the differences in technology and learning models in conventional (face-to-face) classroom learning and E-learning environments. The results of the analyses indicate that the innovation from traditional classroom learning to E-learning is radical for both the learner and instructor, leading to drastic changes in the technology and learning model. For education institutions, the technology is a fundamental change, while the learning model is reinforced. From the dynamic capability perspectives, a set of core capabilities needed for successfully exploiting E-learning is identified. These results provide insight for learners, instructors, and education institutions for enhancing their understanding of E-learning innovation and provide guidelines to help E-learning stakeholders adapt from conventional classrooms to E-learning environments.

DOI: 10.4018/978-1-61520-623-0.ch015

INTRODUCTION

Developments in the field of information and communication technology (ICT) offer new instructional paradigms for education. Internet technology is presently enabling humankind to communicate with anyone, anywhere, and anytime globally, instantaneously and yet inexpensively. Such a rich communication tool can be put to use in education in the form of electronic learning (E-learning). The application of ICT in E-learning is now making it possible for education to transcend space, time, and political boundaries.

The literature on distance education shows how technological, economic, and scientific factors are contributing to the development of a new educational panorama which would offer different teaching contexts to meet different learners' preferences and needs, and which could produce outcomes for students which go beyond simple subject learning (Francescato et al., 2006). For example, distance learning programs are offered worldwide. The situational application of E-learning distance education programs is distinct in different countries. Trends in the USA suggest that E-learning will increase from 31% in 1998 to 90% by 2008 (Cheong, 2002). Currently, totally online degree-seeking students in the USA exceed 350,000 and the students are from all over the world.

A rather large body of literature indicates the dramatic changes in the higher education instructional system caused by the diffusion of new ICTs, as well as the need for schools to radically change in order to stand both the social pressure and the competition from online universities (Bates, 2000; Hazemi et al., 1998). The advantage of E-learning is clear. For instance, Tennyson and Jorczak (in press) write that E-learning matches the needs of nontraditional students, increases the educational facilities available to traditional students, provides companies with cost efficient yet effective train-ing options, and gives students and researchers in developing nations an invaluable means of gaining a first-world education tempered by third-world experience.

E-learning has created unprecedented virtual learning environments, offering new educational models that impact the learning industry (Piccoli et al., 2001). These innovative learning environments may impact the traditional education system and render the capabilities of the stakeholders in the system obsolete. From the dynamic capability perspectives (Teece et al., 1997), in such a new setting, the stakeholders must constantly reconfigure, renew, or learn new capabilities rather than protect their capabilities along with technology, content, and education delivery expertise to embrace emerging educational innovations, such as E-learning.

Understanding the nature of innovation is the crucial first step in managing the change associated with any innovation. In order to apprehend the nature and scope of the opportunities that accompany E-learning innovations, it is necessary to organize them categorically and see them fully. It is necessary for E-learning participants to recognize and evaluate changes in the education and technological landscape and speculate on what extent each stakeholder meets the emerging capability gaps in a timely way. Possessing this knowledge is crucial for stakeholders to successfully adapt from traditional classroom to an E-learning environment. However, research on these issues is extremely limited. Therefore, this study utilizes an E-learning hypercube innovation model, adopted from Afuah and Bahram (1995), with secondary data analysis and comparative analysis to evaluate the differences in two dimensions: technological components and learning model between traditional classroom and E-learning and then explore the core capabilities that are necessary for E-learning stakeholders to successfully adapt and exploit the E-learning innovation.

E-Learning History: An Overview

The history of distance education can be classified into five stages. (1) 1700–1900, distance education programs use US Postal Service to mail correspondence education materials in higher education. (2) 1920–1960, correspondence education programs begin using radio and television technologies to delivery of instruction; states pass laws requiring students to attend face-to-face course situations. US military initiates correspondence education for advanced training and promotion. (3) 1970–1980, distance education programs began using pre-recorded video recordings, cassette recordings and collections delivered over broadcast channels. (4) 1980–1990, educators in all settings initiated delivery of instruction through teleconferencing, video conferencing, cable network programming for K-12 students, and more televised educational programs. The milestone for ICTs was the emergence of Arpanet, which became the World Wide Web. And, (5) 1990 to present, the characteristics of distance education are less expensive computers, greater access to technology, Internet in classrooms, more educational institutions and businesses employing distance learning, computer-based training (CBTs), and synchronous and asynchronous communication. The contemporary ICT is an instructional delivery approach variously called online learning, online education, Web-based education, or E-learning. Dominance of the World Wide Web, wireless technology, and more financing from private industry and universities are additional milestone to enhance distance education.

E-learning is the most recent evolution of distance learning; a learning situation where instructors and learners are separated by distance, time, or both. E-learning uses ICTs to create, deliver, and share learning, anytime and anywhere. E-learning is characterized by speed, technological transformation, and mediated human interactions (Stokes, 2000). In this paper, we use the term E-learning as it is defined by the Commission of the European Communities: "the use of new multimedia technologies and the Internet to improve the quality of learning by facilitating access to resources and services as well as remote exchanges and collaboration" (CEC, 2001). The E-learning environment provides some advantages such as stretching the spatial and temporal barriers, flexibility, interactivity and interoperability (Curran, 2002; Huang & Hu, 2000; Khalifa & Lam, 2002; Kinshuk & Yang, 2003; Wheeler, 2000; Yang & Liu, 2005).

Today, there is almost universal recognition that new advances in ICTs have the potential to address fundamental challenges facing higher education. The current *third* generation of computer-supported learning uses computer supported communication networks to support E-learning (Francescato et al., 2006). E-learning supports the sharing and exchange of information and experience, the development of common projects and the representation and development of a community in which knowledge can be shared (Trentin, 2000). E-learning supporters view learning as a primarily social process in which the computer enables both independent learning and collaborative learning (Calvani & Rotta, 2000; Kiely, 1993; Marjanovic, 1999).

E-learning instructional design employs a variety of electronic forms of telecommunication. That is, instruction is delivered via television, videocassette disc, film, radio, computer networks or other devices that use some audio–video format. In early applications of distance-based learning, the major forms of communication between a student and a remote location were television, video cassettes, audio tape cassettes, or other multimedia. With the growth of the Internet and large networks, learners now have an opportunity to utilize asynchronous and synchronous communication tools, as well as to choose the time, place, and pace of their education. The environment can be a pure virtual environment or a blended virtual and class room environment.

E-learning provides an environment to learn beyond time and geographic limitations, turning the society into a Knowledge and Learning Logistic Center where industry can preserve their roots, namely the critical know-how and core competence. *E-learning for everyone* will be carried out through education and promotion campaigns, cultivating habits of digital learning for an increasing demand, flourishing business and henceforth market economy. To facilitate *E-learning for everyone*, the primary task is to integrate domestic soft/hardware resources which can be leveraged in building community E-learning centers, enabling *Easy access to the Internet, Information available everywhere*. E-learning activities are to facilitate popular learning so that current employees, teachers and students, civil servants, the unemployed, active-duty military personnel, housewives, retirees, and the underprivileged can all engage in diversified E-learning.

E-learning is becoming more important and not only in academic environments. Despite the fact that the use of information technology is increasing in general, professional knowledge is changing so quickly that up to 50% of all job skills may become outdated within a few years (Moe & Blodget, 2000). Thus, flexible, up-to-date learning content is required. E-learning will facilitate adapting content to the rapidly changing demands in professional education (Moe & Blodget, 2000). Especially for teaching image dependent subjects, a Web-based system offers advantages (Grunewald et al., 2003; Harasim et al., 1995).

As anticipated, E-learning differs from traditional classroom-based learning in many ways. Therefore, converting a conventional course to an E-learning environment would cause the content to change, the technology to be redefined, and the way education services delivered to change. E-learning environments not only deliver course material to the learners, but they also provide live, contextual, and interactive environments for the learners. In addition, instructors and learners can control the teaching and learning process as they do in the conventional classroom (Raab et al., 2002; Stokes, 2000). They are ideally suited to the rapid dissemination of knowledge from any place in the world to almost any place else and allow collaboration and discussion over vast spatial and temporal distances (Raab et al., 2001).

Hypercube Innovation Model

As a result of the E-learning evolution, it impacts the existing education systems and learning environments. Indeed, the changes derived from technology-mediated learning can be analyzed from the perspective of the technology itself and the learning environments. To understand the nature of the E-learning innovation and then manage the changes, we adopted a hypercube model (Afuah & Bahram, 1995) to examine E-learning innovation and its impact on E-learning stakeholders. The E-learning hypercube model is a coherent framework that includes three dimensions: technological components, learning model, and stakeholders, as shown in Figure 1.

Technological components refer to the collection of technological tools (hardware and software) used to deliver learning material and to facilitate communication among participants. They are distinct portions of an E-learning system and embody the core design knowledge such as technological infrastructure and content. They are further described as: (1) Technological infrastructure consisting of network infrastructures, application platforms, and devices; and, (2) Content consisting of content creation, content packaging, and content delivery. The E-learning model is based on the technological infrastructure and content, that is, it could become good design function by making the core design knowledge concrete. The learning model is the way in which the core components are built by integrating the components and linking them into a coherent whole to support the learning process. The learning model is further described as consisting of educational environments, course development, teaching and learning, faculty/student interaction, collaborative learning, and evaluation and assessment.

The possible changes in E-learning innovation can be categorized into four types: radical, architectural, modular, and incremental (Afuah & Bahram, 1995; Henderson & Clark, 1990). The classification is based on the intensity in which change overturns the existing technological components and learning model. An E-learning innovation is incremental if it conserves (or reinforces) the existing technological components and learning model, modular if it destroys technological components but conserves (or reinforces) the learning model, architectural if it destroys the learning model but preserves (or reinforces) the technological components, and radical if both the technological components and learning model become obsolete.

As Moe (2000) states, "technology is the driver of the New Economy, and human capital is its fuel. In today's world, not only does knowledge make the difference in how an individual performs but it also makes the difference in how well a company performs and, of that matter, how well a country performs (p. 50)." According to the innovation of the learning environment, it needs a greater involvement of institutional partnerships. Human

capital is the fuel to prompt the success from the traditional learning environment to E-learning. Today's learning and E-learning partnerships include a much wider range of nontraditional educational enterprises. "Partnership and alliances among stakeholders - national and institutional policymakers, teaching and related staff, researchers and students (i.e., learners), and administrative and technical personnel in institutions of higher education, the world of work and community groups - are a powerful force in managing change" (UNESCO, 1998). For the purpose of this study, the E-learning stakeholders we selected include E-learners, E-instructors, and education institutions. E-learners are existing or potential learning end users. E-instructor is the teacher who develops courses, provides learner support, and provides evaluation and assessment. Education institutions provide the platform, services and environment for learners and instructors to obtain what they need (Govindasamy, 2002).

ANALYSIS OF E-LEARNING INNOVATION

Understanding the nature of an innovation is a crucial first step in managing the changes associ-

Figure 1. The e-learning hypercube innovation model

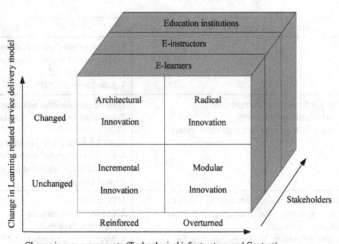

ated with any innovation (Afuah, 2003). In order to explore the nature and impact of E-learning, this section utilizes the E-learning hypercube innovation model to frame a comparative analysis of extant literature and analyze the differences between a traditional class and E-learning in the dimensions: core components and learning model, and then to examine the impact of E-learning on the stakeholders.

Analysis by Technological Components

The ICT can promote educational innovation. Technological infrastructures can integrate the core design concept and all participants in the process of network learning service delivery (Afuah & Bahram, 1995). We compared traditional classroom learning and E-learning based on network infrastructures, application platform, and devices as argued by prior researches (e.g., Cheong, 2002; Chou & Tsai, 2002; Harper et al., 2004; Henry, 2001; Moore & Kearsley, 1996; Piccoli et al., 2001).

Technological improvements in education have taken many forms over the past decades; innovations like radio, television, recorded audiotapes, CD-ROM products, and computer networks

literally have influenced students' learning and instructors' teaching methods (Chou & Tsai, 2002; Moore & Kearsley, 1996). Table 1 summarizes the comparison result, which shows that E-learning could provide geographical freedom, temporal freedom, unlimited class size, and change the way of interaction and learner control. For network infrastructures and application platform, the E-learning environment has momentous differences from the traditional classroom learning because the network infrastructure is not required for the later while they are necessary for the former. However, the difference in devices is not significant.

Based on the prior research (e.g., Aldrich, 2001; Henry, 2001; Rosenberg, 2001), content can be divided into content creation, content packaging, and content delivery. In traditional classrooms, instructors deliver content by narration, shadow, handout and black/white board. With the advance of ICT, the E-learning instructor must integrate multiple media content with richness and engaging media design of websites to attract learners. E-learning environment has two basic features: a communication infrastructure used to broadcast educational materials via television, computer, or both and an educational design based on an analytical approach in which complex topics are broken down into simpler modules.

Table 1. Differences in the technological infrastructure

Factors	Traditional classroom learning	E-learning
Network Infrastructures	N/A	1. Wired or wireless networking 2. Data-oriented and voice-based network 3. Internet channel 4. Standards: TCP/IP
Application Platform	1. No platform infrastructure 2. No technology standards 3. Low ability to integrate with other systems	1. Have the platform infrastructure: LMS, LCMS 2. Learning technology standards: SCORM, CMI, COM, TLSC 3. ASP, JAVA, XML programs 4. Easy to integrated with other TML (Technology Mediated Learning system) (e.g., Streaming Multicast System, Virtual classroom)
Devices	1. PCs, Radio, Video, Microphone, Trumpet 2. Overhead projector, Slide projectors, microfiche, and microfilm 3. Cable television, VCR, and Satellite TV	1. PCs, Server 2. Digital video camera 3. Network facility 4. Microphone, trumpet, and headphones

Learning is organized into a sequence of blocks with an assessment at the end of each block. With this approach, the learning process is defined by the instructors (Francescato et al., 2006).

According to Relan and Gillani (1997), in the student-centered Internet-based learning environments, students help decide how the contents are organized and learned. In addition, French et al. (1999) considered that, in the E-learning environments, students have more choices of and control over their learning time and pace, but also the objectives and learning outcomes. Furthermore, because the Internet-based instruction consists of both asynchronous (such as e-mails) and synchronous (such as video conferencing) communication features, it enables learners to be involved in the social interaction process (Chuang & Tsai, 2005). Table 2 summarizes the difference between both environments.

Analysis by Learning Model

The learning model describes the essential instructional and learning process. Based on prior research (Forman et al., 2002; Govindassamy, 2002; Lepori et al., 2000; Harper et al., 2004;

Raab et al., 2002; Slomon, 2001), the learning model can be analyzed using these components: educational environment, course development, teaching and learning, faculty/student interaction, collaborative learning, and evaluation and assessment activities. In terms of educational environment, the E-learning model can be analyzed from the perspectives of the system itself and the human computer interaction. The former focuses on the functions that the system could offer, while the later focuses on the interaction process between human and system. Traditionally, the learning environment can be characterized by such factors as time, place, and space. Piccoli et al., (2001) further expanded three more dimensions: technology, interaction and control. The Internet is enables humankind to instantaneously communicate globally with anyone, anywhere, anytime. E-learning can bring learners from different nationalities into discussions, hence exposing the learners to the experiences of people from different cultural, socioeconomic, and political backgrounds (Cheong, 2002).

Furthermore, E-learning differs from traditional classroom learning in the process of learning and teaching. For instance, cooperative

Table 2. Differences in the content

Factors	Traditional classroom learning	E-learning
Content creation	1. Text, Audio, Image, Video 2. The cost is low 3. It is difficult to preserve and update 4. The retrieval of learning materials would be restricted in time and place 5. The interactive ability is not high 6. Cognitive-oriented 7. System-oriented 8. It is difficult to integrate because content formats are different	1. Animation, Image, Audio, Video, Text (Web-based teaching materials) 2. The cost is high 3. It is easy to preserve and update 4. The retrieval of learning materials would not be restricted in time and place 5. The interactive ability is high 6. Problem-oriented learning 7. Exploration-oriented learning 8. Be integrated by content integrated system (Asset, SOC, CA) 9. Easy to integrate all learning material
Content packaging	1. Print and binding 2. Video manufacture	1. Systems help learning material packaging 2. The XML format
Content delivery	1. Distribution in person 2. One-to-many distribution 3. It would spend long time	1. Streaming media technologies 2. Synchronous or asynchronous delivery by network 3. One-to-one or one-to-many distribution 4. It would spend short time

learning is a pedagogical technique that allows students to work together in small, fixed groups on a structured learning task with the aim of maximizing their own and each other's learning (Johnson & Johnson, 1986; Johnson et al., 1998). The theoretical advantages of cooperative instruction have long been acknowledged and have been extensively practiced in the classroom. While

cooperative learning promises many benefits for students in academic achievement, self-esteem, active learning, social skill development, and equity achievement (Cohen, 1994; Johnson & Johnson, 1989; Kagan, 1992; Slavin, 1995) in traditional classroom learning, executing cooperative learning is limited in time and place. However, the collaborative learning activities,

Table 3. Differences in learning models

Factors	Activities	Traditional classroom learning	E-learning
Learning environment	1. Human 2. Time 3. Place 4. Space	Localization learning environment	1. Learners from different regions 2. Anytime 3. Learners determine the time of instruction 4. Anyplace and anywhere 5. Students use online teaching modules 6. Students use the same online teaching modules to complete assignments
Course development	1. Course design 2. Select instructional activities and media element	1. Face-to-face courses 2. Different material about the same subject 3. Characterized by the class (often active in full-time)	1. Lecture-based course 2. Consistent content 3. Updated easily and quickly 4. Personalized for the learners
Teaching and learning	Instruction interaction	1. Lecture-based teaching and face-to-face learning 2. The student plays a reactive role in the in-presence paradigm 3. Just-in-time feedback and interactions	1. Online learning and teaching 2. The learner assumes a proactive role in the distance modality 3. Self-paced (E-learning courses can be taken when they are necessary) 4. Encouraging interaction with other e-learners and e-instructors (chat rooms, discussion boards, instant messaging and e-mail all offer effective interaction for e-learner
Interaction	1. Course material delivery 2. Interaction process and method 3. Courses design method	1. Interaction method is face-to-face 2. Need to respond immediately 3. Courses design trend to individual work	1. Using the WWW to deliver course material, and promote learner-to-learner and learner-to-instructor connectivity and interaction 2. Asynchronous and immediate interaction 3. Stress-free interaction 4. To provide 24 hour access to information from any computer connected to the Internet 5. Courses design involve a high degree of team work 6. Course that involve a high degree of team work and encourage arrangement to facilitate interactions
Collaborative learning	Group collaborative learning	Limited in time and place	1. E-learning provide collaborative learning environments to continue learning 2. Geographical and temporal freedom for collaborative learning
Evaluation and assessment	1. The track of instruction schedule progress 2. Evaluation and assessment	More time-consuming	1. Easily and timeliness 2. Quizzes and exams customization (Using intelligent algorithm to generate quizzes and exams with different levels of difficulties)

such as knowledge articulation, explanations, argumentation and other demanding epistemic activities can be supported in different ways using communication tools and shared workspaces in E-learning environments (e.g., Hakkinen, Arvaja, & Makitalo, 2004; Strijbos et al., 2004). Table 3 summarizes the differences in learning model between traditional classroom learning and E-learning environment.

Impact on E-Learning Stakeholders

As mentioned previously, we consider E-learning a radical innovation for E-learners and E-instructors because the traditional learning core components (i.e., technological infrastructures and content) and learning models are overturned. They need to learn about Internet technology, E-learning platform, the integrated devices, and the embedded mechanisms. They need to be aware of diverse content types and learn how to create, package

and distribute course materials in the E-learning environment. They also need to use different strategies, method or model to achieve the effectiveness of E-learning (Collison et al., 2000; Palloff & Pratt, 1999). Therefore, E-learners need to understand and/or install the new technology, learn the mechanisms embedded and perform the learning activity in the E-learning environment. Table 4 summarizes the impact on the E-learners and E-instructors.

With respect to education institutions, the E-learning environment has a fundamental core component change, while the learning model they support is reinforced. The influences on the education institution may include an institution's vision, the core concepts of school operation and management, and technological infrastructure, the interaction and support between instructors, learners and administrative unit. An incumbent education institution would need to learn the characteristics of the new ICTs, the potential

Table 4. Impact on the e-learners and e-instructors

Factors	Activities	Potential impact
Technological infrastructure	Network infrastructures	Learning/Teaching in the Internet and virtual environment
	Application platform	Must learn to use the E-learning platform
	Devices	Need to learn various devices formulating learning environment.
Content	Content creation	1. Types of content have changed 2. Content becomes more diversity and richness
	Content packaging	Method of content packaging has changed
	Content distribution	1. The method of content assessing has changed. 2. Content transfer and interaction method has changed
Learning model	Course development	1. Course requirement has changed 2. Course progress must be more self-control and self-correcting
	Teaching and learning	1. Learning motivation in E-learning environment must be stronger than traditional classroom learning 2. Teaching theory, method, and model has changed
	Faculty/student interaction	1. Interaction with learners and instructors has changed 2. Communication skills have changed 3. Interaction method would be flexible in terms of time and place
	Collaborative learning	1. Learning method becomes collaborative learning. 2. Method of knowledge gathering, usage, assimilation, and sharing in collaborative learning have changed
	Evaluation and assessment	1. Evaluation and assessment method changed 2. Method of evaluation and assessment method become diversified

economic opportunity it may provide, the organization needed to adopt the technological component, and the potential value-added to its E-learners and E-instructors. Table 5 summarizes the impact on the education institutions.

DEVELOPMENT OF E-LEARNING CORE CAPABILITIES

The analysis of E-learning innovation leads to several conclusions regarding the gaps in the technological knowledge and learning model between traditional classroom learning and E-learning. From the dynamic capabilities perspective (Daniel & Wilson, 2003; Wheeler, 2002; Wu, et al., 2005; Wu et al., 2006), there is a growing demand for educational stakeholders to develop new capabilities to fill the gaps. While an E-learning innovation introduces changes to stakeholders, such innovation will fail to contribute to stakeholders' capabilities and performance unless stakeholders are capable of appropriating them. Accordingly, in face of the E-learning innovation, a stakeholder must be aware of the capability-destroying changes; otherwise, any attempt to exploit the innovations may be doomed

to fail. However, to successfully cope with such innovations requires careful coordination with the development of dynamic capabilities (Teece et al., 1997). According to the constructs of the E-learning hypercube model, the stakeholders' abilities related to exploit an E-learning innovation rest on two general categories of capabilities: E-learning delivery and technical capabilities. Based on those categories, we identify the core capabilities that need to be developed in E-learning environment and provide several recommendations for each stakeholder.

Core Capabilities for E-Leaner and E-Instructor

As explained above, the innovation from traditional classroom learning to E-learning is regarded as radical for learners and instructors. In general, the major user groups for E-learning are primarily online users. They may use E-learning anytime and anywhere. Thus, both stakeholders must have or learn delivery capabilities in order to achieve effective learning in the E-learning environment. For instance, learners should have the ability to develop appropriate learning strategies, properly use E-learning course material, engage in self-

Table 5. Impact on the educational institution

Factors	Activities	Potential impact
Institution vision	The core concepts of school operation and management	The institution's vision or mission in relation to E-learning
Technological infra-structures	Infrastructure	Enhance or improve out-of-date prior innovation core concepts
		Infrastructure for enhancing quality (annual monitoring cycle)
Content	Learning material	1. The learning material produced 2. Expertise in developing materials
Learning model	The connection of instructors, learners, and e-learning administrative unit	Enhance or destroy prior connection and communication method
	The service of school administration	Reservation or changed
	The abilities of school management	Enhance or destroy other abilities
	Institutional support	Education institution could or could not provide the need of driving the proceeding of E-learning Education institution could or could not accept research subvention from other institutions

directed learning, work alone or in-groups, be less dependent on the teacher or other people, exhibit self discipline to plan study, learn communication and interaction skills, and develop creativity to improve the quality of assigned assignments (Collison et al., 2000; Forman et al., 2002; Francescato et al., 2006; Hakkinen et al., 2005; Kreijns et al., 2003; Palloff & Pratt, 1999; Yang & Liu, 2005).

Instructors are the other principal actors in the E-learning environment. A teaching strategy employing cooperative learning cannot be effective if it is not designed effectively. Though potentially beneficial, implementing cooperative learning does require substantial modifications or adaptations in how teachers organize their teaching and manage their classroom. ISTE (International Society for Technology in Education) pointed out that course requirement, learning motivation, learning method, socialization model, and learning assistance has changed in the E-learning environment (Relan & Gillani, 1997; Webster & Hackley, 1997). Regardless of the research indicating that cooperative learning improves students' achievement and social skills, the approach must be an integral part of a teachers' repertoire before students can benefit. The instructors should be aware that some potential disadvantages or unexpected episodes might result from a cooperative learning strategy, they should be attentive during the process, and intervene in a timely way or adjust instruction accordingly (Randall, 1999; Yang & Liu, 2005). Table 6 summarizes the learning delivery capabilities for E-learner and E-instructor.

In general, the major user groups for E-learning are primarily online users. They may use E-learning anytime and anywhere. Thus, the capability to estimate profit potential can help education institutions match new market opportunities. Moreover, E-learning services are likely to significantly increase learning performance. Here, the increasing level of communication intensifies the complexity of the industry value network. When Internet, communication type, new collaboration and networks of relationships must be reconfigured to facilitate the E-learning environment, the capability to appraise an education institutions' position in an attractive area and aligned with diverse stakeholders must be seriously considered.

Technical Capabilities

The ICT is both one of the most promising and at the same time the most challenging technologies to be employed in classrooms. The increasing degree of mobility and ubiquity from dynami-

Table 6. E-learning delivery capabilities for e-learner and e-instructor

Activities	Core capabilities
Course development	1. The ability of developing appropriate learning strategies 2. The ability of properly used e-learning resources
Teaching and learning	1. The ability of self-directed learning 2. The ability to work alone or in-groups and be less dependent on the teacher or other people. 3. Problem solving skills
Faculty/student interaction	1. The ability of self discipline (e.g. follow their own plan for study, interaction with other users actively in the E-learning environment) 2. The ability of communication and interaction skill in the e-learning environment
Collaborative learning	1. The ability to challenge one's own knowledge and the views of others 2. Enhance or destroy prior communication and interactive model 3. Enhance or destroy original skills and knowledge through prior learning models. 4. Social skills
Evaluation and assessment	The ability of creativity to improve the quality of assigned assignments

cally changing networking environments will make such capabilities mandatory. Here, education institutions will need the mature ability to upgrade IT infrastructure to develop appropriate services that meet a rich variety of demands for applications across an array of wired networks deployed intra- and inter-educational environment. In terms of technological infrastructure, learners should have technical skills, proficiency in using E-learning platforms, IT skills, and experience in using E-learning environment devices.

ISTE proposed instructor education technology standards and suggested three required information capacities (basic operation and concept of computer technology, technology applications in personal and professional domain, and technology applications in teaching). However in 2000, ISTE modified the original standards and extended three capacities to six capacities in order to maintain the effectiveness of the standard and be consistent with the education technology standard. The six capabilities are basic operation and concept of computer technology, the formulation of learning environment and experience, teaching and learning of courses, evaluation and assessment, productivity and professional practice, and social, ethics, law, and humanity issues. Table 7 summa-

rizes the core technical capabilities for e-learner and e-instructor.

Core Capabilities for Education Institutions

To truly build E-learning environments, it is critical to erect common platforms and service standards that include support for interoperability and transparency. The development and implement of technological components are major topics for education institution administrators. Indeed, E-learning is creating unparalleled learning value and opportunities for E-learning stakeholders to leverage the benefits. To this end, identifying the user value frontier and conveying new value propositions to the market should be given a high priority (Wheeler, 2002). Because of the chain of different stakeholders involved in E-learning environments, configuring new strategic alliances and implementing inter-education institution collaborations with them would become increasingly important. Education institutions must critically position themselves at advantageous locations in viable value networks in order to gain access to core competencies and maintain existing advantages.

Table 7. Technical capabilities for e-learner and e-instructor

Factors	Activities	Capabilities
Technological infrastructure	Network infrastructures	Internet capability: the ability to use the Internet and network
	Application platform	1. e proficient in using an e-learning platform 2. Basic operation and concepts of computer technology, electronic mails, bulletin boards, video or telephone conferencing, and the Internet capability
	Devices	1. Information technology (IT) skills. 2. Capability of using the devices in E-learning environment 3. Capability to formulate and prepare a learning environment
Content	Content creation	1. Ability to seek and know how to get the teaching material 2. Ability to decide what teaching material in E-learning environment is necessary to them (teaching material belongs self-assess oriented)
	Content packaging	1. Ability to make choices and decisions about what to study and how to study 2. Ability to utilize useful storage method in E-learning environment
	Content distribution	1. Ability to get the required teaching material actively 2. Sound communication skills, both written and spoken, as these are the main vehicles for interaction and assessment

In addition, the following technical capabilities are crucial. First, education institutions have to re-think their technology planning to satisfy and achieve their pedagogical goals in E-learning environments. The administrators of education institution must plan the technology environment for E-learning. Second, the abilities of ICT acquisitions and distribution is often an overlooked or under specified area of school management. Third, the ICT maintenance and user support is needed. In some cases, improper adjustment of those settings causes the entire computer to become inoperable, particularly when access to networks is desired. This is a challenge both to policy and management and to the capabilities of school staff. Teachers cannot get the help they need when they need it, which becomes a strong disincentive to the inclusion of technology in their regular teaching practices. Ronnkvist et al., (2000) found that more than two-thirds of instructors nationally who reported needing help with technology could not get that help when they needed it. Thus, how to support users to use e-learning systems is also an important issue. Finally, spanning traditional boundaries is an important capability. Just as inquiry-oriented and communication technologies pose problems for teachers who must learn to communicate in new ways with new audiences, they post similar problems within educational organizations, forcing communication where none was thought to

be necessary before. These organizations had not previously had to cope with the highly interactive and interconnected curriculum and education applications made possible by the Internet in the classroom. Table 8 summarizes the capability for education institution administrators.

IMPLICATIONS AND CONCLUSION

This study utilized the E-learning hypercube innovation model and accompanied it with a secondary data analysis and comparative analysis to analyze the differences between traditional classroom learning and E-learning, investigate the impacts of E-learning on the E-learning stakeholders, and develop the needed core capabilities for them. The results indicate that the innovation from traditional classroom to E-learning for learners and instructors is radical. The move from traditional classroom learning to E-learning is an overturned innovation in technological components that makes established technical and E-learning delivery capabilities obsolete. This may lead to a drastic overhaul of existing ways of doing education. Thus, an existing E-learning participant must seriously rethink how to rebuild new technological and learning delivery capabilities. Attempting to duplicate the previous technological knowledge and learning model is impractical.

Table 8. Core capability for education institution administrators

Factors	Capabilities
Vision	1. Envisioning customer value 2. Ability to develop school operation and management concepts
Technological infrastructures	1. Ability to connect instructors, learners, and e-learning administrative unit 2. Planning for technology 3. Acquisitions and distribution IT 4. IT maintenance and support
Contents	1. Content types and diversify development and management 2. Learning material management
Learning delivery model	1. Span traditional boundaries 2. The abilities of school management 3. Ability to formulate the service that e-learning could offer 4. Institutional support

For an education institution, the technological component has a fundamental change, while the learning delivery activities they support are reinforced. To cope with the innovative changes, assisting education institutions to strengthen or reconfigure their technical capabilities to exploit new educational environments should be given a high priority. For instance, the major change in technological knowledge can be facilitated through a combination of four core IT capabilities. Yet, both technological and E-learning delivery capabilities play critical roles in the E-learning transformation. It is helpful to understand what capabilities obstruct an educational institution in the new E-learning environment. Education institutes' administrators should pay attention to improve their learning delivery functions and core capabilities.

In sum, the contribution of this study is threefold: First, this research develops a comprehensive E-learning innovation hypercube model and then uses it to analyze the impact of the E-learning and examines the critical differences between them by comparing the features of their technological components (technological infrastructure and content) and learning model. This analysis provides a better understanding of how E-learning will impact the capabilities of E-learning stakeholders: learners, instructors, and education institutions. Second, this research indicates that the change derived from E-learning are multidimensional (i.e., technological components and learning model) and identifies their critical differences. These two dimensions are interwoven, and one must not focus exclusively on any single factor in assessing overall E-learning innovation. Finally, this research further explored the core capabilities based on the dynamic capabilities perspective for implementing and managing E-learning innovation. It is helpful to understand what capability obstacles E-learning stakeholders have in transitioning to E-learning environments.

This study provides several inductive results to enhance our understanding and management of E-learning change. These research results can be utilized as a diagnostic tool for practitioners to assess and analyze what aspects of their E-learning applications are most problematical. Practitioners can compare the current level of each element in their learning delivery functions with the expected levels to understand their relative effectiveness or ineffectiveness and take the necessary corrective actions to successfully make the E-learning transformation.

The current study is an exploratory research on developing a systemic model to analyze the E-learning innovations. Several issues deemed worthy of future research are mentioned in the body of this research. For instance, the inference we drew from the secondary data analysis and comparative analysis is based on the assumption that further E-learning innovation evolution does not deviate from the expected course herein. It is not easy to exactly recognize the trajectory of the innovations; hence, the limitation of contextual uncertainties may influence the validity of this study. As more and more education institutions implement E-learning, future empirical research should refine and extend the results and should continue to seek better means of assisting the E-learning transformation to cope with rapid E-learning innovation.

REFERENCES

Afuah, A., & Bahram, N. (1995). The hypercube of innovation. *Residence Policy*, *24*, 51–76. doi:10.1016/0048-7333(93)00749-J

Aldrich, H. E. (2001). How to hand exams back to your class. *College Teaching*, *49*(Summer).

Bates, T. W. (2000). *Managing technological change: Strategies for college and university leaders*. San Francisco: Jossey-Bass.

Calvani, A., & Rotta, M. (2000). *Fare formazione in Internet: Manuale di didattica online*. Rome: Erickson.

CEC. (2001). *The learning action plan: Designing tomorrow's education*. Communication from the commission to the council and the European Parliament. Retrieved from http://europa.eu.int/comm/education/elearning/index.html

Cheong, C. S. (2002). E-learning-a provider's prospective. *The Internet and Higher Education, 4*, 337–352. doi:10.1016/S1096-7516(01)00075-6

Chou, C., & Tsai, C. C. (2002). Developing Web-based curricula: Issues and challenges. *Journal of Curriculum Studies, 34*, 623–636. doi:10.1080/00220270210141909

Chuang, S. C., & Tsai, C. C. (2005). Preferences toward the constructivist Internet-based learning environments among high school students in Taiwan. *Computers in Human Behavior, 21*, 255–272. doi:10.1016/j.chb.2004.02.015

Cohen, E. G. (1994). *Designing groupwork: Strategies for the heterogeneous classroom* (2nd ed.). New York: Teachers College Press.

Collison, G., Elbaum, B., Haavind, S., & Tinker, R. (2000). *Facilitating online learning: Effective strategies for moderators*. Madison, WI: Atwood Pub.

Curran, K. (2002). A web-based collaboration teaching environment. *IEEE MultiMedia, 9*(3). doi:10.1109/MMUL.2002.1022860

Daniel, E. M., & Wilson, H. M. (2003). The role of dynamic capabilities in e-business transformation. *European Journal of Information Systems, 12*, 282–296. doi:10.1057/palgrave.ejis.3000478

Engelbrecht, E. (2003). A look at e-learning models: Investigating their value for developing an e-learning strategy. *Progressio, 25*(2), 38–47.

Forman, D., Nyatanga, L., & Rich, T. (2002). E-learning and educational diversity. *Nurse Education Today, 22*, 76–82. doi:10.1054/nedt.2001.0740

Francescato, D., Porcelli, R., Mebane, M., Cuddetta, M., Klobas, J., & Renzi, P. (2006). Evaluation of the efficacy of collaborative learning in face-to-face and computer-supported university contexts. *Computers in Human Behavior, 22*, 163–176. doi:10.1016/j.chb.2005.03.001

French, D., Hale, C., Johnson, C., & Farr, G. (Eds.). (1999). *Internet based learning: An introduction and framework for higher education and business*. Sterling, VA: Stylus.

Govindassamy, T. (2002). Successful implementation of e-learning pedagogical consideration. *The Internet and Higher Education, 4*, 287–299. doi:10.1016/S1096-7516(01)00071-9

Grunewald, M., Heckemann, R. A., & Gebhard, H. (2003). COMPARE radiology: Creating an interactive web-based training program for radiology with multimedia authoring software. *Academic Radiology, 10*, 443–553. doi:10.1016/S1076-6332(03)80065-X

Hakkinen, P., Arvaja, M., & Makitalo, K. (2004). Prerequisites for CSCL: Research approaches, methodological challenges and pedagogical development. In Littleton, K., Miell, D., & Faulkner, D. (Eds.), *Learning to collaborate: Collaborating to learn* (pp. 161–176). New York: Nova Science.

Harasim, L., Hiltz, S., & Teles, L. (1995). *Learning networks*. Cambridge, MA: MIT Press.

Harper, K. C., Chen, K., & Yen, D. C. (2004). Distance learning, virtual classrooms, and teaching pedagogy in the Internet environment. *Technology in Society, 26*, 585–598. doi:10.1016/S0160-791X(04)00054-5

Hazemi, R., Hailes, S., & Wilbur, S. (Eds.). (1998). *The digital university: Reinventing the academy*. London: Springer.

Henderson, R., & Clark, K. (1990). Architectural innovation: The reconfiguration of existing product technologies and the failure of established firms. *Administrator Science Quarterly, 35*, 9–30. doi:10.2307/2393549

Henry, P. (2001). E-learning technology, content and services. *Education + Training, 43*, 249–255. doi:10.1108/EUM0000000005485

Huang, S., & Hu, H. (2000). Integrating windows streaming media technologies into a virtual classroom environment. *IEEE Transactions on Education, 38*(2).

Johnson, D. W., Johnson, R., & Holubec, E. (1998). *Cooperation in the classroom* (7th ed.). Edina, MN: Interaction Book Co.

Johnson, D. W., & Johnson, R. T. (1986). Computer-assisted cooperative learning. *Educational Technology, 26*(1), 12–18.

Johnson, D. W., & Johnson, R. T. (1989). *Cooperation and competition: Theory and research.* Edina, MN: Interaction Book Co.

Kagan, S. (1992). *Cooperative learning resources for teachers* (7th ed.). San Juan Capistrano, CA: Resources for Teachers, Inc.

Khalifa, M., & Lam, R. (2002). Web-based learning: Effects on learning process and outcome. *IEEE Transactions on Education, 45*(4). doi:10.1109/TE.2002.804395

Kiely, T. (1993). Learning to share. *CIO, 6*(15), 38–44.

Kinshuk, J., & Yang, A. (2003). Web-based asynchronous synchronous environment for online learning. *United States Distance Education Association Journal, 17*(2), 5–17.

Kreijns, K., Kirschner, P. A., & Jochems, W. (2003). Supported collaborative learning environments: A review of the research. *Computers in Human Behavior, 19*, 335–353. doi:10.1016/S0747-5632(02)00057-2

Lepori, B., Cantoni, L., & Succi, C. (2000). The introduction of e-learning in European universities: Models and strategies. *Quality on the Line*, 74-83.

Logan, D. (2001). *E-learning in the knowledge age.* Paper presented at the Gartner Symposium Itxpo 2001, Johannesburg, South Africa.

Marjanovic, O. (1999). Learning and teaching in a synchronous collaborative environment. *Journal of Computer Assisted Learning, 15*(2), 129–138. doi:10.1046/j.1365-2729.1999.152085.x

Moe, M. T., & Blodget, H. (2000). *The knowledge web: People power-fuel for the new economy.* San Francisco: Merrill Lynch.

Moore, M. G., & Kearsley, G. (1996). *Distance education: A systems view.* Belmont, CA: Wadsworth.

Palloff, R. M., & Pratt, K. (1999). *Building learning communities in cyberspace.* San Francisco: Jossey-Bass.

Piccoli, G., Ahmad, R., & Ives, B. (2001). Web-based virtual learning environments: A research framework and a preliminary assessment of effectiveness in basic IT skills training. *Management Information Systems Quarterly, 25*, 401–426. doi:10.2307/3250989

Raab, R. T., Ellis, W. W., & Abdon, B. R. (2002). Multisectoral partnerships in e-learning: A potential force for improved human capital development in the Asia Pacific. *The Internet and Higher Education, 4*, 217–229. doi:10.1016/S1096-7516(01)00067-7

Randall, V. (1999). Cooperative learning abused and overused? *Gifted Child Today Magazine, 22*(2), 14–16.

Relan, A., & Gillani, B. G. (1997). Web-based instruction and the traditional classroom: Similarities and differences. *Web-Based Instruction*, 41-46.

Ronnkvist, A., Dexter, S. L., & Anderson, R. E. (2000). *Technology support: Its depth, breadth and impact in America's schools. Teaching, Learning, and Computing: 1998 National Survey Report #5. Irvine, CA: Center for Research on Information Technology and Organizations*. Irvine: University of California.

Rosenberg, M. J. (2001). *E-learning: Strategies for delivery knowledge in the digital age*. New York: McGraw-Hill.

Slavin, R. E. (1995). *Cooperative learning: Theory, research, and practice* (2nd ed.). Boston: Allyn & Bacon.

Sloman, M. (2001). *The e-learning revolution*. Wimbledon, UK: CIPD.

Stokes, P. J. (2000). How E-learning will transform education. Education week on the Web. *Editorial Projects in Education, 20*. Retrieved October 1, 2001 from http://www.edweek.org/ew/ewstory.cfm?slug=02stokes.h20andkeywords=education%20technology#author

Strijbos, J.-W., Kirschner, P. A., & Martens, R. L. (Eds.). (2004). *What we know about CSCL in higher education*. Boston: Kluwer. doi:10.1007/1-4020-7921-4

Taylor, D. R. (2002). E-learning: The second wave. *Leaning Circuits: ASTD's online magazine*. Retrieved from http:www.learningcircuits.com/2002/oct2002/taylor.html

Teece, D. J., Pisano, G., & Shuen, A. (1997). Dynamic capabilities and strategic management. *Strategic Management Journal, 18*, 509–533. doi:10.1002/(SICI)1097-0266(199708)18:7<509::AID-SMJ882>3.0.CO;2-Z

Tennyson, R. D., & Jorczak, R. L. (in press). Benefits of CSCL for learners with disabilities. In Ordóñez de Pablos, P. (Ed.), *Technology enhanced learning for people with disabilities: Approaches and applications*. Hershey, PA: IGI Global.

Trentin, G. (2000). *Telematica e formazione a distanza*. Florence: La Nuova Italia.

UNESCO. (1998). *World declaration on higher education on higher education for the twenty-first century: Vision and action*. Paris: UNESCO, Division of Higher Education, Unit for the World Conference on Higher Education. Retrieved from http://www.unesco.org/education/educprog/wche/declaration_eng.htm#world%20declaration.

Webster, J., & Hackley, P. (1997). Teaching effectiveness in technology-mediated distance learning. *Academy of Management Review, 40*, 1282–1309. doi:10.2307/257034

Wheeler, B. (2000). WebCT – WebCT clear leader in online learning programs. *The Chronicle of Higher Education, 11*, 34.

Wheeler, C. (2002). NEBIC: A dynamic capabilities theory for assessing net-enablement. *Information Systems Research, 13*, 125–146. doi:10.1287/isre.13.2.125.89

Wu, J.-H., Hsia, T.-L., & Heng, M. (2006). Core dynamic capabilities for exploiting electronic banking. *Journal of Electronic Commerce Research, 7*, 111–122.

Wu, J.-H., & Shiah, T.-L. (2005). Developing E-business dynamic capabilities: An analysis of E-commerce innovation from I-, M-, to U-commerce. *Journal of Organizational Computing and Electronic Commerce*.

Yang, S. C., & Liu, S. F. (2005). The study of interactions and attitudes of third-grade students' learning information technology via a cooperative approach. *Computers in Human Behavior, 21*, 45–72. doi:10.1016/j.chb.2004.02.002

Chapter 16
Design Strategies for Improved Online Instructional Systems

Jen-Her Wu
National Sun Yat-Sen University, Taiwan

Tzyh-Lih Hsia
Chinese Naval Academy, Taiwan

Robert D. Tennyson
University of Minnesota, USA

ABSTRACT

This chapter presents instructional design strategies to improve student learning satisfaction. Conformation factor analysis was performed to test the reliability and validity of the measurement model. The partial least squares method was used to evaluate the causal model. The results indicated that the learning climate, perceived value and perceived ease of use significantly affected learning satisfaction. Computer self-efficacy had a strong impact on perceived behavioral control; computer self-efficacy, perceived behavioral control and social interaction had significant effects on perceived ease of use. System functionality, content feature and social interaction significantly affected perceived value. Social interaction had a significant effect on learning climate. This chapter provides initial insights into those factors that are likely significant antecedents for planning and implementing a blended e-learning system to enhance student learning satisfaction.

INTRODUCTION

Traditional face-to-face learning typically occurs in a teacher-directed environment with interpersonal interaction in a live synchronous environment. This learning environment is costly with less access flexibility. On the other hand, the electronic learning (e-learning) environments that have grown and expanded dramatically as new technologies have expanded the possibilities for communication, interaction and multimedia input. Although the e-learning may increase access flexibility and improve cost effectiveness, it suffers from a lack of social interaction between learners and instructors (Wu, Tennyson, Hsia, & Liao, in press).

With the rapid emergence of technological innovations in information and communication,

DOI: 10.4018/978-1-61520-623-0.ch016

people have searched for another instructional delivery solution to relieve the above problems. The term blended learning has been discussed as a promising alternative. Blended learning refers to courses that combine face-to-face classroom instruction with online learning. In recent years blended e-learning has become part of the educational landscape. Several blended e-learning systems (BELS), such as WebCT (www.webct.com) and Cyber University of NSYSU (cu.nsysu.edu.tw) have been recently developed that integrate a variety of functions to facilitate the learning activities. For example, these systems can be used to integrate instructional material (via audio, video, and text), e-mail, live chat sessions, online discussions, forums, quizzes and assignments. With this kind of system, instructional delivery and communication between instructors and students can be performed at the same time (synchronously) or at different times (asynchronously). Such systems provide a variety of instructional aides and communication methods, and offer learners or instructors great flexibility as to the time and place of instruction. As a result, these online learning systems may better accommodate the needs of learners or instructors who are geographically dispersed and have conflicting schedules (Pituch & Lee, 2006).

While we have recognized a number of advantages in employing BELS, insufficient learning satisfaction has long been an obstacle to the successful adoption of BELS (So, 2006). The explosion of BELS in supporting learning has made it extremely significant to probe the determinants crucial that would entice learners to use BELS and enhance their learning satisfaction. Comprehending the essentials of what determines student learning satisfaction can provide great management insights into developing effective strategies that will allow universities to create new opportunities and value for their students and instructors. Generally, the essential characteristics of BELS differ greatly from the traditional teaching and e-learning system. Thus, any model developed for e-learning or business systems may not apply to a BELS environment. BELS may need to consider BELS-specific factors, such as the social factor. Hence, the goal of this study is to present a research model for assessing student learning satisfaction in a BELS environment. The theory of reasoned action (TRA) and technology acceptance mode (TAM) serve as the theoretical basis for this study that are integrated with factors such as individual differences, system characteristics, and social factors. We also validate the factors that determine learning satisfaction and examined the relationships among those latent variables.

BASIC CONCEPTS AND THEORETICAL FOUNDATION

Blended E-Learning Environments

In contrast with traditional instructions, e-learning provides more learning resources and more opportunities to allow learners and instructors to communicate, collaborate, and interact with and among each other without regard to temporal or physical location. Prior research (e.g., Kinshuk & Yang, 2003, Yang & Liu, 2007, Wu et al., 2008) indicated both positive and negative aspects of the e-learning environments. Among the positive aspects were that e-learning stretched the spatial and temporal barriers, provided greater flexibility and student convenience, more positive overall learning experience, and improved access/interaction with the instructor. However, some negative aspects and disadvantages of e-learning were pointed out such as lack of peer contact and interaction, high initial costs for preparing multimedia content of learning materials and also substantial costs for its maintaining and updating, as well as the need for flexible tutorial support. With the above concerns and dissatisfaction with e-learning in prior studies, people have searched for another instructional delivery solution. Blended e-learning has been discussed as a promising alternative (So, 2006).

Graham (2006) defined the blended e-learning as the combination of instruction from two historically separate models for teaching and learning: traditional face-to-face learning system and e-learning system. It is an important distinction because it is certainly possible to enhance regular face-to-face courses with online resources without displacing classroom contact hours. The BELS emphasizes the central role of computer-based technologies (e-learning system) in blended learning focusing on enabling access and flexibility, enhancing traditional teaching and learning practices, and transforming the way individuals learn (Graham, 2006). Thus, we defined the BELS as the combination of online and face-to-face instruction and the convergence between traditional face-to-face learning and e-learning environments. As blended e-learning emerges as perhaps the most prominent instructional delivery solution, it is vital to explore what determines learning satisfaction in a blended e-learning environment.

Theory of Reasoned Action and Technology Acceptance Mode

The theory of reasoned action (TRA), proposed by Fishbein and Ajzen (1975), is a well-established model that has been used broadly to predict and explain human behavior in various domains. According to the TRA model, attitudes are a function of beliefs, specifically including the behavioral beliefs directly linked to a person's intention to perform a defined behavior. Davis (1989) proposed a technology acceptance mode (TAM) derived from TRA in modeling user technology acceptance behavior. The original TAM consists of perceived ease of use (PEOU), perceived usefulness (PU), attitude toward using (ATU), behavioral intention to use (BI), and actual system use (AU). PU and PEOU are the two most important determinants for AU. The ATU directly predicts users' BI which determines AU.

Venkatesh and Davis (2000) further proposed an extended TAM, i.e. TAM2, which includes social influence processes (subjective norm, voluntarism, and image) and cognitive instrumental processes (job relevance, output quality, result demonstrability, and PEOU), whereas it omits ATU due to weak predictors of either BI or AU. The research indicated that both social influence processes and cognitive instrumental processes significantly influenced user acceptance as well as PU and PEOU indirectly influenced AU through BI. User acceptance can be measured by a positive attitude toward the system based on TAM (Taylor & Todd, 1995). Satisfaction is a good surrogate for user acceptance and was often used to measure learners' attitude in learning-related studies (Chou & Liu, 2005, Piccoli et al., 2001). Prior research in education had found that perceived ease of use and perceived value were positively related to student satisfaction and perceived ease of use was positively related to perceived value (Martins & Kellermanns, 2004).

In this study, we conceptualize the student attitude toward the system as learning satisfaction with the BELS. Learning satisfaction is the sum of student feelings and attitudes that result from aggregating all the benefits that a student hopes to receive from interaction with the BELS. Perceived value is defined as the degree to which a person believes that using a particular system would enhance his or her job performance and perceived ease of use is defined as the degree to which using the technology will be free of effort. Therefore, the following hypotheses are proposed.

H1a:*Perceived ease of use has a positive effect on BELS learning satisfaction.*

H1b:*Perceived ease of use has a positive effect on BELS perceived value.*

H2:*Perceived value has a positive effect on BELS learning satisfaction.*

External Variables

Individual Differences

Individual difference refers to user factors that include traits such as personality, demographic variables and situational variables that account for differences attributable to circumstances such as experience and training. Several individual variables, e.g., computer self-efficacy and perceived behavioral control, are believed to be the most relevant factors affecting information system (IS) success (Alavi & Joachimsthaler 1992). In virtual environments, individual differences have been suggested related to IT acceptance (Chen et al. 2000) and e-learning systems (Pituch & Lee 2006). In an e-learning environment, learning success has been found to depend on (a) the ability to cope with technical difficulty and (b) the learners' perception of the availability of skills, resource facilitating conditions, technology facilitating conditions and opportunities. Therefore, in our study, computer self-efficacy and perceived behavioral control are two individual difference factors that are expected to influence BELS use.

Computer self-efficacy is defined as "the confidence in one's ability to perform certain learning tasks using a BELS" in this research (Compeau & Higgins 1995). Prior research has indicated that computer self-efficacy influences performance or behavior (Francescato et al. 2006, Piccoli et al. 2001, Johnston et al. 2005), including attitude and behavioral intention (Venkatesh & Davis 2000). Other studies have found that computer self-efficacy and perceived ease of use are related (Davis 1989, Hong et al. 2002, Pituch & Lee 2006). Perceived behavioral control, defined as the learners' perception of the availability of skills, resource facilitating conditions, technology facilitating conditions and opportunities. Venkatesh et al., (2003) indicated that the related resources support for BELS learners can influence system utilization. Based on the forgoing discussion, the following hypotheses are proposed

H3a:*Computer self-efficacy has a positive effect on perceived behavioral control with BELS.*

H3b:*Computer self-efficacy has a positive effect on perceived ease of use with BELS.*

H4:*Perceived behavioral control has a positive effect on perceived ease of use with BELS.*

System Characteristics

Prior research has shown that IS characteristics can significantly affect user beliefs in various contexts (Venkatesh & Davis, 2000). For instance, prior researches indicated that system functionality and content features are important external variables that directly affect both perceived ease of use and perceived value of IS (Hong et al., 2002, Pituch & Lee, 2006). In our study, system functionality and content feature are two system characteristics factors that are expected to influence BELS use.

System functionality is defined as the perceived ability of a BELS to provide flexible access to instructional and assessment media (Pituch & Lee, 2006). For example, allow students to access course content, turn in homework assignments, and complete tests and quizzes online. In addition to system functionality, effective BELS must provide high quality content feature. In our study, content feature is defined as the characteristics and presentation of BELS information (Zhang et al., 2000). Empirical evidences have shown that high quality of content features (Zhang et al., 2000) and system functionality (Pituch & Lee, 2006) positively affect both perceived ease of use and perceived value of BELS use. Therefore, we proposed.

H5a:*System functionality has a positive effect on perceived ease of use for BELS.*

H5b:*System functionality has a positive effect on perceived value of BELS.*

H6a:*Content feature has a positive effect on perceived ease of use for BELS.*

H6b:*Content feature has a positive effect on perceived value of BELS.*

Social Factors

There is an increasing focus on facilitating human interaction in the form of online collaboration, virtual communities, and instant messaging in the context of BELS (Graham 2006). From the group interactions perspective, social factors, such as collaborative learning (Francescato et al., 2006), learning climate (Chou & Liu, 2005), and social interaction (Johnston et al. 2005), are important antecedents of beliefs about using a learning system. Prior research (Pituch & Lee 2006) showed that social interaction has a direct effect on the usage of an e-learning system. The interactions among students, between faculty and students, and collaboration in learning resulting from these interactions are the keys to the learning process. In addition, the emotional learning climate is an important indicator of learning effectiveness (Chou & Liu, 2005). In our study, social interaction is defined as the interactions among students themselves, the interactions between faculty and students, and the collaboration in learning (Chou & Liu, 2005). Learning climate is defined as the learning atmosphere in the context of BELS (Prieto & Revilla, 2006).

Johnston et al., (2005) proposed that contact and interaction with the instructors and learners is a valid predictor of perceived value for student satisfaction. In addition, a positive learning climate encourages and stimulates the exchange of ideas, opinions, information and knowledge in the organization as it is characterized by trust and collaboration between learners (Prieto & Revilla, 2006). That is, when learners believe that BELS provides effective student-student and student-instructor interactions and improves learning climate, they will be more satisfied with the BELS. Therefore, the following hypotheses are proposed:

H7a:*Social Interaction has a positive effect on perceived ease of use with BELS.*

H7b: *Social Interaction has a positive effect on perceived value of BELS.*

H7c:*Social Interaction has a positive effect on the BELS learning climate.*

H8:*Learning climate has a positive effect on learning satisfaction with BELS.*

Figure 1. The research model for student learning satisfaction in the BELS context

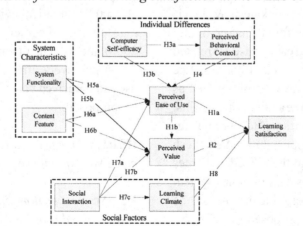

Based on the aforementioned discussion, we propose a research model that suggests that perceived ease of use, perceived value and learning climate influence student learning satisfaction, as shown in Figure 1. Table 1 indicates the constructs and their definitions.

RESEARCH METHODOLOGY

Instrument Development

To validly develop the instrument, a number of prior relevant studies were reviewed to ensure that a comprehensive list of measures was included. For instance, the measures for learning satisfaction were derived from Chiu et al., (2005) and Wu and Wang (2006). Measures for perceived ease of use and perceived value were taken from previous research (e.g., Davis, 1989, Venkatesh & Davis, 2000). The computer self-efficacy construct was captured using four items tailored from Compeau and Higgins (1995). The measures for perceived behavioral control were taken from previous studies (e.g., Taylor & Todd 1995, Venkatesh et al. 2003). The system functionality construct was captured using items, selected from Pituch and Lee (2006). The measures for content feature were adapted from Zhang et al., (2000), and Molla and Licker (2001). The measures for the social interaction were taken from Johnston et al. (2005), Kreijns et al., (2003), and Pituch and Lee, (2006). Finally, the measures for the learning climate were selected from Chou and Liu (2005). The instrument items were shown in the Appendix.

The survey questionnaire consisted of two parts including the respondent's demographic information and the subject's perception of each variable in the model. All items in the second part of the questionnaire are measured via a 7-point scale ranging from 1 (strongly disagree) to 7 (strongly agree).Once the initial questionnaire was generated, an iterative personal interview process with the domain experts from blended e-learning course related instructors and students (including four instructors and five students in three different schools) was conducted to verify the instrument and to confirm the content validity. At the end of the pre-test, there were 9 constructs with 28 items in total to be used for the survey.

Table 1. Constructs in the research model

Construct	Acronym	Definition
Computer Self-efficacy	CSE	The confidence in one's ability to perform certain learning tasks using BELS.
Perceived behavioral control	PBC	The learners' perception of the availability of skills, resource facilitating conditions, technology facilitating conditions and opportunities.
System Functionality	SF	The perceived ability of a BELS to provide flexible access to instructional and assessment media.
Content Feature	CF	The characteristics and presentation of BELS information.
Social Interaction	SI	The interactions among students themselves, the interactions between faculty and students, and the collaboration in learning.
Learning Climate	LC	The learning atmosphere in the context of BELS.
Perceived Ease of Use	PEOU	The degree to which using BELS will be free of effort.
Perceived Value	PV	The degree to which a person believes that using BELS would enhance his or her performance.
Learning Satisfaction	LS	The sum of student feelings and attitudes that result from aggregating all the benefits that a student hopes to receive from interaction with BELS.

Participant Characteristics

The empirical data were collected using a questionnaire survey administered over a span of two semesters. Subjects for this study were students that had the opportunity to take courses via BELS. We distributed 518 questionnaires (paper-based and online questionnaires) to the targeted universities that actually implemented BELS in Taiwan. Sample data were collected via snowball and convenient sampling. Three hundred seven-six questionnaires were returned. Sixty-four responses were incomplete and had to be discarded. This left 212 valid responses for the statistical analysis, and a valid response rate of 40.93% of the initial sample. Among the valid responses, 84 responses are received from physical classrooms and 128 responses are gathered from online learning environment.

The potential non-response bias was assessed by comparing the early versus late respondents that were weighed on several demographic characteristics. The results indicated that there are no statistically significant differences among demographics between the early and late respondents. The profile of respondents and the results of non-response bias analysis are shown as in Table 2.

RESULTS

Partial least squares (PLS) method was applied for the data analysis in this study. PLS performs a Confirmatory Factor Analysis (CFA). In a CFA, the pattern of loadings of the measurement items on the latent constructs was explicitly specified in the model. The fit of this pre-specified model is then examined to determine its convergent and discriminant validities. This factorial validity deals with whether the loading patterns of the measurement items corresponds to the theoretically anticipated factors (Gefen & Straub, 2005). The evaluation of the model fit was conducted in two stages (Chin, 1998, Gefen & Straub, 2005).

First, the measurement model is assessed, in which construct validity and reliability of the measures are assessed. The structural model with hypotheses is then tested. The statistical analysis strategy involved a two-phase approach in which the psychometric properties of all scales were first assessed through CFA and the structural relationships were then validated using bootstrap analysis.

Measurement Validation

For the first phase, the analysis is performed in relation to the attributes of individual item reliability, construct reliability, average variance extracted (AVE), and discriminant validity of the indicators as measures of latent variables through a CFA. The results indicated that all items of the instrument have significant loadings higher than the recommended value of .707. As shown in Table 3, all constructs in the measurement model exhibit good internal consistency as evidenced by their composite reliability scores. The composite reliability coefficients of all constructs and the AVE in the proposed model (Figure 1) are more than adequate, ranging from 0.836 to 0.957 and from 0.631 to 0.849, respectively.

To assess discriminant validity, (1) indicators should load more strongly on their corresponding construct than on other constructs in the model and (2) the AVE should be larger than the inter-construct correlations (Chin 1998). For each specific construct, AVE shows the ratio of the sum of its measurement item variance as extracted by the construct relative to the measurement error attributed to its items. As a rule of thumb, the square root of the AVE of each construct should be much larger than the correlation of the specific construct with any of the other constructs in the model and should be at least .50 (Chin 1998). As the results show in Table 4, all constructs meet the above mentioned requirements. The values for reliability are all above the suggested minimum of 0.7. Thus, the convergent and discriminant

Table 2. Respondents profile and the results of non-response bias analysis (N=212)

Variable	Classification	Total (%)		Early respondents (%)		Late respondents (%)		χ^2 (Sig.)
Gender	Male	106	0.500	73	0.344	33	0.156	0.022 (0.50)
	Female	106	0.500	72	0.340	34	0.160	
Age	18-30	101	0.476	48	0.453	53	0.500	1.344 (0.855)
	31-40	82	0.387	41	0.387	41	0.387	
	41-50	23	0.108	14	0.132	9	0.085	
	51-60	4	0.019	2	0.019	2	0.019	
	>61	2	0.009	1	0.009	1	0.009	
Types of Jobs	Student	8	0.038	3	0.014	5	0.024	4.806 (0.440)
	Industry	30	0.142	12	0.057	18	0.085	
	Manufacturing	57	0.269	27	0.127	30	0.142	
	Service	10	0.047	5	0.024	5	0.024	
	Finance	59	0.278	36	0.170	23	0.108	
	Others	48	0.226	23	0.108	25	0.118	
Education level	Senior high school	0	0.000	0	0.000	0	0.000	8.824 (0.32)
	College (2 years)	10	0.047	1	0.005	9	0.042	
	University (4 years)	116	0.547	60	0.283	56	0.264	
	Graduate school	86	0.406	45	0.212	41	0.193	
BELS experience	Pure physical classroom experience	15	0.071	7	0.033	8	0.038	0.371 (0.946)
	Pure virtual classroom experience	42	0.198	20	0.094	22	0.104	
	Physical experience more than virtual experience	105	0.495	53	0.250	52	0.245	
	Virtual experience more than physical experience	50	0.236	26	0.123	24	0.113	
BELS experience: participating in BELS (Years)	< 0.5 years	35	0.165	18	0.085	17	0.080	2.695 (0.747)
	0.5 ~ 1 years	95	0.448	50	0.236	45	0.212	
	2 years	48	0.226	25	0.118	23	0.108	
	3 years	11	0.052	6	0.028	5	0.024	
	4 years	4	0.019	2	0.009	2	0.009	
	>4 years	19	0.090	5	0.024	14	0.066	
BELS experience: participating in BELS (Times)	1 times	44	0.208	24	0.113	20	0.094	4.710 (0.452)
	2 times	43	0.203	22	0.104	21	0.099	
	3 times	30	0.142	15	0.071	15	0.071	
	4 times	13	0.061	9	0.042	4	0.019	
	5 times	10	0.047	6	0.028	4	0.019	
	>= 6 times	72	0.340	30	0.142	42	0.198	

continued on following page

Table 2. continued

Variable	Classification	Total (%)		Early respondents (%)		Late respondents (%)		χ^2 (Sig.)
BELS experience: spending time in the BELS (1 week)	< 1 hours	62	0.292	33	0.156	29	0.137	4.729 (0.450)
	1 ~ 3 hours	75	0.354	33	0.156	42	0.198	
	3 ~ 5 hours	43	0.203	22	0.104	21	0.099	
	5 ~ 7 hours	20	0.094	10	0.047	10	0.047	
	7 ~ 9 hours	6	0.028	4	0.019	2	0.009	
	> 9 hours	6	0.028	4	0.019	2	0.009	
Average years of computer usage experience		11.79 (years)		13.7 (years)		10.7 (years)		27.076 (0.133)

Table 3. Results of confirmatory factor analysis

Construct	Items	Composite Reliability	AVE
Computer Self-efficacy (CSE)	3	0.836	0.631
Perceived behavioral control (PBC)	4	0.921	0.745
System Functionality (SF)	3	0.905	0.761
Content Feature (CF)	2	0.891	0.803
Social Interaction (SI)	3	0.915	0.782
Learning Climate (LC)	3	0.926	0.807
Perceived Ease of Use (PEOU)	3	0.943	0.846
Perceived Value (PV)	3	0.944	0.848
Learning Satisfaction (LS)	4	0.957	0.849

Table 4. Correlation between constructs

	CSE	PBC	SF	CF	SI	LC	PEOU	PV	LS
CSE	0.794*								
PBC	0.643	0.863							
SF	0.502	0.650	0.872						
CF	0.455	0.534	0.603	0.896					
SI	0.346	0.402	0.507	0.609	0.884				
LC	0.365	0.407	0.513	0.597	0.726	0.898			
PEOU	0.695	0.802	0.580	0.519	0.462	0.440	0.920		
PV	0.364	0.398	0.501	0.580	0.658	0.781	0.411	0.921	
LS	0.403	0.519	0.531	0.603	0.613	0.739	0.497	0.813	0.921

*The shaded numbers in the diagonal row are square roots of the average variance extracted.

validity of all constructs in the proposed model can be assured.

Test of the Structural Model

In the second phase of the statistical analysis, the structural model is assessed to confirm to what extent the causal relationships specified by the proposed model are consistent with the available data. The PLS method does not directly provide significance tests and path coefficient confidence interval estimates in the proposed model. A bootstrapping technique was used to estimate the significance of the path coefficients. Bootstrap analysis was performed with 200 subsamples and the path coefficients were re-estimated using each of these samples. This approach is consistent with recommended practices for estimating significance of path coefficients and indicator loadings (Löhmoeller, 1984).

Hypotheses and corollaries testing were performed by examining the size, the sign, and the significance of the path coefficients and the weights of the dimensions of the constructs, respectively. Results of the analysis for the structural model are presented in Figure 2. The estimated

path coefficient (standardized) and its associated significance level are specified next to each link. The R^2 statistic is indicated next to the dependent construct. We found that all specified paths between constructs in the model had significant path coefficients except for the paths drawn from system functionality and content feature to perceived ease of use and perceived ease of use to perceived value. The results provide good support for our model.

One indicator of the predictive power of path models is to examine the explained variance or R^2 values (Barclay et al. 1995). The results indicate that the model explained 71 percent of the variance in learning satisfaction. Similarly, 71.3 percent of the variance in PEOU ($R^2 = 0.713$) and 49.5 percent of the variance in PU ($R^2 = 0.495$) were explained by the related antecedent constructs. The path coefficient from computer self-efficacy to perceived behavior control was 0.414 and from social interaction to learning climate was 0.526. The magnitude and significance of these path coefficients provides further evidence in support of the nomological validity of the research model. For the individual differences, Hypotheses, H3a, H3b, and H4 are supported.

Figure 2. Results of PLS analysis

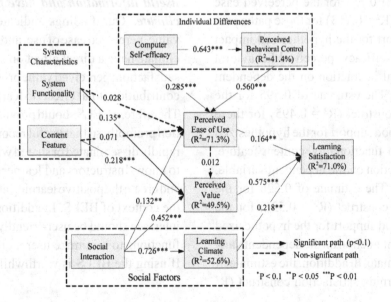

That is, the computer self-efficacy influences the perceived behavioral control and the computer self-efficacy and perceived behavioral control apparently positively influence the perceived ease of use too.

As for the construct of system characteristics, the results also provide support for the Hypotheses, H5b and H6b. Contrary to our predictions, the paths from system functionality (H5a) and content feature (H6a) to perceived ease of use are not supported. For the social factors, Hypotheses, H7a, H7b, and H7c are supported. That is, social interaction apparently influences the perceived ease of use, perceived value, and learning climate, respectively. Concerning the learning satisfaction, the analysis results provide support for the Hypotheses, H1a, H2, and H8. That is, perceived ease of use, perceived value, and learning climate influence learning satisfaction. Contrary to our prediction, the path from perceived ease of use to perceived value (H1b) is not supported.

CONCLUSION

The results provide strong empirical evidence for the nomological validity of each construct and validate the proposed model, as shown in Figure 2. The estimate of 0.713 for the perceived ease of use construct ($R^2 = 0.713$) for these paths provides good support for the hypothesized impact of computer self-efficacy, perceived behavioral control and social interaction on the dependent variable, PEOU. The estimate of 0.495 for the perceive value construct ($R^2 = 0.495$) for these paths provides good support for the hypothesized impact of system functionality, content feature, and social interaction on the dependent variable, perceived value. The estimate of 0.526 for the learning climate construct ($R^2 = 0.526$) for the path provides good support for the hypothesized impact of social interaction on the dependent variable, learning climate. In addition, the estimate of 0.710 for the learning satisfaction construct ($R^2 = 0.710$) denotes that the learning satisfaction as perceived by learners are directly and indirectly mediated by the perceived ease of use, perceived value, and learning climate constructs. Therefore, as a whole, the model has strong explanatory power for the learning satisfaction construct.

It is worth noting that the effect of system characteristics on perceived ease of use was not significant and perceived ease of use did not significantly influence perceived value. This effect subsides over time. In past years, the user interface for IS was the text mode. Presently, most software uses a graphic user interface with an intuitive interface design. These features have significantly improved the functionality of systems and thus enhanced the ease of use. Scarborough and Zimmer (2000) addressed that the introduction of IT has three stages: substitution, adaptation, and revolution. When the substitution stage approaches its end, users are familiar with using the information technology. In our study, about 70% of the subjects had ten years or more computer experience. Thus, ease of use for them is not an important issue and perceived value outweighs ease of use. This may provide a good reason that supports these striking findings. The implications of this study include that:

A BELS should be easy to use and provide useful information and have positive learning climate. Our findings indicate that perceived value, perceived ease of use, and positive learning climate have a direct effect on student's learning satisfaction; perceived value provided the greatest contribution (total effect) to learning satisfaction. Therefore, a BELS should provide useful information promptly so that useful recommendations are rapidly disseminated or shared with those that need to know. Instructors and learners should promote and create the positive learning atmosphere within the context of BELS. In addition, a BELS's user interface should be user-friendly and include key functions to minimize user's efforts in learning. If using the BELS is worthwhile, enjoyable and simple, learners will be more likely to use it resulting in greater satisfaction.

University administrators should provide resources to enhance students' computer self-efficacy. The computer self-efficacy has a significant positive influence on perceived behavioral control. In addition, computer self-efficacy and perceived behavioral control had a direct significant positive influence on perceived ease of use. The perceived behavioral control has the most contribution (total effect) to the perceived ease of use. These finding suggest that (1) a BELS should provide customized functions to allow learners control over the system and built-in help to fit various learners' needs in different learning circumstances; (2) learners should have the computer competency necessary to use the BELS and control over his/her learning activity. Students' computer self-efficacy could reduce their barrier in using the BELS. If students have the higher computer self-efficacy and can control over the BELS, they will perceive the system is easy to use. Therefore, university administrators should provide resources to enhance students' computer self-efficacy; insufficient computer self-efficacy may decrease the students' motivation to use the BELS resulting less satisfaction in learning.

A BELS should offer good content features with multimedia presentation and flexibility in learning activity. The results indicated that system functionality and content feature have a significant positive influence on perceived value. These findings suggest that (1) a BELS should offer useful information with appropriate online feature and good content design that satisfy students' needs; (2) a BELS should provide various types of content presentation functions (e.g., multimedia) and flexible access to fit various learners' needs. Therefore, it seems reasonable to infer that universities may provide relatively efficient technical support, training, and an awareness program for all staff involved and sufficient resources to implement the BELS.

A BELS should provide an environment for social interaction and instructor should motivate positive interaction publicly. The results indicated that social interaction had a significant positive influence on perceived ease of use, perceived value, and learning climate. In addition, social interaction has the most contribution (total effect) to the perceived value. These findings suggest that when implementing the BELS, the instructors should motivate the positive interaction publicly to encourage collaborative learning interaction via the system. If the BELS could offer a good environment to facilitate the interaction among students and instructors, learners will be more likely to perceive better learning climate, greater BELS value, and easier BELS usage.

Although the empirical research develops and validates a model of learning satisfaction in the BELS context, it has several limitations that could be addressed in the future research. First, our results were obtained from one single study that examined some particular e-learning systems and targeted some specific students in Taiwan. Thus, caution needs to be taken when generalizing our findings to other blend e-learning systems or students groups. In addition, the sample size used in this study is another limitation. A cross-cultural validation using a large sample gathered elsewhere is required for greater generalization of the proposed model.

REFERENCES

Alavi, M., & Joachimsthaler, E. A. (1992). Revisiting DSS implementation research: A meta-analysis of the literature and suggests for researchers. *Management Information Systems Quarterly, 16,* 95–116. doi:10.2307/249703

Barclay, D., Higgins, C., & Thomson, R. (1995). The partial least squares approach to causal modeling, personal computer adoption and use as an illustration. *Technology Studies, 2,* 285–309.

Chen, C., Czerwinski, M., & Macredie, R. (2000). Individual differences in virtual environments: Introduction and overview. *Journal of the American Society for Information Science American Society for Information Science, 51,* 499–507. doi:10.1002/(SICI)1097-4571(2000)51:6<499::AID-ASI2>3.0.CO;2-K

Chin, W. W. (1998). The partial least squares approach to structural equation modeling. In Marcoulides, G. A. (Ed.), *Modern methods for business research* (pp. 295–236). Mahwah, NJ: Erlbaum.

Chiu, C. M., Hsu, M. H., & Sun, S. Y. (2005). Usability, quality, value and e-learning continuance decisions. *Computers & Education, 45,* 399–416. doi:10.1016/j.compedu.2004.06.001

Chou, S. W., & Liu, C. H. (2005). Learning effectiveness in a web-based virtual learning environment: A learner control perspective. *Journal of Computer Assisted Learning, 21,* 65–76. doi:10.1111/j.1365-2729.2005.00114.x

Compeau, D. R., & Higgins, C. A. (1995). Computer self-efficacy: Development of a measure and initial test. *Management Information Systems Quarterly, 19,* 189–211. doi:10.2307/249688

Davis, F. D. (1989). Perceived usefulness, perceived ease of use, and user acceptance of information technology. *Management Information Systems Quarterly, 13,* 318–339. doi:10.2307/249008

Fishbein, M., & Ajzen, I. (1975). *Belief, attitude, intention and behavior: An introduction to theory and research.* Reading, MA: Addison-Wesley.

Francescato, D., Porcelli, R., Mebane, M., Cuddetta, M., Klobas, J., & Renzi, P. (2006). Evaluation of the efficacy of collaborative learning in face-to-face and computer-supported university contexts. *Computers in Human Behavior, 22,* 163–176. doi:10.1016/j.chb.2005.03.001

Gefen, D., & Straub, D. W. (2005). A practical guide to factorial validity using PLS-graph: Tutorial and annotated example. *Communications of the Association for Information Systems, 16*(5), 91–109.

Graham, C. R. (2006). Blended learning system: Definition, current trends, future directions. In Bonk, C. J., & Graham, C. R. (Eds.), *Handbook of blended learning* (pp. 3–20). San Francisco, CA: Pfeiffer.

Hong, W., Thong, J. Y. L., Wong, W. M., & Tam, K. Y. (2002). Determinants of user acceptance of digital libraries: An empirical examination of individual differences and system characteristics. *Journal of Management Information Systems, 18*(3), 97–124.

Johnston, J., Killion, J., & Oomen, J. (2005). Student satisfaction in the virtual classroom. *The Internet Journal of Allied Health Sciences and Practice, 3*(2), 17–29.

Kinshuk, D., & Yang, A. (2003). Web-based asynchronous synchronous environment for online learning. *United States Distance Education Association Journal, 17*(2), 5–17.

Kreijns, K., Kirschner, P., & Jochems, W. (2003). Identifying the pitfalls for social interaction in computer-supported collaborative learning environments: A review of the research. *Computers in Human Behavior, 19,* 335–353. doi:10.1016/S0747-5632(02)00057-2

Löhmoeller, J. B. (1984). *LVPS 1.6 program manual: Latent variable path analysis with partial least squares estimation.* Köhn, Germany: Universitaet zu Köhn. Zentralarchiv fuer Empirische Sozialforschung.

Martins, L. L., & Kellermanns, F. W. (2004). A model of business school students' acceptance of a web-based course management system. *Academy of Management Learning & Education, 3*(1), 7–26.

Molla, A., & Licker, P. S. (2001). E-commerce systems success: An attempt to extend and re-specify the DeLone and McLean model of IS success. *Journal of Electronic Commerce Research, 2*(4), 1–11.

Piccoli, G., Ahmad, R., & Ives, B. (2001). Web-based virtual learning environments: A research framework and a preliminary assessment of effectiveness in basic IT skills training. *Management Information Systems Quarterly, 25*, 401–426. doi:10.2307/3250989

Pituch, K. A., & Lee, Y. (2006). The influence of system characteristics on e-learning use. *Computers & Education, 47*, 222–244. doi:10.1016/j.compedu.2004.10.007

Prieto, I. M., & Revilla, E. (2006 February). Formal and informal facilitators of learning capability: The moderating effect of learning climate. *IE Working Paper.* WP06-09.

Rai, A., Patnayakuni, R., & Seth, N. (2006). Firm performance impacts of digitally-enabled supply chain integration capabilities. *Management Information Systems Quarterly, 30*, 225–246.

Scarborough, N. M., & Zimmer, T. W. (2000). *Effective small business management: An entrepreneurial approach.* Upper Saddle River, N J: Prentice-Hall.

So, H. J. (2006). *Student satisfaction in a blended learning course: A qualitative approach focusing on critical factors.* Paper presented at the Annual Meeting of the American Educational Research Association, San Francisco, California.

Taylor, S., & Todd, P. A. (1995). Decomposition and crossover effects in the theory of planned behavior: A study of consumer adoption intentions. *International Journal of Research in Marketing, 12*, 137–156. doi:10.1016/0167-8116(94)00019-K

Venkatesh, V., & Davis, F. D. (2000). A theoretical extension of the technology acceptance model: Four longitudinal field studies. *Management Science, 46*, 186–204. doi:10.1287/mnsc.46.2.186.11926

Venkatesh, V., Morris, M. G., Davis, G. B., & Davis, F. D. (2003). User Acceptance of Information Technology: Toward a Unified View. *Management Information Systems Quarterly, 27*(3), 425–478.

Wu, J. H., Tennyson, R. D., Hsia, T. L., & Liao, Y. W. (in press). Analysis of e-learning innovation and core capability using a hypercube model. *Computers in Human Behavior.*

Wu, J. H., & Wang, S. C. (2005). What drives mobile commerce? An empirical evaluation of the revised technology acceptance model. *Information & Management, 42*, 719–729. doi:10.1016/j.im.2004.07.001

Yang, Z., & Liu, Q. (2007). Research and development of web-based virtual online classroom. *Computers & Education, 48*, 171–184. doi:10.1016/j.compedu.2004.12.007

Zhang, X., Keeling, K. B., & Pavur, R. J. (2000). Information quality of commercial website home pages: An explorative analysis. In *Proceedings of the 21th International Conference on Information Systems*, Brisbane, Australia (pp. 164-175).

APPENDIX

Construct	Instrument Item
Computer Self-efficacy (CSE) 3 items	I could use blended e-learning system (BELS) for learning... 1. if there was no one around to tell me what to do as I go. 2. if I had never used a package like it before. 3. if I could call someone for help if I got stuck.
Perceived Behavioral control (PBC) 4 items	1. I have control over using the BELS. 2. I have the resources necessary to use the BELS. 3. I have the knowledge necessary to use the BELS. 4. Guidance and specialized instruction concerning the system was available to me in the selection of the BELS.
System Functionality (SF) 3 items	1. The BELS allows learner control over his or her learning activity 2. The BELS offers flexibility in learning as to time and place 3. The BELS offers multimedia (audio, video, and text) types of course content
Content Features (CF) 2 items	1. The content of BELS is personalization. 2. The content of BELS is ease of understanding. 3. Key features of good online resources, from a student's perspective, include: accessibility (fast to download, easy to read, easy to navigate), use of appropriate online features and good content design.
Social Interaction (SI) 3 items	1. The BELS enables interactive communication between instructor and students 2. The BELS enables interactive communication among students 3. The BELS environment is a an excellent medium for social interaction
Learning Climate (LC) 3 items	1. The course in BELS is interesting. 2. I felt less pressure in BELS environment. 3. The climate in BELS could help me to learn. 4. The interaction feature in BELS could help me to learn.
Perceived Ease of Use (PEOU) 3 items	1. Learning to operate the BELS would be easy for me. 2. I would find it easy to get the BELS to do what I want it to do. 3. I would find the BELS easy to use
Perceived Value (PV) 3 items	1. Using the BELS would improve my learning performance. 2. Using the BELS would enhance my effectiveness for learning. 3. I would find the BELS useful in my job.
Learning Satisfaction (LS) 4 items	1. I am satisfied that BELS meet my learning needs 2. I am satisfied with BELS efficiency. 3. I am satisfied with BELS effectiveness. 4. Overall, I am satisfied with the BELS.

Compilation of References

Aaker, D. (1991). *Managing Brand Equity: Capitalizing on the Value of a Brand Name.* New York: The Free Press.

Aaker, D. A., & Day, G. S. (1986). The perils of high-growth markets. *Strategic Management Journal,* 409–421.

Afuah, A., & Tucci, C. (2001). *Internet Business Models and Strategies, text and cases.* New York: McGraw-Hill/Irwin.

Afuah, A., & Bahram, N. (1995). The hypercube of innovation. *Residence Policy, 24,* 51–76. doi:10.1016/0048-7333(93)00749-J

Aguilar, J. (2005). A Survey about Fuzzy Cognitive Maps Papers. *International Journal of Computational Cognition, 3*(2), 27–33.

Ahram, T. Z., Karwowski, W., Amaba, B., & Andrzejczak, C. (2010). User-centered Smarter Robotic Medical Systems. In Halimahtun, K., Hedge, A., & Ahram, T. (Eds.), *Advances in Ergonomics & Usability Evaluation.* NJ: Taylor & Francis.

Ahram, T. Z., & Karwowski, W. (2009a). Measuring Human Systems Integration Return on Investment. In *The International Council on Systems Engineering – INCOSE Spring 09 Conference: Virginia Modeling, Analysis and Simulation Center (VMASC),* Suffolk, VA, USA.

Ahram, T. Z., & Karwowski, W. (2009b). Human Systems Integration Return on Investment. Presentaton to the U.S. Department of Defense Human Systems Integration and Human Factors Engineering Technical Advisory Group meeting 61 HFE/HSI (DoD TAG). Seattle, Washington (May 11-14, 2009). Retrieved from http://www.hfetag.com/meetings/docs/program_meet_61.pdf

Ahram, T. Z., Karwowski, W., Amaba, B., & Obeid, P. (2009). Human Systems Integration: Development Based on SysML and the Rational Systems Platform. In *Proceedings of the 2009 Industrial Engineering Research Conference,* Miami, FL. USA.

Alavi, M., & Leidner, D. E. (2001). Review: Knowledge Management and Knowledge Management Systems: Conceptual Foundations and Research Issues. *Management Information Systems Quarterly, 25*(1), 107–136. doi:10.2307/3250961

Alavi, M., & Joachimsthaler, E. A. (1992). Revisiting DSS implementation research: A meta-analysis of the literature and suggests for researchers. *Management Information Systems Quarterly, 16,* 95–116. doi:10.2307/249703

Aldrich, H. E. (2001). How to hand exams back to your class. *College Teaching, 49*(Summer).

Alessi, S. (2000). Building versus using simulations. In Spector, J. M., & Andersen, T. M. (Eds.), *Integrated and holistic perspectives on learning, instruction and technology: Improving understanding in complex domains* (pp. 175–196). Dordrecht, The Netherlands: Kluwer.

Alexandria Small Business Association (ABA). (2009). *ABA Small business enterprises definition.* Retrieved January 15, 2009, from http://www.aba-sme.com/index.htm

Anderson, C. A., & Bushman, B. J. (2001). Effects of violent video games on aggressive behaviour, aggressive cognition, aggressive affect, physiological arousal, and prosocial behaviour: A metaanalysis of the scientific literature. *Psychological Science, 12,* 353–359. doi:10.1111/1467-9280.00366

Anderson, C. (2007). *The Long Tail, Why the Future of Business Is Selling Less of More*. New York: Hyperion Books.

Anderson, C. (2008). *Free! Why $0.00 is the Future of Business*. Retrieved from http://www.wired.com/techbiz/it/magazine/16-03/ff_free

Andreou, A. S., Mateou, N. H., & Zombanakis, G. A. (2003). Evolutionary Fuzzy Cognitive Maps: A Hybrid System for Crisis Management and Political Decision Making. In *Proceedings of the International Conference on Computational Intelligence for Modelling, Control and Automation*, Austria.

Andrews, K. (1971). *The Concept of Corporate Strategy*. Homewood, IL: Dow Jones-Irwin, Inc.

Anthes, G. (2008, July 21). *How to get more out of ITIL with Version 3*. Retrieved July 31, 2008 from http://www.computerworld.com/action/article.do?command=viewArticleBasic&articleId=321499&source=rss_news10

Antonelli, C. (Ed.). (1988). *New Information Technology and Industrial Change: The Italian Case*. London: Kluwer.

Argote, L., & Ingram, P. (2000). Knowledge transfer in organizations: A basis for competitive advantage in firms. *Organizational Behavior and Human Decision Processes*, *82*, 150–169. doi:10.1006/obhd.2000.2893

Arthur, W. B. (1998). Increasing Returns and the New World of Business. *The Knowledge Economy*, 75.

ASL BiSL Foundation. (2007, July 27). *ASL*. Retrieved July 31, 2008, from http://www.aslbislfoundation.org/content/view/11/15/lang,en/

Atkinson, R. D. (2002). *The 2002 State New Economy Index-Benchmarking Economic Transformation in the States*. Retrieved from http://www.neweconomyindex.org/states/2002

AUSE. (2009). *The Arab Union for Small Enterprises*. Retrieved January 2, 2009, from http://www.sfdegypt.org/Arab_Union_e.asp

Axelrod, R. (1976). *Structure of Decision: The Cognitive Maps of Political Elite* (1st ed.). Princeton, NJ: Princeton University Press.

Baader, F., Horrocks, I., & Sattler, U. (2004). Description Logics. In Staab, S., & Studer, R. (Eds.), *Handbook on Ontologies* (pp. 3–28). Berlin: Springer-Verlag.

Baars, B. J. (1997). *In the Theatre of Consciousness*. Oxford, UK: Oxford University Press. doi:10.1093/acprof:oso/9780195102659.001.1

Back, A., Krogh, G., Seufert, A., & Ellen, E. (2005). *Putting Knowledge Networks Into Action: Methodology, Development, Maintenance*. Berlin: Springer-Verlag. doi:10.1007/b138845

Bain, J. S. (1956). *Barriers to New Competition*. Cambridge, MA: Harvard University Press.

Bain, J. S. (1959). *Industrial Organization*. New York: John Wiley & Sons.

Bandura, A. (1993). Perceived self-efficacy in cognitive development and functioning. *Educational Psychologist*, *28*, 117–148. doi:10.1207/s15326985ep2802_3

Bannan-Ritland, B., Dabbagh, N., & Murphy, K. (2000). Learning object systems as constructivist learning environments: related assumptions, theories, and applications. In D. A. Wiley (Ed.), *The Instructional use of learning objects: online version*. Retrieved June 18, 2005, from http://www.reusability.org/read/chapters/bannan-ritland.doc

Barbian, J. (2000). IT in 2000 and beyond. *Computer User, 19*(1).

Barclay, D., Higgins, C., & Thomson, R. (1995). The partial least squares approach to causal modeling, personal computer adoption and use as an illustration. *Technology Studies, 2*, 285–309.

Bates, T. W. (2000). *Managing technological change: Strategies for college and university leaders*. San Francisco: Jossey-Bass.

Baum, J. A. C., & Greve, H. R. (Eds.). (2001). *Multiunit Organizations and Multiunit Strategy: Advances in Strategic Management*. Oxford, UK: Elsevier.

Beckstrom, R., & Brafman, O. (2006). *The Starfish and the Spider, The Unstoppable Power of Leaderless Organizations*. London: Penguin Books.

Becta, D. A. (2001). Computer games in education. *Project Report*. Retrieved July 20, 2005, from http://www.becta.org.uk/page_documents/research/cge/report.pdf

Bensaou, M., & Earl, M. (1998). The right mind-set for managing information technology. *Harvard Business Review, 76*(5).

Berendes, K. (2002). *Lenkungskompetenz in komplexen ökonomischen Systemen*. Wiesbaden, Germany: Gabler.

Berendes, K., & Breuer, K. (1999). Potentiale von system-dynamisch basierten Mikrowelten. In Hohmann, G. (Ed.), *Simulationstechnik* (pp. 113–116). Erlangen, Germany: SCS Publishing House.

Berners-Lee, T. (2007, March 1). The Future of the World Wide Web. *Hearing on the Digital Future of the United States before the United States House of Representatives Commitee on Energy and Commerce Subcommittee on Telecommunications and the Internet*. Cambridge, MA: Massachusetts Institute of Technology.

Bharati, P. (2003). People and information matter: task support satisfaction from the other side. *Journal of Computer Information Systems, 43*(2), 93–102.

Blumenthal, B., & Haspeslagh, P. (1994). *Toward a definition of corporate transformation*. Sloan Management Review.

Bonoma, T. V., Crittenden, V. L., & Dolan, R. J. (1988). Can the authors have Rigor and Relevance in Pricing Resarch? In Devinney, T. M. (Ed.), *Issues in Pricing: theory and research* (pp. 337–359). Toronto, Canada: Lexington Books.

Booher, H. (Ed.). (2003). *Handbook of human systems integration*. Hoboken, NJ: Wiley. doi:10.1002/0471721174

Booher, H. R., & Minninger, J. (2003). Human systems integration in army systems acquisition. In Booher, H. (Ed.), *Handbook of human systems integration* (pp. 663–698). Hoboken, NJ: Wiley. doi:10.1002/0471721174

Boutin, P. (2006, March 29). Web 2.0 - The new Internet boom doesn't live up to its name. *Slate*. Retrieved January 15, 2008, from http://www.slate.com/id/2138951/

Bower, J. L., & Christensen, C. M. (1995). Disruptive technologies: catching the wave. *Harvard Business Review, 73*(1), 43–53.

Bratina, T. A., Hayes, D., & Blumsack, S. L. (2002). *Preparing teachers to use learning objects*. Retrieved January 12, 2002, from http://technologysource.org/article/preparing_teachers_to_use_learning_objects/

Breuer, K., & Kummer, R. (1990). Cognitive effects from process learning with computer-based simulations. *Computers in Human Behavior, 6*, 69–81. doi:10.1016/0747-5632(90)90031-B

Breuer, K. (1985). Computer simulations and cognitive development. In Duncan, K. A., & Harris, D. (Eds.), *The proceedings of the world-conference on computers in education 1985 WCCE/85* (pp. 239–244). Amsterdam: North Holland.

Breuer, K. (1983). Lernen mit computersimulierten komplexen dynamischen Systemen. In Lechner, E., & Zielinski, J. (Eds.), *Wirkungssysteme und Reformansätze in der Pädagogik* (pp. 341–351). Frankfurt, Germany: Peter Lang.

Breuer, K., & Streufert, S. (1995). Strategic management simulations in the German case. In Mulder, M., Nijhoff, W. J., & Brinkerhoff, R. O. (Eds.), *Corporate training for effective performance* (pp. 195–208). Norwell, MA: Kluwer.

Breuer, K., Molkenthin, R., & Tennyson, R. D. (2006). Role of simulations in Web-based learning. In O'Neil, H., & Perez, R. (Eds.), *Web-based learning* (pp. 307–326). Mahwah, NJ: Erlbaum.

Brynjolfsson, E., Hu, Y. J., & Simester, D. (2007, November). Goodbye Pareto Principle, Hello Long Tail: The Effect of Search Costs on the Concentration of Product Sales. *SSRN*. Retrieved from http://ssrn.corn/abstract=953587

Brynjolfsson, E., Hu, Y. J., & Smith, M. D. (2003). Consumer Surplus in the Digital Economy: Estimating the Value of Increased Poduct Variety at Online Bookstores. *Managment Science, 49*(11).

Bunderson, C. V., Inouye, D. K., & Olsen, J. B. (1993). The four generations of computerized educational neasurement. In Linn, R. L. (Ed.), *Educational measurement* (pp. 367–407). Phoenix, AZ: Oryx Press.

Burn, J., Marshall, P., & Barnett, M. (2002). *E-business Strategies for Virtual Organisations.* Oxford: Butterworth-Heinemann.

Burn, J., & Robins, G. (2003). Moving towards e-government: a case study of organizational change processes. *Logistics Information Management, 16*(1), 25–35. doi:10.1108/09576050310453714

Burnes, B. (2000). *Managing Change: A Strategic Approach to Organizational Dynamics.* London: Pearson Education.

Burns, T., & Stalker, G. M. (1961). *The Management of Innovation.* London: Tavistock Publications.

Burns, J., & Gordon, J. (2005). *Human Systems Integration.* Sonalysts, Inc. Presentation to Orlando INCOSE 09 June 2005.

CAEB. (2009). Crédit Agricole Egypt Bank- small business enterprises definition. Retrieved January 15, 2009, from http://www.ca-egypt.com/SME/About-SME.html

Calvani, A., & Rotta, M. (2000). *Fare formazione in Internet: Manuale di didattica online.* Rome: Erickson.

Cameron, K. S., & Freeman, S. J. (1991). Cultural Congruence, Strength, and Type: Relationships to Effectiveness. *Research in Organizational Change and Development, 5,* 23–58.

Cao, L. (2002). Corporate and product identity in the post national economy: rethinking US trade laws. *California Law Review, 90*(2), 401–484. doi:10.2307/3481283

Capaul, R. (2001). Didaktische und methodische Analyse der Planspielmethode. *Erziehungswissenschaft und Beruf, 1,* 3–14.

CAPMAS. (2009). *The Central agency for Public Mobilisation and Statistics - Egyptian Population.* Retrieved May 5, 2009, from http://www.msrintranet.capmas.gov.eg/pls/fdl/tst12e?action=&lname=

Carlsson, C., & Fuller, R. (1996), Adaptive Fuzzy Cognitive Maps for Hyper knowledge Representation in Strategic Formation Process. In *Proceedings of the International Panel Conference on Soft and Intelligent Computing*, Budapest.

CEC. (2001). *The learning action plan: Designing tomorrow's education.* Communication from the commission to the council and the European Parliament. Retrieved from http://europa.eu.int/comm/education/elearning/index.html

Chaffey, D. (2007). *E-business and E-commerce Management: Strategy, Implementation and Practice.* Upper Saddle River, NJ: Financial Times/Prentice Hall.

Chamberlin, E. H. (1933). *Theory of Monopolistic Competition.* Boston, MA: Harvard University Press.

Chapanis, A. (1996). *Human factors in systems engineering.* Hoboken, NJ: Wiley.

Chen, C. M., Lee, H. M., & Chen, Y. H. (2005). Personalized e-learning system using Item Response Theory. *Computers & Education, 44,* 237–255. doi:10.1016/j.compedu.2004.01.006

Chen, C., Czerwinski, M., & Macredie, R. (2000). Individual differences in virtual environments: Introduction and overview. *Journal of the American Society for Information Science American Society for Information Science, 51,* 499–507. doi:10.1002/(SICI)1097-4571(2000)51:6<499::AID-ASI2>3.0.CO;2-K

Cheong, C. S. (2002). E-learning-a provider's prospective. *The Internet and Higher Education, 4,* 337–352. doi:10.1016/S1096-7516(01)00075-6

Chesbrough, H. (2003). *Open Innovation: The New Imperative for Creating and Profiting from Technology.* Watertown, MA: Harvard Business School Press.

Chesbrough, H., & Rosenbloom, R. S. (2002). The Role of the Business Model in Capturing Value from Innovation: Evidence from Xerox Corporation's Technology Spin-off Companies. *Industrial and Corporate Change, 11*(3), 529–555. doi:10.1093/icc/11.3.529

Chin, W. W. (1998). The partial least squares approach to structural equation modeling. In Marcoulides, G. A. (Ed.), *Modern methods for business research* (pp. 295–236). Mahwah, NJ: Erlbaum.

Chiu, C. M., Hsu, M. H., & Sun, S. Y. (2005). Usability, quality, value and e-learning continuance decisions. *Computers & Education, 45*, 399–416. doi:10.1016/j.compedu.2004.06.001

Chou, C., & Tsai, C. C. (2002). Developing Web-based curricula: Issues and challenges. *Journal of Curriculum Studies, 34*, 623–636. doi:10.1080/00220270210141909

Chou, S. W., & Liu, C. H. (2005). Learning effectiveness in a web-based virtual learning environment: A learner control perspective. *Journal of Computer Assisted Learning, 21*, 65–76. doi:10.1111/j.1365-2729.2005.00114.x

Christensen, C., & Raynor, M. (2003). *The Innovator's Solution - Creating and Sustaining Successful Growth.* Boston: Harvard Business School Press.

Chuang, S. C., & Tsai, C. C. (2005). Preferences toward the constructivist Internet-based learning environments among high school students in Taiwan. *Computers in Human Behavior, 21*, 255–272. doi:10.1016/j.chb.2004.02.015

Churchland, P. S. (2002). *Brain-Wise - Studies in Neurophilosophy.* Cambridge, MA: The MIT Press.

Coase, R. H. (1937). The Nature of the Firm. *Economica, 4*(16), 386–405. doi:10.1111/j.1468-0335.1937.tb00002.x

Cohen, W. M., & Levinthal, D. A. (1990). Absorptive capacity: a new perspective on learning and innovation. *Administrative Science Quarterly, 35*(1), 128–152. doi:10.2307/2393553

Cohen, E. G. (1994). *Designing groupwork: Strategies for the heterogeneous classroom* (2nd ed.). New York: Teachers College Press.

Collison, G., Elbaum, B., Haavind, S., & Tinker, R. (2000). *Facilitating online learning: Effective strategies for moderators.* Madison, WI: Atwood Pub.

Coltman, T., Devinney, T., Latukefu, A., & Midgley, D. (2001). E-business: revolution, evolution or hype? *California Management Review, 44*(61).

Compeau, D. R., Higgins, C. A., & Huff, S. (1999). Social cognitive theory and individuals reactions to computing technology: a longitudinal study. *Management Information Systems Quarterly, 23*(2), 145–158. doi:10.2307/249749

Compeau, D. R., & Higgins, C. A. (1995). Computer self-efficacy: Development of a measure and initial test. *Management Information Systems Quarterly, 19*, 189–211. doi:10.2307/249688

Conner, K. R. (1988). Strategies for product cannibalism. *Strategic Management Journal, 9*, 9–26. doi:10.1002/smj.4250090704

Cooper, R. G. (1975). Why new industrial products fail. *Industrial Marketing Management, 4*(4), 315–326. doi:10.1016/0019-8501(75)90005-X

Cordella, A. (2001). Does Information Technology Always Lead to Lower Transaction Costs? In *Proceedings of ECIS,* Bled, Slovenia.

Cordova, D. I., & Lepper, M. R. (1996). Intrinsic motivation and the process of learning: Beneficial effects of contextualization, personalization, and choice. *Journal of Educational Psychology, 88*, 715–730. doi:10.1037/0022-0663.88.4.715

Coulon, F. (2003). *Regional Systems of Innovation: A Case Study of four Science Parks in Belgium and Sweden.* University of Linkoping, Sweden. Retrieved from http://www.esst.uio.no

Crocker, O., Charney, C., & Chiu, J. (1984). *Quality Circles.* New York: Methuen.

Crubezy, M., & Musen, M. A. (2004). Ontologies in Support of Problem Solving. In Staab, S., & Studer, R. (Eds.), *Handbook on Ontologies* (pp. 322–341). Berlin: Springer-Verlag.

Cuban, L. (1993). Computers meet classroom: Classroom wins. *Teachers College Record, 95*(2), 185–210.

Curran, K. (2002). A web-based collaboration teaching environment. *IEEE MultiMedia, 9*(3). doi:10.1109/MMUL.2002.1022860

Daniel, E. M., & Wilson, H. M. (2003). The role of dynamic capabilities in e-business transformation. *European Journal of Information Systems, 12*, 282–296. doi:10.1057/palgrave.ejis.3000478

Dasgrupta, P., & Stiglize, J. (1980). Uncertainty, industrial structure and speed of R&D. *The Bell Journal of Economics, 11*(1), 1–28. doi:10.2307/3003398

Davenport, T. H., DeLong, D. W., & Beers, M. C. (1998). Successful knowledge management projects. *Sloan Management Review, 39*(2), 43–57.

Davies, J., Fensel, D., & Van Harmelen, F. (2003). *Towards the Semantic Web - Ontology Based Knowledge Management. Davies, J., Fensel, D., Van Harmelen, F.* John Wiley & Sons, Ltd.

Davis, F. D., Bagozzi, R. P., & Warsaw, P. R. (1989). User acceptance of computer technology: a comparison of two theoretical models. *Management Science, 35*(8), 983–1003. doi:10.1287/mnsc.35.8.982

Davis, F. D. (1989). Perceived usefulness, perceived ease of use, and user acceptance of information technology. *Management Information Systems Quarterly, 13*, 318–339. doi:10.2307/249008

Day, G., & Schoemaker, P. (2000). Avoiding the pitfalls of emerging technologies. *California Management Review, 42*(52).

de Jong, T. (1991). Learning and instruction with computer simulations. *Education and Computing, 6*, 217–229. doi:10.1016/0167-9287(91)80002-F

De Vaus, D. A. (1991). *Surveys in social research.* New York: Routledge.

Deal, T. E., & Kennedy, A. A. (1982). *Corporate Cultures.* Reading, MA: Addison-Wesley.

Dembo, M. H., Junge, L. G., & Lynch, R. (2006). Becoming a self-regulated learner: Implications for Web-based education. In O'Neil, H. F., & Perez, R. S. (Eds.), *Web-based learning: Theory, research, and practice* (pp. 185–202). Mahwah, NJ: Erlbaum.

Deming, W. E. (1986). *Out of the Crisis.* Cambridge, MA: Cambridge University Press.

Dempsey, P. G., Wogalter, M. S., & Hancock, P. A. (2006). Defining Ergonomics/Human Factors. In Karwowski, W. (Ed.), *The international Encyclopedia of Ergonomics and Human Factors* (2nd ed.). Boca Raton, FL: CRC Press.

Dempsey, D. V., Lucassen, B. A., Haynes, L. L., & Casey, C. S. (1996). *Instructional applications of computer games.* Paper presented at the 1996 annual meeting of the American Educational Research Association, New York.

Dierlamm, J. (2008, May 28). Itil V3 - Good Practices versus gepflegtes Chaos. *Computerwoche.*

Doerner, D. (1996). *The logic of failure: Why things go wrong and what we can do to make them right* (1st ed.). New York: Metropolitan Books.

Dorward, N. (1987). *The Pricing Decision: economic theory and business practice.* London: Harper & Row.

Dosi, G. (1982). Technical paradigms and technological trajectories: a suggested interpretation of the determinants and directions of technical change. *Research Policy, 11*(3), 147–162. doi:10.1016/0048-7333(82)90016-6

DTI-news-release. (2008). *National statistics, The Small Business Service (SBS), The British Department of Trade and Industry.* Retrieved October 14, 2008, from http://www.sbs.gov.uk/SBS_Gov_files/researchandstats/SMEStats2004.pdf

Dutta, S., Abaracki, M. J., & Bergen, M. (2003). Pricing Process as a Capability: a resource-based perspective. *Strategic Management Journal, 24*(7), 615–630. doi:10.1002/smj.323

Eblen, R. A., & Eblen, W. (1994). *The Encyclopaedia of the Environment*. Boston: Houghton Mifflin Company.

Edwards, L. D. (1995). Microworlds as representations. In DiSessa, A. A., Hoyles, C., & Noss, R. (Eds.), *Computers and exploratory learning, computer and systems sciences* (pp. 127–154). Berlin: Springer.

Edwards, R. (2004). *System does matter*. Retrieved July 28, 2005, from http://www.indie-rpgs.com/_articles/system_does_matter.html

Eid, R. (2003). *Business-to-business international internet marketing: adoption, implementation and implications, an empirical study of UK companies*. Bradford, UK: Bradford University.

EINP. (2009). *Egyptian Institute of National Planning - small business enterprises definition*. Retrieved January 25, 2009, from http://www.inplanning.gov.eg/Activities/Publication/Details.aspx

EITP. (2009). *The Egyptian International Trade Points (EITP) - About Us*. Retrieved January 5, 2009, from http://www.tpegypt.gov.eg/EITP.aspx

Emes, C. E. (1997). Is Mr. PacMan eating our children? A review of the effect of video games on children. *Canadian Journal of Psychiatry, 42*, 409–414.

EMI. (2009). *Egyptian ministry of investment - Egyptian economy indicators*. Retrieved May 5, 2009, from http://www.investment.gov.eg/MOI_Portal/en-GB/Egypts+Business/Economy/

EMTI. (2008). *Ministry of Trade and Industry - Small Business Enterprises in Egypt*. Retrieved December 16, 2008, from http://www.mfti.gov.eg/English/index.htm

Engelbrecht, E. (2003). A look at e-learning models: Investigating their value for developing an e-learning strategy. *Progressio, 25*(2), 38–47.

Enright, M. (2000). *Survey of Characterization of Regional Clusters*. University of Hong Kong working paper.

Ernst, H., & Soll, J. H. (2003). An integrated portfolio approach to support market-oriented R&D planning. *International Journal of Technology Management, 26*(5/6), 540–561. doi:10.1504/IJTM.2003.003422

Ettlie, J. E. (1982). The commercialization of federally sponsored technological innovations. *Research Policy, 11*(3), 173–192. doi:10.1016/0048-7333(82)90018-X

European Commission. (2000). *SMEs Access to the Digital Economy*. Brussels: Directorate C of DG Information Society.

EUROPEAN-COMMISSION. (2006). *Small businesses definition*. Retrieved October 14, 2006, from http://ec.europa.eu/enterprise/entrepreneurship/craft/definition.htm

Evans, P., & Warster, T. S. (1999). *Blown to Bits: How the New Economic of Information Transforms Strategy*. Boston, MA: Harvard Business School Press.

Fabricatore, C. (2000). *Learning and videogames: An unexploited synergy*. Retrieved June 20, 2005, from www.learndev.org/ dl/FabricatoreAECT2000.pdf

Farley, J. U., Hulbert, J. M., & Weinstein, D. (1980). Price Setting and Volume Planning by two European Industrial Companies: a study and comparison of decision processes. *Journal of Marketing, 44*(1), 46–54. doi:10.2307/1250033

FEI. (2009). Federation of Egyptian Industries - small business enterprises definition. Retrieved January 14, 2009, from http://www.fei.org.eg/committees_info.asp?id=9&searchtxt=small

Fishbein, M., & Ajzen, I. (1975). *Belief, attitude, intention and behavior: An introduction to theory and research*. Reading, MA: Addison-Wesley.

Flecther, T., & Russell-Jones, N. (1997). *Value Pricing: How to maximize profits through effective pricing policies*. London: Kogan Page.

Folds, D., Gardner, D., & Deal, S. (2008). Building Up to the Human Systems Integration Demonstration. *INCOSE INSIGHT, 11*(2).

Ford, D., Gadde, L.-E., Håkansson, H., Lundgren, A., Snehota, I., Turnbull, P., & Wilson, D. (1998). *Managing Business relationships*. Chichester, UK: John Wiley & Sons, Ltd.

Forman, D., Nyatanga, L., & Rich, T. (2002). E-learning and educational diversity. *Nurse Education Today, 22*, 76–82. doi:10.1054/nedt.2001.0740

Fornell, C., & Larcker, D. F. (1981). Evaluating Structural Equation Models with Unobservable Variable and Measurement Error. *JMR, Journal of Marketing Research, 18*(1), 39–50. doi:10.2307/3151312

Forrester, J. W. (1968). *Principles of systems*. Cambridge, MA: MIT Press.

Forrester. (2008). *Global Enterprise Web 2.0 Market Forecast - 2007-2013.*

Francescato, D., Porcelli, R., Mebane, M., Cuddetta, M., Klobas, J., & Renzi, P. (2006). Evaluation of the efficacy of collaborative learning in face-to-face and computer-supported university contexts. *Computers in Human Behavior, 22*, 163–176. doi:10.1016/j.chb.2005.03.001

Francescato, D., Porcelli, R., Mebane, M., Cuddetta, M., Klobas, J., & Renzi, P. (2006). Evaluation of the efficacy of collaborative learning in face-to-face and computer-supported university contexts. *Computers in Human Behavior, 22*, 163–176. doi:10.1016/j.chb.2005.03.001

Franke, N., & von Hippel, E. (2003). Satisfying heterogeneous user needs via innovation toolkits: the case of Apache security software. *Research Policy, 32*(7), 1199–1215. doi:10.1016/S0048-7333(03)00049-0

French, D., Hale, C., Johnson, C., & Farr, G. (Eds.). (1999). *Internet based learning: An introduction and framework for higher education and business*. Sterling, VA: Stylus.

Frensch, P. A., & Funke, J. (1995). *Complex problem solving. The European perspective*. Hillsdale, NJ: Erlbaum.

Frey, K. (1995). *Die Projektmethode* (6th ed.). Weinheim, Germany: Beltz.

Friedenthal, S., Moore, A., & Steiner, R. (2008). *A Practical Guide to SysML: The Systems Modeling Language*. San Francisco: Morgan Kaufmann, Elsevier Science.

Gabor, A. (1988). *Pricing: Concepts and Methods for Effective Pricing*. Aldershot, UK: Gower.

Garris, R., Ahlers, R., & Driskell, J. E. (2002). Games, motivation, and learning: A research and practice model. *Simulation & Gaming, 33*, 441–467. doi:10.1177/1046878102238607

Gee, J. P. (2003). *What video games have to teach us about learning and literacy*. New York: Macmillan.

Gee, J. P. (2005). Learning by design: Good video games as learning machines. *E-learning, 2*(1), 5–14. doi:10.2304/elea.2005.2.1.5

Gefen, D., & Straub, D. W. (2005). A practical guide to factorial validity using PLS-graph: Tutorial and annotated example. *Communications of the Association for Information Systems, 16*(5), 91–109.

Georgopoulous, V. C., & Malandrak, S. C. D. (2002). A Fuzzy Cognitive Map Approach to Differential Diagnosis of Specific Language Impairment. *Artificial Intelligence in Medicine*, 1–18.

Giles, J. (2005, December 15). Internet encyclopaedias go head to head. *Nature - International weekly journal of science*. Retrieved January 23, 2008, from http://www.nature.com/nature/journal/v438/n7070/full/438900a.html

Gladwell, M. (2000). *The Tipping Point: How Little Things can make a Big Difference*. Boston: Little, Brown and Company.

Gomez-Perez, A. (2004). Ontology Evaluation. In Staab, S., & Studer, R. (Eds.), *Handbook on Ontologies* (pp. 251–273). Berlin: Springer-Verlag.

Gore, E. (1999). Organizational Culture, TQM and Business Process Reengineering. *Team Performance Management: An International Journal, 5*(5), 164–170. doi:10.1108/13527599910288993

Gorton, I., & Motwani, S. (1996). Issues in co-operative software engineering using globally distributed teams. *Information and Software Technology, 38,* 647–655. doi:10.1016/0950-5849(96)01099-3

Govindasamy, T. (2002). Successful implementation of e-learning pedagogical considerations. *The Internet and Higher Education, 4,* 287–299. doi:10.1016/S1096-7516(01)00071-9

Govindassamy, T. (2002). Successful implementation of e-learning pedagogical consideration. *The Internet and Higher Education, 4,* 287–299. doi:10.1016/S1096-7516(01)00071-9

Graham, C. R. (2006). Blended learning system: Definition, current trends, future directions. In Bonk, C. J., & Graham, C. R. (Eds.), *Handbook of blended learning* (pp. 3–20). San Francisco, CA: Pfeiffer.

Graham, P. (2005, November). *Web 2.0.* Retrieved January 7, 2008, from http://www.paulgraham.com/web20.html

Gredler, M. E. (1992). *Designing and evaluating games and simulations. A process approach.* London: Kogan Page.

Gruber, T. R. (1993). A translation approach to portable ontologies. *Knowledge Acquisition, 5*(2), 199–220. doi:10.1006/knac.1993.1008

Grunewald, M., Heckemann, R. A., & Gebhard, H. (2003). COMPARE radiology: Creating an interactive web-based training program for radiology with multimedia authoring software. *Academic Radiology, 10,* 443–553. doi:10.1016/S1076-6332(03)80065-X

Habgood, M. P. J., Ainsworth, S. E., & Benford, S. (2005). Endogenous fantasy and learning in digital games. *Simulation & Gaming, 36,* 483–498. doi:10.1177/1046878105282276

Hair, J. R., Anderson, R., Tatham, R., & Black, W. (1998). *Multivariate Data Analysis* (5th ed.). Upper Saddle River, NJ: Prentice Hall Inc.

Hakkinen, P., Arvaja, M., & Makitalo, K. (2004). Prerequisites for CSCL: Research approaches, methodological challenges and pedagogical development. In Littleton, K., Miell, D., & Faulkner, D. (Eds.), *Learning to collaborate: Collaborating to learn* (pp. 161–176). New York: Nova Science.

Halima, T. (2007). *Safety Culture Ontology - From Theory to Practice.* Licentiate thesis. Tampere University of Technology, Pori, Finland.

Hall, P., & Markusen, A. (Eds.). (1988). *Silicon Landscapes.* Boston: Allen and Unwin Inc.

Handley, H. A., & Smillie, R. J. (2008, May). Architecture framework human view: The NATO approach. *Systems Engineering, 11*(2), 156–164. Retrieved from http://dx.doi.org/10.1002/sys.v11:2. doi:10.1002/sys.20093

Hänninen, S., & Kauranen, I. (2007). Product innovation as micro-strategy. *International Journal of Innovation and Learning, 4*(4), 425–443. doi:10.1504/IJIL.2007.012580

Hänninen, S. (2007). *Innovation commercialisation process from the 'four knowledge bases' perspective.* Doctoral Dissertation Series, Development and Management in Industry. Espoo, Finland: Helsinki University of Technology.

Harasim, L., Hiltz, S., & Teles, L. (1995). *Learning networks.* Cambridge, MA: MIT Press.

Hardman, N., Colombi, J., Jacques, D., & Hill, R. (2008). What Systems Engineers Need to Know About Human – Computer Interaction. *INCOSE INSIGHT, 11*(2).

Haritz, J., & Breuer, K. (1995). Computersimulierte und dynamische Entscheidungssituationen als Element der multikulturellen Personalentwicklung. In Scholz, J. M. (Ed.), *Internationales change-mangement* (pp. 109–120). Stuttgart, Germany: Schäffer-Poeschel.

Harper, K. C., Chen, K., & Yen, D. C. (2004). Distance learning, virtual classrooms, and teaching pedagogy in the Internet environment. *Technology in Society, 26,* 585–598. doi:10.1016/S0160-791X(04)00054-5

Hazemi, R., Hailes, S., & Wilbur, S. (Eds.). (1998). *The digital university: Reinventing the academy.* London: Springer.

Henderson, R. M., & Clark, K. B. (1990). Architectural innovation: the reconfiguration of existing technologies and the failure of established firms. *Administrative Science Quarterly, 35*(1), 9–30. doi:10.2307/2393549

Henderson, R., & Clark, K. (1990). Architectural innovation: The reconfiguration of existing product technologies and the failure of established firms. *Administrator Science Quarterly, 35*, 9–30. doi:10.2307/2393549

Henry, P. (2001). E-learning technology, content and services. *Education + Training, 43*, 249–255. doi:10.1108/EUM0000000005485

Hess, P., & Siciliano, J. (1996). *Management - Responsibility for Performance.* New York: McGraw-Hill.

Hillen, S. (2004). *Systemdynamische Modellbildung und Simulation im kaufmännischen Unterricht.* Frankfurt, Germany: Peter Lang.

Hinchcliffe, D. (2005, September 24). The Web 2.0 Is Here. *Dion Hinchcliffe's Web 2.0 Blog.* Retrieved January 15, 2008, from http://web2.socialcomputingmagazine.com/web2ishere.htm

Hinchcliffe, D. (2006, April 2). The State of Web 2.0. *Dion Hinchcliffe's Web 2.0 Blog.* Retrieved November 12, 2007, from http://web2.socialcomputingmagazine.com/the_state_of_web_20.htm

Hinchcliffe, D. (2006, July 15). Web 2.0's Real Secret Sauce: Network Effects. *Dion Hinchcliffe's Web 2.0 Blog.* Retrieved January 23, 2008, from http://web2.socialcomputingmagazine.com/web_20s_real_secret_sauce_network_effects.htm

Hoegg, R., Martignoni, R., Meckel, M., & Stanoevska-Slabeva, K. (2006). Overview of business models for Web 2.0 communities. In [Dresden, Germany: Universität St. Gallen, Institute of Media and Communication Management.]. *Proceedings of GeNeMe, 2006*, 23–37.

Hofstede, G. (1980). *Culture's Consequences.* Beverly Hills, CA: Sage.

Hong, W., Thong, J. Y. L., Wong, W. M., & Tam, K. Y. (2002). Determinants of user acceptance of digital libraries: An empirical examination of individual differences and system characteristics. *Journal of Management Information Systems, 18*(3), 97–124.

Huang, S., & Hu, H. (2000). Integrating windows streaming media technologies into a virtual classroom environment. *IEEE Transactions on Education, 38*(2).

IBM. (2006). Expanding the Innovation Horizon - The Global CEO Study 2006.

IBM. (2008, July 18). *IBM Service Management.* Retrieved July 31, 2008, from http://www-306.ibm.com/software/tivoli/governance/servicemanagement/itup/tool.html

IDWB. (2009). *The Industrial Development and Workers Bank of Egypt (IDWB) - small business enterprises definition.* Retrieved January 25, 2009, from http://www.idbe-egypt.com/product.htm

Ingenbleek, P. (2002). *Money for Value: pricing from a resource-advantage perspective.* PhD Tilburg University.

ISE. (2009). *Internet Society of Egypt - The Internet in Egypt.* Retrieved March 5, 2009, from http://www.ise.org.eg/inegypt.htm

IWS. (2009a). *Internet World Stats - Egypt Internet and Population Statistics.* Retrieved April 15, 2009, from http://www.internetworldstats.com/africa.htm#eg

IWS. (2009b). *Internet World Stats - Africa top 10 Internet countries.* Retrieved April 15, 2009, from http://www.internetworldstats.com/stats1.htm

Jackson, C. M. (2004). *Systems Thinking: Creative Holism for Managers.* West Sussex, UK: John Wiley & Sons Ltd.

Johnson, D. W., Johnson, R., & Holubec, E. (1998). *Cooperation in the classroom* (7th ed.). Edina, MN: Interaction Book Co.

Johnson, D. W., & Johnson, R. T. (1986). Computer-assisted cooperative learning. *Educational Technology, 26*(1), 12–18.

Johnson, D. W., & Johnson, R. T. (1989). *Cooperation and competition: Theory and research.* Edina, MN: Interaction Book Co.

Johnson-Laird, P. N. (1983). *Mental models. Towards a cognitive science of language. Inferences and consciousness.* Cambridge, MA: University Press.

Johnson-Laird, P. N. (1988). *The computer and the mind. An introduction to cognitive science.* Cambridge, MA: University Press.

Johnston, J., Killion, J., & Oomen, J. (2005). Student satisfaction in the virtual classroom. *The Internet Journal of Allied Health Sciences and Practice, 3*(2), 17–29.

Jonassen, D., & Tennyson, R. D. (Eds.). (1997). *Handbook of research on educational communications and technology.* Washington, DC: Association for Educational Communications and Technology.

Jonassen, D. H. (2002). Learning as activity. *Educational Technology, 42*(2), 45–48.

Jonassen, D. H., Howland, J., Moore, J., & Marra, R. (1999). *Learning to solve problems with technology–A constructivist perspective.* Columbus, OH: Merrill Prentice Hall.

Jones, R. (1996). Digital equipment corporation: creating new business. In *The Internet Strategy Handbook, Lessons from the New Frontier of Business.* Boston, MA: Harvard Business School Press.

Jong-Ae, K. (2005). *User acceptance of web-based subscription databases: extending the technology acceptance model.* Unpublished Doctoral Dissertation, Florida State University, Tallahassee, Florida.

Kafai, Y. B. (2001). *The educational potential of electronic games: From games-to-teach to games-to-learn.* Retrieved May 16, 2006, from http://www.culturalpolicy.uchicago.edu/conf2001/papers/kafai.html

Kagan, S. (1992). *Cooperative learning resources for teachers* (7th ed.). San Juan Capistrano, CA: Resources for Teachers, Inc.

Kalakota, R., & Robinson, M. (1999). *E-business, Roadmap for Success.* Reading, MA: Addison- Wesley.

Kanter, R., Stein, B., & Jick, T. (1992). *The Challenge of Organizational Change: How Companies Experience It and Leaders Guide It.* New York: Maxwell Macmillan Int.

Kantola, J., Karwowski, W., & Vanharanta, H. (2005). Creative Tension in Occupational Work Roles: A Dualistic View of Human Competence Management Technology Based on Soft Computing. *Ergonomia: An International Journal of Ergonomics and Human Factors, 27*(4), 273–286.

Kantola, J. (2005). *Ingenious Management.* Doctoral thesis, Tampere University of Technology at Pori, Finland.

Kantola, J., Karwowski, W., & Vanharanta, H. (2009a). *Evolute Internet pages – MOO Applications.* Retrieved July 10, 2009, from http://www.evolutellc.com/Applications.html

Kantola, J., Karwowski, W., & Vanharanta, H. (2009b). *Evolute Internet pages – Evolute Research Centres.* Retrieved July 10, 2009, from http://www.evolutellc.com/ERCs/ERCs.aspx

Kappel, T. A. (2001). Perspectives on roadmaps: how organizations talk about the future. *Journal of Product Innovation Management, 18*(1), 39–50. doi:10.1016/S0737-6782(00)00066-7

Karwowski, W. (2000). Symvatology: The science of an artifact-human compatibility. *Theoretical Issues in Ergonomics Science, 1,* 76–91. doi:10.1080/146392200308480

Karwowski, W. (2005). Ergonomics and human factors: the paradigms for science, engineering, design, technology and management of human-compatibility systems. *Ergonomics, 48,* 436–463. doi:10.1080/00140130400029167

Karwowski, W. (Ed.). (2006). *International Encyclopedia of Ergonomics and Human Factors* (2nd ed.). Boca Raton, FL: CRC Press. doi:10.1201/9780849375477

Karwowski, W. (Ed.). (2006). *Handbook of Human Factors and Ergonomics Standards and Guideliness*. New York: Lawrence Erlbaum Publishers.

Karwowski, W. (2006). The Discipline of Ergonomics and Human Factors. In Salvendy, G. (Ed.), *Handbook of Human Factors & Ergonomics* (3rd ed., pp. 1–25). New York: John Wiley. doi:10.1002/0470048204.ch1

Karwowski, W. (2006a). The discipline of ergonomics and human factors. In Salvendy, G. (Ed.), *Handbook of Human Factors and Ergonomics* (3rd ed., pp. 3–31). Hoboken, NJ: John Wiley & Sons. doi:10.1002/0470048204.ch1

Kass, A., Burke, R., & Fitzgerald, W. (1996). How to support learning from interactions with simulated characters. In Gorayska, B., & Mey, J. L. (Eds.), *Cognitive technology: In search of a human interface*. Amsterdam: Elsevier. doi:10.1016/S0166-4115(96)80030-6

Katz, M. L., & Shapiro, C. (1985). Network Externalities, Competition, and Compatibility. *Teh American Economic Review*, *75*(3), 424–440.

Keen, A. (2007). *The Cult of the Amateur: How Today's Internet is Killing Our Culture*. New York: Currency.

Khalifa, M., & Lam, R. (2002). Web-based learning: Effects on learning process and outcome. *IEEE Transactions on Education*, *45*(4). doi:10.1109/TE.2002.804395

Khan, B. H. (2000). *A framework for web-based learning*. Englewood Cliffs, NJ: Educational Technology Publications.

Kiely, T. (1993). Learning to share. *CIO*, *6*(15), 38–44.

Kim, W. C., & Mauborgne, R. (1997). Value innovation: the strategic logic of high growth. *Harvard Business Review*, *75*(1), 103–112.

Kinshuk, J., & Yang, A. (2003). Web-based asynchronous synchronous environment for online learning. *United States Distance Education Association Journal*, *17*(2), 5–17.

Kinshuk, D., & Yang, A. (2003). Web-based asynchronous synchronous environment for online learning. *United States Distance Education Association Journal*, *17*(2), 5–17.

Kirriemuir, J. (2003). *The relevance of video games and gaming consoles to the higher and further education learning experiences*. Techwatch Report: TSW 02-01. Retrieved June 30, 2005, from http://www.jisc.ac.uk/uploaded_documents/tsw_02-01.rtf

Klass, B. S., McClendon, J., & Gainey, T. W. (2002). Trust and Role of Professional Employer Organisations: Managing HR in Small and Medium Enterprises. *Journal of Managerial Issues*, *14*(1), 31–48.

Knol, P., Spruit, M., & Scheper, W. (2008). Web 2.0 Revealed. In *Proceedings of the Seventh AIS SIGeBIZ Workshop on e-business (WeB 2008)*, Paris.

Koedinger, K. R., & Corbett, A. (2006). Technology bringing learning sciences to the classroom. In Sawuer, R. K. (Ed.), *The Cambridge handbook of the learning sciences* (pp. 61–77). New York: Cambridge Press.

Kohonen, T. (2001). *Self-Organizing Maps*. Helsinki, Finland: Springer Verlag.

Kosko, B. (1986). Fuzzy Cognitive Maps. *International Journal of Man-Machine Studies*, *24*, 65–75. doi:10.1016/S0020-7373(86)80040-2

Kosko, B. (1997). *Fuzzy engineering*. Upper Saddle River, NJ: Prentice Hall.

Kotter, J. (1996). *Leading Change*. Boston, MA: Harvard Business School Press.

Kotter, J. P., & Heskett, J. L. (1992). *Corporate Culture and Performance*. New York: Macmillan.

Kreijns, K., Kirschner, P. A., & Jochems, W. (2003). Supported collaborative learning environments: A review of the research. *Computers in Human Behavior*, *19*, 335–353. doi:10.1016/S0747-5632(02)00057-2

Kreijns, K., Kirschner, P., & Jochems, W. (2003). Identifying the pitfalls for social interaction in computer-supported collaborative learning environments: A review of the research. *Computers in Human Behavior, 19*, 335–353. doi:10.1016/S0747-5632(02)00057-2

Kriz, W. C. (2001). Die Planspielmethode als Lernumgebung. In Mandl, H., Keller, C., Reiserer, M., & Geier, B. (Eds.), *Planspiele im Internet: Konzepte und Praxisbeispiele für den Einsatz in Aus- und Weiterbildung* (pp. 41–64). Bielefeld, Germany: Bertelsmann.

Kuruppuarachchi, P., Mandal, P., & Smith, R. (2002). IT project implementation strategies for effective changes: a critical review. *Logistics Information Management, 15*(2), 126–137. doi:10.1108/09576050210414006

Ladd, A., & Ward, M. A. (2002). An Investigation Of Environmental Factors Influencing Knowledge Transfer, Air Force Institute of Technology (AFIT)/ENV. *Journal of Knowledge Management Practice.* Retrieved from http://www.tlainc.com/articl38.htm

Lado, A. A., Boyd, N. G., & Hanlon, S. C. (1997). Competition, cooperation, and the search for economic rents: a syncretic model. *Academy of Management Review, 22*(1), 110–141. doi:10.2307/259226

Law 141. (2009). Law number 141 for the year 2004, the Small Business Enterprises Development Law. In Law (Ed.), *Elmatabea Elameriah.*

Lawrence, E., Corbitt, B., Fisher, J., Lawrence, J., & Tidwell, A. (2000). *Internet Commerce: Digital Models for Business* (2nd ed.). Milton, Australia: John Wiley & Sons, Inc.

Leadbeater, C. (2007). *We-Think: the power of mass creativity.* Retrieved from http://www.wethinkthebook.net.

Lecocq, C. (1989). *The New Louvre.* Connaissance des Arts.

Lei, D. (1991). Global strategic alliances: payoffs and pitfalls. *Organizational Dynamics, 19*, 44–62. doi:10.1016/0090-2616(91)90093-O

Lei, D., & Slocum, J. W. Sr. (1992). Global strategy, competence-building and strategic alliances. *California Management Review, 35*, 81–97.

Leonard-Barton, D. (1992). Core capabilities and core rigidities: a paradox in managing new product development. *Strategic Management Journal, 13*(5), 111–125. doi:10.1002/smj.4250131009

Lepori, B., Cantoni, L., & Succi, C. (2000). The introduction of e-learning in European universities: Models and strategies. *Quality on the Line,* 74-83.

Lepper, M. R., & Malone, T. W. (1987). Intrinsic motivation and instructional effectiveness in computer-based education. In Snow, R. E., & Farr, M. J. (Eds.), *Aptitude, learning and instruction: III. Conative and affective process analyses* (pp. 255–286). Hillsdale, NJ: Erlbaum.

Lewis-Beck, M. S. (1995). *Data analysis: An introduction.* Thousand Oaks, CA: Sage.

Liaw, S. S. (2004). Considerations for developing constructivist Web-based learning. *International Journal of Instructional Media, 31*(3), 309–321.

Liaw, S. S., & Huang, H. M. (2003). An investigation of users attitudes towards search engines as an information retrieval tool. *Computers in Human Behavior, 19*(6), 751–765. doi:10.1016/S0747-5632(03)00009-8

Liaw, S. S., Huang, H. M., & Chen, G. D. (2007). Surveying instructor and learner attitudes towards e-learning. *Computers & Education, 49*, 1066–1080. doi:10.1016/j.compedu.2006.01.001

Lieberman, M. B., & Montgomery, D. B. (1988). First-mover advantages. *Strategic Management Journal, 9*, 41–58. doi:10.1002/smj.4250090706

Liebowitz, S. (2002). *Re-Thinking the Network Economy - The True Forces that Drive the Digital Marketplace.* New York: Amacom.

Lierman, B. C. (1993). Designing laboratory and simulation instruction. In Piskurich, G. M. (Ed.), *The ASTD handbook of instructional technology* (pp. 24.1–24.12). New York: McGraw-Hill.

Liikamaa, K. (2006). *Tacit Knowledge and Project Managers' Competencies*. Doctoral Thesis, Tampere University of Technology at Pori, Finland.

Lim, B. (1995). Examining the Organizational Culture and Organizational Performance Link. *Leadership and Organization Development Journal, 16*(5), 16–21. doi:10.1108/01437739510088491

Lin, H., & Sun, C. (2007). Cash Trade within the Magic Circle: Free-to-Play Game Challenges and Massively Multiplayer Online Game Player Responses. In *Proceedings of DiGRA 2007: Situated Play*, The University of Tokyo, September, 2007 (pp. 335-343).

Logan, D. (2001). *E-learning in the knowledge age*. Paper presented at the Gartner Symposium Itxpo 2001, Johannesburg, South Africa.

Löhmoeller, J. B. (1984). *LVPS 1.6 program manual: Latent variable path analysis with partial least squares estimation*. Köhn, Germany: Universitaet zu Köhn. Zentralarchiv fuer Empirische Sozialforschung.

Luftman, J., Bullen, V. C., Liao, D., Nash, E., & Neumann, C. (2004). *Managing the information Technology Resources – Leadership in information age*. Upper Saddle River, NJ: Pearson Prentice Hall.

Lund, D. (2003). Organizational Culture and Job Satisfaction. *Journal of Business and Industrial Marketing, 18*(3), 219–236. doi:10.1108/0885862031047313

Ma, Q., & Liu, L. (2004). The technology acceptance model: A meta analysis of empirical findings. *Journal of Organizational and End User Computing, 16*(1), 59–72.

MacInnes, I. (2005). Dynamic Business Model Framework for Emerging Technologies. *International Journal of Services Technology and Management, 6*(1). doi:10.1504/IJSTM.2005.006541

Malhotra, Y. (Ed.). (2001). *Knowledge Management and Business Model Innovation*. Hershey, PA: Idea Group.

Malone, T. W. (1981). Toward a theory of intrinsically motivating instruction. *Cognitive Science, 5*, 333–369. doi:10.1207/s15516709cog0504_2

Malone, T., & Lepper, M. R. (1987). Making learning fun: A taxonomy of intrinsic motivation for learning. In Snow, R. E., & Farr, M. J. (Eds.), *Aptitude, learning and instruction: III. Conative and affective process analyses* (pp. 223–253). Hillsdale, NJ: Erlbaum.

March, J. R. (1991). Exploration and exploitation in organizational learning. *Organization Science, 2*(1), 71–87. doi:10.1287/orsc.2.1.71

Marjanovic, O. (1999). Learning and teaching in a synchronous collaborative environment. *Journal of Computer Assisted Learning, 15*(2), 129–138. doi:10.1046/j.1365-2729.1999.152085.x

Marshall, A. (1920). *Industry and Trade*. London: Macmillan.

Martins, L. L., & Kellermanns, F. W. (2004). A model of business school students' acceptance of a web-based course management system. *Academy of Management Learning & Education, 3*(1), 7–26.

Maslin, K. T. (2001). *An Introduction to the Philosophy of Mind*. Malden, UK: Blackwell Publishers Inc.

Mason, E. S. (1939, March). Price and production policies of large-scale enterprise. *The American Economic Review, 29*, 61–74.

May, P. (2000). *The Business of E-commerce: From Corporate Strategy to Technology*. New York: Cambridge University Press.

Mayer, R. (2006). Ten research-based priniciples of multimedia learning. In O'Neil, H., & Perez, R. (Eds.), *Web-based learning* (pp. 371–390). Mahwah, NJ: Erlbaum.

McAfee, A. (2006a). Enterprise 2.0: The Dawn of Emergent Collaboration. *MIT Sloan Management Review, 47*(3), 21–28.

McAfee, A. (2006b, March 24). The Trends Underlying Enterprise 2.0. *The Impact of Information Technology (IT) on Businesses and their Leaders*. Retrieved January 17, 2008, from http://blog.hbs.edu/faculty/amcafee/index.php/faculty_amcafee_v3/the_three_trends_underlying_enterprise_20/

McAfee, A., & Brynjolfsson, E. (2008, July/August). Investing in the IT That Makes a Competitive Difference. *Harvard Business Review*.

McCutcheon, D. M., & Meredith, J. R. (1993). Conducting case study research in operations Management. *Journal of Operations Management, 11*, 239–256. doi:10.1016/0272-6963(93)90002-7

McDonald, M., & Wilson, H. (1999). *E-marketing Improving marketing effectiveness in a digital world*.

McGee, J. S. (1988). *Industrial Organization*. New York: Prentice-Hall.

McKinsey. (2007). *How Business are using Web 2.0*.

McLuhan, M. (1964). *Understanding Media: The Extensions of Man*. New York: McGraw Hill.

Menzies, T. (1999). Cost Benefits of Ontologies. *Intelligence, 10*(3), 26–32. doi:10.1145/318964.318969

Merrill, M. D. (1997). Instructional transaction theory: An instructional design model based on knowledge objects. In R. D. Tennyson, F. Schott, N. Seel, & S. Dijkstra (Eds.), *Instructional design: International perspectives. Vol. 1: Theory and research* (pp. 381-394). Hillsdale, NJ: Erlbaum.

Merton, R. K. (1968). The Matthew Effect in Science. *Science, 159*(3810), 56–63. doi:10.1126/science.159.3810.56

Metcalfe, R. (1980). Pup: An Internetwork Architecture. *IEEE Transactions on Communications, 28*(4), 612–624. doi:10.1109/TCOM.1980.1094684

Microsoft Corporation. (2005). *MOF SMF - Change Management*. Redmond, WA: Author.

Microsoft Corporation. (2008a, April 25). *Microsoft Operations Framework 4.0*. Retrieved July 31, 2008 from http://technet.microsoft.com/en-us/library/cc506049.aspx

Microsoft Corporation. (2008b, April 25). *Change and Configuration Service Management Function*. Redmond, WA: Author. Retrieved from http://www.microsoft.com/downloads/details.aspx?FamilyId=457ED61D-27B8-49D1-BACA-B175E8F54C0C&displaylang=en

Miller, G. A., Galanter, E., & Pripram, K. H. (1960). *Plans and the structure of behaviour*. London: Holt, Rinehart & Winston. doi:10.1037/10039-000

Mitchel, A., & Savill-Smith, C. (2004). *The use of computer and video games for learning: A review of the literature*. Retrieved June 30, 2005, from http://www.lsda.org.uk/files/PDF/1529.pdf

Mitchell, W., & Singh, K. (1996). Survival of businesses using collaborative relationships to commercialize complex goods. *Strategic Management Journal, 17*(3), 169–195. doi:10.1002/(SICI)1097-0266(199603)17:3<169::AID-SMJ801>3.0.CO;2-#

Moe, M. T., & Blodget, H. (2000). *The knowledge web: People power-fuel for the new economy*. San Francisco: Merrill Lynch.

Molkenthin, R. (2003). *Zur Entwicklung einer systemdynamischen Unternehmenssimulation als Komponente von e-Learning*. Unpublished master's thesis, Johannes Gutenberg-University, Mainz, Germany.

Molla, A., & Licker, P. S. (2001). E-commerce systems success: An attempt to extend and respecify the DeLone and McLean model of IS success. *Journal of Electronic Commerce Research, 2*(4), 1–11.

Monroe, K. B., & Della Bitta, A. J. (1978). Models for Pricing Decisions. *JMR, Journal of Marketing Research, 15*(3), 413–428. doi:10.2307/3150590

Moon, J. W., & Kim, Y. G. (2001). Extending the TAM for a World-Wide-Web context. *Information & Management, 38*, 217–230. doi:10.1016/S0378-7206(00)00061-6

Moore, G. A. (1991). *Crossing the Chasm: Marketing and Selling High-Tech Products to Mainstream Customers*. New York: Harper Business Essentials.

Moore, M. G., & Kearsley, G. (1996). *Distance education: A systems view*. Belmont, CA: Wadsworth.

Moreno, R., & Mayer, R. E. (2005). Role of guidance, reflection, and interactivity in an agent-based multimedia game. *Journal of Educational Psychology, 97*, 117–128. doi:10.1037/0022-0663.97.1.117

Mun, Y. Y., & Hwang, Y. (2003). Predicting the use of web-based information systems: self-efficacy, enjoyment, learning goal orientation, and the technology acceptance model. *International Journal of Human-Computer Studies, 59*, 431–449. doi:10.1016/S1071-5819(03)00114-9

Nagle, T., & Holden, R. (2002). *The strategy and Tactics of Pricing: a guide to Profitable Decision Making* (3rd ed.). Upper Saddle River, NJ: Prentice Hall.

Narayanan, V. (2001). *Managing Technology and Innovation for Competitive Advantage*. Upper Saddle River, NJ: Prentice Hall.

Naude, P., & Holland, C. (1996). *Business-to-business relationships, Relationship Marketing, Theory and Practice*. London: Paul Chapman Publishing.

Naukkarinen, O., Kantola, J., & Vanharanta, H. (2004). A New Qualitative Decision Support Tool for Evaluating and Managing R&D Investments. In *4th Annual Conference: Governance in Managerial Life, EURAM*, St. Andrews, Scotland, May 2004.

Nault, B. R., & Vandenbosch, M. B. (1996). Eating your own lunch: protection through pre-emption. *Organization Science, 7*(3), 342–358. doi:10.1287/orsc.7.3.342

Nielsen, J. (1993). *Usability Engineering*. San Diego, CA: Academic Press.

Nojima, M. (2007). Pricing models and Motivations for MMO play. In *Proceedings of DiGRA 2007: Situated Play*, The University of Tokyo, September, 2007 (pp. 672-681).

Nonaka, I., & Takeuchi, H. (1995). *The Knowledge-Creating Company: How Japanese Companies Create the Dynamics of Innovation*. New York: Oxford University Press.

Nonaka, I., Toyama, R., & Hirata, T. (2008). *Managing Flow: A Process Theory of the Knowledge-Based Firm*. New York: Palgrave Macmillan.

Normann, R. (1971). Organizational innovativeness: product variation and reorientation. *Administrative Science Quarterly, 16*(2), 203–215. doi:10.2307/2391830

Northup, P. (2002). A framework for designing interactivity into web-based instruction. *Educational Technology, 41*(2), 31–41.

O'Mahony, S. (2003). Guarding the commons: how community managed software projects protect their work. *Research Policy, 32*(7), 1179–1198. doi:10.1016/S0048-7333(03)00048-9

O'Neil, H. F. (1999). Perspectives on computer-based performance assessment of problem solving. *Computers in Human Behavior, 15*, 269–282.

Oberle, D., Volz, R., Staab, S., & Motik, B. (2004). An Extensible Ontology Software Environment. In Staab, S., & Studer, R. (Eds.), *Handbook on Ontologies* (pp. 299–319). Berlin: Springer-Verlag.

Obrst, L. (2003). Ontologies for Semantically Interoperable Systems. In *Proceedings of the 12th international conference on Information and knowledge management*.

OGC - Office of Government Commerce. (2007). *Service Transition*. London: TSO.

OGC - Office of Government Commerce. (2008, June 16). *ITIL*. Retrieved July 31, 2008, from http://www.ogc.gov.uk/guidance_itil.asp

OMG SysML specification. (2007). Retrieved from http://www.omgsysml.org/

Orbach, E. (1977). Some theoretical considerations in the evaluation of instructional simulation games. *Simulation & Games, 8*(3). doi:10.1177/003755007783003

O'Reilly, T. (2005, September 30). What is Web 2.0. *O'Reilly Media*. Retrieved July 4, 2007, from http://www.oreillynet.com/pub/a/oreilly/tim/news/2005/09/30/what-is-web-20.html

O'Reilly, T. (2006, December 10). Web 2.0 Compact Definition: Trying Again. *O'Reilly Radar*. Retrieved January 9, 2008, from http://radar.oreilly.com/archives/2006/12/web_20_compact.html

Ormrod, J. E. (2004). *Human learning* (4th ed.). Upper Saddle River, NJ: Merrill Prentice Hall.

Osterwalder, A., Pigneur, Y., & Tucci, C. L. (2005). Clarifying Business Models: Origins, Present, and Future of the Concept. *Communications of the Association for Information Systems, 16*, 1–25.

Ouchi, W. G. (1981). *Theory Z*. Reading, MA: Addison-Wesley.

Oxenfeldt, A. R. (1973). A Decision-making Structure for Price Decisions. *Journal of Marketing, 37*(1), 48–53. doi:10.2307/1250774

Paajanen, P. (2006). *Dynamic Ontologies of Knowledge Creation and Learning*. Licentiate Thesis. Tampere University of Technology, Pori, Finland.

Paajanen, P., Kantola, J., Karwowski, W., & Vanharanta, H. (2004). LITUUS: A system for the development of learning organizations. In H.-W. Chu, J. Aguilar & J. Ferrer (Eds.)., *ISAS CITSA 2004: 10th international conference on international systems analysis and synthesis*, July 21-25, 2004, Orlando, Florida, USA (pp. 412-416).

Palloff, R. M., & Pratt, K. (1999). *Building learning communities in cyberspace*. San Francisco: Jossey-Bass.

Parkhe, A. (1991). Interfirm diversity, organizational learning, and longevity in global strategic alliances. *Journal of International Business Studies, 22*, 579–601. doi:10.1057/palgrave.jibs.8490315

Parkhe, A. (1993). 'Strategic alliances structuring: a game theoretic and transaction cost examination of interfirm cooperation'. *Academy of Management Journal, 38*, 794–829. doi:10.2307/256759

Parkin, M., Powell, M., & Matthews, K. (2002). *Economics* (6th ed.). Harlow, UK: Pearson Education Ltd.

Parry, D. (2004). A fuzzy ontology for medical document retrieval. In *Proceedings of the second workshop on Australasian information security, Data Mining and Web Intelligence, and Software Internationalisation*, Dunedin, New Zealand, Australian Computer Society, Inc.

Passerini, K., & Granger, M. J. (2000). A development model for distance learning using the Internet. *Computers & Education, 34*, 1–15. doi:10.1016/S0360-1315(99)00024-X

Pearce, R. J. (1997). 'Toward understanding joint venture performance and survival: a bargaining and influence approach to transaction cost theory'. *Academy of Management Review, 22*(1), 203–225. doi:10.2307/259229

Pearlson, K. (2001). *Managing and Using Information Systems: A Strategic Approach*. New York: John Wiley & Sons.

Peters, T. J., & Waterman, R. H. (1982). *In Search of Excellence*. New York: Harper & Row.

Pevzner, B. (2007, June 4). ITIL v3 – Building a successful IT service delivery organization brick by brick, with the Service Portfolio as the cornerstone! *The Boris Files*. Retrieved July 31, 2008, from http://blog.centrata.com/weblog/

Phoha, V. V. (2001). *An Interactive Dynamic Model for Integrating Knowledge Management Methods and Knowledge Sharing Technology in a Traditional Classroom*. Presented at SIGCSE.

Piccoli, G., Ahmad, R., & Ives, B. (2001). Web-based virtual learning environments: A research framework and a preliminary assessment of effectiveness in basic IT skills training. *Management Information Systems Quarterly, 25*, 401–426. doi:10.2307/3250989

Piore, M., & Sabel, C. (1984). *The Second Industrial Divide*. New York: Basic Books.

Pituch, K. A., & Lee, Y. (2006). The influence of system characteristics on e-learning use. *Computers & Education, 47*, 222–244. doi:10.1016/j.compedu.2004.10.007

Porter, M. (1986). *Competition in Global Industries*. Cambridge, MA: Harvard Business School.

Porter, M. (1985). *Competitive Advantage*. New York: Free Press.

Porter, M. (1980). *Competitive Strategy*. New York: The Free Press.

Potomac Institute Study. (2008). *New Concepts in Human Systems Integration*.

Prahalad, C., & Ramaswamy, V. (2004). *The Future of Competition: Co-Creating Unique Value with Customers*. Boston, MA: Harvard Business School Press.

Prahalad, C. K., & Bettis, R. A. (1986). The dominant logic: a new linkage between diversity and performance. *Strategic Management Journal, 7*(6), 485–501.

Prahalad, C. K., & Ramaswamy, V. (2003). The new frontier of experience innovation. *MIT Sloan Management Review, 44*(4), 12–18.

Prensky, M. (2001). *Digital game based learning*. New York: McGraw-Hill.

Prieto, I. M., & Revilla, E. (2006 February). Formal and informal facilitators of learning capability: The moderating effect of learning climate. *IE Working Paper*. WP06-09.

Quinn, C. N. (1997). Engaging learning. *Instructional technology forum*. Retrieved July 30, 2005, from http://it.coe.uga.edu/itforum/paper18/paper18.html

Raab, R. T., Ellis, W. W., & Abdon, B. R. (2002). Multisectoral partnerships in e-learning: A potential force for improved human capital development in the Asia Pacific. *The Internet and Higher Education, 4*, 217–229. doi:10.1016/S1096-7516(01)00067-7

Rai, A., Patnayakuni, R., & Seth, N. (2006). Firm performance impacts of digitally-enabled supply chain integration capabilities. *Management Information Systems Quarterly, 30*, 225–246.

Randall, V. (1999). Cooperative learning abused and overused? *Gifted Child Today Magazine, 22*(2), 14–16.

Rao, V. R. (1984). Pricing Research in Marketing: the State of the art. *The Journal of Business, 57*(1), 39–60. doi:10.1086/296235

Rauhala, L. (1986). *Ihmiskäsitys ihmistyössä* [The Conception of Human Being in Helping People]. Helsinki, Finland: Gaudeamus.

Rauhala, L. (1995). *Tajunnan itsepuolustus* [Self-Defense of the Consciousness]. Helsinki, Finland: Yliopistopaino.

Reedy, J. E., Schullo, S. S., & Zimmerman, K. R. (1999). *Electronic Marketing: Integrating Electronic Resources into the Marketing Process*. Fort Worth, TX: Harcourt College Publishers.

Reimann-Rothmeier, G., & Mandl, H. (1996). Lernen auf der Basis des Konstruktivismus. Wie Lernen aktiver und anwendungsorientierter wird. *Computer und Unterricht, 23*, 41–44.

Reimann-Rothmeier, G., & Mandl, H. (1999). *Unterrichten und Lernumgebungen gestalten*. Göttingen, Germany: Hogrefe.

Relan, A., & Gillani, B. G. (1997). Web-based instruction and the traditional classroom: Similarities and differences. *Web-Based Instruction*, 41-46.

Renkl, A., Gruber, H., Mandl, H., & Hinkhofer, L. (1994). Hilft Wissen bei der Identifikation und Steuerung eines komplexen ökonomischen Systems? *Unterrichtswissenschaft, 22*, 195–202.

Review, H. L. (2001). Antitrust and the Information age, Section 2: Monopolization. *Analyses in the New Economy, 114*, 1623–1646.

Ricci, K., Salas, E., & Cannon-Bowers, J. A. (1996). Do computer-based games facilitate knowledge acquisition and retention? *Military Psychology, 8*, 295–307. doi:10.1207/s15327876mp0804_3

Rieber, L. P. (1991). Animation, incidental learning, and continuing motivation. *Journal of Educational Psychology, 83*, 318–328. doi:10.1037/0022-0663.83.3.318

Rogers, E. M. (1962). *Diffusion of Innovations*. New York: Free Press.

Ronnkvist, A., Dexter, S. L., & Anderson, R. E. (2000). *Technology support: Its depth, breadth and impact in America's schools. Teaching, Learning, and Computing: 1998 National Survey Report #5*. Irvine, CA: Center for Research on Information Technology and Organizations. Irvine: University of California.

Rosenberg, M. J. (2001). *E-learning: Strategies for delivery knowledge in the digital age*. New York: McGraw-Hill.

Rothschild, K. W. (1947). Price Theory and Oligopoly. *The Economic Journal, 57*(227), 299–320. doi:10.2307/2225674

Ryan, M. (2000, September 5). *Retention and Recruiting Update*. Air Force Commanders' Notice to Airmen 00-4.

Saade, R., & Bahli, B. (2005). The impact of cognitive absorption on perceived usefulness and perceived ease of use in on-line learning: an extension of the technology acceptance model. *Information & Management, 42*(2), 317–327. doi:10.1016/j.im.2003.12.013

Sadri, G., & Lees, B. (2001). Developing Corporate Culture as a Competitive Advantage. *Journal of Management Development, 20*(10), 853–859. doi:10.1108/02621710110410851

Saga, V., & Zmud, R. (1994). The nature and determinants of IT acceptance, routinization, and infusion. *IFIP Transactions A (Computer Science and Technology, A*(45), 67-86.

Salvendy, G. (Ed.). (2006). *Handbook of Human Factors and Ergonomics* (3rd ed.). Hoboken, NJ: John Wiley & Sons. doi:10.1002/0470048204

Sashkin, M. (1996). *Organizational Culture Assessment Questionnaire.*

Scarborough, N. M., & Zimmer, T. W. (2000). *Effective small business management: An entrepreneurial approach*. Upper Saddle River, N J: Prentice-Hall.

Schein, E. (1990). Organizational Culture. *The American Psychologist, 45*(2), 10–19. doi:10.1037/0003-066X.45.2.109

Schmitt, B. H., Simonsen, A., & Marcus, J. (1995). Managing corporate image and identity. *Long Range Planning, 28*(5), 82–92. doi:10.1016/0024-6301(95)00040-P

Schwarzer, C., & Buchwald, P. (2001). Beratung. In Krapp, A., & Weidenmann, B. (Eds.), *Pädagogische Psychologie* (4th ed., pp. 565–600). Weinheim, Germany: Beltz Psychologie.

SEDO. (2009). *The Small Enterprise Development Organisation*. Retrieved January 12, 2009, from http://www.sfdegypt.org/groups.htm#4

Senge, P. (1990). *The fifth discipline*. New York: Doubleday.

Senge, P. M. (1994). *The Fifth Discipline the Art and practice of the Learning Organization*. New York: Currency Doubleday.

SFD. (2009a). *The Egyptian Social Fund for Development (SFD)*. Retrieved January 12, 2009, from http://www.sfdegypt.org/about.asp

SFD. (2009b). *The Egyptian Social Fund for Development* Retrieved March 1, 2009, from http://www.sfdegypt.org/PDF/1-12.pdf

Shapiro, C., & Varian, H. (1999). *Information Rules: A Strategic Guide to the Network Economy*. Boston, MA: Harvard Business School Press.

Sherehiy, B., & Karwowski, W. (2006). Knowledge Management for Occupational Safety, Health and Ergonomics. *Human Factors and Ergonomics in Manufacturing, 16*(3), 309–320. doi:10.1002/hfm.20054

Silberston, A. (1951). The Pricing of Manufactured Products: a comment. *The Economic Journal, 61*(242), 426–429. doi:10.2307/2226968

Simon, H. (1991). Bounded Rationality and Organizational Learning. *Organization Science, 2*(1), 125–134. doi:10.1287/orsc.2.1.125

Singh, H. (2000). *Achieving interoperability in e-learning*. Retrieved October 21, 2002, from http://www.learningcircuits.org/2000/mar2000/singh.html

Skouras, T., Avlonitis, G. F., & Indounas, K. (2005). Economics and Marketing: How and Why Do They Differ? *Journal of Product and Brand Management, 14*(6), 362–374. doi:10.1108/10610420510624512

Slavin, R. E. (1995). *Cooperative learning: Theory, research, and practice* (2nd ed.). Boston: Allyn & Bacon.

Sloman, M. (2001). *The e-learning revolution*. Wimbledon, UK: CIPD.

Smith, P. R., & Chaffey, D. (2005). *E-marketing Excellence*. London: Butterworth-Heinemann.

So, H. J. (2006). *Student satisfaction in a blended learning course: A qualitative approach focusing on critical factors*. Paper presented at the Annual Meeting of the American Educational Research Association, San Francisco, California.

Stanley, M. (2005). *China Internet - Creating Consumer Value in Digital China*. Retrieved from http://www.morganstanley.com/institutional/techresearch /pdfs/China_Internet_091205.pdf

Stasser, G., & Stewart, D. D. (1992). Discovery of hidden profiles by decision- making groups: Solving a problem versus making a judgment. *Journal of Personality and Social Psychology, 63*, 426–434. doi:10.1037/0022-3514.63.3.426

Sterman, J. D. (2000). *Business dynamics. System thinking and modeling for a complex world*. Boston: McGraw-Hill.

Stokes, P. J. (2000). How E-learning will transform education. Education week on the Web. *Editorial Projects in Education, 20*. Retrieved October 1, 2001 from http://www.edweek.org/ew/ewstory.cfm?slug=02stokes.h20andkeywords=education%20technology#author

Strauss, J., & Frost, R. (2001). *E-marketing*. Upper Saddle River, NJ: Prentice-Hall.

Streufert, S., & Satish, U. (1997). Graphic representations of processing structure: The time-event matrix. *Journal of Applied Social Psychology, 27*, 2122–2131. doi:10.1111/j.1559-1816.1997.tb01644.x

Strijbos, J.-W., Kirschner, P. A., & Martens, R. L. (Eds.). (2004). *What we know about CSCL in higher education*. Boston: Kluwer. doi:10.1007/1-4020-7921-4

Ström, P., & Ernkvist, M. (2007). The unbound network of product and service interaction of the MMOG industry: with a case study of China. In *Proceedings of DiGRA 2007: Situated Play*, The University of Tokyo, September, 2007 (pp. 639-649).

Surowiecki, J. (2004). *The Wisdom of the Crowds - Why the Many Are Smarter Than the Few and How Collective Wisdom Shapes Business, Economies Societies and Nations*. New York: Doubleday.

Tapscott, D., & Williams, A. D. (2007). *Wikinomics: How Mass Collaboration Changes Everything*. New York: Penguin.

Tauber, E. M. (1983). Editorial: corporate wisdom: the need for 'the brand knowledge base. *Journal of Advertising Research, 23*(1), 7.

Taubman, P. (2008). Top Engineers Shun Military, Concerns Grow. *The New York Times*. Retrieved from http://www.nytimes.com/2008/06/25/us/25engineer.html

Taylor, S., & Todd, P. A. (1995). Decomposition and crossover effects in the theory of planned behavior: A study of consumer adoption intentions. *International Journal of Research in Marketing, 12*, 137–156. doi:10.1016/0167-8116(94)00019-K

Taylor, D. R. (2002). E-learning: The second wave. *Leaning Circuits: ASTD's online magazine*. Retrieved from http:www.learningcircuits.com/2002/oct2002/taylor.html

Teece, D. J., Pisano, G., & Shuen, A. (1997). Dynamic capabilities and strategic management. *Strategic Management Journal, 18*, 509–533. doi:10.1002/(SICI)1097-0266(199708)18:7<509::AID-SMJ882>3.0.CO;2-Z

Tennyson, R. D. (2002). Linking learning theories to instructional design. *Educational Technology, 42*(3), 51–55.

Tennyson, R. D., & Breuer, K. (2002). Improving problem solving and creativity through use of complex-dynamic simulations. *Computers in Human Behavior, 18*, 650–668. doi:10.1016/S0747-5632(02)00022-5

Tennyson, R. D., & Foshay, W. R. (1998). Instructional systems development. In Dean, P. J., & Ripley, D. E. (Eds.), *Performance improvement interventions: Methods for organizational learning* (Vol. 2, pp. 64–106). Washington, DC: The International Society for Performance Improvement.

Tennyson, R. D., & Jorczak, R. L. (in press). Benefits of CSCL for learners with disabilities. In Ordóñez de Pablos, P. (Ed.), *Technology enhanced learning for people with disabilities: Approaches and applications*. Hershey, PA: IGI Global.

Tennyson, R. D. (2005). Learning theories and instructional design: An historical perspective of the thinking model. In J. M. Spector, C. Ohrazda, & A. Van Schaak (Eds.), Innovations in instructional technology: Essays in honor of M. David Merrill (pp. 219–235). Mahwah, NJ: Erlbaum.

Tennyson, R. D., & Breuer, K. (1997). *Psychological foundations for instructional design theory.* In R. D. Tennyson, F. Schott, N. Seel & S. Dijkstra (Eds.), *Instructional design: International Perspective, Volume 1: Theory, research, and models* (pp. 113-133). Mahwah, NJ: Erlbaum.

Thaler, R. (1985). Mental Accounting and Consumer Choice. *Marketing Science, 4*(3), 199–214. doi:10.1287/mksc.4.3.199

The British Council. (1999 October). *Science Parks, Briefing Sheet 7, UK Partnerships*. Retrieved from http://www.ukspa.org.uk

Theng, L. G., & Boon, J. L. W. (1996). An exploratory study of factors affecting the failure of local small and medium enterprises. *Asia Pacific Journal of Management, 13*(2), 47–61. doi:10.1007/BF01733816

Thomas, J. C., Kellogg, W. A., & Erickson, T. (2001). *The knowledge management puzzle: Human and social factors in knowledge management.* IBM Systems Journal, Knowledge Management, 40*(4).*

Thomas-Hunt, M. C., Odgen, T. Y., & Neale, M. A. (2003). Who's Really Sharing? Effects of Social and Expert Status on Knowledge Exchange within Groups. *Management Science, 49*(4), 464–477. doi:10.1287/mnsc.49.4.464.14425

Tirole, J. (1989). *The Theory of Industrial Organization*. Cambridge, MA: MIT Press.

Treacy, M., & Wiersema, F. (1995). *The Discipline of Market Leaders*. Reading, MA: Addison-Wesley.

Trentin, G. (2000). *Telematica e formazione a distanza*. Florence: La Nuova Italia.

Tsadiras, A. K., Kouskouvelis, I., & Margaritis, K. G. (2001). Making Political Decision using Fuzzy Cognitive Maps: The FYROM crisis. In *Proceedings of the 8th Panhellenic Conference on Informatics*, Greece.

Turban, E., King, D., Warkentin, M., & Chung, H. (2002). *E-commerce: A Managerial Perspective*. Upper Saddle River, NJ: Prentice Hall.

Turban, E., Lee, J., King, D., & Chung, H. (2000). *Electronic Commerce: A Managerial Perspective* (International Ed.). Upper Saddle River, NJ: Prentice-Hall International.

Turban, E., McLean, E., & Wetherbe, J. (2000). *Information Technology for Management: Making Connection for Strategic Advantage* (2nd ed.). New York: John Wiley & Sons Inc.

Tushman, M. L., & Anderson, P. (1986). Technological discontinuities and organizational environments. *Administrative Science Quarterly, 31*(3), 439–465. doi:10.2307/2392832

UNESCO. (1998). *World declaration on higher education on higher education for the twenty-first century: Vision and action*. Paris: UNESCO, Division of Higher Education, Unit for the World Conference on Higher Education. Retrieved from http://www.unesco.org/education/educprog/wche/declaration_eng.htm#world%20declaration.

United States Agency for International Development (USAID). (2009). *USAID Small business enterprises definition*. Retrieved January 25, 2009, 2009, from http://www.usaid-eg.org/display.cfm?s=USAID's_Small_and_Micro_Enterprise_%28SME%29_Development_program&pt=2&-sp=2&ppc=%2BqWEgB7wUAc%3D&qs=06oENya4ZG1YS6vOLJwpLiFbgelW6za09oFkf0Q_HyPMgoQS_5rcSSiueh8dRYznz_8jvGx6IcavSpTuD8v0TKAZLvH2M0e5RsYGiYcZN49ZAeXRddZzY0OZ1T_M5oT8FwHc0z-3bu-85bIdmVrPpBK8Ose0vJs5ck21SFewZWnbZ5Ha4FZ31Dil_-5lLQ4FZG_UfGTKuFfVPd6a1ekysXYRO1hE36o,YT0z&vid=1242216953_2X04X1284826321&rpt=2&lpt=1242217007&bd=1%23600%23800%231%230%23741%2357&kt=1

Urden, T. A., & Weggen, C. C. (2000). *Corporate E-learning: Exploring a new frontier*. W. R. Hambrecht and Company Equity Research Report.

Uttal, B. (1983). The Corporate Culture Vultures. *Fortune, 108*(8), 66–79.

van der Boom, G., Paas, F., van Morriënboer, J., & van Gog, T. (2004). Reflection prompts and tutor feedback in a web-based learning environment: effects on students' self-regulated learning competence. *Computers in Human Behavior, 20*, 551–568. doi:10.1016/j.chb.2003.10.001

Vanharanta, H. (2003). Circles of mind. Identity and diversity in organizations – building bridges in Europe. In *11th European congress on work and organizational psychology*, 14-17 May 2003, Lisboa, Portugal.

Velu, C. (2005). *Business Model Innovation in Network Markets*. Cambridge, MA: Cambridge University.

Venkatesh, V., Speicer, C., & Morris, M. G. (2002). User acceptance enablers in individual decision making about technology: towards an integrated model. *Decision Sciences, 33*(2), 297–316. doi:10.1111/j.1540-5915.2002.tb01646.x

Venkatesh, V., & Davis, F. D. (2000). A theoretical extension of the technology acceptance model: Four longitudinal field studies. *Management Science, 46*, 186–204. doi:10.1287/mnsc.46.2.186.11926

Venkatesh, V., Morris, M. G., Davis, G. B., & Davis, F. D. (2003). User Acceptance of Information Technology: Toward a Unified View. *Management Information Systems Quarterly, 27*(3), 425–478.

Verespej, M. (1990). When you Put the Team in Charge. *Industry Week*, 30–33.

Vossen, G., & Hagemann, S. (2007). *Unleashing Web 2.0, From Concepts to Creativity*. Burlington, MA: Morgan Kaufman Publishers.

Waddell, D., Cummings, T., & Worley, C. (2000). *Organisation Development and Change*. Melbourne: Nelson Thomson Learning.

Walsh, J. P. (1995). Managerial and organizational cognition: notes from a trip down memory lane. *Organization Science, 6*(3), 280–321. doi:10.1287/orsc.6.3.280

Wang, Y. S. (2003). Assessment of learner satisfaction with asynchronous electronic learning systems. *Information & Management, 41*, 75–86. doi:10.1016/S0378-7206(03)00028-4

Ward, S., Light, L., & Goldstine, J. (1999). What high-tech managers need to know about brands. *Harvard Business Review, 77*(4), 85–95.

Watson, J., & Everett, J. E. (1996). Do small businesses have high failure rates? *Journal of Small Business Management, 34*(4), 45–62.

Weber, R. A., & Camerer, C. F. (2003). Cultural Conflict and Merger Failure: An Experimental Approach. *Management Science, 49*(4), 400–415. doi:10.1287/mnsc.49.4.400.14430

Webster, J., & Hackley, P. (1997). Teaching effectiveness in technology-mediated distance learning. *Academy of Management Review, 40*, 1282–1309. doi:10.2307/257034

Welp, C. (2007). Gefühltes Glück. *Wirtschaftswoche*, 21.

Wernerfelt, B. (1984). A Resource-Based View of the Firm. *Strategic Management Journal, 5*(2), 171–180. doi:10.1002/smj.4250050207

Wheeler, B. (2000). WebCT – WebCT clear leader in online learning programs. *The Chronicle of Higher Education, 11*, 34.

Wheeler, C. (2002). NEBIC: A dynamic capabilities theory for assessing net-enablement. *Information Systems Research, 13*, 125–146. doi:10.1287/isre.13.2.125.89

Whipple, J. M., & Frankel, R. (2000). Strategic alliance success factors. *Journal of Supply Chain Management*, 21-26.

Whiteley, R. (1991). *The Customer Driven Company*. Reading, MA: Addison-Wesley.

Wilbers, K. (2001). E-Learning didaktisch gestalten. In Hohenstein, A., & Wilbers, K. (Eds.), *Handbuch E-Learning: Expertenwissen aus Wissenschaft und Praxis*. Köln, Germany: Fachverlag Deutscher Wirtschaftsdienst.

Wiley, D. (2001). *Peer –to-peer and learning objects: the new potential for collaborative constructivist learning online*. Paper presented at the Proceedings of the IEEE International Conference on Advanced Learning Technology.

Wilkinson, I., & Young, L. (2002). On cooperating: Firms, relations and networks. *Journal of Business Research*.

Williams, A., Dobson, P., & Walters, M. (1993). *Changing Culture: New Organisational Approaches*. London: Institute of Personnel Management.

Williamson, O. E. (1985). *The Economic Institutions of Capitalism - Firms, Markets, Relational Contracting*. New York: Free Press.

Wright, R. (2004). *Business to Business Marketing, A step by step guide*. Harlow, UK: Prentice Hall.

Wu, J.-H., Hsia, T.-L., & Heng, M. (2006). Core dynamic capabilities for exploiting electronic banking. *Journal of Electronic Commerce Research, 7*, 111–122.

Wu, J. H., Tennyson, R. D., Hsia, T. L., & Liao, Y. W. (in press). Analysis of e-learning innovation and core capability using a hypercube model. *Computers in Human Behavior*.

Wu, J. H., & Wang, S. C. (2005). What drives mobile commerce? An empirical evaluation of the revised technology acceptance model. *Information & Management, 42*, 719–729. doi:10.1016/j.im.2004.07.001

Wu, J.-H., & Shiah, T.-L. (2005). Developing E-business dynamic capabilities: An analysis of E-commerce innovation from I-, M-, to U-commerce. *Journal of Organizational Computing and Electronic Commerce*.

Yang, S. C., & Liu, S. F. (2005). The study of interactions and attitudes of third-grade students' learning information technology via a cooperative approach. *Computers in Human Behavior, 21*, 45–72. doi:10.1016/j.chb.2004.02.002

Yang, Z., & Liu, Q. (2007). Research and development of web-based virtual online classroom. *Computers & Education, 48*, 171–184. doi:10.1016/j.compedu.2004.12.007

Yin, R. K. (1994). *Case Study Research - Design and Methods*. Thousand Oaks, CA: Sage Publications.

Yin, R. K. (1984). *Case Study Research: Design and Methods*. Thousand Oaks, CA: Sage Publications.

Zadeh, L. A. (1965). Fuzzy sets. *Information and Control, 8*, 338–353. doi:10.1016/S0019-9958(65)90241-X

Zadeh, L. A. (1973). Outline of a new approach to the analysis of complex systems and decision processes. *IEEE Transactions on Systems, Man, and Cybernetics, 1*(1), 28–44.

Zhang, X., Keeling, K. B., & Pavur, R. J. (2000). Information quality of commercial website home pages: An explorative analysis. In *Proceedings of the 21th International Conference on Information Systems*, Brisbane, Australia (pp. 164-175).

Zinkhan, M. G. (2002). Promoting services via the internet: new opportunities and challenges. *Journal of Services Marketing, 16*(5), 412–423. doi:10.1108/08876040210436885

About the Contributors

Patricia Ordóñez de Pablos is a Professor in the Department of Business Administration and Accountability in the Faculty of Economics of the University of Oviedo, Spain. Her teaching and research interests focus on the areas of strategic management, knowledge management, intellectual capital measuring and reporting, organisational learning and human resources management. She serves as Executive Editor of the International Journal of Learning and Intellectual and the International Journal of Strategic Change Management. She also serves as Associate Editor of Behaviour and Information Technology.

Miltiadis D. Lytras is a professor in the American College of Greece. His research focuses on semantic web, knowledge management and e-learning, with more than 100 publications in these areas. He has co-edited /co-edits, 25 special issues in International Journals (e.g. IEEE Transaction on Knowledge and Data Engineering, IEEE Internet Computing, IEEE Transactions on Education, Computers in Human Behaviour, Interactive Learning Environments, Journal of Knowledge Management, Journal of Computer Assisted Learning, etc) and has authored/[co-]edited 25 books [e.g. Open Source for Knowledge and Learning Management, Ubiquitous and Pervasive Knowledge Management, Intelligent Learning Infrastructures for Knowledge Intensive Organizations, Semantic Web Based Information Systems, China Information technology Handbook, Real World Applications of Semantic Web and Ontologies, Web 2.0: The Business Model, etc] . He is the founder and officer of the Semantic Web and Information Systems Special Interest Group in the Association for Information Systems (http://www.sigsemis.org). He serves as the (Co) Editor in Chief of 12 international journals [e.g. International Journal of Knowledge and Learning, International Journal of Technology Enhanced Learning, International Journal on Social and Humanistic Computing, International Journal on Semantic Web and Information Systems, International Journal on Digital Culture and Electronic Tourism, International Journal of Electronic Democracy, International Journal of Electronic Banking, International Journal of Electronic Trade etc] while he is associate editor or editorial board member in seven more.

Rongbin W.B. Lee is the Chair Professor and Director of the Knowledge Management Research Centre, of The Hong Kong Polytechnic University. He is currently a council member of the Hong Kong Productivity Council and a member of the assessment panel of the Innovation and Technology Fund of the Hong Kong SAR Government. He established the Knowledge Solution Laboratory, the first of its kind in Hong Kong, and pioneered the research and practice of knowledge management in various organisations in manufacturing, trading, public utilities, various government departments and healthcare. Professor Lee and his team have launched Asia's first online MSc Programme in Knowledge Management. His research interests include manufacturing strategy, knowledge management, organisational learning and intellectual capital-based management.

Waldemar Karwowski, PhD, DSc, PE is Professor and Chairman, Department of Industrial Engineering and Management Systems and Executive Director of the Institute for Advanced Systems Engineering at the University of Central Florida, USA. He holds an MS (1978) inProduction Engineering and Management from the Technical University of Wroclaw, Poland, and a Ph.D. (1982) in Industrial Engineering from Texas Tech University. He was awarded D.Sc. (dr habil.) degree in management science by the State Institute for Organization and Management in Industry, Poland (2004). He also received Honorary Doctorate degrees from three European universities. He is the author or coauthor of over 350 scientific publications, and is Certified Professional Ergonomist (BCPE). Dr. Karwowski was named the J. B. Speed School of Engineering Alumni Scholar for Research, University of Louisville (2004–2006). He served as member of the Board of Directors of the American Association of Engineering Societies (2006–2007), and Executive Board of the Council of Scientific Society Presidents, Washington, D.C. (2007-2009). Dr. Karwowski currently serves on the Committee on Human Systems Integration, National Research Council of the National Academies, USA (2007–2009), and as Editor of the Human Factors and Ergonomics in Manufacturing Journal, and Editor-in-Chief of Theoretical Issues in Ergonomics Science journal. He is Past President of the International Ergonomics Association (2000-2003), and Past President of the Human Factors and Ergonomics Society (2007).

* * *

Tareq Ahram, PhD, is a Post Doctoral Research Fellow working with the Institute for Advanced Systems Engineering at the University of Central Florida and the president of the Systems Engineering Chapter of INCOSE Orlando at the University of Central Florida. He holds a Master of Science degree in Human Engineering from the University of Central Florida, Master of Science degree in Engineering Management from the University of Jordan and Ph.D. (2008) in Industrial Engineering from the University of Central Florida. Tareq holds a 6-Sigma Green Belt certification from Harrington Group. Since 2005, he has worked as a research associate at the Industrial Engineering & Management Systems Department at UCF. His research has focused on the development of the Human Systems Integration framework based on Systems Engineering modeling language and model-based systems engineering concepts.

Chris Andrzejczak is a current PhD student at the University of Central Florida, in the Industrial Engineering and Management Systems department. His undergraduate degree is in Scientific and Philosophical Studies of Mind from Franklin & Marshall College. He holds a Master of Science degree in Human Factors and Engineering Systems from Embry-Riddle Aeronautical University. Chris also holds a Private Pilot License and hopes to continue his flight training. His employer since 2005 is the Boeing Company, where he is a member of the 787 Reliability, Maintainability, and Testability team. His research interests include usability studies, improving ease of maintenance on ground, air, and space vehicles, and most recently the use of Non-Linear Dynamics and Chaos Theory to model and describe human cognitive and physical processes.

Hatem El-Gohary is the Editor-in-Chief of the International Journal of Online Marketing (IJOM) and the UK Director for the Institute for Research on Global Business (IRGB - UK). He have more than 18 years of experience in academia, worked as the marketing Director of a multinational company as well as a marketing consultant for a number of national and multinational companies. His research interest include: Electronic Marketing, Electronic Business, Electronic Commerce, Internet Marketing and Small Business Enterprises. He has published several articles and book chapters and presented several research papers in various international conferences. He holds a PhD, MSc, PGDip, BSc as well as PGCHE. He is also a Certified E-Marketer (CeM), an AABPP Fellow, CIM member (MCIM) and has a significant record of experience in voluntary work in Egypt and the UK. With regards to awards and honours Dr. El-Gohary won: the Routledge Best Paper Award 2007, The American Academy of Business and Public Policy Best Paper Award 2009, the Ideal Student for Cairo University Award 1992, the Ideal Student for Cairo University Business School Award (twice for the years 1991 and 1992) as well as The SLED Best New Mentor Award 2007.

Martin Görnitz is a consultant with Krallmann AG, Berlin, Germany. He received a MSc in Computer Science from the Berlin Institute of Technology in 2008. His research interests are in the areas of IT management methods and business-IT alignment.

Jon G. Hall, Fellow of the British Computer Society and of International Academy, Research and Industry Association, is a Senior Lecturer and Researcher in the Computing Department at The Open University in the UK. He is the Editor-in-Chief of Expert Systems: The Journal of Knowledge Engineering and of the IARIA International Journal of Software Advances. He has published over 70 academic papers in areas that include Petri Nets, Logic, Formal Methods for Safety-Critical Systems, Requirements, Software, Systems and Knowledge Engineering, Design, and Multi-Agent Systems, and has edited many special issues and books. His current research mission is to provide complementary practical and theoretical foundations for computing as an engineering discipline. His current goal is to provide an overarching theory of engineering design into which all traditional and modern engineering disciplines fit, and within which their interrelatedness and complementarity can be explored.

Seppo J. Hänninen is Researcher at Helsinki University of Technology Department of Industrial Engineering and Management. He holds a Doctor of Science in Technology degree from the Helsinki University of Technology with distinction. His research and teaching activities focus on the areas of new product development, commercializing technological inventions, micro-strategy management, entrepreneurship, and networks. He cooperates with several Finnish firms that develop innovations in technology programs. Before joining the research team at Helsinki University of Technology, he worked eight years in advertising industry and ten years as entrepreneur in international business. He has an extensive teaching experience at the HAMK University of Applied Sciences.

Philip Hardwick is a Professor of Economics and Director of Postgraduate Research at Bournemouth University. His research interests concern the econometric analysis of the relative performance of financial services firms, in terms of economies of scale and scope, and cost, profit and revenue efficiencies. He has published widely in academic journals in finance and economics, including Oxford Economic Papers, Applied Financial Economics, the Journal of Management Studies, Abacus, the Journal of Risk and Insurance, the Journal of Business Finance and Accounting and the Journal of Banking and Finance.

Tzyh-Lih Hsia is an associate professor in the Department of Information Management at the Chinese Naval Academy in Taiwan. He holds a PhD from National Sun Yat-Sen University. He has published papers in professional journals such as Information & Management, Computers in Human Behavior,

Journal of Organization Computing and Electronic Commerce, Electronic Commerce Research and Applications, and others. His current research includes electronic commerce, electronic learning, and information system innovation.

Salaheldin Ismail is a Professor of Production/Operations Management and the Chair of Department of Management &Marketing at College of Business & Economics at the Qatar University. He has an MSc degree in Production/Operations Management from the College of Commerce & Business Administration at Helwan University, Cairo, Egypt. Dr. Salaheldin earned a PhD in Operations Management from the Glasgow Business School at Glasgow University, UK. His publications have appeared in, among others, International Journal of Operations and Production Management, Journal of Industrial Management & Data Systems, International Journal of Management & Decision Making, International Journal of Learning & Intellectual Capital, International Journal of Productivity and & Performance Management, Journal of Measuring Business Excellence, Journal of International Business and Entrepreneurship Development, International Journal of Global Business and Management Research, International Journal of Customer Relationship Marketing and Management, Journal of Manufacturing Technology Management, and Journal of TQM.

Robert L. Jorczak is a private consultant. He is also a lecturer at the University of Minnesota on topics dealing with educational technology, learning and instructional theories, advanced computer mediated learning. His published work includes journal and book chapters on computer games, designing collaborative learning environments, and adult learning.

Jussi Kantola is an associate professor at KAIST (Korea Advanced Institute of Science and Technology) in the new department of Knowledge service engineering. Earlier he worked in Finland at Tampere University of Technology, Pori and at University of Turku as a research director.Before that he worked as an IT consultant in US for Romac International and as a process consultant for ABB in Finland.

Thanos Kriemadis is Associate Professor teaching Total Quality Management and Strategic management at the University of Peloponnese and the University of Athens. He received his MA, PhD, and MBA from USA Universities. He was specialized in Strategic Management under the guidance of Dr. Ansoff (The Father of Strategic Management). He was also an active member of the San Diego Deming User Group where he was introduced to Total Quality Management by Dr. Deming's disciples. He is Quality Auditor for Quality Management Systems (ISO 9001:2000) as well as Quality Assessor of the European Quality Award promoted by the European Foundation for Quality Management (EFQM) specialized in Small and Medium Enterprises and the Public sector-Education. Before moving to academia Dr. Kriemadis held several management posts in both the public and private sectors in the USA and Greece. In USA, he worked in the Quality Department of Motorola, Inc. using the six-sigma methodology. He also served as a quality and strategy consultant developing and auditing quality systems and strategic plans in Greece, European Union and USA. Research interests include Total Quality Management and Strategic Management issues applied in service organizations.

P. Kyriazopoulos: After his studies in Greece (B.A.B.A.) and his post-Graduate studies in U.K. (Marketing and Economics) he jointed to multination company where he worked for several years. Later on, he got his PhD in TQM from University of Thessalonica. In 1978 he joined to Technological

Education Institute of Piraeus as Professor of Marketing. He is publishing more than 20 text books, many articles in Greek and International scientific magazines and he presented more than 22 research work in International conferences. He is the course leader of M.Sc. in International Marketing which is running in collaboration with University of Paisley, Scotland.

Peter Knol, MSc, currently holds a position as web strategy consultant at Deloitte Consulting in the Netherlands. He is involved in projects implementing valuable use of emerging and social possibilities of Internet for large organizations. He recently obtained his masters degree in the field of Business Informatics at the Institute of Information and Computing Sciences of Utrecht University. His master thesis focused on Web 2.0 in relation to business model innovation.

Masoud Mohammadian has received his Bachelor of Computer Science from Flinders University of Australia, Master of Computer Science and his PhD from Central Queensland University in Australia. He is a Senior Lecturer at the Faculty of Information Sciences and Engineering at the University of Canberra in Australia. His research interests lie in adaptive self-learning systems, fuzzy logic, genetic algorithms, neural networks and intelligent agents and their applications in industrial, financial and business problems. He has chaired 12 international conferences on computational intelligence and intelligent agents. He has published a large number of research papers in conferences, journal and books as well as editing 17 books. He has over 17 years of academic experience. He was the chair of IEEE ACT Section and he was the recipient of a number of international awards including Awards from IEEE from USA and Ministry of Commerce and education from Austria.

Theodore Pelagidis is Professor of Economics at the University of Piraeus. He received his M.Phil. from Sussex University, UK, and his PhD from Paris University, France, being at the same time an EU SPES researcher. He has also conducted post-doctoral research on the EMU at the Center for European Studies, Harvard University, USA, (1993-94 and 1995-96 as a NATO scholar). He has published expensively in professional journals such as, The Journal of Policy Modelling, Cambridge Journal of Economics, International Review of Law and Economics, Journal of Economic Studies, The Cato Journal, European Journal of Law and Economics, Journal of Post-Keynesian Economics, Challenge. The Magazine of Economic Affairs, Industrial Relations, Review of International Studies, Current Politics and Economics of Europe, Economy and Society, International Review of Economics and Business, Cahiers Economiques de Bruxelles, Actualite Economique. Review d'Analyse Economique, etc. He is also co-editor of the Welfare State and Democracy in Crisis, Aldershot, Ashgate, 2001, and co-author of Strong Growth and Weak Institutions in Greece, MacMillan/Palgrave, 2010 (forthcoming).

Qun Ren got her Master degree in International business Finance from Bournemouth University in 2005. Currently, she is a PhD researcher in the Business school of Bournemouth University, UK. Her research interests focus on business strategy in fast-paced competitive IT industries, pricing in Internet services and national cultural issues in management.

I. Samanta is a faculty member of the Department of Business Administration, Graduate Technological Education Institute of Piraeus, she received her Bachelor in Business Administration from the Graduate Technological Education Institute of Piraeus, her Master degree from University of Paisley, UK. She is a PhD candidate from University of the West of Scotland, UK. Her current scientific research activities include e-marketing, B2B relationship, Marketing Communication, Innovation Culture. Her research has been presented in more than 16 European and global conferences with proceedings. In addition, she has published a number of articles in scientific Journals. She is member of the Editorial Committee in Strategic Outsourcing, an International Journal (EMERALD Group Publishing) and responsible for suggesting acceptance or rejection of each submission

Wim Scheper is partner at Deloitte Consulting in the Netherlands and professor in the field of business/IT-alignment at the Institute of Information and Computing Sciences of Utrecht University. In his consulting practice, he is involved in implementations of ICT solutions from the vision that within an organization the strategy, the control, the establishment of processes, the qualifications of employees, and the IT must be aligned to each other for the best investment return to earn and improve efficiency. He recently founded Deloitte Innovation Netherlands from the view that focus on breakthrough innovations are essential for growth and that special attention and a dedicated innovation process appear to be indispensable.

Khurram Sharif is an Assistant Professor of Marketing in the Management & Marketing Department, Qatar University. He is also a marketing research consultant and has worked with a number of UK pharmaceutical and cable communications companies on a variety of projects. His current research interests include marketing research design and methodologies, customer experience management, managing business-to-business relationships and learning technologies within higher education domain.

Marco Spruit is an Assistant Professor in the Organisation & Information research group at the Institute of Information and Computing Sciences of Utrecht University. His information systems research currently focuses on business aspects regarding Natural language technologies, Data mining, Social computing and Method engineering, among others. His PhD research in the field of Computational Linguistics at the University of Amsterdam was awarded an Association for Linguistic and Literary Computing Bursary Award in 2005. Before, he has been a professional software developer for fourteen years in the fields of Information Retrieval & Intelligence, and an independent product software vendor for SME's. He also regularly contributed to the Dutch Personal Computer Magazine (PCM) for seven years as a freelance editor.

Vladimir Stantchev is a senior scientist at the Berlin Institute of Technology where he heads the Public Services and SOA Group. He is also a senior lecturer at the FOM Fachhochschule für Ökonomie und Management in Berlin, Germany. Vladimir received a MA in Computer Science from the Humboldt University in Berlin, Germany in 2005 and a PhD in Computer Science from the Berlin Institute of Technology in 2007. In 2008 he was a visiting postdoctoral scholar - Fellow at the University of California, Berkeley and at the International Computer Science Institute in Berkeley. His research interests are in the areas of service-oriented computing, software engineering, and IT management.

Robert D. Tennyson is Professor of Educational Psychology at the University of Minnesota. He is editor of a professional journal, Computers in Human Behavior. He also serves on editorial boards for four other journals. His research and publications include topics on problem solving, concept learning, intelligent systems, testing and measurement, instructional design, and advanced learning technologies. He has directed NATO sponsored workshops and advanced study institutes on automated instructional design and delivery in Spain and Norway. He has authored over 200 journal articles, books and book chapters.

Hannu Vanharanta, 1949, began his professional career in 1973 as Technical Assistant at the Turku office of the Finnish Ministry of Trade and Industry. 1975–1992 he worked for Finnish international engineering companies, i.e. Jaakko Pöyry, Rintekno and Ekono as process engineer, section manager and leading consultant. His doctoral thesis was approved 1995. In 1995-1996 he was professor in Business Economics in the University of Joensuu. In 1996-1998 he served as Purchasing and Supply Management professor in the Lappeenranta University of Technology. Since 1998 he has been professor in Industrial Management and Engineering in Tampere University of Technology at Pori. The research interests are: Human Resource Management, Knowledge Management, Strategic Management, Financial Analysis, E-Business, Soft Computing, Management Ontologies and Decision Support Systems.

Jen-Her Wu is Professor of Information Management at National Sun Yat-Sen University, Taiwan. His current research is in the areas of electronic commerce and innovation, IT service, system development and management. He is the author of three books and over 50 referred journal articles. His research articles have appeared in such journals as Information & Management, Decision Support Systems, and Computers in Human Behavior. He also serves as an associate editor of Computers in Human Behavior and on the editorial board of Information & Management.

Index

A

actual system use (AU) 224
advance organizer 3
affect component 20
Alexandria Small Business Association (ABA)
    189, 203
alternating current (AC) 113
Arab Union for Small Enterprises (AUSE)
    186, 187, 203
asynchronously 223
attitude toward using (ATU) 224
avatars 22
average variance extracted (AVE) 228, 230

B

B2B e-commerce 54, 55, 66
B2B firms 54, 60, 63, 64, 65, 66
B2B relationships 54, 55, 56, 60, 62, 65
behavioral intention to use (BI) 224
black-box models 7
blended e-learning systems (BELS) 223, 224,
    225, 226, 227, 228, 229, 230, 232, 233,
    236
blue butterfly (Maculinea arion) 71
brand knowledge 162
broadcast 207, 210
business-logic knowledge 163
business simulations 1, 5, 6, 7, 8

C

Canon 127
case study 181, 197
CATIA 48, 49

CDC Corporation 138
CD-ROM products 210
Central Agency for Public Moblisation and
    Statistics (CAPMAS) 184, 189, 203
Charles Frederick Worth 73
Chief Information Officers (CIOs) 90, 91, 92,
    93, 94, 95, 96, 97, 98
Chinese online game market 135, 138, 141,
    142, 143
Circles of Mind metaphor 80
Clan culture 102
classroom technology 147, 150, 155
cognitive strategies 19
Comanche Rotor System Design (CRSD) 41
Commercial-Off-The-Shelf (COTS) 47
Commission of the European Communities
    207
communication infrastructure 210
Computer Aided Design (CAD) 48
Computer Aided Engineering (CAE) 48
Computer Aided Manufacturing (CAM) 48
computer-based training (CBTs) 207
Computer Numerically Controlled (CNC) 2, 6
computer science 182
COMSCORE, Inc. 137
Confirmatory Factor Analysis (CFA) 228
content analysis 181, 197
Cost-Based Pricing 140
Crédit Agricole Egypt Bank (CAEB) 190, 203
Cultural Strength 104
Customer Orientation 103, 104
Customer Relationships 128, 129, 130
Customer Segments 127, 128, 129
Cyber University of NSYSU 223
Cycloid 82, 83, 86